The King of Fighters

Nikolay Polikarpov and his Aircraft Designs

Volume 2: The Monoplane Era

Mikhail Maslov

Helion & Company

Helion & Company Limited
Unit 8 Amherst Business Centre
Budbrooke Road
Warwick
CV34 5WE
England
Tel. 01926 499 619
Email: info@helion.co.uk
Website: www.helion.co.uk
Twitter: @helionbooks

Published by Helion & Company 2021
Designed and typeset by Farr out Publications, Wokingham, Berkshire
Cover designed by Paul Hewitt, Battlefield Design (www.battlefield-design.co.uk)

Text © Mikhail Maslov 2021
Photographs provided courtesy of the Russian State Documentary Film and Photo Archive, Central Armed Forces Museum, and Russian State Military Archive.
Aircraft scale drawings were prepared by the author with the active participation of Vadim Egorov.
Colour profiles drawn by Andrey Yurgenson.

Every reasonable effort has been made to trace copyright holders and to obtain their permission for the use of copyright material. The author and publisher apologize for any errors or omissions in this work, and would be grateful if notified of any corrections that should be incorporated in future reprints or editions of this book.

ISBN 978-1-913336-19-6

British Library Cataloguing-in-Publication Data.
A catalogue record for this book is available from the British Library.

All rights reserved. No part of this publication may be reproduced, stored in a retrieval system, or transmitted, in any form, or by any means, electronic, mechanical, photocopying, recording or otherwise, without the express written consent of Helion & Company Limited.

For details of other military history titles published by Helion & Company Limited contact the above address, or visit our website: http://www.helion.co.uk.

We always welcome receiving book proposals from prospective authors.

Contents

Abbreviations	v
Acknowledgements	vi
1. The I-16 fighter	7
1.1. Introduction	7
1.2. Development, manufacturing and improvements	7
1.2.1. The TsKB-12 prototype	7
1.2.2. Launch of production. Introduction of the I-16 Type 4	10
1.2.3. Improvements. The 'Red Fives' and the I-16 s/n 123954	13
1.2.4. The last TsKBs. The cannon-armed TsKB-12P	25
1.2.5. Aviation Factory No.21 in 1936: mastering the production of the I-16 Type 5 and Type 12	26
1.2.6. The problems of the 1937	30
1.2.7. Wing reinforcements	37
1.2.8. The **Grizodubova** airplane	39
1.2.9. The hard year of 1938	41
1.2.10. Airplane No.7211	44
1.2.11. The I-16 with the M-62 and M-63 Engines	46
1.2.12. Abundancy of types in 1939	49
1.2.13. The I-16 Type 24	57
1.2.14. The Moscow finale: cannons, machine guns and superchargers	59
1.2.15. The end of series production; 1940–41	63
1.2.15.1. Changes at Aviation Factory No.21	63
1.2.15.2. The I-16 Type 29	66
1.2.15.3. Aviation Factory No.153	70
1.2.15.4. The UTI-4 fighter trainer	70
1.2.15.5. Aviation Factory No.458	74
1.2.14.6. Aviation Factory No.600	76
1.2.15.7. The production figures	77
1.3. Technical description	78
1.4. Camouflage and markings	85
1.5. Types of I-16 aircraft built by Factory No.21 during the period of series production	90
1.6. Combat use	93
1.6.1. The Spanish debut	93
1.6.2. In China	102
1.6.3. Conflict in Mongolia in summer 1939	105
1.6.4. The Winter War of 1939–40	113
1.6.5. The I-16s in service with the Finnish Air Force	117
1.6.6. The Great Patriotic War of 1941–45	120
1.6.7. 'Vakhmistrov's Circus'	134
1.6.8. The I-16s with rocket projectiles	140
Comparisons	148
2. The I-17 fighter	159
The inline engine and the first TsKB-15 prototype	159
The I-17 (TsKB-19) suspended fighter	161
The speed record episode	161

    The I-17 (TsKB-19) second prototype 162
    The I-17 (TsKB-19bis) third prototype 164
    The I-172 and I-173 projects 165

3. The I-180 fighter 171
    The I-180 variants – differences and details 180

4. The I-185 – the best fighter of designer Polikarpov 192
    The engines 193
    Design period 193
    The first flights 195
    Initiative-based developments 196
    Front-line tests of the I-185 198
    The last attempt 201
    The last versions 202

5. The ITP fighter 214

6. The last biplanes of Nikolay Polikarpov 218
    6.1. The I-190 218
    6.2. The I-170 222
    6.3. The I-195 223

7. The bomber designs of the 1930s 225
    7.1. The VIT air destroyer of tanks 225
    7.2. The SPB high-speed dive-bomber 227
    7.3. The *Ivánov* single-engine bomber 237

8. Prototypes and projects of the 1940s 243
    8.1. The ODB single-engine daytime bomber 243
    8.2. The NB night bomber 244
    8.3. The BDP combat troop-carrier glider 248
    8.5. The TIS heavy escort fighter 254
    8.6. The last projects 258

Abbreviations

CG	centre of gravity
GUAP	Chief Administration of Aviation Industry (*Glavnoye Upravlenie Aviapromyshlennosti*)
GUAS	Chief Directorate of Aviation Supplies (*Glavnoye Upravleniye AviaSnabzheniya*)
GVF	Civil Air Fleet (*Grazhdanskiy Vozdushniy Flot*)
LII	Flight Research Institute (*Lyotno-Issledovatelskiy Institut*)
MAC	Mean Aerodynamic Chord
NII GVF	Scientific Research Institute of the Civil Air Fleet (*Nauchno-Issledovatelskiy Institut Grazhdanskogo Vozdushnogo Flota*)
NII VVS	Air Force Scientific and Testing Institute (*Nauchno-Ispytatelny Institut Voyenno-Vozdushnykh Sil*)
NKAP	People's Commissariat of Aviation Industry (*Narodniy Komissariat Aviatsionnoy Promyshlennosti*)
PGU NKOP	1st Chief Directorate of People's Commissariate of Defence Industry (*Pervoye Glanoye Upravleniye Narodnogo Komissariata Oboronnoy Promyshlennosti*)
TsAGI	Central Aerohydrodynamic Institute (*Tsentralniy Aerogidrodinamicheskiy Institut*)
TsIAM	Central Institute of Aviation Motor-building (*Tsentralniy Institut Aviatsionnogo Motorostroeniya*)
TsKB	Central Design Bureau (*Tsentralnoye Konstruktorskoye Byuro*)
VVS RKKA	Workers' and Peasants' Red Army Air Force (*Voenno-Vozdushniye Sily Raboche-Krestyanskoy Krasnoy Armii*)

Acknowledgements

This publication was prepared using materials from the Russian State Archive of Economy, Russian State Military Archive, Central Naval Archive, Central State Archive for Scientific-Technical Documentation, Russian State Archive for Moscow Area and State Archive of Nizhny Novgorod Area, and materials provided by Professor E. Zhukovsky's Scientific Memorial Museum.

Photos are provided courtesy of the Russian State Documentary Film and Photo Archive, Central Armed Forces Museum and Russian State Military Archive.

Aircraft scale drawings were prepared by the author and Andrey Yurgenson, with active participation by Vadim Egorov, while the colour views were created by Andrey Yurgenson.

The author would like to extend his sincere thanks for the help in preparation of this book to the following persons (in Russian alphabetical order): S.V. Abrosov, A.N. Averin, N.T. Gordyukov, V.V. Egorov, P.V. Zaika, V.P. Ivanov, V.N. Krutikhin, M.V. Orlov, G.F. Petrov, N.N. Polikarpov, G.O. Sloutskiy, D.B. Khazanov and A.A. Yurgenson.

1

The I-16 fighter

1.1. Introduction

The Polikarpov I-16 fighter is one of the most famous aircraft of the Soviet period in the history of Russia. Thanks to the short stubby fuselage, which was smoothly interfaced to the wide wings by means of powerful fillets, the massive empennage and the retractable landing gear, the I-16 had an absolutely unique and eye-catching appearance. The high maneuverability that was reckoned among the main advantages of the I-16 was primarily due to the aft centre-of-gravity position, which, on the other hand, made the aircraft extremely unstable in flight. This peculiarity brought about a lot of practical difficulties in the course of pilots' training; however, it also had some positive effect. Pilots who managed to master the I-16 well usually had refined piloting skills and later were able to easily convert to other, even more complex aircraft. They dubbed the I-16 *Ishachok* (Donkey) – a nickname that fitted the aircraft, which was capricious but at the same time unpretentious in terms of repair and maintenance.

Production of the aircraft continued from 1934 until 1941. Throughout those years, Soviet aviation factories built over 10,000 I-16s of all versions, making the aircraft the most mass-produced pre-war fighter in world history. Combat use of the I-16 began in 1936 and continued till 1944–45. Some aircraft of pre-war manufacture kept taking to the air as late as the 1950s. Currently, at the beginning of the twenty-first century, Russian museums have two original I-16s on display. Several more aircraft, restored by aviation enthusiasts, still fly in the skies over New Zealand, Spain and the USA.

1.2. Development, manufacturing and improvements

1.2.1. The TsKB-12 prototype

The first calculations and preliminary sketches of the monoplane fighter which was eventually designated the I-15 were prepared by Nikolay Polikarpov in May 1932. There were many reasons why such an experimental project emerged. Firstly, Polikarpov was the pioneer among Soviet designers who developed, in practice, a cantilever monoplane fighter referred to as the IL-400 in 1923. The aircraft, later designated the I-1, found no proper understanding in the Red Army Air Force due to certain individual drawbacks, and was never accepted into production. During the years that followed, Polikarpov worked on improving sesquiplane (a biplane with one wing less than half the area of the other) fighters, creating, as a result, one of the best such aircraft, namely, the I-15. However, monoplanes never left his drawing board or calculation sheets. Up to 1928, the designer was drawing and calculating possible variants for further development of the I-1. One of the later sketches represents an elegant low-wing monoplane, demonstrating the perfection of the selected configuration with its sweeping contours.

In summer 1929, Polikarpov carried out initial calculations for the I-9 fighter included in the experimental aircraft building plan for 1930–33. The I-9 was determined as a high-speed aircraft; for this reason, to design it in one of the suggested variants, Polikarpov again chose the monoplane configuration.

In autumn 1929, the designer was arrested under a contrived charge, imprisoned and started working in TsKB-39 – one of the so-called *sharagas* (a secret experimental design bureau in the Soviet labour camp system), where with Polikarpov's participation the VT-11 (I-5) fighter was designed within a short period of time. This 'prison aircraft' proved to be decent enough and was cleared for production; the arrested designers were gradually discharged. In May 1931, Polikarpov was appointed Pavel Sukhoi's deputy at the Design Brigade No.3 of the Central Design Bureau – Central Aerohydrodynamic Institute (TsKB-TsAGI, *Tsentralnoye Konstruktorskoye Byuro – Tsentralniy Aerogidrodinamicheskiy Institut*). At that time, the Design Brigade had already been working on designing the I-14 monoplane fighter, which featured an all-metal construction (conventional for TsAGI) and corrugated wing and tail skin. Apparently, such work gave another impetus for Polikarpov to begin designing his 'own' monoplane fighter of mixed construction, with retractable landing gear.

After the splitting up of TsKB-TsAGI into two independent organisations, Polikarpov became Head of TsKB Design Brigade No.2, which specialised in fighter aircraft. Along with developing the new TsKB-3 (I-15) sesquiplane already included in the experimental building plan, he continued pilot work on designing the devised monoplane. In May 1933, the Soviet Air Force displayed an interest in this aircraft, and handed out an assignment for it to Polikarpov, without including it, however, in the already finalised experimental activities plan of the Chief Administration of Aviation Industry (*Glavnoye Upravlenie Aviapromyshlennosti*, GUAP).

By summer 1933, the prototype – codenamed TsKB-12 – had acquired clear-cut features. The low-wing monoplane with a short tapered fuselage, closed cockpit canopy and retractable landing gear was presented in two variants in terms of the engine cowling configuration: with the Townend ring and with the NACA cowling. The decision to build at least one prototype with the lightweight and narrow Townend ring remained in force until December 1933. In practice, however, the first two prototypes were both fitted with the wider NACA cowling.

For the power plant, the designer believed the American-built Wright Cyclone air-cooled engines to be the most acceptable. Launched in 1925, the radial Cyclones were undergoing improvements on a continuous basis; in 1933, they were ranked among the most advanced engines in the world. In 1932–33, Soviet representatives were conducting negotiations with Curtiss-Wright, which resulted in purchasing an entire engine-building works complete with all equipment and licenses to manufacture the 625hp Cyclone R-1820 F-3 engines.

However, it turned out that receiving even one such engine for the TsKB-12 pilot project in the first half of 1933 was a challenging task. Commander of the Workers' and Peasants' Red Army Air Force (VVS RKKA, *Voenno-Vozdushniye Sily Raboche-Krestyanskoy Krasnoy Armii*) Yakov Alksnis put forward a suggestion that Polikarpov should build the first prototype with the less powerful (480hp) but widely used M-22 engine, which, according to calculations, was quite able to ensure the required speed of 300km/h at an altitude of 5km.

Full-scale work on the TsKB-12 began in June 1933. The military were watching the aircraft building process closely. Inspection of the TsKB-12's wooden mock-up in November convinced them conclusively of the correctness of their choice. The fighter being designed was found to fully conform to the requirements established for it, especially in terms of maximum speed. On 22 November 1933, the Council of Labour and Defence of the USSR made a decision to accept the new fighter into production under the designation I-16.

Meanwhile, negotiations regarding purchasing the first batch of the Wright Cyclone engines had, for the most part, come to a close, with delivery of the engines expected in the months to come. There were thus still hopes to fit the TsKB-12 prototype with the American-built engine. On 20 September 1933, the director of Aviation Factory No.39, Margolin, sent the following report to the head of the GUAP and the Commander of the Air Force:

> In the course of designing the TsKB-12 (I-16) aircraft, the Design Brigade No.2 of TsKB performed several variants of calculations for various engines. The calculations show that, with the Wright Cyclone F-5, we will have an excellent fighter, way ahead of European and American aircraft, with a maximum speed of 410km/h at an altitude of five kilometers, and with a service ceiling of 9,000m. I hereby request you to purchase one engine not later than December and to install it on one of the TsKB-12s being built.

Margolin suggested that the latest Wright engine variant (the F-5 altitude version) should be purchased. However, this request was not accepted, and Soviet technical crews only acquired it much later – in 1938 in Spain.

In 1933, there was only one F-3 engine in Moscow, undergoing evaluation testing in the Central Institute of Aviation Motor-building (TsIAM, *Tsentralniy Institut Aviatsionnogo Motorostroeniya*). It was suggested that the tests should be completed upon reaching 50 running hours, with the engine then installed on the TsKB-12. Meanwhile, the designer of the aircraft managed to arrange for a Wright Cyclone F-2 engine (the low-altitude version) to be procured, and decided to install it on the second prototype (the TsKB-12bis).

Before the end of 1933, both prototypes were completed. The two aircraft had no differences in terms of external appearance, both being stubby and stocky, with engines covered with cylindrical NACA cowlings. However, the TsKB-12bis with the American-built engine was easily distinguishable by the three-bladed Hamilton Standard propeller. Since it was mid-winter, aircraft were fitted with fixed skis, which did not allow the determining of maximum flight speed, but on the other hand allowed flight testing to begin immediately.

On 30 December 1933, the M-22-powered TsKB-12 first took to the air with Valery Chkalov, test pilot of Aviation Factory No.39, at the controls. The debut flight of the TsKB-12bis fitted with the Wright Cyclone F-2 took place in early January 1934. In flight, the two aircraft behaved almost identically; Chkalov found both difficult to fly. In February 1934, the aircraft were prepared for state tests, the objective being to discover the main flight performance parameters of the TsKB-12 and to make a final decision on whether it should be cleared for production.

On 16 February, test pilot V. Kokkinaki began to fly the M-22-powered TsKB-12. The aircraft with the Wright Cyclone engine was tried out by another test pilot of the Air Force Scientific and Testing Institute (NII VVS, *Nauchno-Ispytatelny Institut Voyenno-Vozdushnykh Sil*), V.A. Stepanchonok. For the flight testing, the aircraft were fitted with skis. The weather in February that year did not favour the test pilots, with flights often postponed due to persistent low cloud cover. Nevertheless, several important conclusions could be drawn. Between 25 and 27 February, the aircraft were handed over to Factory No.39 for rectification of defects and preparation for more thorough tests utilising wheeled landing gear.

So what was found out in respect of the two prototypes after several hours of flying in each of them? Both TsKB-12s, the one powered by the M-22 and that with the Wright Cyclone engine, turned out to be rather similar in terms of piloting. They responded actively to control surface operations and switched easily from one aerobatic manoeuvre to another, but did not tolerate abrupt control inputs. A pilot had to be especially careful during landing. Intolerant to high-altitude flare-out, the aircraft tended to drop the wing. On the other hand, the pilots noted that the I-16 was more stable at take-off and landing than the TsAGI-developed I-14 fighter. During turns, the I-16 also proved to be more forgiving than its rival. Out of the two TsKB-12 prototypes, the M-22-powered aircraft inspired greater confidence (the Wright Cyclone engine brought about unwanted vibration in the second prototype). Consequently, pilots Yumashev and Chernavsky performed some minor flying in it during those first days of flight testing. The pilots' unanimous opinion was that the aircraft still held a lot of mysteries and was rather dangerous to fly. Therefore, performing any aerobatics in it (including steep turns) was forbidden for an indefinite time. However, the decision to accept the aircraft into production remained in force. For this reason, the test approval certificate contained an order by Commander of the Air Force Alksnis to begin selection of highly trained pilots to master the new fighter. This decision was substantiated by the fact that the flight performance parameters, among which flight speed was the critical one, recorded during the 10-day tests proved to be rather decent:

	TsKB-12 (M-22)	TsKB-12bis (Wright Cyclone F-2)
Maximum speed at an altitude of 1,000m (km/h)	303	361
Maximum speed at an altitude of 5,000m (km/h)	283	314
Time to climb to 5,000m (minutes)	10.9	7.9
Time to perform a turn (seconds)	16.5	16.5

Among the drawbacks found in the prototypes were the imperfect fuel supply system, the flimsy structure of the canopy, the poor attachment of the gunsight and the uncomfortable shoulder harness. To make the process of climbing into the cockpit more convenient, pilots recommended providing a special step or a stepladder against the fuselage. However, in view of the desire to ensure streamlined aerodynamic contours, such a device was never mounted on the fuselage. To get in, a pilot had first to step onto the wing fillet edge, and then pull himself up and over into the cockpit.

Another aspect mentioned among the disadvantages of the I-16 was the doubt regarding its safe recovery from a spin. In particular, TsAGI aerodynamicist Zhuravchenko concluded, from results of wind tunnel tests, that the aircraft – with its short tail – would be prone to enter a flat spin, and even suggested that the vertical stabiliser should be relocated upward, as was the case with the I-14. During meetings on 17 January and 21 February 1934, which were dedicated to the problem of spin in the I-16, none of the engineers or pilots could say anything definite in favour of the Polikarpov fighter. As a last resort, in order to clear up this question, it was decided to perform flight tests involving entering a spin intentionally.

During two days (1 and 2 March 1934), test pilot Valery Chkalov performed 75 spins in the M-22-powered aircraft. The tests showed that the I-16 did not enter spin in the case of speed loss with the controls in the neutral position: after dipping a wing and making half a turn, the aircraft resumed straight flight. In the case of an intentional spin (when the pilot pulled the control stick and pushed the pedal), the I-16 entered a steady spin. The spins could be easily terminated by placing the controls in the neutral position. No tendency to enter a flat spin was noted.

After rectification of major drawbacks and installation of wheeled retractable landing gear, both TsKB-12 prototypes were sent to the Crimea to continue testing on the airfield of Military Aviation School of Pilots No.1 near Sevastopol. The school was better known as the Kacha School; in popular parlance, both the airfield and the school were referred to simply as 'Kacha'. Operational tests began there on 22 March. The M-22-powered aircraft (under leading pilot Kokkinaki) was flown with retracted undercarriage in order to obtain overall speed performance parameters. The results turned out to be promising: maximum speed near ground level was 359km/h; maximum speed at the target altitude of 5km was 325km/h.

However, the landing gear retraction system proved to be unreliable, as the lifting mechanism, which utilised a cable wound onto a drum, often jammed and failed. The landing gear retraction process on the first prototypes even caused considerable difficulties for a physically strong pilot such as Chkalov. For this reason, a decision was made not to retract the landing gear during the testing of the second prototype – the Cyclone-powered TsKB-12bis (flown by leading pilot Chernavsky). But even with such precautions taken, the aircraft did not escape trouble. On 14 April, the right landing gear leg attachment fitting failed during the last stage of the landing run, and the aircraft found itself on its belly. Damage turned out to be minor: only the propeller blades were bent and the fuselage bottom was slightly dented. However, for this prototype, the Crimean tests came to an end at that point.

A week later, flight tests of the M-22-powered aircraft were also completed. The damaged TsKB-12bis was packaged in a crate and sent by rail to the factory for repair, whereas the TsKB-12 M-22 was ferried by Chkalov to Moscow. On 1 May, the M-22-powered prototype, together with the TsKB-3 (I-15) sesquiplane and the TsAGI I-14, was first demonstrated in flight above Red Square in Moscow.

After the return to Moscow, the TsKB-12bis prototype underwent considerable modifications. The aircraft was fitted with a new Wright Cyclone F-3 engine featuring a tunnel cowling, which in terms of configuration was close to the so-called 'Vatter' cowling. In such cowlings, each engine cylinder was cooled via an individual hole in the forward portion. Furthermore, the airflow and exhaust gases were discharged via special 'buckets' with teardrop-shaped cut-outs on the cylindrical surface of the cowling. This type of cowling was designed by Russian emigrant Mikhail Vatter, who moved to the USA in the early 1920s. The invention returned to Russia as a 'foreign' product, so its name was spelled and read as 'Watter'.

The engine of the TsKB-12bis was fitted with a two-blade propeller manufactured at Factory No.28. The propeller blades could be set to lower or higher pitch on the ground, depending on the flight mission. The propeller hub was covered with a spinner. Furthermore, the aircraft wing was reinforced; the leading edge of the outer wing panels was covered with sheet duralumin up to the first spar; the landing gear was modified; and the slots in the ailerons and in the tail control surfaces were covered with movable duralumin panels. Other modifications included, *inter alia*, removal of the spoilers which were arranged forward of the front spar of the outer wing. Deployed across the stream, they had been intended to slow down the aircraft rotation if it entered a spin. As there were now no more concerns regarding recovery from a spin, the spoilers were finally abandoned.

On 7 September 1934, the TsKB-12bis was ferried to the NII VVS airfield in Shchelkovo near Moscow to conduct state tests, which lasted until 12 October. This time, the opinion on the I-16 turned out to be categorical and more stringent. The higher landing speed and the unreliable landing gear retraction system did not suit the military. Having admitted that the aircraft had failed the tests due to the unrefined condition of certain individual components of structure and equipment, Commander of the Air Force Yakov Alksnis demanded that its armament should be modified. He concluded that the I-16 "could not be deemed a military fighter aircraft" until its reliable operation was ensured. In spite of the fact that the TsKB-12bis was able to develop a maximum speed of 437km/h at an altitude of 3,000m, the military, who had shortly before been happy with the achievement of 300km/h, now demanded higher performance. They suggested that the I-16 should be fitted with the new Soviet-built Nazarov M-58 engine, with which the aircraft was required to reach a maximum speed of 470km/h.

All these issues were applicable only to improvement of the aircraft as a type, whereas the top-priority task was to put the I-16 into production, which was duly launched at Aviation Factory No.39 in Moscow and Aviation Factory No.21 in Nizhny Novgorod. The latter city, on the River Volga, had during the Soviet era been renamed Gorky, and the aviation factory was referred to as 'Gorkovsky'. Currently, it again bears the name of Nizhny Novgorod. The author rather favours the city's original name; for this reason, he reserves the right to hereafter refer to it as Nizhny Novgorod.

1.2.2. Launch of production. Introduction of the I-16 Type 4

The leading Moscow Aviation Factory No.39 was tasked, for the year of 1934, with manufacturing 50 I-16s with the M-22 engines. The TsKB, quartered at the factory facilities, was carrying out aircraft design modifications and preparing technical documentation for full-scale production.

Aircraft manufactured by Aviation Factory No.39 bore serial numbers in accordance with the sequence numbering scheme adopted by TsKB. Throughout 1934, the factory manufactured the planned 50 I-16s bearing serial numbers from 123901–123950 (which was an abbreviation from 'TskB-12 aircraft built at Factory No.39, s/n 12-39-XX'). In 1935–36, the Moscow factory built another eight aircraft (four aircraft each year), ending the series with s/n 123958. Of course, the abovementioned I-16s were by no means duplicates of the M-22-powered prototype. Moreover, the series included, among others, prototype aircraft developed by Polikarpov's Design Brigade.

Aviation Factory No.21 in Nizhny Novgorod, named after Enukidze (renamed after Ordzhonikidze from 1935), proved unable to immediately join the process of mastering production of the new fighter aircraft for several reasons. Suffice it to say that it was only in 1932 that Factory No.21 began to operate as a fully fledged enterprise; two years later, it was only beginning to become a large-scale manufacturing facility. In 1934, young and insufficiently trained personnel aged 18–22 made up over 70% of the factory's overall headcount. However, by that time, the factory had been manufacturing the I-5 fighter aircraft for two years. In early 1934, it began to master production of the KhAI-1 and the I-14. In spring the same year, the factory began to receive materials and technical documentation for the I-16.

Under GUAP Order No.1106 dated 11 June 1934, Factory No.21 was tasked with introducing the I-16 M-22 into large-scale production before the end of the year. An interesting fact is that, early that year, the factory was given an assignment to manufacture 250 such aircraft; later, factory Director Evgeny Miroshnikov managed to convince the management to reduce the ordered quantity to 80 aircraft. The GUAP order in June again scaled up the plan for the factory, which now had to supply 225 I-16s before the end of the year. Furthermore, the assignment for manufacturing three KhAI-1 and 300 I-5 airplanes also remained in effect. The I-14, however, was withdrawn from the plan, with the order for its manufacture handed over to Factory No.125 in Irkutsk.

It was only on 17 July that the factory in Nizhny Novgorod began to formally work on the new aircraft. Needless to say, given the stringent plan for manufacture of the I-5s, the factory proved unable to comply with the management's ambitious intentions. However, throughout this period, the factory specialists managed, with help from the TsKB Design Brigade No.2, to develop a complete package of working drawings, prepare production tooling and master new labour-intensive technologies such as wing spar welding.

Because the I-16 M-22 was the fourth type of aircraft manufactured by Factory No.21 (after the I-5, KhAI-1 and I-14), it received the designation I-16 Type 4. Aircraft of this type were produced by the factory from 1934–35, with a total of 505 built during this period. Taking into account aircraft of similar type manufactured in Moscow, the overall quantity of I-16 M-22s built may be estimated at 555. It was during the period when the I-16 was being put into production that the new type designation system came into effect at the factory. It should be noted that, initially, personnel tended to forget about this when drawing up technical documentation. Thus, for example, a document of November 1934 mentions the I-5 s/n 121633, which passed acceptance inspection (that was the pre-production aircraft of the 19th series, equipped with brake wheels), whereas in another document, reference to the next manufactured I-5 is made without specifying the type, that is, just '21634'.

The first I-16 Type 4s manufactured by Aviation Factory No.21 as presented for acceptance in November and December 1934 had many drawbacks, and were for this reason unmercifully rejected by acceptance inspectors (only 41 aircraft were successfully accepted). The drawbacks were, for the most part, familiar ones: the unsteadily operating landing gear retraction mechanism and armament failures. On 4 October that year, special-purpose tests of the pre-production I-16 s/n 4211 began, to determine reliability of the new landing gear raising mechanism developed by engineers of the factory design bureau A. Borovkov and I. Florov. The tests were attended by Leading Engineer Kupriyanov and test pilot Pavlushev representing the factory, and Leading Engineer Voyevodin and test pilot Kokkinaki representing NII VVS. It was recognised that retracting the landing gear at an increased speed of over 200km/h was extremely difficult.

Eventually, personnel at Factory No.21 adjusted the landing gear retraction kinematics so that it operated almost faultlessly, and remained unchanged in the I-16s of all types until production was discontinued. Besides, in November 1934 (during the period of 'landing gear problems'), at the suggestion of Borovkov and Florov, the I-16 s/n 4217 was built. This featured non-retractable wheels enclosed in wide spats ('pants'). Among the advantages of this version were the ease of installation of the spats by combat unit personnel and the possibility to successfully use the combination of such wheels with fixed skis. There were attempts to hand over the aircraft to military acceptance inspectors with the first batch of 15 aircraft as part of the plan for the year. However, the Air Force took a surprising interest in the aircraft and recommended that it should undergo state tests.

The tests of the I-16 s/n 4217 were conducted at NII VVS in October 1935. The aircraft was flown by pilot Altynov, representing the factory, andtest pilot Stefanovsky, from NII VVS. The non-retractable landing gear in the I-16 was evaluated positively. The aircraft with the 'pants' offered a noticeably higher stability in aerobatic manoeuvres, and there was also an obvious reduction in gross weight. Upon the conclusion of the test results, it was stated that accepting the aircraft into production in such a configuration was expedient. Commander of the Air Force Alksnis recommended that aircraft should be brought up to final condition and then tested in combat units.

However, in 1935, many of the abovementioned problems were successfully rectified, and only aircraft with retractable landing gear were put into production. One such aircraft – the I-16 M-22 s/n 421230 – was tested at NII VVS from 29 October until 13 November that year. Among other things, this aircraft featured better workmanship and had a number of improvements, including reinforced skin and bracing wires on the empennage to enhance vertical stabilizer rigidity. In the course of the tests, the aircraft was compared with an I-16 manufactured by Factory No.39. The comparison came down in favour of the aircraft from Nizhny Novgorod.

Commander of the Air Force Alksnis approved the I-16 s/n 421230 test report on 21 December. Among other requirements, he demanded that the machine-gun mount of the fighter aircraft should undergo improvements in the shortest possible time.

Comparison table for the I-16 prototype built at Factory No.39 and aircraft s/n 42130 and s/n 4217				
	Prototype built at Factory No.39	Prototype built at Factory No.39, with skis	I-16 s/n 421230	I-16 s/n 4217
Maximum speed at H=0m (km/h)	359	306	362	345
Maximum speed at H=3,000m (km/h)	339	296	346	335
Maximum speed at H=5,000m (km/h)	325	283	330	317.5
Time to climb to 5,000m (minutes)	9.4	10.9	9.2	10.0
Service ceiling (m)	7,180	6,350	7,440	7,110
Gross weight (kg)	1,311.7	1,322.8	1,354.8	1,335.1

The I-16's peculiarity consisted in that it was, from the very beginning, fitted with the cutting-edge 7.62mm ShKAS machine gun. Developed in 1932 by armament designers Shpitalniy and Komaritsky, the machine gun featured the world's highest rate of fire of 1,800 rounds per minute. The ShKAS was put into production almost concurrently with the I-16 in 1934. Initially, the machine gun had numerous defects, which were rectified in the course of operation. The estimated cost of the new machine gun was five times as high as that of the PV-1 machine gun which had already been mastered by industry (in 1934, the cost of a ShKAS machine gun was 5,000 roubles); on the other hand, its weight was lower than the latter by one-third, and in terms of rate of fire it was worth two of the older machine guns.

Initially, the wing-mounted ShKAS machine guns often failed during firing. This was caused by the aircraft designers having installed the machine gun in the inverted position, as it was thus easier to fit it into the overall design within the confined space of the wing centre section. Positioned 'upside down', the sophisticated mechanisms tended to fail. Armament designers finally realised the problem and voiced their protests. However, there was at this stage to be no going back, and the first I-16s manufactured in 1934 kept flying with the 'capricious' armament. The drawback was, however, eventually rectified; mounted correctly, ShKAS machine guns operated more reliably.

As early as the spring of 1934, TsKB developed the TsKB-18 ground-attack aircraft fitted with four machine guns and featuring a larger-size wingspan of 10 metres. The armament consisted of four wing-mounted ShKAS machine guns (in another version, four PV-1 machine guns), whose line of fire was beyond the rotating propeller disc area. The cockpit was provided with armour protection, and there were provisions for installation of the DER-32 bomb racks to accommodate four 25kg bombs. The service ceiling was estimated to reach 7,200m, the time to climb to 5,000m was 12.5 minutes, and the maximum speed near ground level was reduced by 9km/h.

Due to lack of support from the Red Army Air Force, the TsKB-18 received no further development. There was an opinion that the DI-6 two-seat biplane was more suitable for use in the role of a ground-attack aircraft.

In 1935, upon the request of Air Force representatives, specialists at Factory No.21 developed and built, using their own resources, a fighter version fitted with four ShKAS machine guns under the designation I-161. The aircraft underwent testing at NII VVS from 22–26 July that year. Unfortunately, the additional ShKAS machine guns operated poorly, with the rate of fire dropping from 1,800 to 1,200 rounds per minute. The Air Force Administration demanded that the drawbacks be rectified, and that the I-161 then be presented again for tests. Apparently, no further improvements followed, and no other I-161s were ever built.

Apart from mastering the fighter, the factory designers were tasked with creating a two-seat trainer variant, having already produced such an aircraft. In early 1934, an aircraft of trainer configuration was built on the I-5 platform. The two-seat I-5 s/n 6211 was tested by pilot Pavlushev from 5–8 August 1934. Later, a small series of 20 aircraft was manufactured and successfully used for training purposes in flying schools.

In May 1935, an M-22-powered two-seat I-16 under the designation UT-2 s/n 8211 was presented for tests. The aircraft's cockpit was fully covered by a single canopy. The UT-2 s/n 8211 underwent testing between 1 July and 16 August. The aircraft had a gross weight of 1,370.5kg, empty weight of 970.3kg, inflight centre of gravity (CG) position of 31.3 mean aerodynamic chord (MAC), maximum speed near ground level of 349km/h and landing speed of 127km/h. The aircraft was flown by Pavlushev and Laryushin, who found its stability acceptable. Among disadvantages, they noted a nose-up tendency at speeds over 220km/h and the penetration of exhaust gases into the cockpit. It was suggested that the aircraft should undergo improvements and be further used for conversion to the I-16.

Afterwards, two more such aircraft were built. It is known that one of them – the UT-2 s/n 82120 manufactured in December 1935 – crashed on 17 July 1936. Factory handover test pilot F. Mech had been training pilot D. Chebotenko to fly the aircraft. During low-altitude approach, the aircraft fell into a spin and crashed, killing both pilots instantly.

In late 1935, another two-seater variant, the UTI-3 s/n 11211 powered by the M-58 Soviet-built engine, also underwent tests. During the tests, in which Chkalov took part and which lasted until spring 1936, the aircraft flew a total of 33 hours. The engine's additional running time on the ground totalled 40 hours. Although the UTI-3 was found to be superior to the UT-2 s/n 8211, no other aircraft of this version were built due to unavailability of the required quantity of M-58 engines.

The variant that was actually put into production was designated the UTI-2 Type 4 and had only individual pilots' windscreens instead of the common canopy. Its landing gear was initially non-retractable. In 1935, 22 two-seat aircraft were built, among them three UTI-2s and an UTI-3. Throughout 1936, 27 UTI-2s were produced. From these figures, it can be seen that the total number of M-22-powered fighter trainers manufactured was 45. In the same year, production of the M-25-powered aircraft under the designation UTI-4 was launched. The first eight aircraft were completed before the end of 1936, and they passed handover inspection together with the rest of the aircraft of this series in 1937.

Later, when an UTI-2 with retractable landing gear was built (having undergone state tests in July 1937), it was found out that there were no more M-22 engines in stock – moreover, production of the engine was discontinued. Thus, the attempt to obtain a cheaper fighter trainer did not take place (there were other suggested savings, for example fitting the aircraft with the M-26 engine),, so consequently the M-25-powered UTI-4 Type 15 was accepted into production.

In 1934, when plans for re-equipment of fighter units were being drawn up, there were intentions to begin with the Far East, Primorsky Krai and the 404th Fighter Air Brigade in Baku. It was planned that, before 1 January 1935, the Soviet Air

Forces should have at their disposal 10 I-14s, 60 I-15s and 275 I-16s. In practice, however, in late 1934 and early 1935, the aircraft were just beginning to be supplied to combat units. The process of conversion to the new aircraft involved certain difficulties. Both flight speeds and landing speeds increased, so airfields with better and larger runways were required.

In spring 1935, a decision was made to organise a flypast over Red Square by 60 I-16s. Because there were not enough sufficiently trained pilots at the time, familiarisation with the new aircraft had to take place directly at Factory No.21. The newly arrived group of 70 trainee pilots were instructed by factory pilots, led by Pavlushev. Factory documents show that the two-seat I-16 version was used. It is highly likely that flights were performed in the UT-2 s/n 8211, even before it passed formal tests.

During the period from 28 August until 3 November 1935, 10 I-16 M-22s built at Factory No.39 underwent operational tests with the 107th Squadron of the Bryansk Air Brigade. All strengths and weaknesses of the aircraft and possible options for its combat application were studied. Thus, for example, it was found out that the ailerons, lowered at take-off (in the I-16 Type 4 and Type 5, the ailerons also served as flaps), actually contributed to the shortening of the take-off and landing distances. This finding became a weighty argument for advocates of the I-16, since work for expansion of the existing airfields for the new fighters had just begun.

In the opinion of pilots who flew the aircraft, the following was noted: "The aircraft is easily controllable; it responds sensitively to operation of the control surfaces … [but] is not forgiving in respect of the slightest mistakes … Pulling the control stick excessively during a turn or at landing entails the risk of falling into a spin." Such sharp response of the aircraft to minor movements of the control stick made it difficult to use mechanically operated triggers for machine-gun firing. Instead, smoother electric triggers were required. The I-16 performed rotation about the longitudinal axis (that is, the roll manoeuvre) in 1–1.2 seconds. It should be noted that, in the course of performing such a manoeuvre, the aircraft could at any time also be retained in an intermediate position. The army pilots noted (as test pilots had earlier done) that during flights at maximum speed, the upper skin on the wings was 'sucked away' by the airflow and tended to swell up. Pilots suggested that wing ribs should be arranged more densely to overcome this, but it was only in 1937–38 that such a suggestion was implemented.

Special attention was paid to spin performance. The following are the principal opinions of the test pilots:

> The aircraft spins well at all altitudes … In the process of spinning, with the pedal pressure reduced, the aircraft demonstrates a noticeable tendency to recover from spin … the right spin is performed up to 12 turns without any delay in recovery. The left spin is more energetic … the entry and the recovery are the same as for the left spin; however, pulling the stick fully is not desirable because, at this moment, the aircraft raises its nose between the horizon and the normal spin; the rotation becomes flat, and the recovery takes place with a delay – two turns of delay after five turns; … there were no instances of failure of the controls during a spin.

The overall opinion for the I-16 was that it offered excellent piloting performance.

To conclude the description of the M-22-powered aircraft, it should be noted that the I-16 Type 4 turned out, on the whole, to be a very decent airplane. With a take-off weight of 1,333kg (empty weight 961kg), the load on the wing was only 91kg/sq.m; thus, the aircraft was manoeuvrable and possessed good aerobatic qualities. The I-16s were efficiently operated in combat units for several years, and later on in training units. As of September 1940, flying schools and flight training organisations mustered a total of 253 such aircraft (227 aircraft in service with the VVS RKKA, and 26 in service with the Naval Aviation).

The Type 4 was never introduced to foreign use (in Spain and China), yet a small number of them were still found in combat units and flying schools at the time of the German invasion of the Soviet Union. It is quite conceivable that some of the I-16 Type 4s might have taken part in combat operations during the summer of 1941.

1.2.3. Improvements. The 'Red Fives' and the I-16 s/n 123954

Let us go back to the autumn of 1934 and the events surrounding the Wright Cyclone F-3-powered TsKB-12bis. In spite of the outstanding speed parameters and satisfactory operational performance, the aircraft did not arouse much enthusiasm among the Air Force management. This attitude was rooted in the shortage of state-of-the-art engines which would be able to ensure the intended high performance of the new aircraft. The Soviet aviation engine-building industry did not demonstrate any particular success. Consequently, in 1933–34, the Soviet Union purchased licenses for the French Gnome-Rhône Mistral Major and Hispano-Suiza 12Ybrs engines, and for the already mentioned Wright Cyclone F-3 from the USA.

Production of the Cyclone, which was intended first and foremost for fighter aircraft, began in the city of Perm in the Urals. To launch production of the engine, now designated the M-25, construction of the new Factory No.19 was begun there. The factory was provided with appropriate machinery and modern equipment. Small batches of original Cyclones were also purchased in America. However, all these engines were intended to be used during the following 12 months for

14   The King of Fighters Volume 2

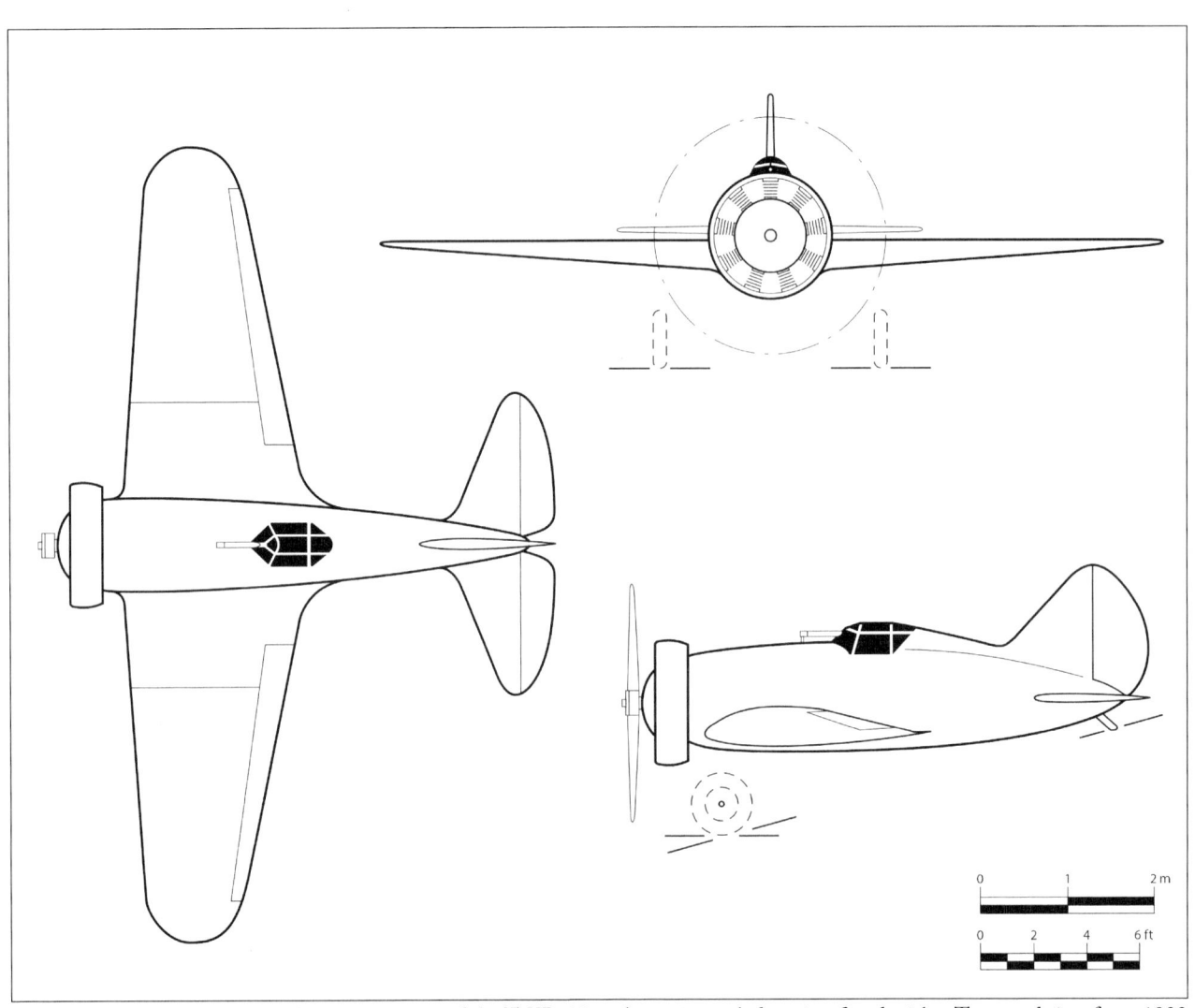

Three-view drawings of the preliminary project of the TsKB-12 with an air-cooled engine fitted with a Townend ring from 1933.

The first TsKB-12 prototype with the M-22 engine and fixed ski landing gear before the beginning of tests in December 1933.

The second TsKB-12bis prototype with the Wright Cyclone F-2 engine before tests in January 1934. The man in the cockpit is Valery Chkalov, who transferred to the factory from NII VVS as a test pilot. He is nearly 30 here, and his 'moment of glory' is still to come.

TsAGI aerodynamicist A. Zhuravchenko preparing the I-5 model for spin tests.

The first TsKB-12 prototype with the M-22 engine during operational tests in the Crimea in March 1934.

The TsKB-12bis with a modified cowling of the Wright Cyclone F-3 engine during state tests in October 1934.

The first TsKB-12 prototype with the M-22 engine during operational tests in the Crimea in March 1934.

The Wright Cyclone F-3-powered TsKB-12bis prototype suffered an accident due to landing gear failure on 14 April 1934.

16   The King of Fighters Volume 2

The TsKB-12bis with the Wright Cyclone F-3 engine is positioned on trestles to have its landing gear retraction mechanism checked.

The production I-16 s/n 4217 featured non-retractable landing gear enclosed in spats, which were referred to as 'pants', seen here in 1934.

The process of landing gear retraction in the TsKB-12bis.

The I-16 s/n 421230 built at Aviation Factory No.21 during state tests at NII VVS in October 1935.

An I-16 Type 4 in flight. The peculiarity of this aircraft consists in the absence of side doors in the cockpit. This was not characteristic of this type of aircraft, on which only the left hinged door was arranged.

A production I-16 M-22 built at Aviation Factory No.39. The enigmatic inscription '3c' on the rudder indicates that this is the third production aircraft of the type manufactured at the factory named after Menzhinsky.

A worn-out I-16 Type 4 at the very end of its career, serving as a visual aid at an aircraft technicians' school. Note the R-Z reconnaissance aircraft in the background.

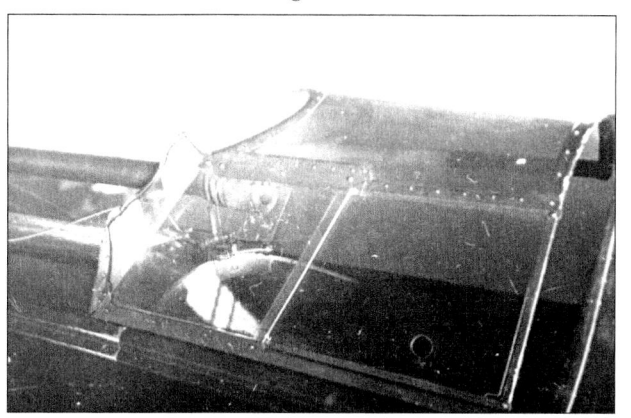

The sliding canopy of the I-16 Type 4 cockpit. The small visible hole served as a stop in the course of opening the side window.

The ShKAS machine-gun mount in the I-16 Type 4 wing centre section.

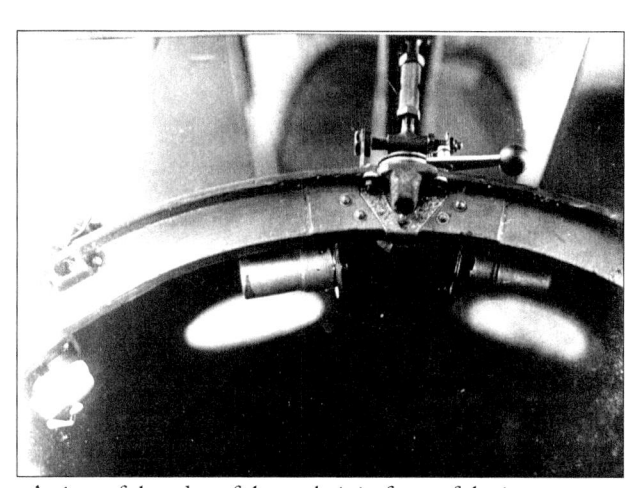

A view of the edge of the cockpit in front of the instrument panel. The device with the ball lever was used to set the OP-1 gunsight before firing. The two light spots are nothing but windows, via which the instrument panel was lit.

18   The King of Fighters Volume 2

The OP-1 gunsight with a cylindrical foam rubber eyepiece.

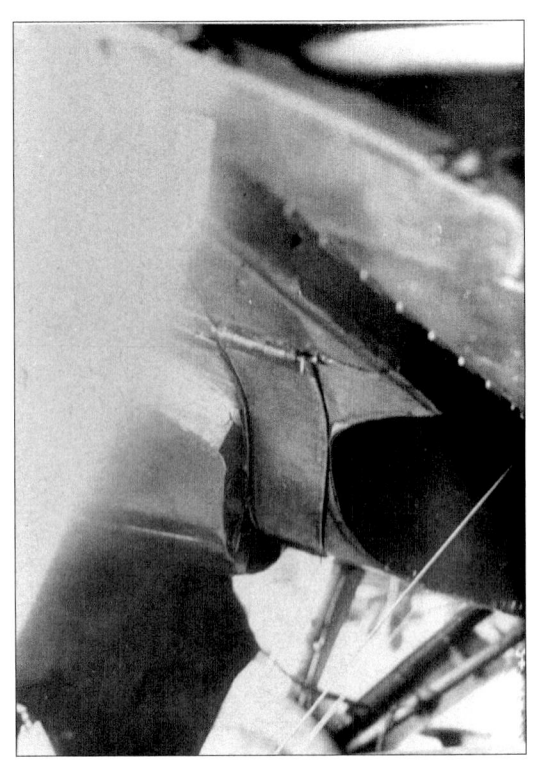

The lower portion of the fuselage near the landing gear well and the cowling edge. In between there is the ammunition box, which was lowered in the course of filling.

The forward portion of the I-16 Type 4 cowling. Note the crankcase fairing provided with cooling windows. The metal propeller is fitted with a ratchet for starting the engine from a motor car starter.

A view of the rear portion of the M-22 engine with the outer and inner cowl flaps removed.

Inside view of the hinged door on the left side of the cockpit.

The instrument panel in the cockpit of an I-16 Type 4.

The tail unit of the I-16 M-22 s/n 123914 built at Aviation Factory No.39. This aircraft featured a long fairing (fillet) covering the entire slot between the vertical stabiliser and the rudder.

A removable duralumin fairing on the rear portion of the I-16 M-22, with a white KhS-35 navigation light and the visible teardrop-shaped small fairing for the elevator control lever.

A tail skid fitted with a *lyzhonok* (Russian for 'tiny ski') for winter flying.

Under-wing flares for night flying under the right wing of the aircraft s/n 123914.

The UT-2 trainer s/n 8211 during tests in May 1935.

The UTI-2 M-22 fighter trainer with retractable landing gear in 1937.

The M-58-powered UTI-3 trainer s/n 11211.

the manufacture of I-14s and I-15s. As for the I-16, it was deemed to have been put into production and provided with the M-22 engine (albeit not a state-of-the-art one) by the manufacturer, and that was, for the time being, quite enough.

Under the circumstances, it was suggested that in the course of further improvements of the I-16, the designers should be oriented towards the M-58 engine. This decision raised considerable doubts in Nikolay Polikarpov, since problems with Soviet-built engines were widely known. The M-58 nine-cylinder air-cooled engine had a dry weight of 465kg, a maximum power of 785hp and a rated power of 630hp. After appropriate improvements, it was decided that the M-58 should be put into production at Factory No.29 in Zaporozhye. However, production of the French Gnome-Rhône Mistral Major engine was launched at the factory in 1935, leaving no place for the Soviet engine.

Further development of the I-16 was thus suspended due to unavailability of a suitable engine. Several events then took place which contributed to a change of situation for the better for the model.

There were intense discussions in 1934 about the I-16 and the problems pertaining thereto, both in the GUAP and the Air Force, for whom the appearance of this new type was not just a routine event. After the state tests of the TsKB-12bis, on 1 October 1934, head of the GUAP G. Korolyov sent the following message to Soviet leader Joseph Stalin: "Please be informed that the Wright Cyclone-powered I-16 fighter built by Factory No.39 has developed a speed of 430km/h at an altitude of 3,000m, thus winning first place for us in the world in terms of fighter aircraft." Stalin responded with a sarcastic remark to the effect that the world speed record was 500km/h, and it was not the Soviet Union that held it. However, Stalin was aware of the difference between a special-purpose record-setting aircraft and an aircraft intended for combat operations. Therefore, he decided to personally see the I-16.

One day in November 1934 (according to the recollections of pilot and designer Vladimir Shevchenko, it took place shortly after the first November snow had suddenly thawed), luxury government cars arrived at Khodynka airfield in Moscow. Among the visitors were Stalin, Sergo Ordzhonikidze, Lazar Kaganovich, Anastas Mikoyan and other party leaders, who all wanted to see the I-16. Chkalov took his seat at the controls and performed demonstration aerobatics before the government delegation. When it was time to land, the capricious landing gear became stuck in the process of extension, as happened quite often. Chkalov performed several spectacular loops to produce acceleration and thus extend the landing gear completely, as he had done before more than once. Stalin was particularly impressed by the show; after the landing, he wished to personally get acquainted with the pilot. Stalin then began to ask other factory pilots and NII VVS pilots who attended the flight demonstration about their opinion of the new fighter aircraft. By that time, approximately 20 pilots had tried out the aircraft, either formally or informally.

All the respondents spoke highly of the aircraft. To Stalin's question, "So what do you think, do we need such an aircraft?", the general consensus was, "We need it very much, comrade Stalin!" This was also when it was suggested that five special-purpose lightweight I-16s should be built for performance of group demonstration flights. It is not known who was the first to raise the issue; however, almost all experienced Soviet aerobatic pilots were present at that time on the airfield. Stalin also had an idea of the subject under discussion: the previous summer, on Aviation Day (18 August), he had been watching the parade aerobatic team flying spectacular aerial stunts in the I-5 fighters.

The order for manufacture of the five special-purpose I-16s, which were to be built before the May Day demonstration of 1935, was placed with Factory No.39. Shortly afterwards, in January 1935, Director of Factory No.39 Margolin was appointed interim head of the GUAP. From that moment on, work on the order, which was informally dubbed 'Stalin's Assignment', was carried out meticulously and under special supervision.

All five aircraft were fitted with Wright Cyclone F-3 American-built engines. Basically, their configuration duplicated that of the TsKB-12bis, but with all the required modifications and improvements made to the structure and the equipment. In March 1935, when the brand-new I-16s came from the factory, the group of five pilots to fly them consisted of Vladimir Kokkinaki, Vladimir Shevchenko, Stepan Suprun, Vladimir Evseev and Edgard Preman. Kokkinaki was the leading pilot for the group. The aircraft were painted bright red; only the cowlings, in accordance with the unwritten traditions in existence at Factory No.39, were black.

Training began almost immediately after the arrival of the aircraft. In the morning, all of the group of five, who were NII VVS test pilots, set out on their duty assignments. It was only in the afternoon that they gathered to practice group aerobatics. It should be noted that masterly skills in aircraft piloting were not the only thing required to be a member of the aerobatic team. Each member had to have absolute confidence in the team leader and to be able to repeat all his manoeuvres without any delay or doubt, all the more so because, as time went on, the aerobatic manoeuvres were growing more sophisticated, and at times the distance between the team members' aircraft wingtips did not exceed 1 or 2 metres.

The most spectacular manoeuvre was the slow ascending roll performed by the entire team, with all five aircraft rushing into the sky while rotating as a single whole. For the May Day demonstration in Red Square, a rather complicated and hazardous stunt was devised, with the consent of Air Force Commander Y. Alksnis. It was decided that the aircraft should fly into Red Square via the passageway between the State Department Store and the Historical Museum at a height lower than that of the buildings. In other words, the aircraft were going to use the route that was typically employed by tank columns during parades to enter Red Square. The passageway mentioned above does not now exist: Iverskaya Chapel, which was previously situated there, has been restored at its place.

It was clear that the pilots faced an extremely difficult task. Therefore, two poles were installed on the airfield and for several days the entire team of five aircraft practiced flying between them over and over again. The distance between the poles was gradually reduced until it was equal to the width of the passageway to Red Square. On 30 April 1935, pilots of the team visited the venue of the forthcoming event. At Kokkinaki's request, a thick white strip was painted on the cobblestones, which was intended to serve as a reference mark for the pilots.

On the next day, which was May Day (1 May), the team of five bright red I-16s descended to a height below the roofs of the buildings, stormed into Red Square with a deafening roar and, rotating all together, corkscrewed into the sky. The effect was amazing!

Upon return to the airfield, the pilots were about to leave for their homes so as to join their families at holiday tables when an aide sent by Marshal Voroshilov arrived. He brought collar patches indicating extraordinary promotions and a cash bonus of 5,000 roubles for each of the pilots. Simultaneously, there was a phone call from Voroshilov. He asked for Kokkinaki to be put on the phone and said, "Comrade Stalin is delighted with the pilots' skills, and is requesting them to fly above Moscow once again."

After that, the team of five flew above Moscow streets again and again. The aircraft were seen in different districts of the city. Their flights even later gave rise to a legend that there were several 'Red Fives' flying above Moscow on 1 May 1935.

In the evening, members of the aerobatic team – including Valery Chkalov – were invited to a banquet in the Kremlin, where Stalin proposed a toast to the health of the Soviet pilots. The triumphant pilots themselves only had a taste of the wine, as they intended to repeat their flights on the following day.

On 2 May, Soviet leaders headed by Stalin inspected aircraft on the Central Airfield in Moscow. Valery Chkalov was among the pilots who took part in demonstration flights. Stalin had already paid attention to him; he had not forgotten their meeting in November the previous year. It was not only Chkalov's high-flying skills but also his open and courageous behaviour that obviously appealed to the Soviet leader. This time, Stalin kissed the pilot in public after landing and talked to him for some time. It is believed that it was on that day that Stalin pronounced his famous and later widely circulated phrase to the effect that the life of a Soviet pilot was more valuable than any aircraft. From that moment on, Chkalov was the most renowned pilot in the Soviet Union. As for the I-16, the author hesitates to make a positive assertion, but it is probable that the aircraft also, at that moment, won special favour with the Kremlin leaders.

Four members of the first 'Red Five' on 18 August 1935. From left to right: Vladimir Kokkinaki, Stepan Suprun, Vladimir Evseev and Vladimir Shevchenko. The fifth member, Edgard Preman, is absent for some unknown reason.

Pilots of a later 'Red Five' led by Major Mikhail Yakushin, who is on the far left, during Aviation Day on 18 August 1939.

The 'Red Five' team of the I-16 fighters in mid-air.

Major Yakushin near his I-16 Type 10. In Spain, Yakushin flew the I-15 fighter, in which he scored several air victories. On the night of 25/26 July 1937, he was the first of the Republican pilots to shoot down a Ju 52 bomber.

Lieutenant Colonel V. Klevtsov near the I-16 Type 10 s/n 1021242. The wide canvas belt thrown over the fuselage was used to lift the aircraft tail.

The I-16 fighter   23

Power plant of the TsKB-12 s/n 123954. The side doors of the engine cowling are removed.

A production I-14 M-25 fighter during state tests at NII VVS in 1936.

The TsKB-12 s/n 123954 near hangar gates in Factory No. 39. The aircraft, fitted with the Wright Cyclone F-3 engine, became a reference aircraft for the production of the I-16 Type 5 series.

The forward portion of the TsKB-12 s/n 123954. The movable shutters which regulated the engine cooling are fully opened.

Nikolay Polikarpov with the Order of Lenin awarded to him in May 1935 for creation of the I-16 fighter aircraft.

The meeting at Khodynka on 2 May also had positive consequences for Nikolay Polikarpov. On 3 May, People's Commissar of Heavy Industry Sergo Ordzhonikidze wrote a note to the Central Committee recommending the awarding of the Order of Lenin to Polikarpov and Chkalov.

On 5 May, newspapers published the following official statement by the Central Executive Committee of the Union of Soviet Socialist Republics:

The Central Executive Committee of the USSR has decreed as follows: The Order of Lenin shall be awarded to:

- Design Engineer Nikolay Polikarpov – for outstanding achievements in the sphere of designing new high-quality aircraft constructions; and
- Test Pilot Valery Chkalov – for repeatedly demonstrated exceptional courage and bravery during tests of new aircraft types.

In late May, Stalin decided to demonstrate the masterly aerial team to the Prime Minister of France, Pierre Laval, who was at that time on a visit in Moscow. The decision to make the demonstration was an unexpected one, and came as a surprise for the pilots.

According to Vladimir Shevchenko, the team members were at the time practicing clockwise rotation in the ascending roll. On the day that the pilots were informed that they would have to fly before the French delegation, it was discovered during aircraft inspection that the right vertical stabiliser attachment fitting on Stepan Suprun's aircraft was damaged. The team was then stationed in Shchelkovo, and needed to set out as soon as possible. What was to be done? After some thought, Kokkinaki made a decision to perform the rotation in the reverse direction. In order to somehow protect the damaged aircraft against failure, the rotation direction had to be changed. The load would now be taken primarily by the left vertical stabiliser attachment fitting. Kokkinaki's decision was thus implemented, and the pilots performed the aerobatics before the French delegation in the counter-clockwise direction with no less success – in spite of the fact that they had never flown like that before.

From 1935 onwards, the 'Red Fives' became an indispensable element of all Soviet air festivals and parades. Squadrons flying I-16s were raised in all military districts. There was an opinion that the demonstration aerobatics, apart from being a spectacular show, helped dispel the mistrust of ordinary pilots in respect of the I-16.

The 'Red Fives; existed until 1941. The aircraft in the teams were flown by different pilots, who rightfully regarded their involvement in such activities as the highest appreciation of their professional skills.

Returning to the aircraft, it should be noted that for over a year from the time when the first TsKB-12 prototypes were completed and one of them was modified to be fitted with the Wright Cyclone F-3 engine, no more I-16 prototypes were built.

The manufacture of the five aircraft for the aerobatic team in spring 1935 contributed to further promotion of the I-16 into real-life application. It was largely thanks to that order that Factory No.39 promptly built an improved I-16, which was further deemed a reference aircraft for production. The I-16 s/n 123954, in some of the documents referred to as 'Aircraft No.54', was rolled out on 25 April 1935. It featured a modified engine cowling with adjustable front cooling shutters, altered aileron attachments and fairings on the hinges of the tail control surfaces. During factory tests, 'Aircraft No.54', with a gross weight of 1,452kg, developed a maximum speed of 456km/h at an altitude of 3,000m. In other words, the maximum speed value had come very close to the target figure of 470km/h.

The new I-16 was considerably superior, in terms of performance, to the I-14 fighter, which had a top flight speed of 445km/h with a gross weight of 1,540kg. For a long time, the I-14's special advantage over the I-16 was believed to consist in its armament, namely the 45mm APK-11 aircraft recoilless guns designed by Leonid Kurchevsky. However, due to unrepairable defects in the APK guns, these had to be abandoned. Consequently, the Resolution of the Council of Labour and Defence of 7 March 1935 prescribed that the I-14s should be fitted with machine guns. This decision, however, did not expedite introducing the I-14 into production at Factory No.125 in Irkutsk. No production aircraft were supplied by the factory in 1935. Later, during state tests, it was found out that the production I-14s had a considerable spin recovery delay. After building 22 aircraft, production of the I-14s was discontinued in 1937.

Meanwhile, production of the M-25 engines at Factory No.19 was gradually gaining pace. Before the end of 1935, the factory manufactured 660 M-25s, often utilising American-made parts. Thus, in the middle of the year, there was confidence that the I-16s would be provided with such engines in 1936.

In view of all the above circumstances, the question regarding the I-16 powered by the Wright Cyclone F-3 (M-25) was discussed in July 1935 at a government session, upon the recommendation of People's Commissar of Defense K. Voroshilov. The discussion resulted in a resolution to launch production of the aircraft in the shortest possible time.

State tests of the I-16 s/n 123954 began on 12 September 1935 and continued until 3 January 1936.

The main recorded performance parameters of the aircraft were as follows: with a gross weight of 1,432kg (empty weight 1,053kg), the maximum speed totalled 359km/h near ground level, 456km/h at an altitude of 3,600m and 445km/h at 5,000m. The aircraft climbed to 5,000m in 5.9 minutes, and the service ceiling was 9,250m. The results obtained during flight tests of the I-16 s/n 123954 offered hope that, in late 1935, the Soviet Union had built the world's best fighter, and was about to put it into large-scale production.

The I-16 was also sent to Italy in 1935 to take part in the international air show at Milan. The Soviet Union presented several exhibits there, including the Yakovlev AIR-9bis, the Chetverikov OSGA-101 and the Putilov Stal-3. The brightly painted I-16 was displayed as an 'ASB sport aircraft' developing a maximum speed of 467km/h. Compared to the elongated, streamlined racing aircraft, it looked plain and did not arouse much interest in other visitors to the show. Few would have thought that large-scale production of the aircraft had already been launched, and that in slightly over a year it would be encountered in real combat.

1.2.4. The last TsKBs. The cannon-armed TsKB-12P

The Design Brigade No.2 of TsKB existed from 1932 until mid-1936. It was in January 1935 that the GUAP decided that all further work to improve the I-16 would be conducted at Aviation Factory No.21, with some consultations from specialists of Factory No.39 and Head of the Design Brigade No.2 of TsKB Polikarpov. It was suggested that the TsKB should prepare the I-16 Wright Cyclone F-3 s/n 123954 for state tests, build a prototype with the Gnome-Rhône engine and a prototype with reinforced landing gear legs ('forks') and a pneumatic retraction system for the undercarriage, and then discontinue all work related to the I-16 in Moscow.

Polikarpov was tasked with designing the I-16 with the 850hp Gnome-Rhône Mistral Major engine in late 1934. The project of the aircraft designated the I-19 (TsKB-25) was ready in April 1935. The aircraft was expected to have a maximum speed of 483km/h at an altitude of 3,000m. In practice, the engine became available only in 1936; for this reason, the airplane was never actually built. The designation I-19 (TsKB-25) was later used for the variant of the I-17 with the M-34 uprated engine designed for glycol cooling.

In late 1934, TsKB began to develop the TsKB-29 aircraft featuring a new landing gear with a pneumatic retraction system and fork-shaped struts. The landing gear configuration was almost entirely 'borrowed' from the I-17 (TsKB-19) fighter prototype which was then being built at Factory No.39. The TsKB-29 was intended to have the Wright Cyclone F-54 altitude engine and had a design speed of 475km/h at an altitude of 5,000m. The design process ended in July 1935; there is no available data regarding the building of the TsKB-29.

In 1935, TsKB was also developing another aircraft designated the TsKB-44, which was an I-16 with four wing-mounted machine guns and the Wright Cyclone F-54 engine. It was intended for use as an unarmoured ground-attack aircraft. It is believed that design documentation for the TsKB-44 was later used in the course of creating the I-162 aircraft at Factory No.21.

Among the projects implemented in practice was the I-16 with retractable skis, which was designed in late 1935. On 2 February 1936, the new winter landing gear was mounted on one of the M-22-powered fighter aircraft. The ski attachment to the landing gear leg was fitted with a special-purpose pivot mechanism, and the rear lower portion of the engine cowling was made shorter.

The tests conducted on two aircraft (s/n 123904 and 123906) demonstrated the efficiency of the mechanism, and the assignment to implement the idea in production aircraft was subsequently given to Factory No.21. For two years afterwards, aircraft in combat units were flying with non-retractable skis. However, in 1938, the problem of retraction was finally resolved. Aircraft manufactured in the second half of the year had a recess in the lower portion of the engine cowling for this purpose. The retraction mechanism was properly adjusted too. From that time on, all production I-16s (except the Type 39) could be flown with skis in the winter season without any tangible impairment of their flight performance.

On 11 May 1936, a resolution of the Council of Labour and Defence was issued related to specialisation of aviation factories and assignment of chief designers to specific production facilities. In connection with this resolution, the majority of Design Brigades in TsKB and TsAGI were reorganised into design bureaus and relocated to various aircraft factories. There was nothing new about this: back in 1934, Design Brigade No.3 under V. Chizhevsky was sent to Smolensk to build the BOK-1 high-altitude aircraft, whereas Design Brigade No.5 led by G. Beriev went to Taganrog to master the MBR-2 flying boat. In 1936, Design Brigade No.1 headed by S. Kocherigin was assigned to Factory No.1; Polikarpov was posted to Factory No.21.

By that time, Nikolay Polikarpov had entered upon the development of several advanced aircraft at once, and was aware that, in Nizhny Novgorod, his opportunities would be considerably limited. For this reason, he made a decision to relocate to the facilities of Aviation Factory No.4 in Khimki, near Moscow. Design Brigade No.2 split accordingly: the majority of the specialists stayed with Polikarpov, while others moved to Factory No.21.

However, before the split of the team took place, TsKB had completed a job which consisted of designing a cannon-armed fighter aircraft under the designation TsKB-12P (I-16P). The explanatory note for the preliminary project prepared in April 1936 read:

The TsKB-12P aircraft is a further development of the TsKB-12 high-speed fighter featuring enhanced flight performance and improved armament. This allows using the available stock of production aircraft built by Factory No.21 and to convert to manufacture of the latest series without any major changes in technological processes and without disturbing the normal pace of work at the factory.

Armament in the I-16P was mounted in the wing in such a way as to enable firing beyond the rotating propeller disc area. The 20mm ShVAK cannons were positioned in the wing centre section, in place of the previously installed ShKAS machine guns. The latter were relocated to the outer wing. The ammunition belt for them was stowed in a long rack-type magazine arranged along the wing span, and it was placed into the aircraft via a hatch in the upper surface of the wingtip. Since the TsKB-12P was intended to be used in the role of a ground-attack aircraft, it was fitted with four bomb racks, which could accommodate 2x100kg or 8x10kg combinations.

For re-equipment, an I-16 Type 5 powered by the Wright Cyclone F-54 engine with the Hamilton Standard variable-pitch propeller was used. The TsKB-12P underwent cannon armament tests during the period from 9 June until September 1936. Flight performance parameters were not measured in their entirety because the aircraft was not new, its landing gear was non-retractable and the fabric skinning required replacement. However, the main objective was achieved: the cannon-armed I-16 was created. Concurrently, the configuration with attached 100kg bombs passed dive tests quite successfully.

After final adjustment of the cannons and ammunition feed mechanisms, tests of the TsKB-12P continued until 8 February 1937. It was then decided that further measurement of flight performance parameters would be taken in a production aircraft, which was expected to arrive from Factory No.21.

1.2.5. Aviation Factory No.21 in 1936: mastering the production of the I-16 Type 5 and Type 12

Creation of the I-16 s/n 123954, which was determined as the reference aircraft for the series, allowed reckoning on the prompt introduction of such aircraft into production in Nizhny Novgorod. The senior officials in Moscow acted in their usual manner, tasking Aviation Factory No.21 with manufacturing 150 M-25-powered aircraft in 1935. One of the causes for such an unexpected turn of events was the decision to discontinue manufacture of the I-15s, thanks to which a sufficient quantity of Soviet-made Wright Cyclones, which were built in Perm, became available. The plans customarily were not fulfilled: until the end of the year, the factory was building the Type 4 aircraft; the new I-16s, designated the Type 5, were formally introduced into production in 1936.

Throughout the year, Factory No.21 supplied to the customer 861 I-16 Type 5s and 27 UTI M-22s. These nearly 900 machines included all the modified and specially outfitted aircraft.

In accordance with the already mentioned resolution relating to chief designers, some of the designers from Polikarpov's Design Brigade were posted to Nizhny Novgorod. The Drawing and Design Department at the factory was split into two separate departments: the Bureau of Experimental Designs and the Production Support Bureau. The Bureau of Experimental Designs was later renamed the Experimental Design Bureau. Its personnel included 43 specialists from the Drawing and Design Bureau and 10 more who had arrived from Moscow. I. Florov was appointed head of the Experimental Design Bureau and, accordingly, Polikarpov's deputy at the factory. A. Borovkov became head of the Production Support Department.

The activities of the Experimental Design Bureau in 1936 included the following:

- Introduction of the TsKB-12P into production.
- Building the I-16 with the *Luch* radio (communication range of up to 40km).
- Introduction of the UTI-4 M-25 into production (eight aircraft were built and supplied to the customer in 1937).
- Introduction of the retractable ski landing gear.
- Introduction of the cockpit heating equipment.
- The I-16bis (I-162).

From among the above-listed activities, the building of a series of the TsKB-12P type cannon-armed aircraft and introduction of the retractable skis were deemed the most important.

The cannon-armed TsKB-12P, when put into production at Factory No.21, was designated the I-16 Type 12. It was nearly autumn when the factory began to produce it, so none of these aircraft were supplied to the customer in 1936. In the records, in particular, it was specified that five Type 12 aircraft were 85% complete. All these aircraft were handed over to the customer in 1937, when a total of 10 I-16 Type 12s were supplied. The factory was instructed to present the first production aircraft for tests in May; however, it was only in the second half of the summer that it was ready for full-fledged testing. State tests of the pre-production I-16 s/n 12219 were conducted during August and September 1937 (under leading pilot Suprun). The aircraft had an empty weight of 1,263kg and a take-off weight of 1,696kg. It developed a speed of 393km/h

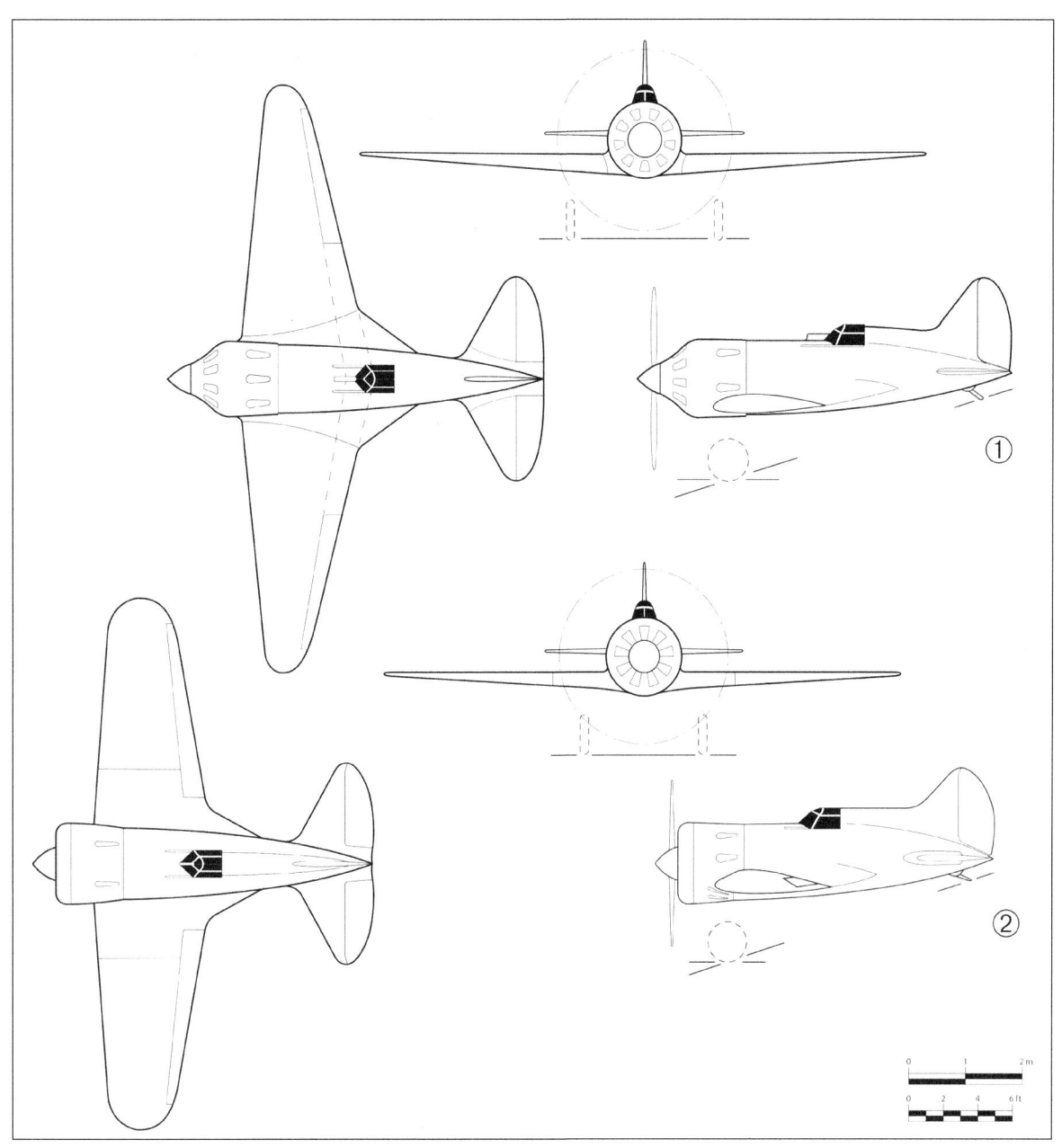

1. Three-view drawings of the I-19 (TsKB-25) project with the 850hp Gnome-Rhône Mistral Major engine in 1935.
2. Three-view drawings of the TsKB-29 project in 1935 featured modified fuselage contours and a new landing gear configuration with pneumatic retraction mechanism.

The ammunition belt for a ShVAK cannon is stowed into the ammunition box arranged in the TsKB-12P fuselage, forward of the fuel tank.

Stowage of the ammunition belt for a ShKAS machine gun with the help of a rack-type guide was implemented only in the TsKB-12P.

28 The King of Fighters Volume 2

The TsKB-12P in the course of cannon armament tests in summer 1936. The landing gear retraction mechanism turned out to be defective; for this reason, landing gear was not retracted at the second stage of the tests.

The ski landing gear retraction process during bench tests in February 1936. The I-16 s/n 123904 is positioned on trestles.

near ground level, 431.5km/h at an altitude of 2,800m and 413km/h at 5,000m. It took the aircraft 7.7 minutes to climb to 5,000m.

The Red Army Air Force planned to order 300 I-16 Type 12s for 1937. Nevertheless, the total number of aircraft produced throughout the year did not go any further than the already mentioned 10 aircraft of the operational testing series. Things took a turn for the better in 1938, with a total of 12 I-16 Type 12s and 27 Type 17s built. But the process of placing the aircraft in service with combat units was a slow one; in mid-1938, the Red Army Air Force mustered only six cannon-armed aircraft. Later chapters will describe how the cannon armament was undergoing improvements in the I-16.

It took nearly two years to introduce the retractable skis. In spring 1937, a decision was made that the I-16s should be fitted with such skis, starting from the 35th series, but the factory failed to meet the schedule. Director of the factory Miroshnikov complained that the retractable skis were a sophisticated mechanism, and that it was an intolerable burden for the factory, given the dramatic shortage of design engineers and production personnel. He was insisting that a decision should be made to install the skis only on aircraft to be supplied to northern regions of the Soviet Union with persistent seasonal snow cover. The issue continued until autumn 1937 when it was resolved, once again, that the retractable skis would be mounted on the I-16s starting from the 37th series. In practice, it was in 1938 that aircraft equipped with retractable skis finally began to be produced.

Concurrently, while experiencing difficulties with manufacture of aircraft included in the Air Force's supply plans, the factory in Nizhny Novgorod continued to progress with its own developments.

Making use of the experience in creation of the I-161, the factory built another aircraft with two additional wing-mounted machine guns, which was designated the I-162 (I-16bis). In the second half of 1936, the aircraft underwent factory tests. Subsequently, by order of Director of the factory Miroshnikov, the I-162s of the operational testing series were produced, which were included in the overall number of the I-16 Type 5s. Five I-162s were supplied to the Bryansk Air Brigade, while another two were handed over to NII VVS.

There is a mention of the I-162 in the verbatim transcript of talks between the Air Force command and pilots who returned from Spain. Director of Factory No.21 Miroshnikov was also present at those meetings. In response to the suggestion to enhance armament in the I-16, Miroshnikov noted, "We supplied five aircraft equipped with four machine guns each … Tarkhov said those were good ones but NII rejected them." To that, pilot Chernykh replied, "They are in Bryansk. I had occasion to perform only one high-altitude flight in it. I never flew it any more. We need [an] electric trigger in it."

The I-162s with four machine guns left no perceptible impact. However, the very fact that they had been built without obtaining approval from the chief designer complicated the relations between Polikarpov and the factory management noticeably. The desire of Evgeny Miroshnikov to make others accept the need for the I-162s frayed, in turn, his relations with the Red Army Air Force command. Later, when officials from the People's Commissariat of Internal Affairs (the Soviet secret police; NKVD, *Narodniy Komissariat Vnutrennikh Del*) got at him in 1937, it turned out that the episode had also been scored up against him.

Another aircraft built at Factory No.21 in 1936 was the I-16 s/n 9211 fitted with six machine guns, which was designed under supervision of A. Borovkov and I. Florov. The ShKAS machine guns, arranged in batteries of three guns each in the wing centre section, could turn downward through 9° in the vertical plane in order to fire on ground targets. The aircraft featured non-retractable landing gear with wheels enclosed in fairings ('pants'). The space under the fuselage, free from the wheels in the retracted position, was used to accommodate racks for six 25kg bomb.

Improvements of the machine guns' turning mechanism and elimination of firing delays took a considerable time. It was only on 27 December 1937 that the I-16 s/n 9211 first flew. In 1938, it was tested at an aviation armament range, aroused much interest and was found to be a good ground-attack aircraft. It was intended that the aircraft would undergo refinement; however, by that time, Borovkov and Florov had transferred to Factory No.207. For this reason, no further improvements were made to the I-16 s/n 9211.

All the above events connected with various improvements and modifications of the I-16 did not relieve the factory of the main task, which consisted of production of the I-16 Type 5. But the mastering of the Type 5 was clouded by a misfortune which marked the beginning of a series of tragic accidents accompanying the flights of the new Polikarpov fighters in the following years.

On 13 February 1936, pilot P. Pavlushev set out in the I-16 s/n 52161 on a mission to reach a ceiling of 8,500m. In general, the flight was going in accordance with the planned figures; however, ground observers noted that the return took place after 55 minutes of flying, which was earlier than the intended time. It was recorded that, on its way back, between 2:00 and 2:10 p.m., the aircraft entered an uncontrollable fall and "crashed into the ground on the edge of the forest near the settlement of Rykovskoye in Sormovo District, at a distance of 3km from the airfield".

Several assumptions were put forward in respect of the catastrophe. However, a malfunction of the oxygen equipment was deemed the most realistic cause. It was believed that at high altitude, the pilot had lost consciousness. He had managed to take off the oxygen regulator but then lost control during his descent. The aircraft had fallen into a spin and crashed. This was the opinion that was shared, among others, by Polikarpov.

In 1931, Pavlushev, who was at that time Commander of the 73rd Air Detachment of the 5th Air Brigade, conducted tests of the I-5 fighter. Later, Pavlushev was invited to Factory No.21, where he was appointed Head of the Flight Test Facility. He was described not only as a skilled pilot but also as the leader of the factory test team. After his death, Tuomas Susi was invited to take over as Head of the Flight Test Facility. Unfortunately, he suffered nearly the same fate as Pavlushev. Susi was killed on 5 September 1939 in a crash during tests of the I-180 fighter prototype. His accident was also brought about by a failure of the oxygen equipment in a flight to an altitude of 10,000 metres.

Operational tests of 10 I-16 Type 5s were conducted by the 34th Air Squadron (under Captain Chivel) of the 56th Air Brigade of the Kiev Military District during the period from 16 May to 21 November 1936. The aircraft were grouped into a detachment under the command of Captain Evsevyev. The aircraft that underwent the tests were those built at Factory No.21 (aircraft s/n 52104, 52110, 52111, 52117, 52120, 52122, 52125 and 52128). One of the aircraft crashed due to the dislocation of a fuel tank in flight. Others flew 40–60 hours each.

The operational tests revealed numerous defects, some of which were rectified when possible. The low firepower (two ShKAS machine guns) and the time-consuming process of manual retraction of the landing gear were mentioned among the main disadvantages of the Type5.

In respect of flight performance, the following was stated:

Taking off in the I-16 M-25 is a complicated process; the aircraft has a long take-off run and tends to turn to the left during the landing run. Low-altitude flying requires special attention on the part of the pilot, since the aircraft quickly loses speed with the control stick slightly overpulled, and falls into a spin. At medium and high altitudes, piloting is fairly easy … Landing in the I-16 is difficult. The aircraft rushes above the ground for a long time; the landing speed is too high; the landing run is too long and unstable in terms of direction.

Completion of the operational tests coincided with the commencement of combat application of the I-16 in Spain. That was where the real tests of the aircraft began. They are described in more detail in the chapter dedicated to events during the Spanish Civil War.

1.2.6. The problems of the 1937

It was in 1936 that the output of engines at Factory No.19 came close to the planned figures, totalling 1,621 M-25s. Concurrently, the engine was undergoing improvements. The factory mastered production of the M-25A version, with an increased take-off power of 715hp at a rotational speed of 2,100rpm. This was followed by the M-25V, which developed 775hp at take-off at a rotational speed of 2,200rpm. In 1937, 2,502 M-25As and 467 M-25Vs were manufactured in Perm.

The factory in Nizhny Novgorod was meanwhile upgrading fighter aircraft and ramping up output. In 1937, Aviation Factory No.21 manufactured the following:

- I-16 M-25A: 1,665 aircraft;
- I-16 Type 12: 10 aircraft;
- UTI-4: 206 aircraft.

It should be noted that the above list mentions the I-16 M-25As. This is done to emphasise the fact that not all of these aircraft corresponded to the main reference aircraft, the I-16 Type 5. Among the modified airplanes there were the following variants:

- 109 aircraft with synchronised armament;
- 41 lightweight aircraft carrying no armament, intended for aerobatic teams;
- one aircraft for V. Grizodubova;
- three aircraft with SN machine guns (completed in 1939);
- one UShA aircraft (the ground-attack version);
- eight aircraft with VISh variable-pitch propellers;
- 20 aircraft with a fixed windscreen accommodating the PAK-1 gunsight;
- three aircraft with 12.7mm ShVAK machine guns (completed in 1939).

One of the first jobs completed in early 1937 was the I-16 Type 5 with additional bomb armament. The aircraft, fitted with underwing bomb racks providing for accommodation of 280kg of bombs, was tested at NII VVS between 10 February and 3 March. The aircraft had four DER-32 racks for four AO-10 bombs and one DER-3 rack for a FAB-100 bomb under each wing. Such a configuration, however, was never put into series production.

The I-16 fighter 31

A movable mount with three ShKAS machine guns in the wing centre section of the I-16 s/n 9211.

An I-16 Type 5 with a fixed windscreen and an OP-1 gunsight. The aircraft is positioned nearly horizontally in order to enable possible armament tryout, complete fuel draining or calibration of instruments.

The I-16 s/n 9211 armed with six ShKAS machine guns during factory tests in autumn 1937.

Senior Lieutenant Lysenko in the cockpit of an I-16 Type 5 in the Byelorussian Military District in December 1939.

The I-16 fighters on the airfield of the Baltic Fleet Air Force in summer 1941. The cowling of the closest aircraft identifies it as a Type 5. Note the cavities for retractable skis in the lower portion of this aircraft, which were typical for later series.

An I-16 Type 5 in the Far East in 1942, fitted with a PAU-22 gun camera on top of the fuselage behind the pilot's seat. Note that the colour of the propeller and its hub is the same as that of the aircraft camouflage.

This picture, providing a good view on the I-16 Type 5's movable canopy, was widely used in the public media, both Soviet and foreign. Note the size of the gap between the engine cowling edge and the wooden skin of the fuselage. The antenna cable lead-ins visible on the fuselage side and on its upper fairing indicate that there is a radio on board.

The next notable event was another modification of armament. Reports from Spain on insufficient firepower with the I-16 were followed by Y. Alksnis' order to immediately tackle this problem. According to the factory correspondence, the version with an additional PV-1 synchronised machine gun was developed in Moscow under the supervision of Polikarpov. It was stated, in respect of these 'special-purpose' aircraft, that there was a need to manufacture them in the shortest possible time, even at the expense of other orders. For this urgent work, Director of the factory Miroshnikov requested that the yearly plan should be reduced by 225 aircraft. Apparently, the officials in the GUAP promised to meet him halfway, but the plan for manufacture of the I-16s was not cut down. It is known that Miroshnikov later claimed that he had been deceived.

In total, 94 aircraft with an additional synchronised PV-1 machine gun were built. This figure differs from the abovementioned quantity of 109 aircraft 'with synchronised armament'. It is possible that the 15 aircraft comprising the difference were equipped with a ShKAS machine gun.

There are other accounts of how the I-16s with three machine guns were built. For example, I. Rabkin relates a story originally told by I. Florov:

> In late December 1937, our factory was visited by representatives of the Air Force and the GUAP. They summoned me and, stating that there was an appropriate order by the management, set the task of equipping the I-16 (which the factory had already been building for two years) with an additional machine gun for synchronised firing through the propeller.
>
> "I instantly began to think over the aspects as were customary for a designer, that is: where it would be better to arrange the machine gun, which relocations would be required for that purpose, how the machine gun should be secured, and how ammunition should be fed to it. In the course of such thinking, I saw an annoying obstacle, that is, one of the fuselage frames. We would have to cut it, then reinforce it, and conduct static tests of the fuselage nose in connection with that. Only upon completion of this work, would we be able to begin testing the machine-gun mount at a shooting range.
>
> I kept thinking while the 'guests' were waiting patiently. Having reckoned the entire amount of work mentally I said that this would take two or three months. The comrades grinned and ordered the director of the factory to cope with the set task before the first of January, that is, in three days. After giving such order, they left.
>
> The director summoned all his assistants and instructed them to obey me unquestioningly and to allocate as many specialists and production facilities for my purposes as I might request. He also ordered that all participants of the activities should work on a twenty-four-hour basis, and arranged for good meals for them.
>
> For seventy-two hours, we did not leave the factory floor, and managed to achieve what we would never have achieved in other conditions and under other circumstances.
>
> The 'miracle' happened. Three days later, one of the production I-16s equipped with an additional machine gun was rolled out to the airfield and handed over to Stepan Suprun, who had arrived to conduct flight tests of the machine-gun mount. Concurrently, reliability tests of the mount at a shooting range and static tests of the fuselage nose were carried out.
>
> Everything proved to be normal. A month after the tests, thirty aircraft with the most powerful armament left factory gates and were sent to Spain.

These I-16s equipped with three machine guns are sometimes determined as Type 6 aircraft. According to other data, the 'Type 6' designation refers to aircraft featuring improved quality of assembly ('export version'), in which the entire set of modifications and upgrades was implemented. At any rate, the Type 6 is not mentioned in any consolidated list, and can be determined as an informal 'Spanish' type. It should be noted, however, that the I-16s with three machine guns are not found in any records relating to Spain either. Most probably, the transport ship with such aircraft was among the Soviet vessels heading for Spain that were sunk (the *Komsomolets*, *Timiryazev* and *Blagoev*). In the factory correspondence related to Spanish orders is the following phrase: "The 30 aircraft were on board the ship that was sunk near Palma de Mallorca."

The events in Spain brought about numerous comments to the effect that the I-16 needed improvement, and that its technical characteristics and combat capabilities required an upgrade. It should be noted that, at an earlier time, there had been more than enough criticism in respect of workmanship of the fighter aircraft. The poor bonding of the veneer sheets, the unskilfully fitted units and mechanisms, and the slovenly assembly and finishing were mentioned among the disadvantages. Such drawbacks were rooted in the enormous and unrealistic plans for aircraft output and the daily race in the hope of fulfilling such plans in conditions of lack of capacity, quality materials and equipment. Indeed, the phrase '*Davai, davai!*' (Russian for 'Move it faster!'), which were pronounced hatefully for the following several decades by all production employees in the Soviet Union, had already been known at that time.

On 3 March 1937, the so-called 'Resolution by two People's Commissars' (Kaganovich and Alksnis) No.01763 was issued, which prescribed making considerable changes to the design of the I-16. The main points from the extensive list of requirements included the following: installing larger 700x150mm wheels instead of 700x100mm ones; installing an improved tail skid; removing the backlash in the controls; and reinforcing the landing gear, the seatback, the vertical stabiliser attachment and the exhaust pipes. There was also a paragraph that prescribed reinforcing the control sticks.

The first accidents brought about by defective control sticks took place in the 142nd Air Brigade in Bobruisk, which received the I-16s in mid-1936. Chief Engineer of the Brigade, I. Prachik, described his participation in the events as follows:

December saw a severe cold set in, which was not typical of the local climate ... However, we kept flying. During one of the flying shifts, the pilots were practicing area flying techniques. There were no forebodings of anything bad. The aircraft took off and headed for the flying area; suddenly, many of the observers from the ground noticed that the *Ishachok* was flying with a much greater climbing angle than usual. Then the aircraft lost speed and began to fall backward, tail first, like in the 'bell tailslide' manoeuvre. After that, it nosed down abruptly and entered a vertical dive. By all appearances, the pilot was making no attempts to undertake anything to save the aircraft or his own life. The fighter crashed into the ground and exploded. The cause of the accident was never identified. Maybe, the equipment had failed; maybe, the pilot had lost consciousness ...

A short time passed. We began to fly again. There was another misfortune in store for us! On that day, two experienced pilots were killed. The squadron leader together with the regimental commissar went in one direction; Evgeny Ptukhin and I made for the place where the other aircraft fell. A short while after we passed the Dnieper, we noticed a cavalry squadron galloping towards us. Then they dismounted from their horses and began to scrutinise something. Soon we also saw the fighter debris, which was scattered by the wind over dozens of metres.

As if through a shroud of mist, I was viewing the cavalrymen, who were telling something ruefully to Brigade Commander Ptukhin. Their words failed to reach my mind; I kept looking for the pilot with my eyes. He lay at a distance of about twenty metres from the crash site holding a fragment of the aircraft control lever in his hand ...

Soon, a commission from the Air Force Administration and a commission from the design bureau arrived at our base; NII VVS also delegated its best specialists ... we received strength analyses for parts and subassemblies of the I-16 fighter from the Polikarpov Design Bureau. These analyses became a major point of contention in the investigation conducted by the commissions: the operational testing series airplane had been tested by Valery Chkalov. And the representatives from Moscow were repeating, in a more and more persistent manner, that our misfortunes were rooted in the incorrect training procedures for flight crews, and that it would not be inappropriate to carry out a thorough check of the brigade pilots' flying technique. Such opinion, however, was unconvincing for us; we kept searching for the true cause indefatigably.

On one of the days, when it was already well into the evening, I put on all the warm clothes that I had, and went to the cold hangar. I climbed into an I-16 cockpit unhurriedly, operated the pedals and the control stick, and suddenly noticed that it was only with a considerable difficulty that I could pull it. 'Probably, it is because of the frost,' I thought. 'But how, then, should it behave at a high altitude, where it is much colder, and the loads on the control surfaces are much higher? Maybe, it is only the case with a single aircraft?' I moved to the cockpit of another *Ishachok*; the situation in it turned out to be the same: the control surfaces operated with difficulty. 'Thus,' I concluded dubiously, 'the problem is brought about by the low temperature.' I kept operating the control surfaces in a more abrupt and energetic manner, as if performing aerobatic manoeuvres with a maximum load. And suddenly ... I heard some crunching sound, like sand between the teeth. I could scarcely trust my eyes: in my right hand, there was a considerable fragment of the control stick, much the same as had been in the hand of the killed pilot. I climbed into the cockpit of yet another aircraft and made several energetic and abrupt movements – and there was the second fragment in my hand ...

Of course, the guess regarding the cause of the accidents had come to my mind earlier than I decided to find a proof for it personally in the I-16 cockpit. Now the hypothesis became a truth: the base of the aircraft control stick tended to fail under a considerable load in low-temperature conditions ... After all the control sticks in the fighter aircraft of this series were replaced, Brigade Commander Ptukhin resumed his practice of coming to the aircraft parking area together with technicians, getting into the cockpit of any randomly chosen fighter, and performing aerobatic manoeuvres above the airfield. That was his method to inspire confidence that our combat aircraft were reliable.

The process of control sticks replacement continued until the beginning of 1938. In total, 2,025 new sets were sent to combat units; these were followed by another order for 250 additional sets. Controls of the newly manufactured aircraft were appropriately modified and reinforced.

Replacement of wheels with the larger 700x150mm ones began in October 1937, from the 31st series. As for other modifications, their number turned out to be considerable: according to estimates by the factory design bureau, over 3,000 changes were made to the structure and equipment of the I-16 before the end of the year.

There were considerable complaints in respect of the movable cockpit canopy, which was installed on the Type 4 and Type 5. The canopy moved over the pilot by means of special rails to a stop at Frame 6 of the fuselage. Apart from the mechanical fixation in a closed position, the canopy was retained by air flow. Rubber-cord shock absorbers facilitated moving the canopy into the open position. The idea was initially not bad, but there were difficulties with moving the canopy forward in flight. There were cases when it was stuck in the closed position, thus preventing the possibility for the pilot to bail out in an emergency situation. Furthermore, the quality of the celluloid used in the canopy left much to be desired; when spattered with motor oil, it provided poor visibility from the aircraft. All these circumstances could hardly inspire confidence in pilots in respect of the canopy, so they tended to retain it in the open position.

Consequently, a fixed windscreen was designed. Its author was Director of the factory E. Miroshnikov. Rather simple and comprising only two parts, the windscreen became the last component which complemented the final external appearance of the fighter. The new windscreen was mounted in the I-16 s/n 521096 in early 1937. In February, the aircraft was handed over to NII VVS. Pilots pointed out the acceptable levels of wind blowing-in into the cockpit and a noticeable improvement of visibility. In September 1937, these windscreens were installed in 20 production aircraft, while series production of the windscreens began in 1938 for the I-16 Type 10. Due to a shortage of the PAK-1 collimator gunsights, the I-16 Type 5s with fixed windscreens were fitted, for the most part, with old OP-1 optical gunsights.

In summer 1937, apart from the elementary windscreens, several modified-design variants of cockpit canopy were suggested for introduction on the I-16. Specialists at NII VVS developed and manufactured a canopy with a fixed windscreen and a rearward-movable middle portion. In terms of size, such canopy, mounted in the I-16 s/n 210601, was smaller than the previous variant. Pilots Tabarovsky, Suprun and Nikashin, who test-flew the aircraft in March 1938, unanimously rejected the new design. In their opinion, closing the canopy required much effort; its size was small and hampered the pilot's head movements; and visibility (especially during landing) was poor. Besides, the celluloid was still not transparent enough; it even more hindered and distorted the view from the cockpit. The canopy was found unfit for service, and all further experiments with it were abandoned.

Later, five variants of the windscreen with flat side faces and 62–64mm thick transparent frontal armour were developed at NII VVS for the I-16. Another version with a 55mm thick armored glass was built at Factory No.21. The trihedral version, weighing 10.8kg with the PAK-1 gunsight and 9kg with the PAN-23 gunsight, was approved. The windscreen was manufactured and tested in combat conditions during the Winter War, but was never put into production.

Special mention should be made of the activities to reduce the weight of the I-16 structure. In particular, Polikarpov believed that a reduction in weight might help achieve a considerable improvement of the aircraft's performance. Many pilots agreed with him. In practice, however, the I-16 was gaining weight from series to series.

In 1937, work to reduce its weight was carried out within the framework of the order for aircraft intended for aerobatic teams. In early August, the factory provided, for flight evaluation, nine weight-reduced I-16s after making 63 modifications and additions to their design. Head of NII VVS Division Commander Bazhanov and Senior Lieutenant Suprun test-flew the aircraft and were happy with it. Stepan Suprun was impressed to the extent that he even declared that these aircraft were more manoeuvrable than the I-15s.

In October 1937, state tests of one of the weight-reduced aircraft (the I-16 s/n 5210660 with the M-25A engine) were completed. Thanks to the stripped-off equipment, the aircraft take-off weight was reduced to 1,490kg. The reduction in weight and a more thorough finish helped increase the maximum speed by 15–20km/h, while the time to perform a turn totalled 12.3 seconds. The aircraft had a more forward centre of gravity, which had a positive impact on the increase of inflight stability.

The weight reduction experiments continued in the course of introduction of the I-16 Type 10. To obtain comparison characteristics, three aircraft (s/ns 1021241, 1021242 and 1021243) were built in late 1937 through to early 1938. In these airplanes, various measures to reduce weight were implemented. In particular, the instrument panel was made smaller; the number of instruments was reduced; the storage battery, flares and navigation lights were removed; the floor was cropped; and the section of the tubes for attachment of the upper machine guns and the diameters of the pressure gauge tubes were reduced. Furthermore, the cowling recesses were made of B-1 duralumin instead of sheet steel; the electric starter was removed; and more lightweight fabric was used for the wing skin. In the I-16 s/n 1021241, the oil cooler was removed; the cast oxygen cylinder was replaced with a welded one; and the depth of the landing gear well dome was reduced by 25mm. Besides all this, wheels with rims made of the Elektron alloy were used, and a lighter old-design tail skid was installed. The ammunition load in all three aircraft was reduced; furthermore, two of them were flying with two machine guns. The eesults of the weight reduction were as follows:

- I-16 M-25V s/n 1021242: weight reduction by 139kg (with four machine guns);
- I-16 M-25V s/n 1021241: weight reduction by 193kg (with two machine guns and without the oil cooler);
- I-16 M-25A s/n 1021243: weight reduction by 194kg (with two machine guns).

In the course of the state tests at NII VVS in July 1938, the weight-reduced I-16s were flown by Taborovsky, Kravchenko, Kokkinaki and Susi. The aircraft were compared with the standard production I-16 M-25V s/n 1021191, and the results are set out in the table below:

I-16 M-25V	s/n 1021191	s/n 1021241	s/n 1021242	s/n 1021243
Gross weight (kg)	1,668	1,507	1,561	1,506
CG position (% MAC)	30.6	27.1	26.6	26.4
Time to climb to 5,000m (minutes)	7.0	5.4	6.3	6.2
Time to climb to 10,000m (minutes)	17–17.2	14.5–15	15.8–16	14.1–14.5
Take-off run (m)	330	220	300	255

State tests of the I-16 Type 5 with additional bomb armament in February 1937. Two FAB-100 bombs are attached under the wing on the DER-3 racks.

The I-16 Type 5s with movable cockpit canopies and installed gun cameras from the 61st Air Brigade of the Red Banner Baltic Fleet Air Force. The distinctive aircraft feature black engine cowlings, red rudders and propeller hubs of various colours.

An I-16 Type 5 with the tactical number '50' with some of the later I-16 Type 10s.

The weight-reduced I-16 s/n 1021242 during
the course of evaluation tests in 1938.

A weight-reduced I-16 Type 5 built in 1937. Intended
for the aerobatic 'fives', the aircraft is painted
red. The insignia stars are of a silver colour.

It was pointed out that the weight-reduced I-16s demonstrated a considerable improvement in rate-of-climb, manoeuvrability and stability. The new landing flaps increased the aircraft weight by 30kg, but on the other hand they allowed landing on limited-size fields. In particular, the landing run of the production I-16 Type 10 fitted with the landing flaps was equal to that of a weight-reduced aircraft without such flaps. Efficiency of the new ailerons dropped by 20%, but according to the test-flying pilots, remained quite sufficient. In respect of the I-16 s/n 1021241, it was pointed out that flying at the maximum speed without an oil cooler for over five minutes was not possible.

It was recommended to further use the majority of the weight-reducing methods, and to use the I-16 s/n 1021242 with mechanical flap control as a reference aircraft for production. In practice, the gross weight of the production I-16 Type 10 exceeded 1,700kg. This considerably degraded the combat capabilities of the I-16 Type 10, which pilots noticed in the course of encounters with the Nakajima Ki-27 Japanese fighters at Khalkhin Gol in mid-1939.

1.2.7. Wing reinforcements

This topic continues the narration of the I-16 drawbacks detected in 1937. However, the specific severity of the events, which had noticeable consequences, persuaded the author to describe it in a separate chapter.

Spring 1937 saw a series of mysterious crashes in combat units operating the I-16. In aircraft s/n 521999, 5210229 and 5210243, wing separation occurred during the course of performing an ascending roll. As this manoeuvre had never been performed before, the failure was attributed to nothing but performance of the rolls accompanied by high acceleration at the wingtips. Throughout May, four more crashes brought about by wing failures occurred in Red Army Air Force units, with no confirmation of performance by those aircraft of any extreme manoeuvres. A short while later, more crashes were reported in Spain. Several Soviet and Spanish pilots were killed in these incidents.

Spanish pilot Antonio Arias, who had with fellow young countrymen completed flying training in the Soviet Union, arrived at the El Carmolí airfield near Los Alcázares, south-east Spain, in May 1937. In his memoirs, he described the following tragic events:

> It was during the days of preparation for combat sorties that we saw, among other things, aircraft crashes. They cast a considerable gloom over us. The crashes occurred in that very group that was preparing to leave for the north. During the flight above the Mar Menor lagoon, which was the final one in the training cycle, one of the fighter aircraft failed to recover from [a] spin and fell into the sea. We saw that with our own eyes but it took us some time to become aware that something irreparable had just happened.
>
> "This is horrible!" pronounced Luis Frutos. We were standing silent, petrified, expecting for some miracle to happen, for the fighter to come up in a little while and to take to the air again. But no miracle happened. The combat aircraft disappeared forever in the depths of the sea together with the pilot.
>
> We had hardly recovered from the shock when another fighter fell into the sea. We were simply dismayed. That could have happened to any one of us.

The accident boards in the Soviet Union and Spain found similar failures during the course of aircraft inspections. Nearly all of the crashed I-16s demonstrated ruptures in the skin of the wingtip leading edge and failures of rib attachments near the aileron hinge fittings. It was clear that the crashes were brought about by insufficient structural strength.

On 18 May 1937, the first meeting on the issue of wing reinforcements took place in Moscow, with employees of the Polikarpov Design Bureau and representatives of the factories and the Red Army Air Force command taking part. It was recognised that grave workmanship defects had been found in the course of examination of the crashed aircraft. It was pointed out that the adjustment of the internal bracing wires had been incorrect; the duralumin skin had been secured using clips instead or rivets, while duralumin debris, fabric shreds and metal washers had been found inside the wing. After the inspection, in the Byelorussian Military District, of 85 I-16s built in 1936–37, 46 were rejected.

The next meeting was held on 20 May, when a plan of activities for wing reinforcement was drawn up. Initially, it was intended that the work should be done directly in combat units, with factory teams to be delegated there. However,

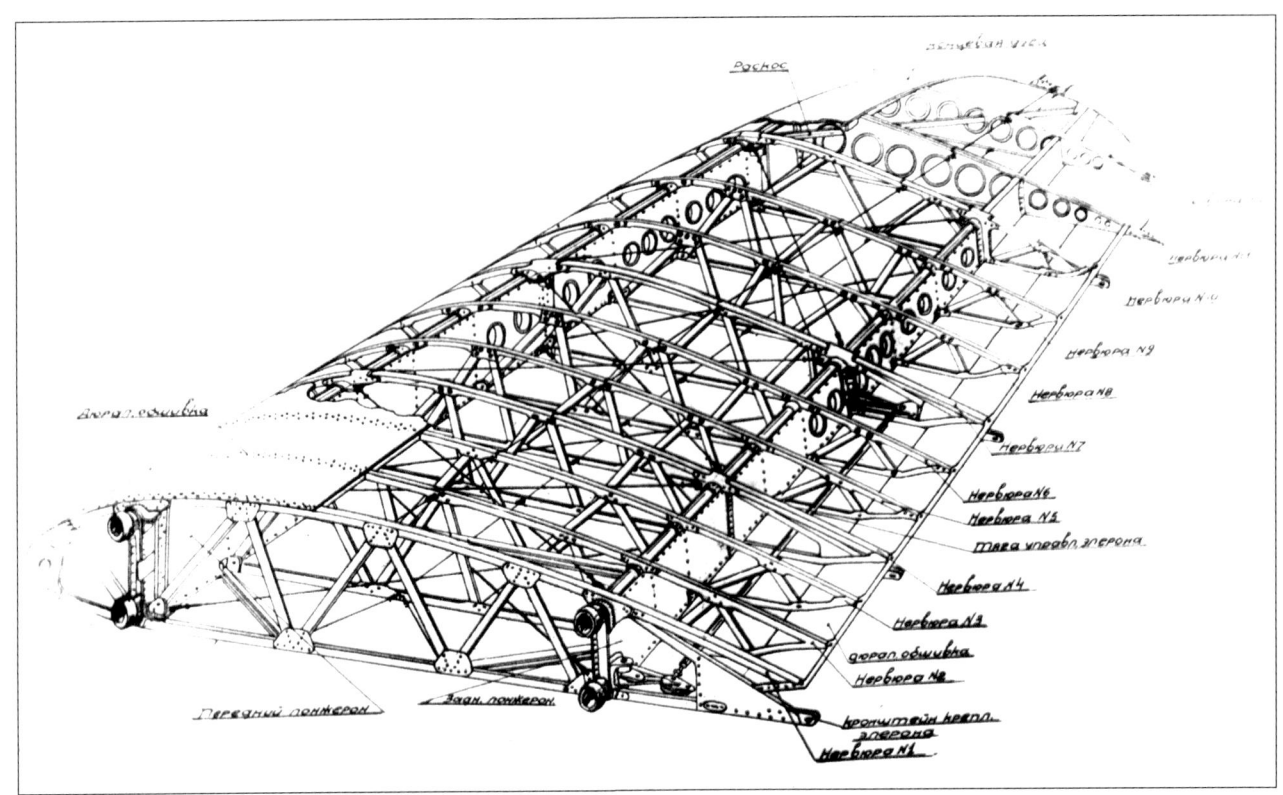

An original drawing of the structure of the earlier-series I-16 wing.

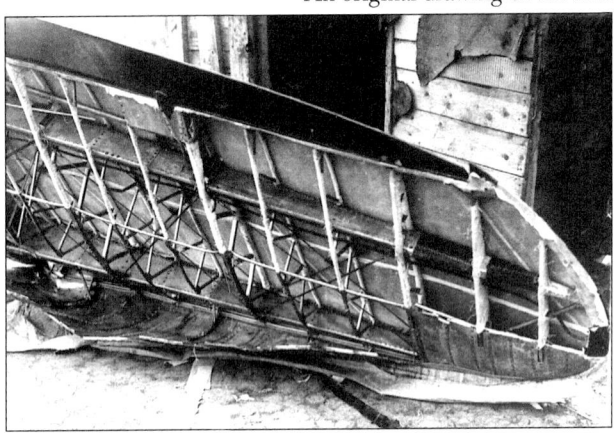

A fragment of wing of a crashed aircraft.

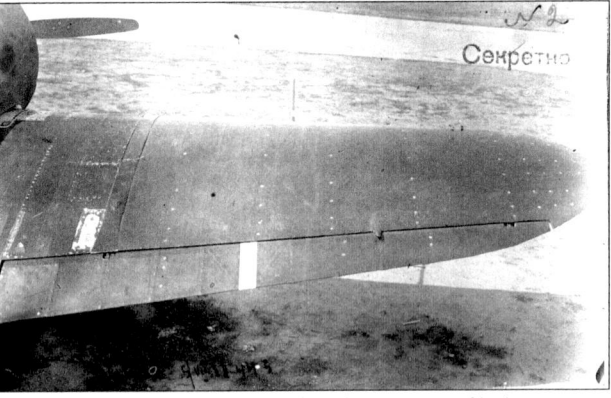

An I-16 wing equipped with a system of holes (vents) to determine air pressure changes at various speeds in the summer of 1937.

The new pilot windscreen with the PAK-1 gunsight which began to be introduced in late 1937.

a decision was finally made to carry out the corrective work in permanent-site conditions at several aviation factories. Consequently, specialists at Factory No.21 began to arrange a wing reinforcement workshop and created an exchange pool of 100 reinforced wings.

The first checks of wing strength showed that they withstood 100% of ultimate load, and failure occurred only with the load increased to 157%. After strength recalculation according to new updated standards of 1937, it turned out that the wing withstood only 80–90% of the load.

However, the results required additional confirmation, so specialists of the TsAGI were tasked with examining the wings of the I-16. From 26 July to 4 August 1937, TsAGI conducted static tests of outer wing panels, dynamic tests of wing centre sections and outer wing panels, and inflight tests of a specially equipped aircraft.

The tests included comparing reinforced and non-reinforced wing tips; they were loaded as per all flight conditions in accordance with strength standards of 1934 and 1937. From among all the tested specimens, a specially selected non-reinforced wingtip with visible workmanship defects failed first. It withstood only 80.6% of the normal value. The wing centre sections, even including those with visible defects and cracks in welded assemblies, successfully withstood the loads.

For inflight testing, a special wing equipped with a vent system and a so-called 'pressure recorder' was prepared. The flights allowed the determining of air pressure changes during various aircraft manoeuvres. In conditions of a very abrupt pullout at a speed of over 400km/h, local pressure on the wingtip exceeded the normal value by 43%, which was accompanied by a shift of the centre of pressure towards the leading edge. In the opinion of the scientists, this phenomenon was brought about by a change in the airfoil due to deformation at high accelerations. Thus, the main methods to be used for achieving sufficient strength of the I-16 wing were successfully determined.

Among the first assignments, Factory No.21 was, under a special instruction of the VVS RKKA, tasked with manufacturing 68 sets of reinforced wings in the shortest possible time to be supplied to Spain (150 wings were reinforced and covered with fabric *in situ* using local resources). The next task was to replace 725 wings, first of all on the aircraft of the 28th through to the 32nd series. The spars were first reinforced and the skin was replaced on the already built aircraft. Additional inner inserts (bougies) were placed inside spar tubes; hence the adoption of the term 'bougied wing'. Thickness of the duralumin spar walls was increased from 0.8mm to 1.5mm on the front spar, and from 1.0mm to 1.2mm on the rear spar. Some wings were provided with additional 1.0mm thick strips, and the attachment of Rib 11 and Rib 12 was reinforced. These activities were carried out not only in Nizhny Novgorod, but also at Aviation Factory No.81 in Moscow and Aviation Factory No.153 in Novosibirsk. Thus, the structure of 1,754 wings was reinforced in 1937.

The next assignment for Aviation Factory No.21 in 1937 consisted of the manufacture of 500 new wing sets in excess of the plan for the year. In total, to replace all the previously made outer wing panels, 2,742 wing sets (the sets consisted of two outer wing panels: the left and right) had to be manufactured. As a result, at Aviation Factory No.21, two-thirds of the experimental shop was busy manufacturing spare wings. Furthermore, control over the quality of handed-over products became much tougher.

Before mid-1938, Factories Nos.21, 81 and 153 continued their work on wing replacement. During that period, 2,829 sets of reinforced wings were manufactured and supplied to military districts operating the I-16s. New series I-16s with the reinforced structure began to be built in May 1938.

1.2.8. The Grizodubova *airplane*

In the mid-1930s, reaching world records became an indispensable feature in the development of the Soviet aviation industry. While the highest figures for flight range and lifting cargo to great altitude had already begun to yield to Soviet aviation, the situation regarding speed records was less promising, mainly due to the Soviets lagging behind in engine-building technology. However, there were certain individual categories where Soviet aviators were able to bring more aviation fame to the Soviet Union. For instance, women's records, which added noticeable variety to the international table of the world's achievements, became of vital importance.

The Soviets aimed to have an I-16 beat the result achieved by French female pilot Hélène Boucher (445km/h). Boucher had been flying in a Caudron C.450 monoplane powered by a 415hp engine in 1934–35. It is not quite clear how the Soviet organizers of the attempt intended to circumvent the nuances of segregation per weight categories. The French pilot, with her speed, was in the category of light aircraft having a gross weight of below 560kg, whereas the I-16 gross weight was approximately a ton and a half. Most probably, it was the absolute speed figure that was of most interest at the time and had a specific political significance whenever any national record was set.

Valentina Grizodubova, a 26-year-old pilot, was put forward to break the record for the Soviets. She had the most extensive experience of female Soviet aviators and the highest number of flying hours (approximately 6,000), and was thus considered an ideal candidate for setting aviation records. For several years, Grizodubova had been flying in the propaganda squadron named after Maxim Gorky, but in 1936 she joined the VVS RKKA.

The new 1,200hp M-62F uprated engine became the basic prerequisite for breaking the speed record. Creation of this engine was central to attempts to improve radial engines of this type. Factory No.19 in Perm guaranteed that, as delivered,

The record-breaking I-16 s/n 5210671 at the accident site near the factory airfield in Nizhny Novgorod on 3 October 1937.

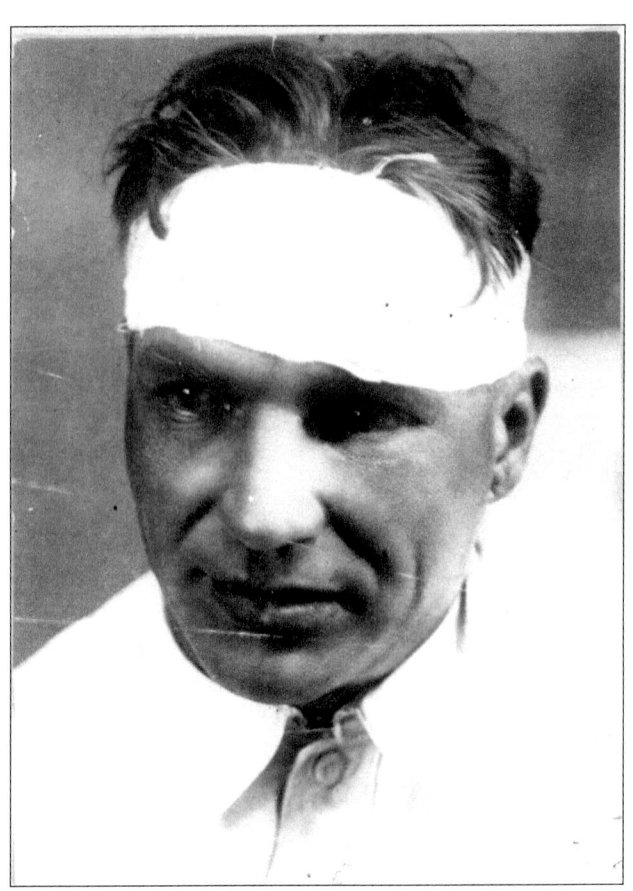

Valery Chkalov after the accident on 3 October 1937.

the M-62F would be capable of 1,170hp at the maximum rotational speed of 2,350 rpm. The allowable continuous running time in such conditions was not more than three minutes, with the total running time in the same conditions being up to 30 minutes and operational time at the rated setting not exceeding 90 minutes.

As soon as the possibility to manufacture both the engine and a special-purpose aircraft was confirmed, the mechanism of preparations for breaking the record sprang into operation. On 28 June 1937, the 1st Chief Directorate of the People's Commissariat of Defence Industry (*Pervoye Glanoye Upravleniye Narodnogo Komissariata Oboronnoy Promyshlennosti*, PGU NKOP) issued Order No.169, which set the timelines and responsibilities of the involved parties:

- Director of Factory No.19 Poberezhny was ordered to manufacture two 1,200hp M-62 engines before 25 July 1937;
- Director of Aviation Factory No.21 Miroshnikov was tasked with building the special-purpose I-16 before 5 August 1937;
- Chief Designer Polikarpov was given responsibility for design and reliability of the record-breaking aircraft.

Aircraft preparation activities were carried out under the supervision of Head of General Layouts Group A. Khramov. For the record-breaking attempt, the I-16 s/n 5210671 was used. It was stripped of armament and unnecessary equipment, and a new windscreen made of organic glass was installed. The landing gear was equipped with lightweight 700x100mm wheels, while to eliminate suction of the fabric skin at high speeds, outer wing panels were fitted with additional structural sections (later, such sections began to be installed on all the I-16s). It should be noted that these were not additional ribs but literally structural sections, which were installed only on top in the space between the ribs.

With the M-62I engine s/n 195800 (having a dry weight of 485kg) and a 2.7m-diameter special-purpose propeller, the gross weight of the I-16 s/n 5210671 was 1,450kg. The engine was fed with the so-called *Maglobek* fuel, with an additive in the form of an ethyl liquid which allowed increasing the octane number to 95. It was expected that, in such configuration, the I-16 would be able to develop a maximum speed of 570km/h at a height of 250–500m.

It was during the course of preparations for testing – in August – that the aircraft received the designation I-167 M-62F. However, this name never caught on. Instead, the unusual name *Grizodubova* was mentioned in some documents and became the more popular designation. The engine itself also went down in history under a different designation, being known as the M-62I (not to be confused with M-62IR).

For tests and preparations for the record-breaking flight, test pilot Valery Chkalov was delegated to Nizhny Novgorod. On 3 October 1937, Chkalov was tasked with testing the aircraft, including passing along at low altitude the 1km measured course which was marked along the roadway to Moscow some 10–15km from the airfield.

After take-off, Chkalov flew along the measured course at a speed of 460km/h during the first pass, with engine rotation speed of 2,270 rpm. During the second pass, according to Chkalov, the speed was 440–450km/h. While making the last pass, he heard an unexpected rattle in the engine, after which the engine stalled. As the altitude was so low, there was very little time to him to decide what to do. The Moscow roadway was nearby, with vehicles running along it and people walking on the roadside. The pilot therefore decided to land in a small forested area near the roadway. At the moment of landing, the aircraft was swung around. It struck a tree trunk, causing the fuselage to disintegrate. Chkalov received a head wound, but was lucky to escape more serious injuries. When the first vehicle came rushing to the accident site from the airfield, the pilot was standing near the aircraft with blood issuing from the wound to his head.

Consequently, preparations for breaking the speed record were brought to a halt. A decision was made not to take any further risks, as even with a much more powerful engine, no noticeable increase in flight speed had been achieved for the I-16.

1.2.9. *The hard year of 1938*

In 1938, as well as the re-equipment of more than 2,000 fighters with new wing sets being 'carried over' to Aviation Factory No.21 from the previous year, there was also a considerable amount of problematic and incomplete work related to prototype aircraft. All such airplanes, created in accordance with plans from the Polikarpov Design Bureau, had numerical designations from '163' to '166'.

The I-163-1 (initially dubbed as 'I-163') was intended as a reference aircraft for series production in 1937. This was the first aircraft fitted with landing flaps. In terms of appearance, it resembled an ordinary Type 5, but among further differences were a modified landing gear design, an enlarged area of the control surfaces and the presence of an aerial mast (signifying that the installation of a radio was planned). In the weight-reduced version with two wing-mounted ShKAS machine guns, the I-163 had a gross weight of approximately 1,600kg. The aircraft was powered by the M-25E high-altitude engine, which developed 710hp at an altitude of 5,000m. Starting from April, this aircraft made approximately 1,000 flights throughout 1937, but fell short of meeting the hopes to reach a speed of 490km/h at an altitude of 6,800m due to unstable engine running. In early 1938, it was believed that, in spite of the failure to implement its improvements into series production of the I-16 Type 5s, the I-163-1 prototype had fulfilled its task.

The I-163-2 was an aircraft which had enlarged landing flaps and a landing gear equipped with an oleo-pneumatic retraction system. Due to multiple defects, it never flew.

The I-164-1 (the first aircraft powered by the M-25V engine), also referred to as the I-16s ('s' for *soprovoditel*, Russian for 'escort aircraft'), was equipped with two additional fuel tanks in the wings. Initially, the I-164 was rejected due to poor workmanship and sent back to the workshop for rectification of defects. After the second presentation, factory tests were conducted in February 1938, the aircraft being flown by test pilot Tuomas Susi. With a total fuel amount of 500kg, the aircraft achieved a flight range of 2,000km. The aircraft was later withdrawn from flying due to leakages in the fuel tanks, which were integrated into the wing. It turned out that repairing the tanks without their complete removal was not possible.

The I-164-2 was originally designed for the M-62 engine, then for the M-88. The aircraft was never built, the project with the M-88 engine being transferred, under an order of the GUAP, to engineer A. Silvansky for further study.

The I-165-1 powered by the M-62 engine was also referred to as the I-16bis (not the first Soviet aircraft with such a designation). It had additional wing tanks, a new refined wing (the so-called 'high-speed wing') with rigid skin, modified fuselage shape and engine cowling, and oleo-pneumatic landing gear retraction system. As of 24 November 1935, the I-165-1 had made three flights, after which engine replacement was required. In 1938, it was planned that the aircraft should receive a new wing with modern airfoil and rigid skin, but due to detected defects connected with poor quality of assembly (a lot of parts were manufactured on the spot, without drawings) the aircraft was found unfit for further flying.

The I-165-2 was initially designed for the M-62. However, in early 1938, assembly of the 80%-ready aircraft was suspended. Nikolay Polikarpov believed that more drastic steps were required to improve the airplane, so he decided that it should be fitted with the M-88 engine. This decision led to a thorough recalculation of the centre of gravity position and the strength of assemblies. All these activities slowed down the production process. Furthermore, with the introduction in late 1938 of the I-180 fighter prototype at Factory No.156, such work became irrelevant.

The I-166 fitted with the M-25V engine was a weight-reduced (with a gross weight of 1,383kg) aircraft built under an assignment from TsAGI. Its main difference from the rest of the I-16s consisted of an engine cowling with adjustable shutter-type cooling doors, an exhaust gases manifold and a frontal annular oil cooler. In the course of factory tests, the aircraft was flown by Tuomas Susi.

Apart from the above modifications of the I-16, the fuselage was built and several individual components were manufactured at Factory No.21 in early 1938 for the Ivánov single-engine bomber designed by Polikarpov. During the

The I-163 prototype featured a modified landing gear, landing flaps and an aerial mast for a radio.

The I-16 Type 12 during tests at NII VVS.

The cowling of an I-166 prototype with the M-25V was fitted with adjustable shutter-type cooling doors.

The forced landing of an I-16 Type 10 at the airfield of Design Bureau 29 in Podlipki near Moscow.

An I-16 Type 10 being filled with oil. The fairings of the top-mounted ShKAS machine guns became a characteristic feature of this aircraft.

same period, specialists of the factory studied landing gear kinematics for the I-172 fighter prototype powered by the M-105 engine.

In 1938, considerable work was done in Nizhny Novgorod to put all drawings and design documentation in order; in particular, to ensure dimensional stability of clearances and identity of contours, mould lofts and templates were made to be further used as references during checks of drawings and fixtures. Full recalculation of structural components according to the strength standards of 1937 was carried out too.

However, the main task for Factory No.21 in Nizhny Novgorod for 1938 was introducing the new I-16 Type 10 into series production. This version featured the M-25V engine, which had take-off power of 750hp, two additional fuselage-mounted synchronised ShKAS machine guns, landing flaps, reinforced wings and the windscreen with the PAK-1 collimator gunsight. Additional differences from other I-16 versions consisted of installation of an oil cooler and the provision of an air intake for it in the lower portion of the engine cowling. The first such aircraft, built on the platform of the I-16 s/n 5210436 and determined as a reference for series production, passed state tests in early 1938. The maximum speed increased slightly, reaching 448km/h at an altitude of 3,160m.

In spite of the considerable amount of preparatory work done, introduction of the aircraft into series production – which was scheduled for the beginning of the year – lagged. In January 1938, half a million roubles were allocated to the factory to be used for bonuses in order to encourage employees in the course of introducing into production the first series of the I-16 Type 10. Perhaps that incentive helped: handover and acceptance of the first production aircraft began on 1 February that year.

Concurrently with introduction of the Type 10, a suggestion was put forward that all the earlier-built I-16 Type 5s should be modified into a variant with four machine guns. On 20 February, a note was prepared on the availability of aircraft equipped with two machine guns in service with the Red Army Air Force. According to this document, 2,590 I-16 Type 5s had been built. Of those, 1,340 aircraft belonged to the earlier series (up to the 32nd series), in which installation of synchronisers was impossible: they had an engine mount that was shortened by 200mm, K-25 carburettors with an air heating system, and the fuel pumps and wirings were arranged on the engine rear cover. The number of fighter aircraft belonging to later series (after the 32nd series) was estimated at 1,250. Among them, there were 110 I-16s with additional PV-1 machine guns, 100 I-16s with additional ShKAS machine guns and 30 unserviceable aircraft. Thus, there remained 1,000 I-16 Type 5s, in respect of which it was suggested that they should be rearmed in workshops of military districts; for this purpose, 10 special repair brigades had to be formed. It was expected that all this wide-scale work should be completed in late 1939.

In practice, the rearmament never took place. The factory, which would have had to bear the burden of additional work (in particular, manufacturing new fuel tanks would have been required), was already making great efforts to comply with the yearly plan. Output of aircraft in 1938 proved to be much more modest compared to the previous year, and totalled 1,068 I-16s of all types:

- 169 I-16 Type 5s;
- 508 I-16 Type 10s;
- 12 I-16 Type 12s;
- 27 I-16 Type 17s;
- 352 I-16 Type 15s (UTI-4).

Manufacture of the I-16 Type 5 was discontinued in March 1938, except for one aircraft built in August and another built in November. The airplanes featured fixed windscreens and reinforced wings, and some of them were equipped with reduced-span ailerons.

Production of the I-16 Type 10 began in February 1938 (32 aircraft), after which 40 or 50 aircraft were manufactured per month.

Manufacture of the I-16 Type 12 was discontinued in March; in total, 12 aircraft were supplied.

The I-16 Type 17 entered production in October 1938.

It is worth noting the figures regarding production costs of various aircraft types manufactured in 1938 at Factory No.21. The I-16 Type 5 was estimated at 50,000 roubles, the Type 10 at 90,000 roubles, the Type 17 at 135,000 roubles and the Type 15 (UTI-4) at 40,000 roubles. Judging by the considerable difference between the cost of the instruction and training aircraft and the combat types, it can be seen that machine guns and cannons accounted for a substantial share in the cost of the latter.

There were also events of a different nature in 1938, with the wave of repressions – or purges – reaching Nizhny Novgorod. In April, Director of the factory Miroshnikov and engineer Uspassky were arrested. They were held to account for the wing failures, the failures with the I-162s with four machine guns and the crash of aircraft No.7211. Petr Golubkov was appointed the new Director of Factory No.21.

1.2.10. Airplane No.7211

The plans to install a powerful Gnome-Rhône Mistral Major radial engine (Series K-9 or K-14) on the I-16 have already been mentioned above. In 1936, the Experimental Design Bureau of the factory was given a similar task to design a fighter version powered by the M-85 engine (the license-built K-14). The new power plant utilising such an engine was actually developed by designers A. Borovkov and I. Florov. However, they did not stop at that, creating their own fighter version.

As envisioned by its creators, the aircraft, which was apparently designed using the I-16 as a guide, combined the advantages of a high-speed monoplane and a manoeuvrable biplane. To harmonise the conflicting objectives, they chose the configuration of a biplane with cantilever wings, without the conventional struts and bracing wires. Unusual novelties included the cockpit, which was shifted aft to the maximum possible extent in order to provide better visibility for the pilot, the forward-sliding windscreen and the all-metal wing with smooth skin. The wings were designed as a rigid box, with the skin supported by internal corrugations. Such a design, which later found many advocates, was used in the USSR for the first time here.

The mock-up of an unconventional but rather eye-catching airplane was viewed by Commander of Air Force Yakov Alksnis during his visit to Nizhny Novgorod. Alksnis subsequently authorised manufacturing the aircraft. The one and only prototype was built in early 1937 as 'Airplane No.7211', where '7' stood for Type 7, '21' for Factory No.21 and '1' for the first prototype.

The power plant comprised the Mikulin M-85 double-row radial air-cooled engine with rated power of 800hp at an altitude of 3,850m. The engine was joined to the central truss of the fuselage, to which the upper and lower wing were attached. The tail portion was – the same as in the I-16 – a wooden monocoque covered in birch veneer sheets. The landing gear was non-retractable, with spats over the wheels and legs. The tail skid also had a fairing as well; it was designed as a lower fragment of the rudder and could move upwards when its shock absorber was compressed.

In March 1937, airplane No.7211 was transferred to the airfield. After taxiing runs and further improvements, it was prepared for flight. The aircraft first took to the air with test pilot L. Maksimov at the controls on 6 May that year. Thereafter, during a month of trials, the prototype made 22 flights. The main results of the tests consisted of confirmation of the expedience of the selected configuration and the functional capability of structural components. Special mention was made of the aircraft's flight performance, including easiness of take-off and landing, excellent lateral stability and controllability

The airplane No.7211 prototype with the M-85 engine during the course of factory tests in 1937.

NII VVS test pilot, member of the aerobatic 'five' and participant of high-altitude flights Edgar Yuganovich Preman in front of an I-15.

at all speeds. The aft-moved cockpit did not cause any unpleasant feelings in the course of performing aerobatic manoeuvres (as it had been originally expected to), while ensuring the predicted excellent visibility.

In terms of manoeuvrability, the aircraft was somewhere in between the I-15 and I-16, with the time to perform a turn at an altitude of 2,000m totalling 14 seconds and the time to climb to 5,000m being four minutes and 37 seconds. The maximum speed of 416km/h obtained at 4,000m was found insufficient, all the more so because the designers had expected a speed of 480–500km/h. However, the declared performance parameters were considered as quite realistic provided that wing workmanship could be improved and the propeller be thoroughly selected.

On 1 June 1937, the Type 7 was test-flown by NII VVS pilot Petr Stefanovsky, who gave a positive opinion of the aircraft and suggested ferrying it to Shchelkovo airfield. One of the most experienced test pilots – Edgar Preman – arrived at the airfield of Factory No.21 to carry out the ferry flight. On 22 June, Preman took off in No.7211 to perform the first familiarisation flight. However, the 24th flight of the airplane became its last one, ending in a crash. While making a second approach to land, after an unsuccessful first attempt, the engine stalled. The height was insufficient, the aircraft crashed into a railroad embankment and Edgar Preman was killed.

The cause of the tragedy was found to be that the M-85's carburetor spraying nozzle had been clogged. While the investigation continued, the fate of those involved in the creation of airplane No.7211 remained uncertain. In 1937, for building an aircraft that crashed, one could easily be labelled as the 'people's enemy'. The primary initiator of the construction of the Type 7 – Commander of the Air Force Yakov Alksnis – was arrested, among many other Soviet leaders.

Eight months after the crash of the first prototype, Borovkov and Florov were summoned to Moscow, where it was suggested that they should continue improving the original biplane. On 13 September 1938, the designers prepared an upgraded preliminary project of the Type 7 airplane with the M-88 engine and a pressurised cockpit. At that point, Director of the factory P. Golubkov declared that building another prototype was too much for the factory, and contacted the GUAP with a request to withdraw the airplane from the plan. Subsequently, it was suggested that Borovkov and Florov should move to Factory No.207 situated in Dolgoprudny, near Moscow, taking a minimum number of employees with them. They continued their experiments at Factory No.207 and built several biplanes under the designation I-207.

Immediately after the dismissal of the two leading employees, Mikhail Pashinin arrived to take up the post of the deputy of Chief Designer Polikarpov at Factory No.21. A short while later, Pashinin was appointed Chief Designer of Factory No.21. Such an appointment implied his special powers and authorities.

1.2.11. The I-16 with the M-62 and M-63 Engines

The M-62 engine with take-off power of 1,000hp became the next step in the development of the M-25 engine. The M-62 had improved kinematics and lubricating system, was fitted with a two-speed supercharger that increased the boost pressure and critical altitude, and was designed for the installation of VV-1 and AV-1 variable-pitch propellers designed by Bas-Dubov and Zhdanov (Factory No.28). The M-62 featured enhanced ribbing of cylinder heads and several structural reinforcements, while its weight, compared to that of the M-25V, grew from 450kg to 520kg. It was in the introduction of the M-62 that specific hopes were placed for considerable improvement of the flight performance of aircraft – both those being designed and those already put into production.

As early as 1937, the M-62 was already mentioned in the industry prospective plans. Factory No.24 in Moscow was being prepared for series production of the engine, while A. Shvetsov's Design Bureau kept upgrading the engine in several ways. In the same year, Factory No.19 built 25 M-62s, which were included in the output for the year along with the M-25s. Apparently, these were prototype engines (among them, the one for Grizodubova's attempted record-breaking aircraft), which still had to go through many stages of improvement. Formally, it was planned that the new M-62s and M-63s (at that time the latter was already being mentioned in plans) would be put into series production in 1939.

Installation of the M-62s on the I-16s at Nizhny Novgorod was going on at an unhurried pace. One I-16 Type 5 was re-equipped there in late 1938, while another aircraft (Type 10) was fitted with an M-62 in early 1939. The engines' service life did not exceed 60 hours: they had a lot of design shortcomings, and the two-speed supercharger was prone to frequent failures and malfunctions. Due to imperfection and capricious behaviour of the first M-62s, the tests with them lagged. This was not helped by neither the Air Force command nor aviation industry officials demonstrating any particular interest in them.

In practice, fit-for-use M-62s prepared for mounting on series production aircraft appeared in the first half of 1939. That was when they began to be installed on the Polikarpov I-153 sesquiplane fighters. In July 1939, 20 I-153s – among them ones powered by the M-62 – were sent to the area of the Soviet–Japanese conflict on the Mongolian border near the Khalkhin Gol river. Together with the aircraft, the spare M-62s also arrived. These were from the latest series manufactured at Factory No.19. In terms of size, the M-62 had almost no differences from the M-25V. For this reason, there arose a bold but implementable idea to install the new engines on the I-16s.

The position of the Air Force Chief Engineer with the 1st Army Group in Mongolia was held at that time by I. Prachik. He enthusiastically undertook to implement the idea within the shortest possible time. Later, Prachik described the events as follows:

We had a hard job to do, that is, to upgrade the I-16 fighter aircraft by installing the M-62 engine on it using the resources of mobile aircraft repair shops. This engine offered a much higher power and critical altitude while fitting within the attachment points of the M-25 engine mount. All we had to do was to make the appropriate design changes to certain installation diagrams. A serious issue that was a concern to me was taking care about the strength of some assemblies of the airframe in connection with installation of the more powerful engine.

After making numerous comparisons and theoretical calculations I came to the conclusion and a firm conviction that upgrading the I-16 fighter was possible, and sent all my calculations to Corps Commander Smushkevich. The Air Force Commander in Mongolia apparently liked my suggestion, since I was promptly summoned to the headquarters.

'I have reviewed all of your calculations and consulted the pilots. They approve the idea. Let us together consider the details of the upgrade more deeply,' the Corps Commander suggested, and listened attentively to me, asking numerous questions as I was speaking. 'I promise you my assistance,' he said in conclusion. 'This is surely an idea that is worth supporting!'

Imagine, then, my surprise and joy when, on the following morning, two M-62 engines were brought to Tamtsak-Bulak airfield in a TB-3 aircraft. On that very evening, there landed an I-16, which was intended to be subjected to our modifications …

In three days, under the supervision of Head of the PARM-1 mobile aircraft repair shop Pavlov, the engine and all the fighter systems were installed, and the aircraft was prepared for flight testing …

And here was the fighter, with Hero of the Soviet Union S. Gritsevets at the controls, taxiing out to the runway. After a short take-off run, the aircraft lifted off easily and gracefully, and I noted at once that the angle of climb and the speed were much higher than before. After reaching 3,000 metres, Gritsevets began to perform the task right above the airfield. Aerobatic manoeuvres were following one another. One cannot imagine what Sergey was performing in mid-air: there were dives, inverted flying and zooms. Then finally the *Ishachok* gained speed and vanished from sight.

We began to worry.

'Fuel … Maybe he has run short of fuel …' I was alarmed.

'Or, maybe, he landed at the airfield of his own 70th Regiment?' the Corps Commander supposed.

Indeed, Gritsevets soon called us on the phone. We understood it by the Corps Commander's curt phrases.

'Smushkevich speaking. Why have you landed there? So, you are not going to return it, and you are ready to go to the guardhouse? Where should I find such a house, then, and what have you taken it into your head for, Gritsevets?'

the Corps Commander hung up. He looked at everybody pensively:

'the Major has landed at his regiment airfield. He was afraid that the aircraft would be taken away from him. And he is ready, you see, to undergo punishment!'

Our Corps Commander, he was a forgiving man. Of course, there were no punishments for Gritsevets; the results of the upgrade of the I-16 fighter were reported by Smushkevich to Moscow. Specialists become interested in how a fighter with the M-62 engine, re-equipped in field conditions, would fly at the front. Two days later, the Head of NII VVS arrived at Khalkhin Gol. Then the prototype of the upgraded I-16 fighter was thoroughly checked and tested in flight again.

Pilots who had flown combat sorties in this aircraft were interviewed. I remember Hero of the Soviet Union N. Gerasimov reporting to the Head of NII VVS: 'This aircraft had not enough speed and power. The numerous modifications just made the excellent airplane heavier. They installed [an] additional machine gun and got the excessive weight; then mounted [an] oxygen cylinder and increased the weight further, so the fighter was 'hanging' on the stick. That was because the engine was not powerful enough. But now, after the upgrade, we really enjoy flying this aircraft to fight the enemy. Once you apply full throttle, you can feel it!'

The content of the conversation between Smushkevich and the Head of NII VVS remained unknown to me. However, soon [our] Corps Commander invited me for a *tête-à-tête* talk and suggested that I should go to Moscow promptly. There, in one of the stationary Air Force repair shops, I was expected to repeat the upgrade of the I-16 fighter aircraft. I agreed gladly, and left for the capital on the following day.

I was provided with excellent production facilities of the aircraft repair shops of Moscow Military District. A group of specialists as required to perform the work was also allocated. We were concurrently upgrading not a single aircraft but a group of three I-16s …

At the end of the fifth day from the start of the work, all the three fighters were at the airfield, fully ready for flight tests. The I-16s were tested by military pilots of an Air Brigade under supervision of experienced pilot Mariysky. They confirmed the good performance parameters as obtained during the tests of the first prototype in Mongolia. The M-62-powered I-16 had undeniable advantages in terms of speed, altitude, rate-of-climb, and other parameters over aircraft of the same type but fitted with the M-25 engine.

A training alert in a fighter air regiment. The I-16 Type 10s are being fired up using a self-starter.

A cannon-armed I-16 Type 27 in mid-air. While not shown at Khalkhin Gol, this is what the fighters looked like in the summer of 1939 in Mongolia after installation of the M-62 engines – without spinners for the AV-1 propellers and with a protruding oil cooler under the cowling.

Commanding officers of the 13th Fighter Air Regiment of the Red Banner Baltic Fleet Air Force inspecting the landing gear of an I-16 Type 18.

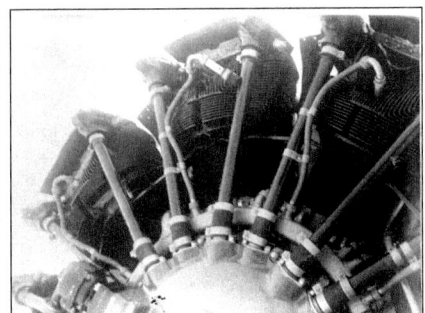

View of a damaged M-63 of an I-16 – the nose part of the propeller shaft was shorn off in flight, which resulted in the loss of the propeller.

The episode related by I. Prachik suggests that military engineers, in an unexpected flash of insight, decided to install the M-62, and thus even left the industry specialists behind in this area. The impression becomes even stronger when reading his further recollections: "It somehow became known at the aviation factory that activities for improving the I-16 had been well under way in the repair shops near Moscow. Factory engineers promptly arrived at the repair shops to view the re-equipment techniques but, to their disappointment, they turned out to be late. What was demonstrated to the engineers were finished aircraft."

In fact, what engineers from the Polikarpov Design Bureau came for was to determine whether those 'makeshift' modifications were fit for flying or not. As for Factory No.21, the activities for installation of the M-62 engines on the I-16s were gaining momentum there as well (this will be described in more detail in the next chapter). However, it was indeed progressing at a rather unhurried pace at the factory. It should be noted that it was the very re-equipment of the aircraft with the M-62 at a temporary base that had unexpected consequences.

After the events in Mongolia, a question arose regarding mass introduction of the new engines into service with the Red Army Air Force, and on their mounting on the I-16 Type 5 and Type 10. To replace the M-25 with the M-62, it was required to reinforce the engine mount upper attachment joints and to install the R-2 speed governor, a new cowling ring and a new spinner for the AV-1 variable-pitch propeller. On 10 September 1939, the Military Council of the VVS RKKA approved a plan which envisaged re-equipping 750 I-16 Type 10s and 1,000 I-16 Type 5s with the M-62 engines. Furthermore, the Type 5, in order to convert it into a fully fledged (almost) Type 18, had to be equipped with additional fuselage-mounted ShKAS synchronised machine guns.

A short time later, it was found out that the majority of the I-16 Type 5s were in service with training units, whereas the aircraft at combat units were noticeably worn out. For this reason, only 750 I-16 Type 10s were left in the re-equipment plans. In the final version, the decision came in the form of Resolution of the Defence Committee of the Council of People's Commissars of the USSR No.225ss of 8 July 1940. Before 7 July 1940, 283 M-62 engines were distributed to various military districts for this purpose. Until that date, the M-62 engines had been installed on 31 I-16 Type 10s (28 aircraft in the Moscow Military District and three in the Leningrad Military District). Before 20 September that year, another 42 I-16s were re-equipped in this way.

The year that had passed allowed viewing the problem in a more sober and comprehensive manner. Indeed, M-25-powered aircraft had, for the most part, been in operation for two or three years, and were noticeably worn out. At the same time, operation of the M-25 engines themselves caused no difficulties, with them being deemed reliable and well-mastered. The M-62 engines, in terms of reliability, did not inspire such confidence; it was stated that they remained not fully refined, while their installation was rather labour-consuming and complicated. Doubts appeared regarding expediency of the replacement: with the M-62, speed increased from 446km/h to 465km/h. In respect of the M-63, the number of questions and claims was still greater. There were cases of the master rod bushing's failure during operation of the M-63 engines, while piston rings and cylinders tended to wear out quickly, thus causing rough engine operation. In October 1940, a considerable number of the M-63-powered fighter aircraft, which had failed to pass acceptance due to power plant defects, accumulated at factories (628 aircraft in total, with 504 at Factory No.21 and 124 at Factory No.153). As a temporary measure to enhance reliability of operation, it was suggested that the power of the M-63 should be reduced to that of the M-62 by means of decreasing rpm and boost.

The experience of using the engines in combat units showed that, in the course of military operations in the North-western Front (that is slightly over three months of the Winter War), 48 M-62 engines of the I-16s and I-153s became unserviceable. During the period from April–June 1940, 94 M-62s and 44 M-63s were found to be unserviceable. The total number of unserviceable M-62 and M-63 engines in early July 1940 was 205. As of 1 July 1940, the Red Army Air Force mustered 1,821 I-153 M-62s and 940 I-16 M-62s and M-63s. Throughout 10 months of 1940, four crashes and 10 accidents involving the I-16s and I-153s occurred in combat units of the VVS RKKA by reason of failures of the M-62 or M-63 engines.

Gradually, it was understood that given their insufficient workmanship and reliability, introduction of the new engines had proved to be premature. The expediency of mounting the M-62s in 1940 began to be challenged by almost all authorities. This is confirmed by the correspondence of Smushkevich, Head of the Chief Directorate of the VVS RKKA Pavel Rychagov, People's Commissar of Defence Marshal Timoshenko and Deputy Head of the Council of People's Commissars Marshal Kliment Voroshilov, in which they all agreed that continuing engine replacement was not practical. As a result, under a resolution of the Defense Committee of 11 October 1940, all activities for conversion of the I-16s from the M-25A and M-25V to the M-62 were discontinued.

1.2.12. Abundancy of types in 1939

In early 1939, the factory in Nizhny Novgorod saw another change of management. Back in December 1938, after the departure of Borovkov and Florov to Dolgoprudny, Mikhail Pashinin became Chief Designer of the factory, but he did not remain a flawless advocate of upgrading the *Ishaks*. In mid-1939, he developed a design of the IP-21 cannon-armed fighter, which could replace the I-16 in production.

On 11 January 1939, under order No.15/K of People's Commissar of Defence Industry M. Kaganovich, Petr Golubkov was relieved from responsibilities as Director of Factory No.21 and was sent as Head of Design Bureau 29 to Podlipki, near Moscow. On 16 February that year, already being People's Commissar of Aviation Industry (the People's Commissariat of Aviation Industry – NKAP, *Narodniy Komissariat Aviatsionnoy Promyshlennosti* – existed from 21 January 1939), Kaganovich appointed Vasily Voronin (who had been Director of Aviation Factory No.23 in Leningrad) as Director of Factory No.21.

The situation at the aviation factory in Nizhny Novgorod during this period could hardly be called serene. While output plans kept growing, the factory was experiencing lack of funding and shortage of up-to-date equipment and tools. Furthermore, the problem of accommodation for employees was especially sensitive. Therefore, it is no surprise that commissions confirmed that there was a high turnover of employees in Nizhny Novgorod, accompanied by a severe shortage of skilled workers, engineers and technicians. Thus, the factory had to deal numerous problems throughout 1939 that were not directly related to aviation.

At the same time, during the sixth year of production of the fighter, an extensive set of activities for improvement of the I-16 was envisaged. Many of them, such as installation of the SN machine guns and retractable skis, had long been expecting completion. Below is a list of the main events in 1939, wherever possible in chronological order.

1. One of the top priority tasks was the installation of the M-62 engine on the I-16. Under the order of Chief Engineer of the factory B. Kupriyanov, signed by Chief Designer Pashinin, of 21 January 1939, the M-62-powered aircraft was designated Type 18. It should be noted, however, that the first aircraft fitted with the M-62 engine, which was presented for tests on 15 May, was converted from an I-16 Type 10, for which reason it was referred to as s/n 1021539. Also in May, an updated definition was established, to the effect that Type 18 meant a Type 10 with the M-62 engine, while Type 24 meant a Type 10 with the M-63 engine. In July the same year, Aviation Factory No.21 began the conversion to the M-62 and M-63, which were to be mounted on the conventional Type 10 and Type 17 aircraft.

The introduction of the new engines was progressing, to put it mildly, half-heartedly. On the one hand, no guaranteed deliveries of the M-62 engines had yet been given, but there was plenty of other work to do. In particular, during the height of events in Mongolia, the factory overhauled and upgraded 134 I-16s of the older series – this programme was done beyond the factory schedule.

The Soviet leaders in Moscow were, in summer 1939, concerned with other problems. During a meeting in the Kremlin in May, Joseph Stalin quite explicitly pointed out that it was time to replace old fighter aircraft with new ones, and that young designers should be first and foremost involved in developing such modern aircraft. The I-16, with its numerous problems, certainly qualified as 'old'. A new fighter designed by Nikolay Polikarpov, namely the M-88-powered I-180, was already available to replace it. The factory was given an assignment to build this aircraft on 23 July 1939. On the same day, under an order from Director of Factory No.21 Voronin, the I-180 received the factory designation Type 25. Further events, however, showed that the I-180 was 'not the only pebble on the beach'. People's Commissar of Aviation Industry Kaganovich began to quite deliberately support Mikhail Pashinin, who was designing a fighter powered by the M-105 engine. It was with such liquid-cooled engines that the specific hopes of aircraft designers were pinned in mid-1939.

However, the summer – with its relaxing heat and dreams of a better future – ended unexpectedly in August. The Red Army Air Force command then enquired of aviation industry officials: "Where are the M-62-powered fighters? Why are our specialists able to mount such engines on the I-16s in field conditions whereas your factory has not supplied a single aircraft yet?" After the question was put like this, Kaganovich ordered Factory No.21 to immediately expedite building the M-62-powered I-16s. It is known that, in August, six I-16 Type 10s were urgently converted at the factory into Type 18s and forthwith sent to the front, that is, to Mongolia, where hostilities against Japan were still going on.

In the same eventful August of 1939, it became known that the M-63, having take-off power of 1,100hp, had successfully passed 100 hours of tests. Furthermore, it was reported that the Perm factory already had a stock of 20 M-63s to undergo operational tests. After receiving this information, Kaganovich acted decisively. Apparently, he decided that the M-62 was already a historical 'relic', and that the still more powerful M-63 should be focused on instead. He cancelled the previous resolution and gave the factory a new task, which consisted of presenting three M-63-powered I-16s for state tests in August 1939. The maximum speed at which such aircraft were expected to fly was 505–515km/h. On 9 September, Kaganovich ordered Director of Factory No.21 Voronin to promptly prepare the production facilities for building the M-63-powered I-16s and to supply the first 10 production aircraft in September.

The rapidly evolving events coincided with emergence of new financial resources at the disposal of the NKAP. For mastering the production of the I-16s with the M-63 engines, the factory management in the person of Voronin was promised numerous benefits, including increase salaries and wages, growth of the design bureau headcount, healthy bonuses, andnew tools and equipment for the installation of an assembly line. The factory was provided with additional electrical power and heat supply, 50 new living apartments and half a million roubles for individual house construction. Furthermore, construction began of 10 dormitories for workers, a pioneer camp and a holiday centre.

By the end of the year, the factory had built over 400 aircraft powered by the M-62 or M-63 engines. The aircraft had a higher rate-of-climb and service ceiling, but the maximum speed still did not reach the coveted 500km/h. The first M-62-powered I-16 completed state testing in October 1939. With a take-off weight of 1,830kg, the aircraft demonstrated the following flight performance parameters: maximum speed near ground level, 411km/h; maximum speed at 1,000m, 428km/h; maximum speed at 4,400m, 464km/h. The service ceiling totalled 9,470m, and it took the aircraft 5.2 minutes to climb to 5,000m.

The I-16s with powerful engines were also prepared for the traditional November parade. An NKAP resolution of 25 October 1939 gave orders, for purposes of a parade flyover above Red Square on 7 November, to "ferry 12 M-62-powered I-16s to Moscow. The aircraft shall be painted red, and shall carry no armament. The said aircraft shall be test-flown on a top priority basis".

2. Another activity comprised building the I-16s with 12.7mm synchronised large-calibre ShVAK machine guns (in all documents, they were referred to as cannons). Under the order of Chief Engineer of the factory Kupriyanov, signed by Chief Designer Pashinin on 21 January 1939, the aircraft fitted with 12.7mm synchronised ShVAK machine guns were designated Type 16. A total of three aircraft were built: s/n 16211, 16212 and 16213. After completion of the factory testing under a shortened programme, the I-16 Type 16s were handed over to NII VVS for operational tests.

3. The story of the three aircraft equipped with wing-mounted SN machine guns stretched over two more years. In 1935, designers Savin and Norov manufactured the prototype SN machine gun with a rate of fire of 2,800–3,000 rounds per minute. In the following year, the SN was tested, and the Defence Committee cleared it for production in 1937. The I-16s were equipped with these machine guns in 1938. In terms of external appearance, these aircraft had only minor differences from other I-16s. The SN machine guns were installed instead of the wing-mounted ShKAS machine guns, but the existing ammunition feed system was preserved.

On 21 January 1939, the aircraft with wing-mounted SN machine guns were given the designation Type 19. A month later, three such aircraft (s/n 19211, 19212 and 19213) were prepared for test flights. During the period from 15–26 March, they were test-flown by the chief pilot of the factory Flight Test Station, Colonel Tuomas Susi. Later, under the designation I-16SN, the fighters were supplied to combat units and took part in the Winter War of 1939–40.

In February 1939, a decision was made to install SN machine guns in the fuselage for synchronised firing through the propeller. Four such aircraft were built at Factory No.21, and were given the designation Type 20. For several reasons, the synchronised mount was rejected. In August that year, the designation Type 20 was used for aircraft with external fuel tanks.

On 7 March 1939, Director of the factory Voronin issued Order No.11, which, in an abridged version, read as follows: "To build an I-16 with four synchronised ShKAS machine guns at the suggestion of a group of designers from the 4th Department, all design studies shall be carried out in respect of this aircraft. The work shall be done in a shortest possible time without compromising production orders. Before 1 April 1939, all drawings shall be handed over to production." Under this order, the I-16 with four synchronised ShKAS machine guns was given the designation Type 21. The aircraft remained in the experimental activities plan throughout 1939, but no further development followed.

On 3 March 1939, a resolution was issued for the building of an I-16 with a combined mount comprising synchronised ShKAS and SN machine guns. The aircraft was designated Type 22 but never entered production.

The designation I-16 Type 23 was used in April 1939, when two Type 10 prototypes were equipped with underwing racks for RS-82 rocket projectiles. Simultaneously, an order was placed with the factory for building 35 production Type 23 aircraft to be presented for acceptance in May that year. In August, the designation Type 23 was cancelled. However, as late as September 1939, such aircraft were sometimes erroneously referred to as Type 23.

4. The problem of building the I-16 with an increased flight range was mentioned in the annual plans of TsKB and Factory No.21 for several consecutive years. Usually, such an aircraft was referred to as escort airplane, which was not a common term. Attempts to install additional fuel tanks in the wing did not yield any positive results, but the topic remained one that was much discussed.

Other design teams also made attempts to achieve an increase in the I-16's flight range. During the winter of 1938/39, external tanks (100 litres each) of two types were manufactured at NII VVS workshops at the suggestion of engineer Zapanovanny. Tanks of the first type were of a cylindrical shape, while those of the second type were nearly flat and were arranged immediately adjacent to the fuselage. Due to an unacceptable aft centre of gravity position, such extra tanks failed their tests.

The task of manufacturing underwing extra fuel tanks was transferred to Nizhny Novgorod. The tanks which were manufactured at Factory No.21 resembled, in terms of appearance, those of similar purpose used on the Japanese Type 97 Fighter. However, that was only an external resemblance. Underwing tanks on the I-16 were made of plywood and pressed, glue-impregnated board (fibreboard). These tanks were installed for the first time on the modified production I-16 s/n

M. Kaganovich congratulating pilot V. Kokkinaki on coming back after a non-stop flight in the Ilyushin DB-3 *Moskva* aircraft. This photograph, taken in summer 1938, bears no direct relationship to the history of the I-16. However, it shows together the People's Commissar of the Soviet Aviation Industry (before 1940) and the commander of a 'Red Five' of the 1935 style.

An SN machine gun mounted in the wing centre section of an I-16.

The lower portion of the I-16 wing with mounting points for attachment of PSB-21 fuel tanks.

An I-16 Type 19 with wing-mounted SN machine guns in 1939.

Additional fuel tanks designed by engineer Zapanovanny being tested in 1939.

The upper portion of a PSB-21 fuel tank had a curved shape, repeating the wing airfoil, in order to ensure a closer contact.

The first I-16 Type 20 prototype with PSB-21 external mounted fuel tanks in spring 1939.

54   The King of Fighters Volume 2

An I-16 Type 17 on skis, with landing flaps fully extended.

Aftermath of an accident with the I-16 M-25V s/n 1021717 on 11 March 1939. During an acceptance flight at the airfield of Factory No.39, pilot Frolov lifted off at a too low speed, which resulted in the twisting of the ski landing gear.

A view on the wing centre section of the I-16 Type 17. The landing gear wells are equipped with additional panels for placing the ski in the retracted position.

The right portion of the I-16 Type 17 wing centre section.

State testing of an I-16 Type 17 of the pre-production series with a retractable ski landing gear in February 1939.

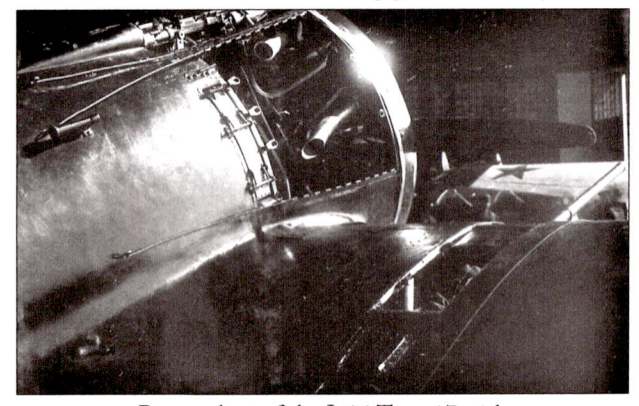

Power plant of the I-16 Type 17 with the engine cowlings removed.

Belly view of the fuselage of the I-16 Type 17. The arrow indicates the well for placing the ski nose part in the retracted position.

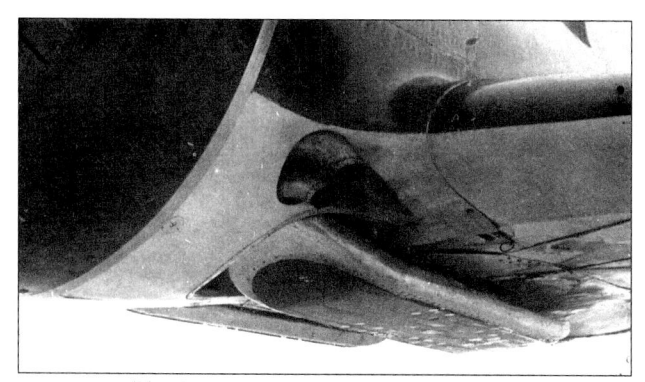

The R-39 skis in the retracted position.

The right side of the I-16 Type 17 cockpit with ski landing gear control levers.

The upper portion of the I-16 Type 17 fuselage with the cowling and ShKAS machine-gun fairings removed. On the aircraft centreline are the oil filler neck and the fuel tank cover. The access door that is closest to the observer covers the compartment for stowage of the ammunition belt for ShVAK cannons.

Tests of the I-16 s/n 1021781 equipped with an RSI-3 radio and provided with bonding and screening. The opened side access door was used in later types; its size is 400x550mm.

1021681, and tests were conducted in June and July 1939. The aircraft was referred to as an 'escort fighter', and at the test stage it was given the designation Type 20.

The drop tanks, designated PSB-21, were attached between the second and third ribs of the wing, had a dry weight of 19.5kg and each held 93 litres of fuel. They were connected to the general fuel system; the pilot could, at his discretion, switch over to the main tank or, when necessary, could easily jettison the extra tanks. It was pointed out that flying with only one tank was possible. With two tanks, the I-16 was able to dive at an angle of 60° and perform turns with a banking angle of up to 80°. Maximum speed at an altitude of 5,000m was 21km/h lower, but the aircraft's flying time increased by one hour.

On 27 July 1939, during the height of the hostilities at Khalkhin Gol, the factory was given an urgent task to build 20 escort fighters before 1 August. The factory thus manufactured 100 tanks (assuming that three sets should be required per aircraft).

The next order was given to the factory in December 1939 with the beginning of the Winter War. Before the end of the year, Factory No.21 supplied to the Red Army Air Force 80 I-16s with external tanks. From January 1940, the wings of all I-16 types began to be equipped with such arrangements. The parts set for each aircraft included six external tanks. Before 1 April that year, 1,000 of them were manufactured.

Starting from 1938, there were also attempts to replace the main (fuselage-mounted) fuel tanks with fiberboard ones. During the same period, development of the most efficient self-sealing methods (for applying a special coating eliminating fuel leaks in case of combat damage) was conducted. One of the self-sealing material variants included the following: 5.5–6mm thick specially impregnated cowhide leather (the so-called bark-tanned side leather) and 0.5mm thick vulcanised rubber, with the external cover made of steel metal mesh and 2.5mm rubber. The work on self-sealing fuel tanks continued in 1939. It was specified that, starting from 1 January that year, self-sealing fuel tanks without any losses in capacity would be installed. Starting from the second half of the year, they were deemed duly mastered and were put into series production.

5. In 1939, the finally modified cannon-armed Type 17 fighters began to be manufactured. State tests of the I-16 Type 17 (of the 27th series) were conducted in February at the NII VVS airfield in Shchelkovo. The aircraft was equipped with type R-39 retractable skis coated in LIR-2 plastic manufactured at Factory No.163. This aircraft was determined as a reference for the year 1939. Test pilot Tuomas Susi noted that the aircraft became noticeably heavier and less manoeuvrable. Indeed, two ShVAK cannons weighed 83kg, and 180 rounds accounted for an additional 39kg. Taking into account the fasteners and excluding the removed ShKAS machine guns, the gross weight grew by nearly 100kg. As it turned out, that was enough for combat pilots to dub the I-16 Type 17 as 'Iron'.

Under Resolution of the VVS RKKA No.230192s of 16 December 1938, the following values of gross weight were established to be observed by the manufacturer: for the I-16 Type 10, 1,640kg; for the I-16 Type 17, 1,730kg. In practice, however, the gross weight grew; usually, the gross weight of the I-16 Type 10 exceeded 1,700kg, whereas that of the I-16 Type 17 was over 1,800kg.

6. In 1939, experiments with the installation of radios continued. To install the transmitter, an upwards-opening 400x550mm access door was arranged on the right side of the fuselage behind the cockpit. With an RSI radio installed 'in the old style', stable communication with the 11-AK ground station at reduced engine rpm did not exceed a distance of 10–15km. The new ARS radio ensured communication at a distance of 30–40km under the same conditions. After a series of screening and bonding measures, stable communication at a distance of 100–120km was achieved. In August 1939, three aircraft provided with bonding and screening underwent tests at NII VVS. Afterwards, the factory was ordered to build all aircraft with bonding and screening measures in order to ensure stable radio communication.

7. In the I-16 Type 10s of the earlier series, landing flaps (commonly just named 'flaps') were extended by means of compressed air. The deployment was abrupt; for an unexperienced pilot, there was a risk of loss of control and subsequent spin stall. For this reason, a mechanical control system was developed, which allowed extending the flaps slowly and fixing them in different positions depending on the situation. The first aircraft (s/n 102175) equipped with such a mechanism was successfully tested at NII VVS in early 1939. Starting from 1 February 1939, mechanically controlled landing flaps were used in production aircraft.

Apart from the above modifications, some of the aircraft were equipped with mounting points for installation of a PAU-22 gun camera in 1939, as well as with a cone sleeve target for aerial gunnery training.

In connection with the emergence of the new I-16 versions, the following numbering of aircraft types was established under a resolution of the factory management of 20 August 1939:

1. For machine-gun armed versions:
    The I-16 M-25, Type 10; the I-16 M-62, Type 18; the I-16 M-63, Type 24.
    For cannon-armed versions:
    The I-16 M-25, Type 17; the I-16 M-62, Type 27; the I-16 M-63, Type 28.

2. For aircraft equipped with RS rocket projectiles, the letter R was added to the serial number; for aircraft with external tanks, the letter P was added. Individual type designations for aircraft equipped with external tanks (Type 20) and RS rocket projectiles (Type 23) were cancelled.

3. The I-16 Type 18 and Type 27 were designated by sequential numbers, continuing the numbering for Type 10 and Type 17.
    Aircraft belonging to Type 24, Type 25 or Type 28 received new numbering:
    Type 24, s/n 24211, 2, 3, etc.
    Type 25, s/n 25211, 2, 3, etc.
    Type 28, s/n 28211, 2, 3, etc.

Under an additional resolution of 23 September 1939, the I-16 Type 10 and Type 17 retained the existing numbering up to discontinuation of production of the M-25 engines.

A further 166 I-16s with the M-63 engine were built but not accepted due to defective engines or propellers.

Output of the I-16s in 1939 was as follows:

Version	Engine	Quantity
Type 10	M-25V	426
Type 18	M-62	177
Type 24	M-63	155

Type 17	M-25V	314
Type 27	M-62	59
Type 28	M-63	16
UTI-4 (Type 15)	M-25	424
TOTAL:		1,571

1.2.13. The I-16 Type 24

On 19 April 1939, following a resolution from NKAP officials, an order was issued by the management of Factory No.21 to upgrade the I-16 in the shortest possible time, and to build two aircraft with heavier armament and the powerful M-63 engine. The new version, which was expected to considerably exceed the I-16 Type 10 in terms of performance, was given the designation Type 24. In particular, its maximum speed at that stage was estimated at 520–525km/h.

The new type was determined as a reference for Factory No.21 for the fourth quarter of 1939 and the entire following year. Preparations for introducing it into production were conducted under the supervision of Chief Designer Mikhail Pashinin. It was intended that no later than in summer 1939, the I-16 Type 24 would complete the entire cycle of all prescribed tests. To put the aircraft into production in the quickest possible time, 300,000 roubles were allocated to the factory from a special fund of the NKAP for bonuses.

The Type 24 also received new shock struts of increased travel. Earlier, the shock strut piston in all the I-15s and I-16s had splines, which served as guides and protected the shock strut with the wheel from turning around its axis. The mechanism itself was named a splined joint. In the Type 24, an ordinary torque link was installed, which was used in the same role with no less efficiency. Interestingly, the torque link continued to be named, in the old manner, as a splined joint (in spite of the fact that it had no splines at all), and this term was even widely used in the manuals for future designers.

Concurrently, a new tail skid design with an oleo-pneumatic shock strut and a small duralumin wheel was introduced.

Among fundamental changes, design improvements were made to the outer wing structure. There were plans to install a wooden stressed-skin wing or a rigid wing with metal formed ribs, but neither of these variants was developed any further.

The I-16 s/n 24213 built and tested in autumn 1939. The wing of this aircraft had plywood skin on the top surface, which allowed a maximum speed of 489km/h.

An I-16 Type 24 of the 16th Fighter Air Regiment, which was used during check tests in summer 1940.

A production I-16 Type 24 equipped with PSB-21 drop tanks.

The I-16 Type 24 which belonged to the Commander of the 13th Fighter Air Regiment of the Red Banner Baltic Fleet Air Force.

On some prototypes, a rigid plywood skin was installed. It was expected that such a skin would ensure, *inter alia*, airfoil cleanness and allow achievement of a higher flight speed.

In May 1939, static tests were conducted of the fuselage with two hinged doors in the cockpit. Starting from the introduction of the Type 24 into production, all I-16s were equipped with such doors on the left and right side.

The prototype I-16 M-63 Type 24 s/n 24213 was tested in early July 1939. Due to uneven engine operation, the factory tests lagged. Later, from 19 August until 14 September, s/n 24213 underwent joint testing by the factory and NII VVS. It was pointed out that the aircraft was powered by the M-63 non-geared engine with a 2.8m-diameter AV-1 propeller. It had an increased-stroke landing gear without splines, tail wheel, mechanically controlled flap and the RI self-starter. The upper skin of the outer wing panels was made of plywood. With a gross weight of 1,878kg, the aircraft developed a maximum speed near ground level of 440km/h. At the critical altitude, with the supercharger operating at the second speed, the maximum flight speed achieved was 489km/h. The maximum service ceiling obtained was 10,800m, and it took the aircraft 5.15 minutes to climb to 5,000m. The time to perform a turn was 17–19 seconds at an altitude of 1,000m. In spite of the increase in the rate-of-climb and service ceiling, only a minor gain in maximum speed was achieved; as before, it failed to reach even 500km/h.

On 3 November 1939, the factory began to test the I-16 s/n 24214. A decision was made to use this prototype for joint testing of the power plant and airframe. However, at that point, the story of the I-16 Type 24 unexpectedly came to a halt. On 3 December, due to numerous defects, it was ordered that all the M-63 engines should be removed from the aircraft. The engines were to be mothballed and sent to Perm for rebuilding. For this reason, Workshop No.40 (Final Assembly) was assembling aircraft without engines until the end of the year.

In April, NII VVS received an I-16 Type 24 as a reference for series production in 1940. During tests, the aircraft achieved a maximum speed of 462km/h. Another production aircraft with a gross weight of 1,882kg, taken from the 16th Air Regiment of the Lyubertsy Air Brigade, recorded a maximum speed of 470km/h. A short while later, tests of the prototype s/n 24213 (which was built in 1939) were conducted. After nearly a year in operation (and a total flying time of 41 hours and 21 minutes) and engine replacement, and without the propeller spinner, the aircraft managed a speed of 481km/h. This achievement was obviously in favour of the rigid plywood skin (and even higher results could have been obtained with a higher-quality metal wing). With fabric covering, the airfoil cleanliness was tangibly degraded due to seams, especially transverse ones. However, aircraft with wings covered in fabric continued to be built until the discontinuation of series production.

The table below shows deliveries of the I-16 Type 24 and I-16 Type 27 during the period from 1 January to 1 June 1940. The designation 'RO' stands for aircraft equipped with racks for RS-82 rocket projectiles. The designation 'RSI-3' indicates aircraft equipped with radios.

	Total	Type 24	Type 28	RO	RSI-3
149th Fighter Air Regiment (Detskoye Selo)	28	28	–	–	–
146th Fighter Air Regiment (Lyubertsy)	63	63	–	–	–
Aircraft armament test range (Noginsk)	1	–	1	–	–
45th Fighter Air Regiment (Kishly)	57	57	–	1	12
60th Air Brigade (Kishly)	23	23	–	10	–
87th Fighter Air Regiment (Uman)	63	63	–	–	–
NII VVS	6	6	–	–	–
OKB-29 (Podlipki)	2	2	–	–	–
88th Fighter Air Regiment (Vinnitsa)	63	63	–	–	–
166th Fighter Air Regiment (Seyma)	14	14	–	–	–
122nd Fighter Air Regiment (Berezina)	67	58	9	–	3
2nd Air Brigade (Kubinka)	30	–	30	–	–
131st Fighter Air Regiment (Mokraya)	63	63	–	20	–
150th Fighter Air Regiment (Nasosnaya)	25	19	6	–	–
153rd Air Brigade (Navtlug)	14	14	–	14	–
116th Fighter Air Regiment (Stalinabad)	33	33	–	–	–
? (Oktyabrskiye Kazarmy)	12	12	–	–	–
22nd Air Brigade (Vasilkovo)	9	9	–	–	9
69th Fighter Air Regiment (Odessa)	33	33	–	–	16

67th Fighter Air Regiment (Odessa)	63	41	22	3	7
149th Fighter Air Regiment (Zhitomir)	15	15	–	–	2
? (Sebezh)	13	7	6	–	1
14th Separate Air Squadron (Krymskaya)	15	11	4	–	–
TOTAL	712	634	78	48	50

The following were not included in the number of supplied aircraft:

- five I-16 Type 5s converted into Type 18 (of those, three aircraft were handed over to Lyubertsy and two went to Kubinka);
- two UTI-4s were sent to Kingisepp.

It is known that several dozens of the I-16 Type 24s with additional fuel tanks were, during the period from 7–18 July, sent to the Far East.

1.2.14. The Moscow finale: cannons, machine guns and superchargers

In late 1937, Nikolay Polikarpov was appointed Chief Designer at Aviation Factory No.156, which had been formerly known as the TsAGI Factory of Experimental Designs. The design bureau moved to the new facility in late December that year and early January 1938. At the new quarters, specialists began to design the I-180 and I-190 fighters and continued development of the Ivánov single-engine multi-purpose aircraft and refinements of the VIT-2 two-engine tank destroyer. Among other activities, the design bureau carried out improvement works on the I-16. These were conducted in two areas: mounting synchronised cannons and large-calibre machine guns, and equipping the aircraft with superchargers to increase the service ceiling. Apart from this, the Polikarpov Design Bureau never again addressed issues with the I-16.

The fuselage-mounted synchronised armament, due to concentration of load in the aircraft's centre of mass, made it more manoeuvrable compared to the basic version. At the same time, the problems of improving the accuracy and density of fire were solved.

Re-equipment of the two I-16s received from the Air Brigade that was stationed in Lyubertsy near Moscow began in December 1938. The aircraft s/n 1021332 was used for mounting two synchronised 12.7mm Berezin TKB-150 machine guns. The guns were mounted along the fuselage sides forward of the pilot, somewhat below the aircraft centreline. To accommodate the ammunition (440 rounds) and the machine guns themselves, the size of the fuselage fuel tank had to be considerably reduced. Part of the fuel was transferred to the centre wing auxiliary fuel tanks. The wing-mounted ShKAS machine guns together with ammunition boxes were removed.

The aircraft was given the designation I-16SO (*Synkhronniy Opytniy* – synchronised, experimental). During the period from 4–14 March 1939, its armament was successfully tested at a shooting range. The empty weight (without fuel, oil and the pilot, but with full ammunition allowance) totalled 1,535kg. The aircraft's gross weight was 1,835kg, while the centre of gravity position was 31.9% MAC.

The flights were conducted with the landing gear extended because, in the retracted position, the ski tip interfered with case ejection chutes of the TKB-150 machine guns. Between 21 and 27 March, the aircraft was flown by N. Zvonarev.

Aerial firing tests revealed serious problems with the new armament variant. The standard propeller spinner was torn off during firing, and cracks appeared in the cowling. Unburnt powder particles were also getting into the carburetor intake. It was suggested that the defects should be rectified, after which an operational testing series should be built.

On 15 May 1939, pilots Chernavsky, Alekseev and Belozerov test-flew the aircraft to evaluate the I-16SO piloting technique. When Belozerov was performing crosswind landing, the aircraft's right landing gear leg collapsed. As a result, the propeller and the right wing tip were bent. After repair, the I-16SO remained at the flight station of Factory No.156 on the Central Airfield. Its eventual fate is unknown.

Almost concurrently with the I-16SO, the I-16 s/n 521570 was converted into a cannon-armed version. The ShVAK cannons were installed through the cockpit, along the fuselage's side. To enable their maintenance, small access doors were cut out in the sides, with ammunition being fed from two magazines, with 175 rounds in each. The aircraft was given the designation I-16PS (*Pushechniy Sinkhronniy* – cannon-armed, synchronised). In terms of external appearance, it had almost no differences from series production aircraft. Tests were conducted during the period from 10 February to 4 April 1939. Firing from the cannons revealed the same problems as in the I-16SO; however, the quantity of powder gases penetrating into the cockpit was noticeably greater. In the course of firing tests, synchroniser operation was deliberately violated, but it turned out that the aircraft was able to continue flying with the propeller blades punctured.

60 The King of Fighters Volume 2

The aftermath of the accident with the I-16SO (s/n 1021332) at the Central Airfield on 20 May 1939. A landing gear leg collapsed during pilot I. Belozerov's crosswind landing.

The I-16TK (s/n 521A250) being assembled in the workshop of the TsAGI New Equipment Bureau at Radio Street in Moscow in spring 1939.

The I-16PS (s/n 521570) with synchronised ShVAK cannons in summer 1939.

Installation of cassettes with cannon rounds into the fuselage of the I-16PS.

ShVAK cannons being installed into the fuselage of the I-16PS.

The I-16 fighter 61

TK-1 turbosuperchargers mounted on the
M-25V engine of the I-16 s/n 1021582.
646. The left side of the cockpit on the I-16 TK s/n 1021582.

The left side of the cockpit on the I-16 TK s/n 1021582.

TK-1 turbosuperchargers mounted on the I-16 s/n 521A250.

The I-16 s/n 1021582 fitted with TK-1 turbosuperchargers during testing in August 1939.

As a result of the tests conducted, cannons were never again installed in the I-16 fuselage. The engineering solutions related to their mounting, ammunition feed and synchronisation were used by Polikarpov in early 1940 in the design of the I-185 fighter.

The installation of additional large-calibre Berezin machine guns in the fuselage was found to be successful. For this reason, a decision was made to use such a variant, but with only one machine gun, in the production I-16s. The first aircraft with a single synchronised TKB-150 was built at Factory No.121 in the early 1940s. Range tests were conducted from 23–27 March 1940. The tests consisted of firing from all conceivable positions in mid-air, including at an altitude of 9,400m, at temperatures reaching minus 55°C.

During the test period, in April 1940, a governmental decree was issued for acceptance of the TKB-150 into service and introducing it into production. A directive was promptly distributed to all aviation factories and design bureaus prescribing a mandatory installation of the Berezin machine gun in all aircraft being designed or upgraded. In the I-16s, the Berezin machine gun, under the designation BS (Berezin, Synchronised), began to be mounted in mid-1940 (on the I-16 Type 29).

Creation of a high-altitude fighter was the

second area of activity in the course of modernisation of the I-16 as conducted at Factory No.156. To accomplish this goal, TsIAM developed the TK-1 turbosuperchargers driven by the exhaust gases from the aircraft engine. There was an opinion that such turbosuperchargers could be installed in aircraft in service with combat units, and thus could enhance the possibilities of aircraft at altitudes of up to 10km.

In 1938, type TK-1 turbosuperchargers were adapted for mounting on the M-25V engines. Two TK-1s (one on each side of the engine) were attached in such a way that the work turbine impeller protruded beyond the aircraft contours to the minimum possible extent. The turbosuperchargers were driven by the engine exhaust gases, with each of them connected to a manifold uniting four cylinders.

The first I-16 s/n 521A250 was fitted with turbosuperchargers in mid-1938. This was the first high-altitude fighter in the USSR. The aircraft had no armament, which led to an additional shift of the flight centre of gravity position aft: according to weighing results, it was 32.18% MAC. Although no special attention was paid to this circumstance, it should have been – such a value called for especially careful piloting.

On 27 July 1939, the first I-16 took to the air. At the controls was the famous test pilot M. Alekseev, who had taken part in many altitude and load-lifting capacity record-setting flights on Tupolev bombers. Unfortunately, he had not flown much in the I-16s and was not familiar with the aircraft's vicious behaviour. Upon approach, during the final turn, the aircraft dropped a wing at a height of 40–50m and crashed into the ground. Pilot Alekseev was killed.

Tests of the next I-16 s/n 1021582 with turbosuperchargers began on 4 August 1939. The aircraft was fitted with the M-25V engine and had the AV-1 variable-pitch propeller. Tests were conducted with the participation of the TsAGI 8th High-Altitude Department, with the aircraft flown by test pilot Stankevich.

Before 3 October, the I-16 TK performed 30 flights, during which the maximum speed reached at an altitude of 8,600m was 494km/h. After installation of the M-62 engine, the speed somewhat increased, exceeding 500km/h at a design altitude of approximately 9,000m.

In spite of these quite encouraging results and the need for high-altitude fighters, turbosuperchargers were never again used in the I-16s. There was an opinion in 1939 that newer fighter types, which had already been ordered from several design teams, would be equipped for high-altitude flying.

Concurrently with working on turbosuperchargers, activities relating to pressurised cabins were being conducted in the USSR. The I-16 was evaluated in terms of the feasibility of installing a pressurised cabin. However, elementary calculations showed that such an installation was all but impossible. With the minimum weight of such an assembly totalling approximately 30kg, the fighter's centre of gravity position reached the catastrophic value of 35% MAC, which was totally unacceptable.

1.2.15. The end of series production; 1940–41

1.2.15.1. Changes at Aviation Factory No.21

In 1940, Aviation Factory No.21, which had already existed for more than seven years, was one of the most powerful and modern Soviet aviation enterprises. As of 1 September, its headcount included 1,884 engineers and technicians, 12,000 workers and 1,030 office employees. The factory had an impressive amount of machinery (370 metal-cutting machines) and relatively modern equipment at its disposal. It is clear that the factory was an attractive proposition for introducing some new aircraft types into series production.

Mastering the production of the Polikarpov I-180 fighter, which was intended to supersede the I-16, began in Nizhny Novgorod in the second half of 1939. In spite of the continuity of design and technology facilitating introduction of this airplane, there were no notable achievements in the manufacture of the I-180.

In late 1939, Stalin replaced People's Commissar of Aviation Industry M. Kaganovich with Alexey Shakhurin. Director of Aviation Factory No.21 Pavel Voronin became Deputy People's Commissar of Production, while designer Alexander Yakovlev was given the post of Deputy People's Commissar of Experimental Aircraft Building.

On 30 January 1940, the new management of the People's Commissariat of Aviation Industry decided to expedite the long-drawn-out process of building the I-180s and tasked Aviation Factory No.21 with completing the first series of 10 aircraft for operational tests as early as February. The next series of 20 aircraft was intended to be built in March. However, once again no noticeable actions followed.

Probably the most important circumstance that accounted for the lags in the production of the I-180 was the unavailability of the M-88 engines. In spring 1940, there were only three such engines in Nizhny Novgorod, which had been manufactured in the previous year and were not highly rated in terms of reliability. The first three aircraft (s/n 25211, 25212 and 25213), sometimes referred to as the I-180S ('S' for *seriynyye*, series production), were completed in late April. For the expected flypast over Red Square on 1 May 1940, the aircraft were sent to Moscow. However, no demonstration took place before the government. Indeed, the I-180S aircraft performed almost no flights and one after another soon sank into oblivion almost unnoticed.

On 25 May 1940, another document (No.223ss) was originated by the People's Commissariat. The document established the plan for production of 110 I-180s during the year. Nevertheless, the consequences were meagre: only a handful of aircraft, without engines, were built before the end of the year.

Concurrently, large-scale work on building the IP-21 fighter designed by M. Pashinin was being carried out. After Kaganovich's resignation, the project was supported by P. Voronin, first in the capacity of factory director, then as Deputy People's Commissar of Aviation Industry. It was believed that the aircraft had noticeably better prospects of success than the I-180.

The IP-21 prototype was completed in June 1940, and its first 18-minute flight from the airfield of Aviation Factory No.21 took place on 11 July that year. The aircraft was flown by test pilot P. Fokin. Before August, 33 flights comprising a total of 16 flying hours were performed within the scope of factory tests. Starting from 3 August, Fokin performed several aerobatic flights. According to his opinion, the IP-21 possessed good controllability, was stable in a dive and demonstrated easier take-off and landing than the I-16. At Factory No.21, the IP-21 was given the designation Type 30. During the pre-production phase, it was planned to use fixtures of the I-16 for manufacturing the IP-21.

In the second half of August 1940, the first IP-21 prototype was sent to Moscow, where it was test-flown by NII VVS pilots. They pointed out the aircraft's tendency for wing stall at high angles of attack. To rectify this drawback, it was suggested that Pashinin should equip the second prototype with automatic slats on the outer wing panels.

The events that followed predetermined the hope for success with the introduction of the IP-21 into series production. In September 1940, under A. Shakhurin's orders, production of the I-180 was discontinued, with Pashinin's fighter superseding it.

However, the emergence of the IP-21 was somewhat late. At nearly the same time, A. Yakovlev (with the I-26), A. Mikoyan (with the I-200) and S. Lavochkin (with the I-301) laid claims to Aviation Factory No.21. In respect of the I-301 fighter prototype, results of state tests showed that it had the highest flight performance parameters among Soviet aircraft powered by the M-105 engine. In particular, its maximum speed at 4,905m was 605km/h. For this reason, under the designation LaGG-3, it was put into production at Factory No.21. There, the Lavochkin–Gorbunov–Gudkov LaGG-3 fighter was given the designation Type 31 and its manufacture began in December 1940. In terms of construction, the fighter was made of 36% wood (in the construction of the I-16, there were 10% wooden parts). This, in a striking manner, confirmed Polikarpov's age-old statement to the effect that, in Russian conditions, an aircraft for warfare should have a wooden construction.

While plans for superseding the I-16 were being drafted during the year, production of the fighter continued. In 1940, the I-16s were manufactured in the following configurations:

Version	Engine	Configuration
Type 18	M-62	with external tanks
Type 24	M-63	without external tanks
Type 24	M-63	with external tanks
Type 24	M-63	with rocket projectiles
Type 24	M-63	with external tanks and RSI-3 radio
Type 24	M-63	with rocket projectiles and external tanks
Type 27	M-62	with external tanks
Type 28	M-63	with external tanks
Type 28	M-63	without external tanks
Type 28	M-63	with external tanks and RSI-3 radio
Type 15	M-25V	UTI-4 trainer

Starting from the second half of 1940, the M-63-powered I-16 Type 29 began to be manufactured instead of the previous variety. The aggregate number of I-16s built throughout 1940 was 2,210. The breakdown per types was as follows:

- Type 18 and Type 24, 760;
- Type 28, 277;
- Type 25 (I-180), 1;
- Type 29, 570;
- Type 15 (UTI-4), 600.

Total: 2,208 aircraft.

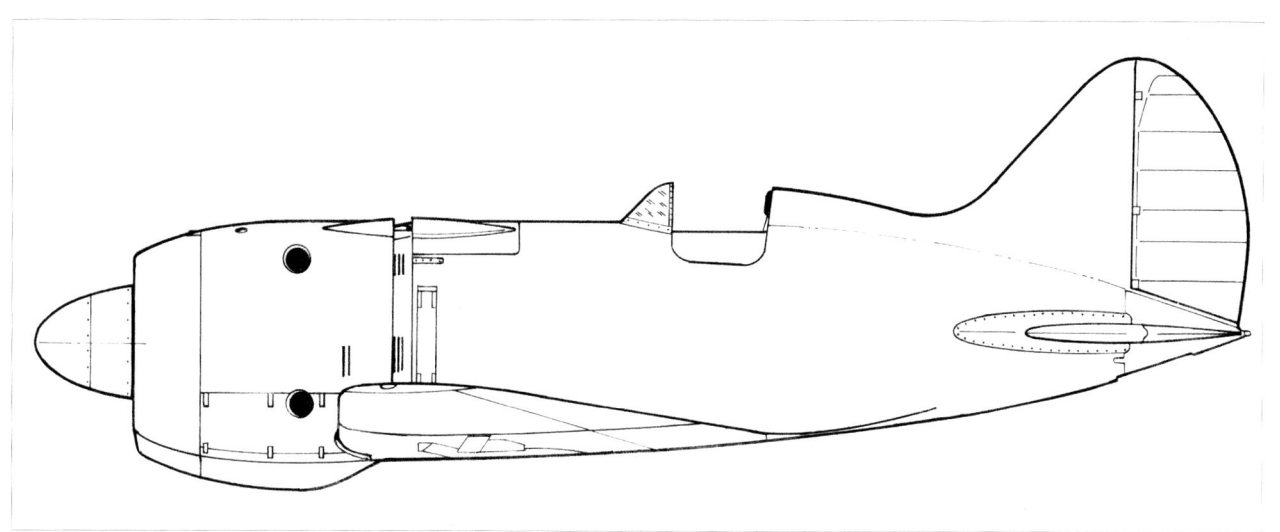

Side view drawing of the I-180 second prototype fitted with the M-87 engine.

The third prototype of IP-21 fighter designed by Mikhail Pashinin.

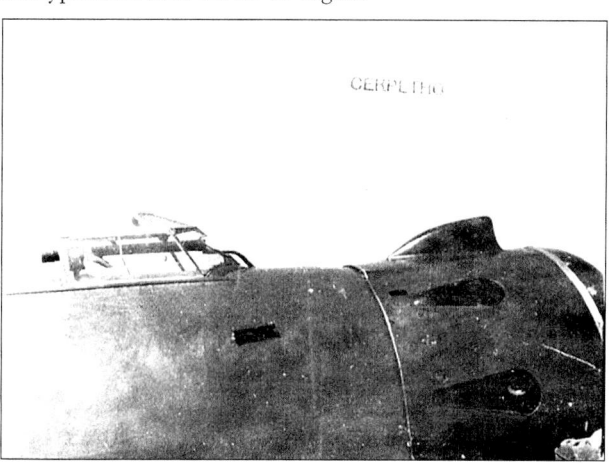

The I-16 with TsAGI carburetor air intake in 1940.

The I-301 fighter prototype during state tests in 1940. In production, the aircraft was designated the LaGG-3; at Factory No.21, it was referred to as Type 31.

The FAB-100 under the fuselage of an I-16 attached to designer Orlov's bomb rack in 1940.

Two I-16 Type 29s were not handed over to the customer as they were tested until they were worn out. Another 125 aircraft (45 Type 15s and 80 Type 29s) were completed but not handed over, and were thus carried over to the plan of 1941. Furthermore, the factory manufactured 7,590 fibreboard external tanks and 165 equipment sets for RSI-3 radios. Besides this, 294 sets of parts were prepared for conversion of the I-16 Type 10 into Type 18 by means of mounting the M-62 engines instead of the M-25V.

After the production of the I-16s was discontinued in the fourth quarter of 1940, Factory No.21 made use of all the available in-process stock related to the aircraft. In early 1941, the last 80 I-16 Type 29s and 256 UTI-4s were built. After this time, only the LaGGs were rolled out to the airfield from the factory workshop.

Apart from the major modifications of the I-16, the following changes were made to the aircraft during the final period of its manufacture. These changes were not implemented on series production aircraft:

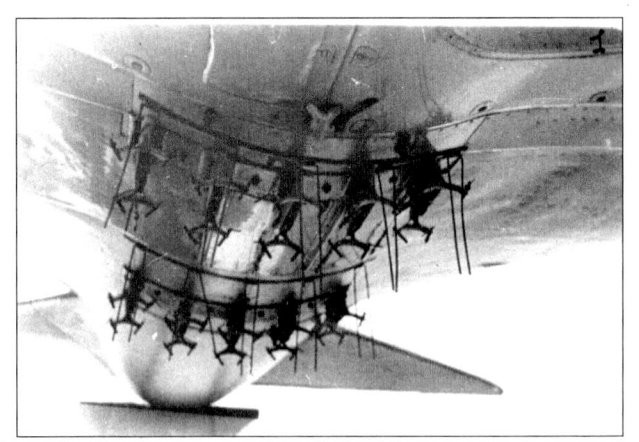

Ten 15kg bombs attached under the fuselage of an I-16, as suggested by Orlov, of the 62nd Air Brigade of the Black Sea Fleet Air Force in 1940.

- TsAGI experiments with the carburetor air intake, which was installed on the upper surface of the engine cowling instead of the frontal-mounted.
- Installation, in 1940, of a 200mm-diameter tailwheel.
- Installation of a flat glare-free windscreen.
- In summer 1940, two I-16 Type 24s were equipped with designer Orlov's bomb racks in the repair shops of the Black Sea Fleet Air Force. The aircraft could carry 10 15kg bombs or a single 100kg bomb. The installations were tested by the 62nd Air Brigade of the Black Sea Fleet Air Force.
- In the first half of 1941, some of the I-16s were equipped with bomb racks (of the same type as on the I-153), which allowed the attaching of teardrop external PLBG-100 fuel tanks or two bombs weighing 100kg each.
- In August 1940, the I-16 No.44 (s/n 4427) powered by the M-62TK was fitted with the so-called N. Efremov's reactor. This equipment utilised the heat energy of exhaust gases to increase flight speed. In spite of the fact that the aircraft frontal portion became larger, a 16km/h increase in the maximum speed at an altitude of 3,000m was reached.

1.2.15.2. The I-16 Type 29

The first I-16 M-63 prototype (s/n 2721G95) with a BS synchronised large-calibre machine gun and two fuselage-mounted ShKAS machine guns was built in January 1940. This airplane had no landing flaps, the ailerons were extended up to the second rib of the wing centre section, and non-standard 610mm-diameter wheels were mounted. The aircraft had an empty weight of 1,370.4kg, take-off weight of 1,780kg and flight centre of gravity position of 26.4% MAC. The wing load totalled 122kg/sq.m, which was less than in the Type 17.

Factory tests of the new aircraft from 8–10 February 1940 were conducted by pilot Fokin. It was then test-flown by NII VVS test pilot V. Inshakov. In the latter's opinion, this I-16 without landing flaps and external tanks turned out to be rather easy to control and excelled the I-16 Type 24 in terms of manoeuvrability.

Further improvement of the aircraft involved mounting additional items and equipment, which entailed an increase in weight to 1,900kg. This aircraft, which was given the designation I-16 Type 29, had the following main distinguishing features:

- The BS machine gun was placed in the space between the landing gear wells below the cap of the wing centre section front spar, and was displaced by 17mm. To enable installation of a magazine for 230–240 rounds, the second fuselage frame was shifted by 54mm. To fit the BS machine gun, the landing gear wells were moved apart; the distance from the normal axis to the wheels' axis in the retracted position increased from 380mm to 421mm. Accordingly, the landing gear legs were made 32mm shorter, while the propeller diameter was reduced to 2.7m to ensure the required clearance from the ground (268mm). This did not entail any noticeable change in the thrust, since 250mm-wide ('widened') blades were used. The distance between the landing gear wells was covered with a removable fairing, which was attached using retaining bars and Fairey locks. In connection with the above modifications, the skin of the wing centre section also underwent changes.
- The oil cooler, which had earlier been arranged along the aircraft centreline, was moved to the position between the fourth and the fifth engine cylinders. The air supplying pipe of the oil cooler was accordingly moved to the space between the ports of these cylinders. Some of the aircraft of the later series had no air supply pipe; the air was fed via cut-out holes. In connection with relocation of the oil cooler, the system for manual engine starting using the RI-type inertia starter was removed.
- Radio-equipped aircraft had an aerial mast installed on the right portion of the engine cowling.

- The wing of the I-16 Type 29 was fully freed from machine-gun and cannon armament. However, the new configuration had under-wing locks for external tanks and six 'flute'-type rail launchers (three on each side) for carrying RS-32 rocket projectiles.

The aircraft with fully implemented modifications – the I-16 s/n 292116 with the M-63 s/n 631698 engine – arrived at NII VVS for tests on 27 August, having been ferried from Factory No.21 to Chkalovskaya. The tests continued for several weeks until 4 October. Throughout this period, leading pilot Major Gruzdev and test pilots Nikashin and Stefanovsky made a total of 55 flights.

The test report specified all the main differences from the previous I-16 types. Apart from those which have already been mentioned above, it was pointed out that the BS machine gun had an ammunition load of 120–230 rounds, while the ShKAS machine guns had 475 rounds for the left-mounted gun and 500 rounds for the right-mounted unit. There was an RSI-3 radio with a fixed antenna, and the radio receiver was arranged under the instrument panel. The aircraft was equipped with external fuel tanks, rail launchers for six rocket projectiles and a PAU-22 gun camera. The centre of gravity position for the gross weight of 1,966kg was 29.15% MAC.

During the course of the tests, the following flight performance parameters were obtained, depending on the configuration of equipment and operational items:

- Variant 1 (antenna, rail launchers without rocket projectiles);
- Variant 2 (antenna, external tanks, rail launchers without rocket projectiles);
- Variant 3 (no antenna, external tanks, rail launchers).

The table below shows the results for each variant:

Parameter	Variant 1	Variant 2	Variant 3
Gross weight (kg)	1,966	2,115	1,940
Load on wing (kg/sq.m)	135.2	146.1	133.5
Maximum speed at H=0 (km/h)	408	382	419
Maximum speed * (km/h)	461	429	470
Time to climb to 5,000m (minutes)	6.2	7.25	5.8
Service ceiling (m)	9,800		
Landing speed with landing flaps (km/h)	130		
Landing speed without landing flaps (km/h)	135.5		
Time to perform a turn at 1,000m (seconds)	16		
Take-off run with landing flaps retracted (m)	243		
Take-off run with landing flaps set to 10° (m)	201		
Landing run with landing flaps and brakes (m)	400		
Reached dive speed (km/h)	580		
Flight range without external fuel tanks at an altitude of 4,700m at 90% maximum speed (km)	510 **		

* At the engine critical altitude (4,350m for Variant 1, 4,150m for Variant 2, 4,480m for Variant 3).
** The report specifies the range for Type 24 M-63.

However, the tests were not without incident. On 11 September, in a flight at the maximum speed, a portion of the cowling became separated and broke the windscreen.

In the conclusions of the test results it was pointed out that the maximum speed in the configuration with the radio antenna decreased from 481km/h (for I-16 Type 24) to 470km/h. The decrease in speed was accounted for by the worsening of the wing aerodynamics due to cut-outs and hatches in the wing. It was suggested that the dive speed should be reduced to 550km/h due to the hazard of tuck-under.

In general, it was considered that the I-16 Type 29 had passed the state tests successfully and could be accepted for service. Nearly all the built aircraft were supplied to the Red Army Air Force during the winter of 1940–41. Given the extraordinarily snowy and sleety weather that winter, the I-16 Type 29s were, for the most part, only mastered by combat units in spring 1941. This circumstance allowed the Type 29s to be considered as one of the newest fighters in service with the Red Army Air Force during the initial period of the war.

68 The King of Fighters Volume 2

A view of the upper part of the I-16 Type 29's power plant with the cowlings removed. Note the cable running from the butt plate of the ShKAS machine gun to the cockpit, which was connected with the machine-gun rearming handle.

A view of the instrument panel and the right side of the cockpit of the I-16 Type 29. In the centre of the floor, note the bracket-mounted receiver of the RSI-3 Oryol radio which worked on five fixed channels.

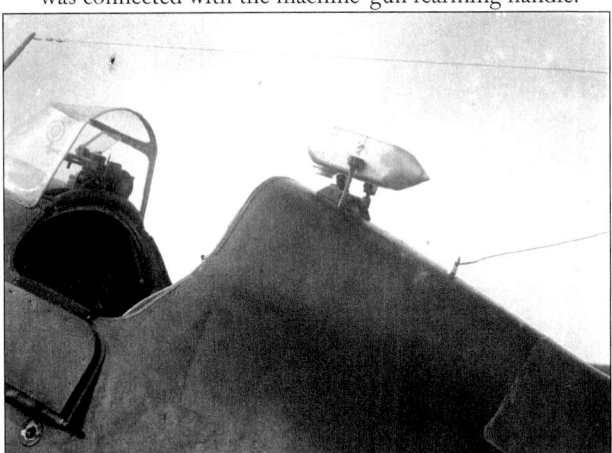

A PAU-22 gun camera mounted on the fuselage upper fairing of the I-16 Type 29.

A 12.7mm BS large-calibre machine gun mounted in the space between the landing gear wells. The machine-gun fairing has been removed.

The cockpit left side. Note the rearming handle in the centre.

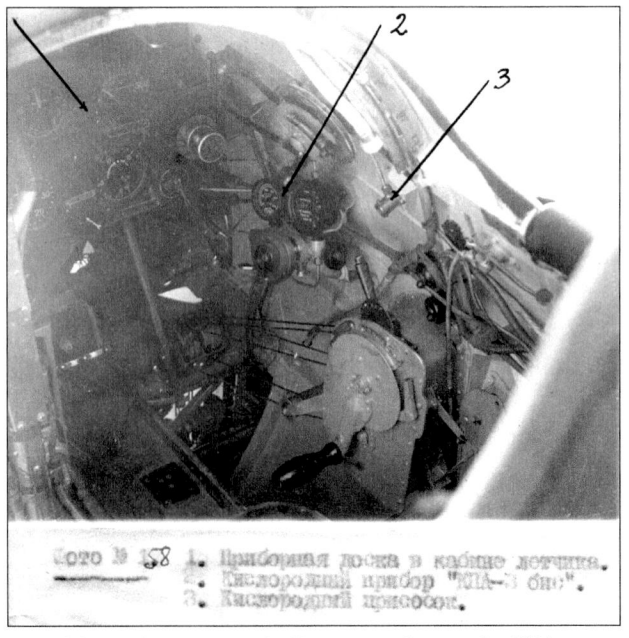

The cockpit right side. Figure 2 indicates the KPA-3bis oxygen control unit, while figure 3 shows the oxygen connector for connecting the mask hose.

The I-16 fighter 69

The RSI-3 radio receiver. Figure 2 indicates the instrument panel.

Aerial masts were installed, for the most part, on the I-16 Type 29. Figure 2 indicates the Venturi tube, which was used to spin up the single-degree-of-freedom gyroscope of the turn indicator.

The left side of the engine cowling with a partly torn-off panel which had covered the ammunition box of the left synchronised ShKAS machine gun.

View of the tail of the aircraft s/n 292116.

A view of the right lower portion of the power plant of I-16 Type 29. The BS machine gun is covered with a cowling. This is one of the few photos which show that the air downstream from the oil cooler was directed to the right landing gear well.

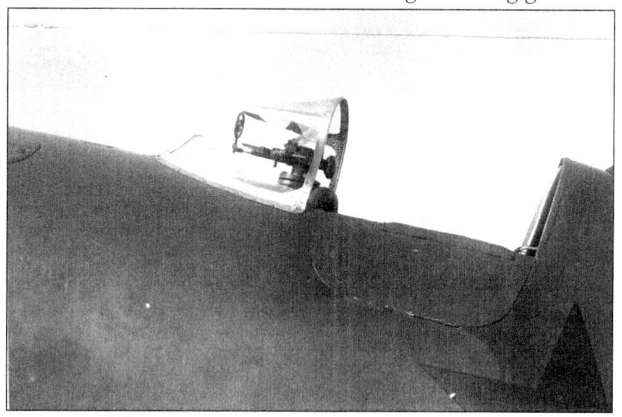

The windscreen after the collision with a fragment of the torn-off cover panel.

A rear view of the I-16 Type 29 during the course of the state tests. Note the external thermometer installed on the cover strip of the left wing.

A side view of the I-16 Type 29.

A front view of the I-16 Type 29.

A power battery installed on the I-16 Type 29.

1.2.15.3. Aviation Factory No.153

In accordance with strategic plans for the creation of industry in the eastern regions of the Soviet Union, several aviation factories were built in Siberian industrial centres in the mid-1930s.

One such aviation factory, which was given the designation No.153, began to operate in 1936 in Novosibirsk. Oriented towards manufacture of the I-16s, the factory initially demonstrated modest results in terms of both quantity and quality of its products. In 1937, 27 I-16 Type 5s were built in Novosibirsk, of which only six were accepted after military inspection. The following year proved none the less difficult for the Siberian aviation industry, which had to manufacture aircraft concurrently with fitting out the factory itself. As a result, the 105 built I-16s constituted only a half of the expected quantity.

In 1938, the factory in Novosibirsk began building the I-220 fighter prototype designed by A. Silvansky. As has already been noted, the aircraft was created on the basis of the M-88-powered I-165 design. However, the I-220 proved to be an unsuccessful aircraft in all aspects and flew very little.

In 1939, Factory No.153 handed over for military inspection 264 I-16s, of which 53 aircraft were defined as Type 5. As for the 500 I-16 Type 24 fighters planned for 1940, a decision was made not to build them due to the problems with the M-63 engines. Instead, the factory in Novosibirsk manufactured 503 UTI-4 trainers. In 1941, Aviation Factory No.153 produced 404 UTI-4s and 19 I-16 Type 24s. Starting from the second half of 1941, Novosibirsk fully converted to manufacture of the LaGG-3 (265 aircraft were built before the end of the year) and Yak-7b fighters (21 aircraft completed before the end of the year).

1.2.15.4. The UTI-4 fighter trainer

The UTI-4 fighter trainer was the most series-produced version of the I-16. Throughout the years of series production, the factories built over 3,400 such aircraft.

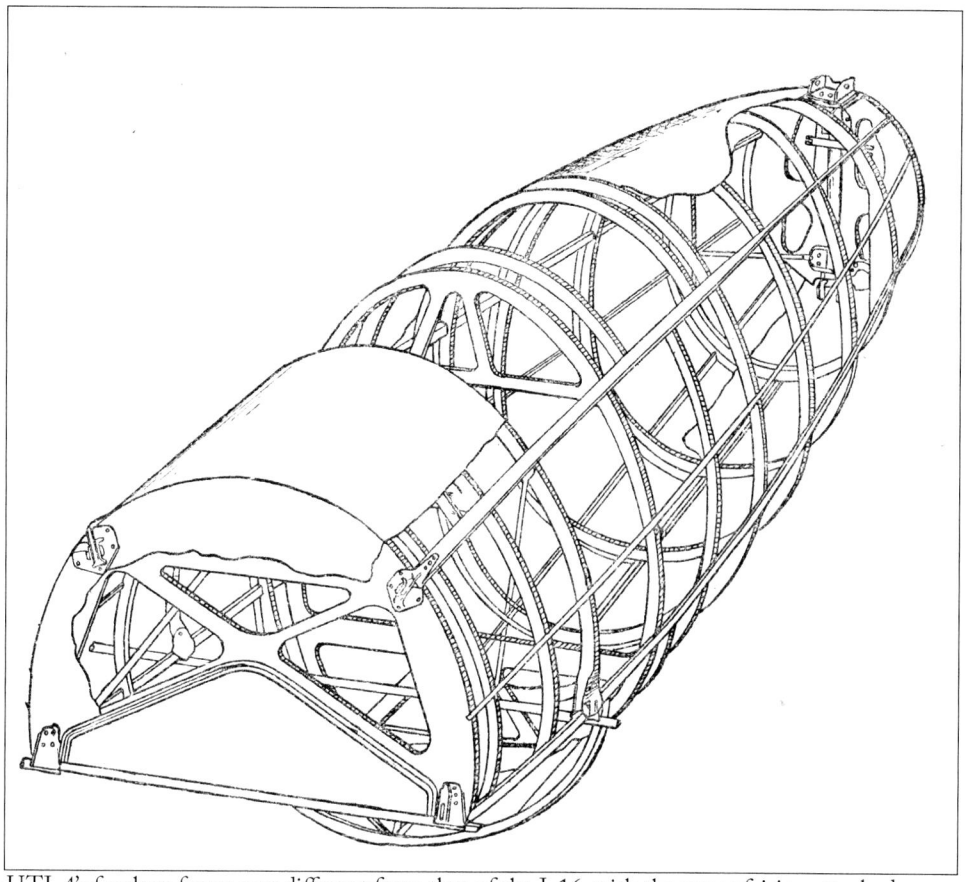

The UTI-4's fuselage frame was different from that of the I-16, with the upper fairing attached separately.

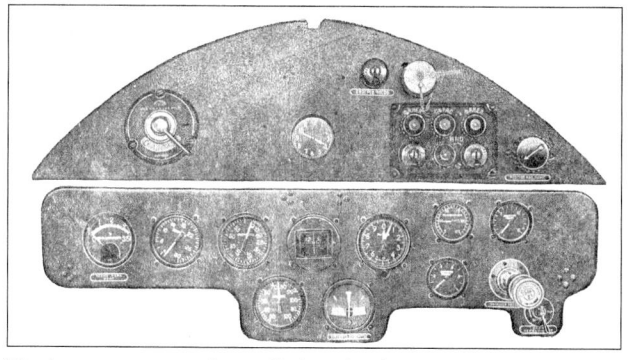

The instrument panel installed in the front cabin of the UTI-4.

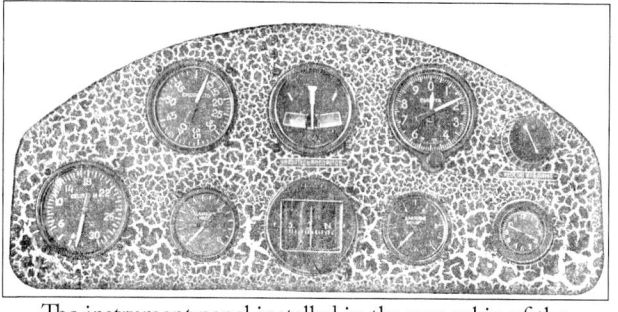

The instrument panel installed in the rear cabin of the UTI-4. The instrument panel itself is painted with black matt paint, providing for a 'moiré style'.

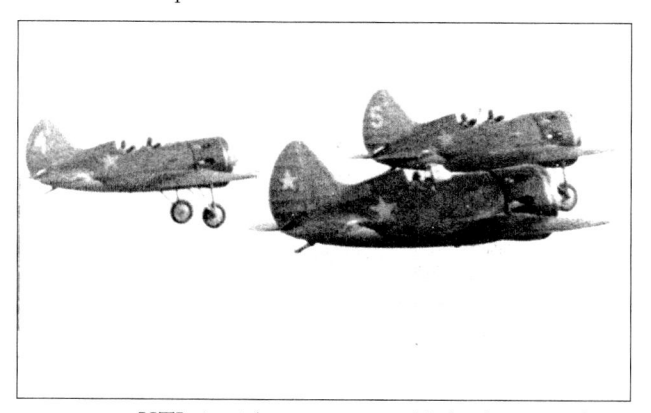

UTI-4s with a non-retractable landing gear flying in formation with a combat I-16. At least three UTI-4s were taking part in the flight; the photo was taken from the third such aircraft. According to the original caption, this is the "alert wing above Sevastopol". However, the episode is more likely to represent the group's flight to another base. It should be noted that four UTI-4s left for the Crimea in the course of the evacuation of the 69th Fighter Air Regiment from Odessa in early September 1941.

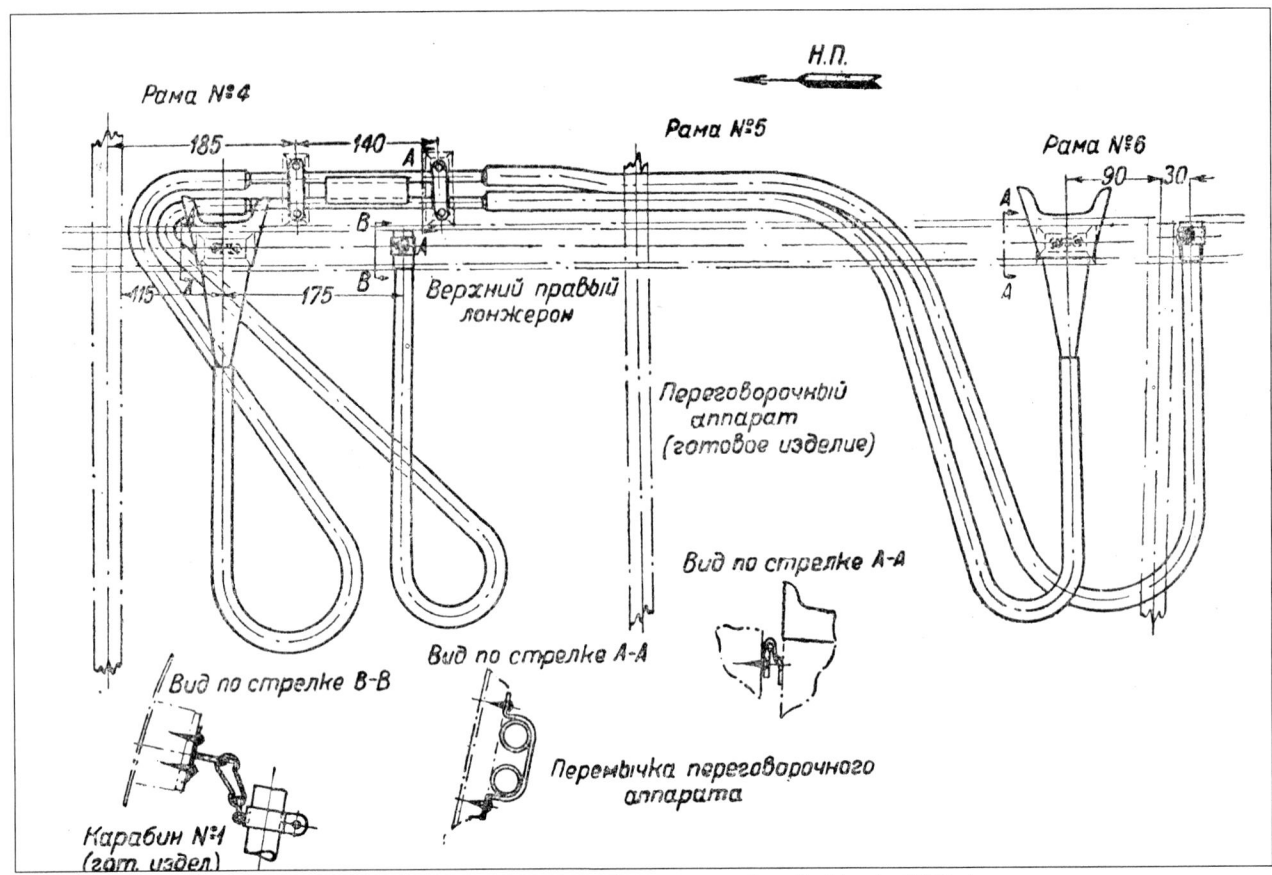

A plan of the intercommunication apparatus installed in the UTI-4.

The M-25 engine being started from a ground motor-car starter. Note that the UTI-4 in the photo has provisions for installation of a retractable ski landing gear.

The I-16 fighter 73

A UTI-4 captured by the Finns in autumn 1941 on the Svir river. The aircraft has a damaged propeller, for which reason it was abandoned during the retreat.

A UTI-4 of the 2nd Guards Fighter Air Regiment of the Northern Fleet Air Force with a fabric 'hood' above the aft cabin for 'blind flying' training. Captain Maksimovich is getting ready for a flight with a young pilot.

Another photo taken from a UTI-4 in mid-air on the Southern Front during 1942. Note an I-16 Type 5 with the tail number '17' in the background. When viewing the photograph closely, it can be seen that the fighter is equipped with a shortened movable canopy, a PAK-1 gunsight and additional external fuel tanks. 680. A UTI-4 with non-retractable ski landing gear at the flying school in Engels during 1942.

Young pilots Zaitsev and Manichev during the course of training, with a UTI-4 in the background, in February 1943.

Four UTI-4s from the flying school at Engels were ferried to Moscow for participation in an aviation parade dedicated to the victory over Nazi Germany. This photograph was taken at Bykovo Airfield in August 1945.

The UTI-4 was fitted with the M-25A or M-25V engine. In terms of design, it was in many aspects identical to the I-16 Type 5 without armament. Due to the absence of machine guns, there were no access hatches for their maintenance on the wing centre section. Ailerons were of enlarged span, the mechanism for their differential lowering at landing was not used and landing flaps were not installed. There were also dual aircraft and engine controls. The landing gear retraction lever and the landing gear retraction mechanical indicator were arranged in the aft cabin. No radio was installed; for communication between the instructor and the trainee, a standard apparatus was provided which was essentially a system of tubes and funnels.

During the course of production, the UTI-4 underwent certain modifications. The M-25V-powered aircraft had the oil cooler air intake on the frontal portion of the cowling; the landing gear with splines was later replaced with a landing gear with a torque link; and the tail skid with rubber shock absorption was replaced with one having oleo-pneumatic shock absorption.

Starting from the UTI-4 s/n 1521109, small fuel tanks (39 litres each) were installed in the wing centre section. The total amount of fuel with such tanks was 220 litres. In August 1939, pilot Frolov and observer Mikhaylov conducted flight range tests in the UTI-4 s/n 15210Ж81. The aircraft, with a take-off weight of 1,503kg, carried 150kg of fuel. In an en-route flight, the range totalled 420km, with the time in flight of one hour and 18 minutes.

Starting from 1 January 1939, the UTI-4s were provided with electrical equipment for night flying and with a non-retractable landing gear.

In summer 1940, tests were conducted of an UTI-4 with the AV-1 propeller having the blades set in a fixed position. For a 2.8m-diameter propeller with a blade width of 220mm, the most efficient blade angle of 32° was determined experimentally. Such a setting was found to be optimal for training flights, circuit flight and simple aerobatics.

The UTI-4s were used for conversion training of pilots in Spain and China. In autumn 1940, Red Army Air Force training schools mustered 1,047 UTI-4 M-25s and 22 UTI-2M-22s, while the Naval Aviation had 129 UTI-4 M-25s and three UTI-2 M-22s. The use of the UTI-4s for training of Soviet pilots continued throughout the war until 1946.

1.2.15.5. Aviation Factory No.458

In 1939, to increase aircraft output, some factories from other sectors of the Soviet economy were put under the jurisdiction of the aviation industry authorities. Thus, the RAZ motor vehicle assembly factory in Rostov-on-Don, which had earlier specialised in assembly of trucks built at Nizhny Novgorod, was handed over to the NKAP. The factory was assigned the designation No.458, and was intended to manufacture the UTI-4 fighter trainer.

In 1940, the factory continued to assemble the GAZ-AA and the GAZ-MM trucks. It should be noted that the number of vehicles assembled at the factory (20,250) indicates a considerable production scale. In the same year, technical documentation, tooling and sets of parts for manufacture of the UTI-4s began to arrive at Rostov-on-Don from Aviation Factory No.21.

Full-fledged aircraft manufacture began on 21 March. To render assistance to the new aviation factory, the Rostov-based factory named after Uritsky (fuselage manufacturer) and Factory No.457 in Zaporozhye (landing gear manufacturer) were

I-16s, prepared for handover/acceptance tests, at the factory airfield.

Final assembly of the I-16 Type 24 in Urumqi in spring 1941. The original caption reads, "A propeller is being installed on the aircraft".

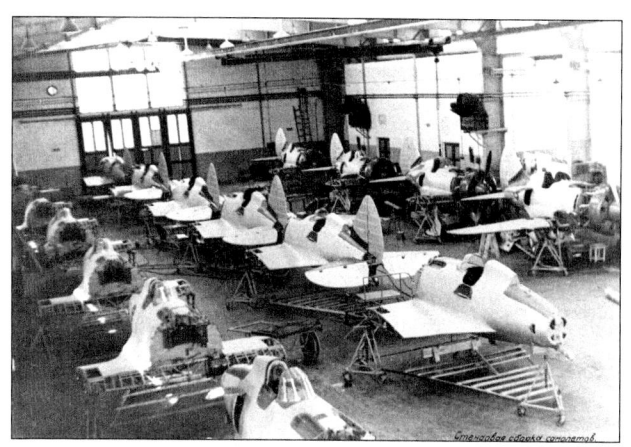

Aircraft being assembled on mobile assembly stands.

An assembled aircraft is prepared for a test flight. The I-16 Type 24 was fitted with locks for mounting external fuel tanks.

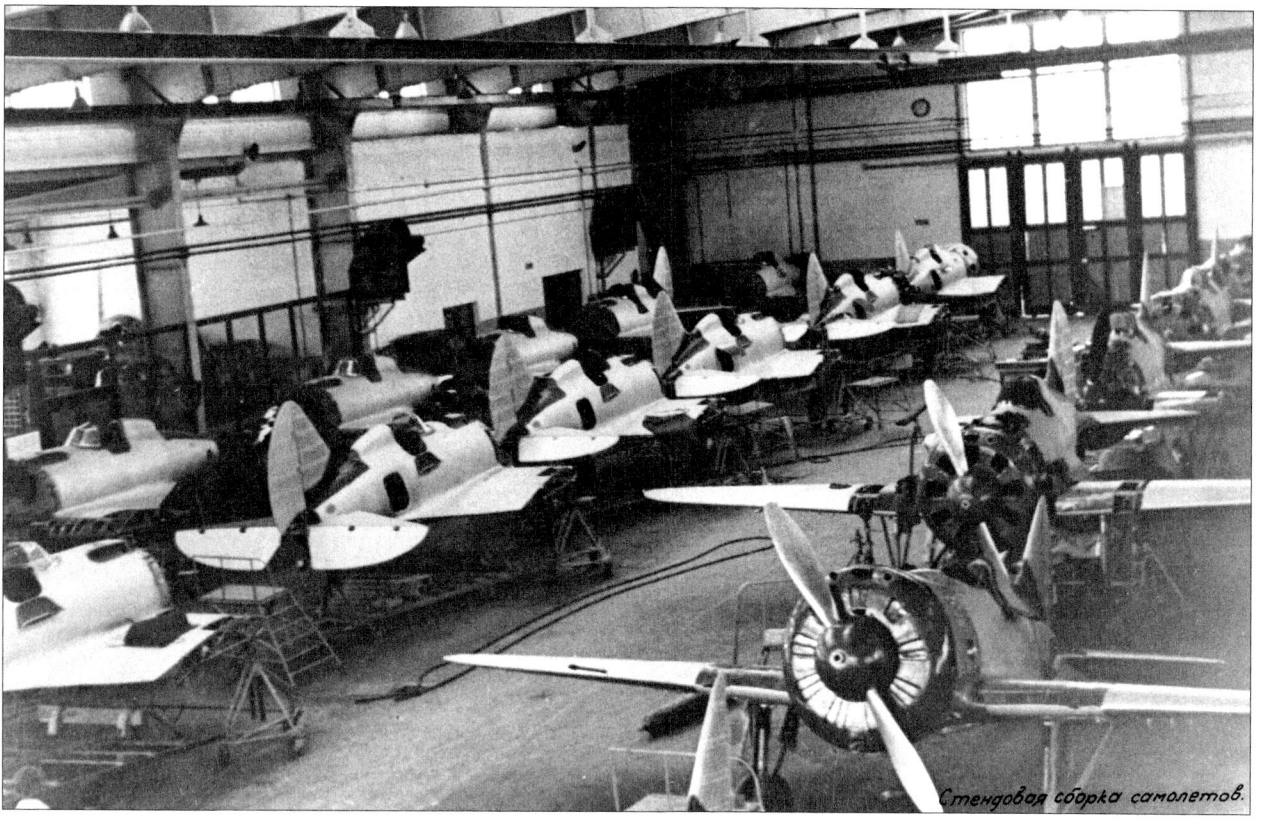

The final stage of aircraft assembly before painting.

Twenty I-16s are prepared for ferrying.

assigned. With the outbreak of the war with Germany, Aviation Factory No.458 was evacuated to Baku in the Caucasus, where it continued to produce the UTI-4s.

Before its evacuation, the factory in Rostov-on-Don built 310 UTI-4s, while another 146 airplanes underwent overhaul. At the new location, 46 training aircraft were manufactured before the end of 1941. In Baku, the last version of the I-16 – the combat version of the UTI-4 designated Type 15B ('B' for *boyevoy*, combat) – was also prepared.

The fighter-trainer underwent numerous modifications. Two large-calibre non-synchronised Berezin BK machine guns were mounted in the wing centre section. Six launchers for RS-82 rocket projectiles (three on each side) and bomb racks for 50kg bombs (one rack on each side) were arranged under the wing. For firing and bombing purposes, a PBP-1A collimator gunsight was installed in the front cabin. In case of combat use, the aft cabin could be covered with a duralumin hood. This version of the UTI-4 was tested at the airfield of the 480th Air Regiment in Kishly and by the 266th Air Regiment in Shekhikay, near Baku.

In January 1942, it was admitted that the Type 15B was superior to all other I-16 variants in terms of firepower. Thereafter, the range of aircraft applications expanded, and standard UTI-4s could be converted into Type 15Bs.

The last 83 UTI-4s were built in Baku in 1942, althjough the number of combat Type 15Bs among them is not known. Factory No.458 was then combined with other evacuated factories. Its products subsequently included fuel tanks for Tupolev SB bombers and parts for PPSh submachine guns and Katyusha rocket launchers, among many other items.

1.2.14.6. Aviation Factory No.600

In 1941, the RKKA VVS received an additional 150 Ishaks, despite them by then being an outdated type. These aircraft came from China, from an aircraft assembly factory located 47km from the city of Urumqi. This factory had been built specifically for the assembly of the I-16s and was an outpost of the Soviet aviation industry in the very centre of Asia. In official documents, the enterprise was designated as Aviation Factory No.600 in Western China. Air ferry of the completed I-16s to this factory in 1940 practically ceased, and the fighters were now delivered by truck in the form of sets of parts and assembled at the Factory No.600.

In 1941, it was a 'brand new' factory with its own power station and an independent water supply system, located in a strategically important area but at the same time deep in the rear. The factory was still under construction and was in the long run intended for carrying out full-fledged aircraft manufacturing.

In April 1941, there were 143 mothballed I-16s in Urumqi, which had already been stored there for six to eight months. A decision was then made to return these aircraft to the Soviet Union, but it was not until after the outbreak of the war that the transfer began. The aircraft were assembled, test-flown, camouflaged and then accepted by military pilots and ferried to

Alma-Ata in modern Kazakhstan. By 1 September 1941, 111 aircraft had been ferried. One I-16 was lost in the mountains. The remaining 30 fighters and two UTI-4s arrived in Alma-Ata before the end of the year.

In 1942, Factory No.600 was engaged in the manufacture of individual assemblies for the I-16, LaGG-3 and Yak-7 fighters. Furthermore, it performed repair of five I-16s and four Tupolev SB bombers. In late 1942, the factory began to manufacture the UT-2 trainer.

1.2.15.7. The production figures

To complete the story of the last years of the I-16 production, it is worth recalling the conventional opinion of many pilots in the early 1940s that it was enough to put a more powerful engine on the *Ishachok*, and the problem of the new fighter would then be solved. At the same time, production engineers were looking for their own ways of prolonging the age of the I-16. Thus, already during the war, specialists from Aviation Factory No.163 in Irkutsk had developed an all-wooden tail unit and wings for the I-16 in 1942. The Novosibirsk branch of TsAGI conducted static tests of these wooden structures. The new wing, fully covered in 2.5mm of plywood, weighed 65kg. This was only 3kg higher than the weight of the previous wing, while the strength was equal. Weight of the wooden tail unit was also slightly higher than that of the duralumin one. In April 1943, the management of Factory No.163 suggested resuming production of the I-16 in an all-wooden form using the tooling of Aviation Factory No.153. However, the idea gathered no enthusiasm from the higher authorities: production of the I-16 fighter was irrevocably discontinued.

In concluding the review on the production and improvements of the I-16, it should be repeated that it was the first fighter in the world to be manufactured on such a massive scale. Together with its instruction and training version – the UTI-4 – the total number of I-16s built during the period from 1934 to 1942 was 10,292.

Production of I-16s from 1934–42										
Factory	1934	1935	1936	1937	1938	1939	1940	1941	1942	Total
No.39 in Moscow	50	4	4	–	–	–	–	–	–	58
No.21 in Nizhny Novgorod	–	527	902	1,881	1,070	1,571	2,207	336	–	8,494
No.53 in Novosibirsk	–	–	–	6	105	264	503	423	–	1,301
No.458* in Rostov-on-Don/Baku	–	–	–	–	–	–	–	356	83	439
Total	50	531	906	1,887	1,175	1,835	2,710	1,115	83	10,292

* Factory No.458 built only UTI-4s.

According to the official factory reports, production of the I-16s per types was as follows:

Year	1934	1935	1936	1937	1938	1939	1940	1941	1942	Total
Type 4	41	464								505[1]
Type 5			861	1,665[2]	169[3]					2,695
Type 10					508	426				934
Type 12				10	12					22
Type 14 (UTI-2)		22[4]	27							49
Type 15 (UTI-4)				206	352	635	1,103	1,016	83	3,395
Type 17					27	314				341
Type 18						177				177
Type 24						155	760[5]	19		934
Type 27						59				59
Type 28						16	277[6]			293
Type 29							570	80		650

1. Taking into account 50 I-16 M-22s manufactured by Factory No.39 in 1934, the number is 555.
2. This figure includes the 186 aircraft with modifications (see the chapter on 1937).

3. According to some records of Factory No.21, the number of I-16 Type 5s produced in 1938 was 150 or even just 100 aircraft.

4. This figure includes the UTI-3 M-58 s/n 11211 and UT-2 M-22 s/n 8211.

5. In 1940, output of the I-16 Type 18 is summed with Type 24.

6. In 1940, output of the I-16 Type 27 is summed with Type 28.

1.3. Technical description

The aircraft was an example of a classical mixed construction which was designed based on the resources and capabilities of Soviet aviation industry in the first half of the 1930s. When creating the I-16, Polikarpov remained faithful to his principle of building aircraft using domestic materials, that is, to a considerable extent, wood, and utilising reasonable amounts of duralumin and structural steel, which were in short supply at the time. It was the harmonious combination of wood, steel and duralumin that made it possible to consider such aircraft cheaper than an all-metal one, and therefore more acceptable to industry. At the same time, the I-16 manufacturing technology was not fraught with any unpleasant surprises for the production specialists and workers. Wooden monocoque fuselages, truss structures made of steel pipes, duralumin cowlings and tail units had been made at Soviet aviation factories for several years. The fabric covering of the wing, which facilitated aircraft repair to the maximum possible extent, also turned out to be appropriate. All of the above features were combined as outlined below.

The I-16 spindle-shaped fuselage was constructed by putting a preformed shell onto an open-worked skeleton assembled from 11 frames, four spars and eight stringers. The materials of the skeleton included pinewood, ashwood, Prima birch plywood and steel reinforcing struts.

The fuselage skin (the so-called 'shell') was made by means of pasting birch veneer sheets with casein glue over a special forming 'plug'. The layers of veneer were oriented perpendicular to each other, and at an angle of 45° to the aircraft centreline. The shell consisted of the left half and the right half; its thickness from the first frame 1 to the seventh frame was 5.5mm in the upper part and 2.5mm in the lower part. The tail portion starting from the seventh frame was 2mm thick. The skin was installed onto the skeleton using casein glue and galvanised nails. All joints, edges and cut-outs were reinforced with plywood plates. The wing-to-fuselage fairing was also formed separately and attached after connecting the wing centre section to the fuselage. After assembly, the skin was covered with nitro-glue on the outer surface, puttied and then pasted over with non-printed cotton fabric, once again puttied and then painted.

The internal fuselage surface during the first few years of production was painted with grey oil paint. Starting from February 1939, to increase the moisture resistance, the surface was first coated with ALG-2 yellow primer and then painted with AE-9 grey enamel.

The wing centre section was the main load-bearing element of the I-16, interconnecting the wing, fuselage, landing gear and power plant. The load-bearing portion of the wing centre section consisted of two steel trussed spars, connected by ribs and tubular bracing struts into a rigid structure. The upper skin of the wing centre section at the interface with the fuselage was wooden; starting from the second rib, it was made of duralumin. At the interface with the outer wing panel in the upper portion of the wing centre section was a hatch for access to the machine guns or cannons. The UTI trainer and I-16 Type 29 were not provided with such hatches. In the lower portion of the wing centre section were skin sections and domes to accommodate landing gear wheels in the retracted position. The domes were provided with cut-out windows covered with transparent celluloid to enable the pilot to see whether the landing gear was retracted.

The outer wing panels were similar to the wing centre section in design, and were connected to it using special sleeves with a threaded head on the butt ends of tubular spars. The slot between the outer wing and the wing centre section was covered with a 100mm-wide duralumin band.

The front section of the wing was covered – on the upper surface by 44.5% and on the lower surface by 14.5% – with a 0.6mm duralumin skin; the rest of the wing was covered in fabric. After covering with fabric, the wing was coated with four layers of colourless dope, then (before the general painting of the aircraft) with two layers of protective green dope on the upper surface and three layers of light grey dope and one layer of colourless oil-based dope No.17 on the lower surface.

The ailerons and the tail unit were made of duralumin and covered in fabric. On Type 4 and Type 5 aircraft, the ailerons had a greater span and were equipped with a droop mechanism. By drooping at landing, they, in addition to their main functions, played the role of flaps, reducing speed. Starting from the I-16 Type 10, the ailerons' span was made smaller; in order to reduce the landing speed, landing flaps with a maximum deflection angle of 60° were installed.

The vertical stabiliser was installed with an offset relative to the aircraft centreline in order to eliminate the engine torque. Since the M-22 and M-25 (M-62) engines had a different direction of rotation, the vertical stabiliser of the I-16 Type 4 was turned 2° to the right; for all later types, the vertical stabiliser was turned 2° to the left. The horizontal stabiliser could be adjusted on the ground within the limits of 3°, which allowed achieving the most acceptable control stick load for different centre of gravity positions. To make installation and adjustment of the unit easier, the tail portion of the aircraft had a removable duralumin fairing.

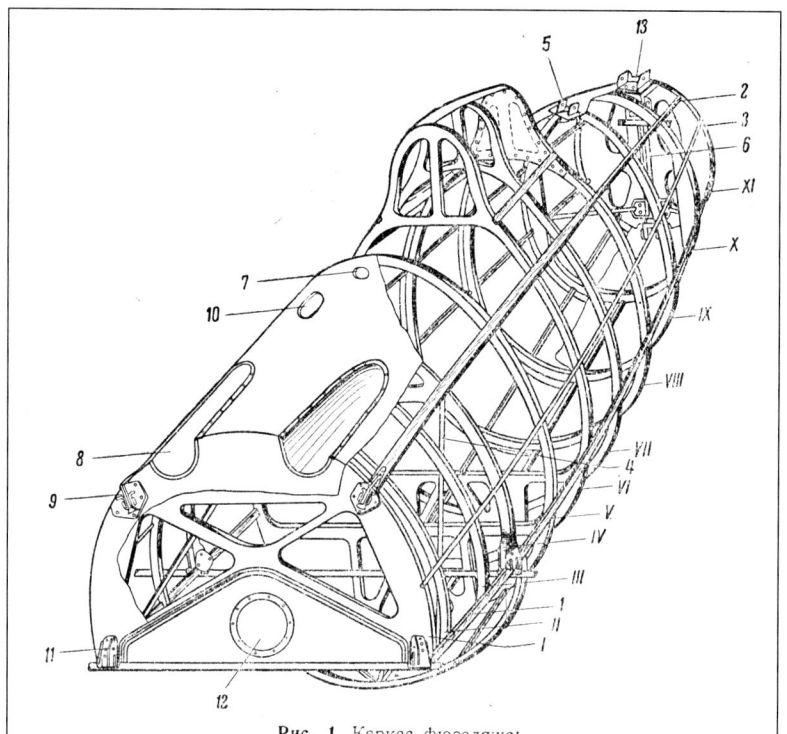

Рис. 1. Каркас фюзеляжа:

1 — нижний лонжерон; 2 — верхний лонжерон; 3 — стрингер; 4 — подкос между 1-й и 4-й рамами; 5 — передний узел крепления киля; 6 — труба костыля; 7 — отверстие для прицела ПАК-1; 8 — желоба для пулеметов; 9 — верхний узел крепления моторамы; 10 — окно освещения доски приборов; 11 — нижний узел крепления моторамы и стыка с центропланом; 12 — лючок для снятия стартера «Эклипс»; 13 — задний узел крепления киля; I—XI — рамы фюзеляжа.

The wooden skeleton of the fuselage.

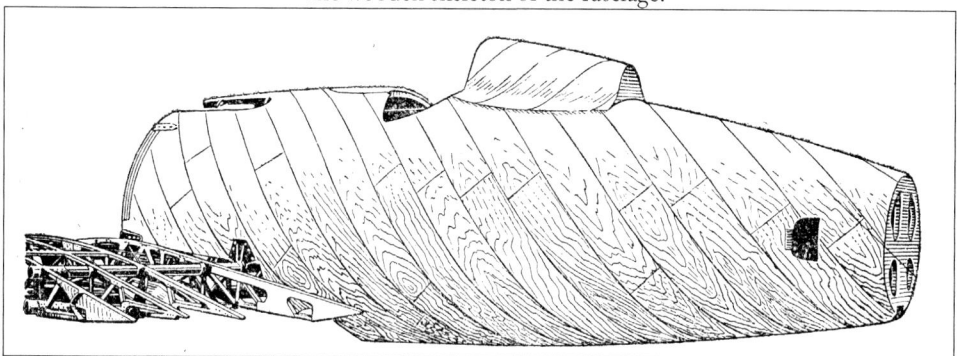

Fuselage skin.

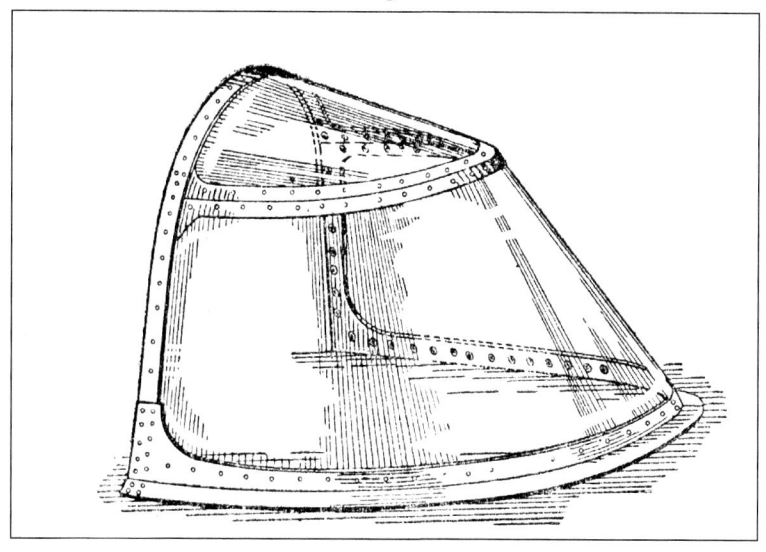

Windscreen.

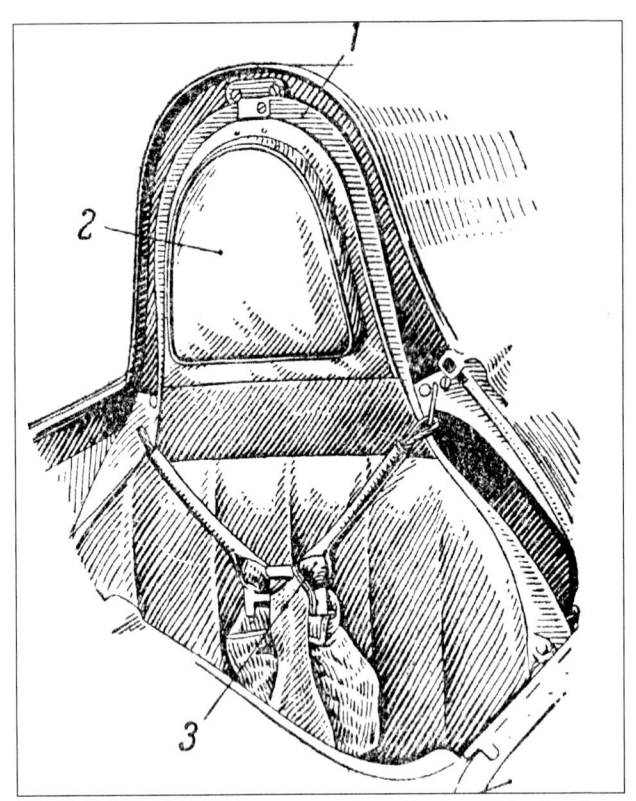

The upper portion of the armoured seat back and the headrest.

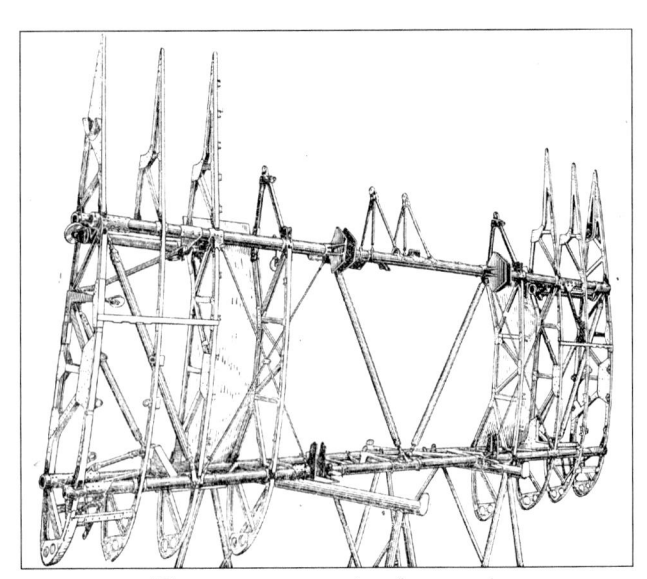

The wing centre section framework.

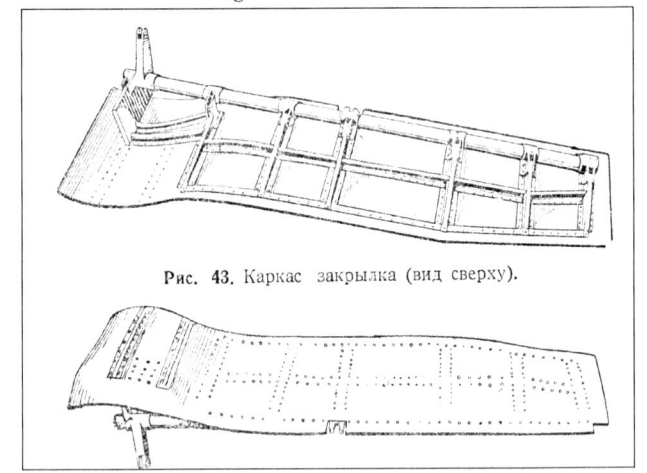

Рис. 43. Каркас закрылка (вид сверху).

General view of the right portion of the flap.

General view of the wing with aileron for the I-16 Type 5 and the UTI-4.

The retractable landing gear of the I-16 had the configuration of two three-rod pyramids. A mechanical jack on the right side of the cockpit was used to retract and extend the landing gear; 44 (actually 42–46) manual turns were required for retraction. The tail leg was actually a tail skid; only the latest versions were provided with a small 150mm-diameter tailwheel.

Wheels of the main landing gear had mechanical brakes. On earlier types, their size was 700x100mm; with all subsequent types, 700x150mm. The toe brakes were installed on the aircraft control pedals.

The pilot's seat was made of duralumin and was provided with a pan for a PL-1 seat-pack parachute (9.5kg). Initially, it had a light removable seat back with a soft leatherette cushion. It was later fitted with an 8mm-thick 18kg armoured seat back. A vertical-adjustment lever on the right side of the seat provided for a travel of 110mm.

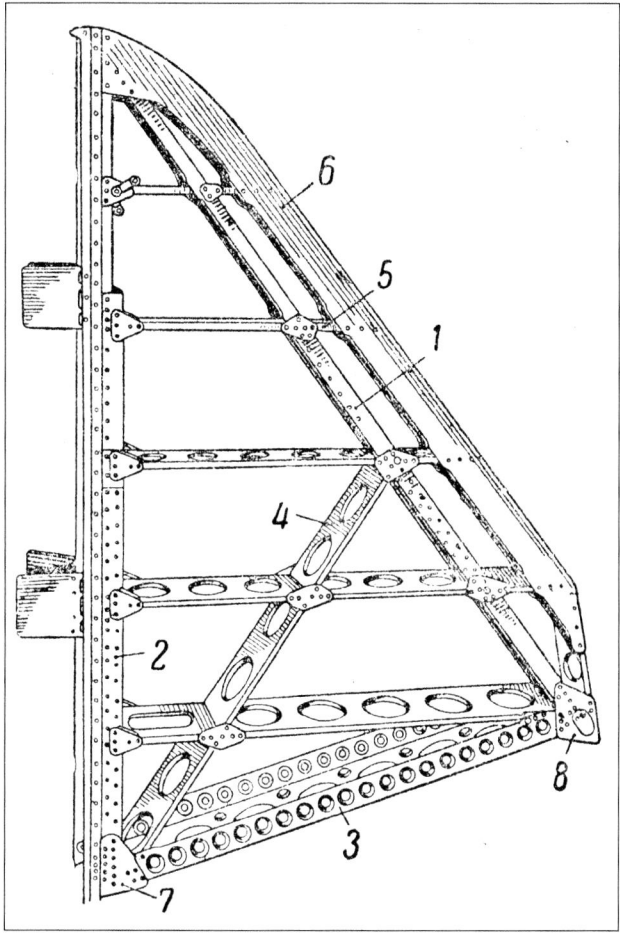

The vertical stabiliser.

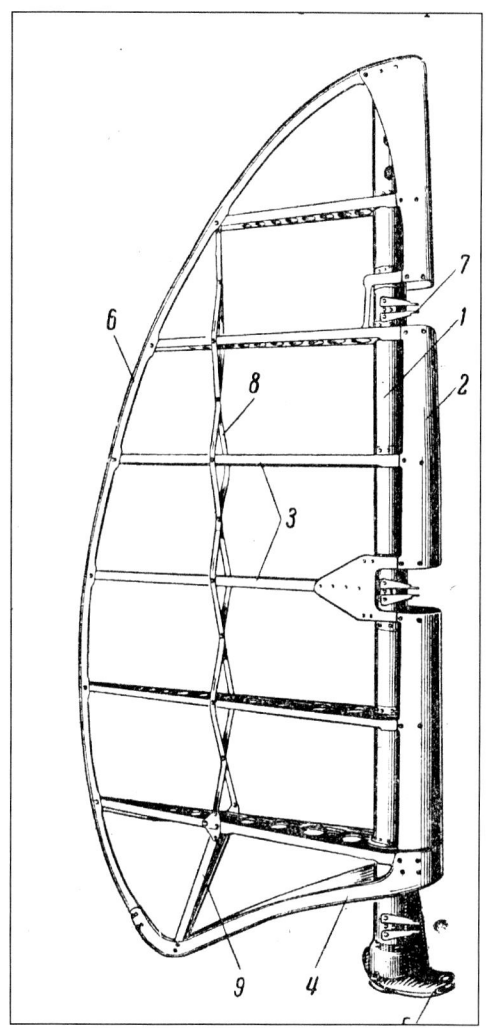

The rudder.

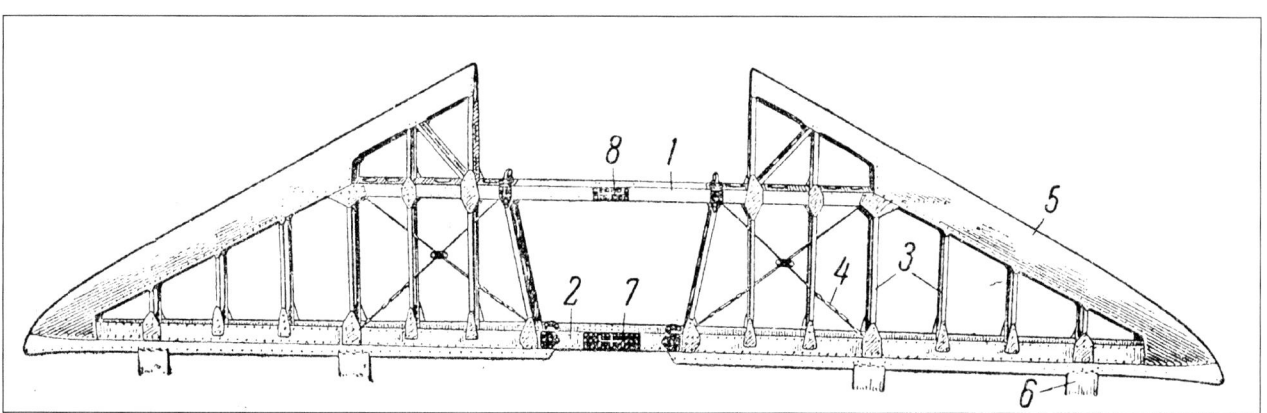

The horizontal stabiliser.

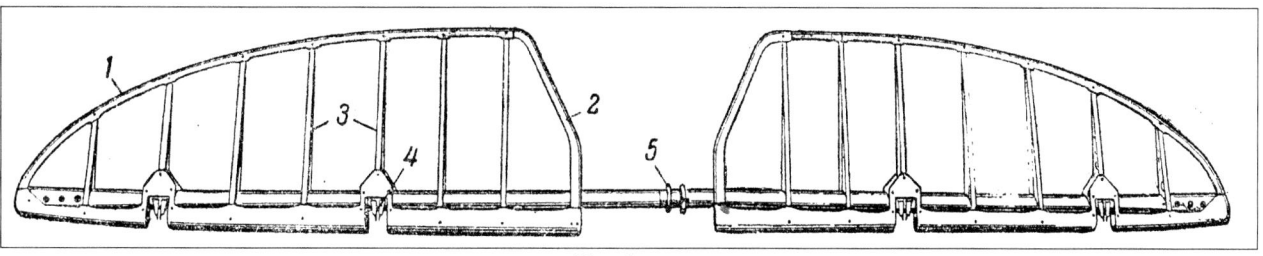

The elevator.

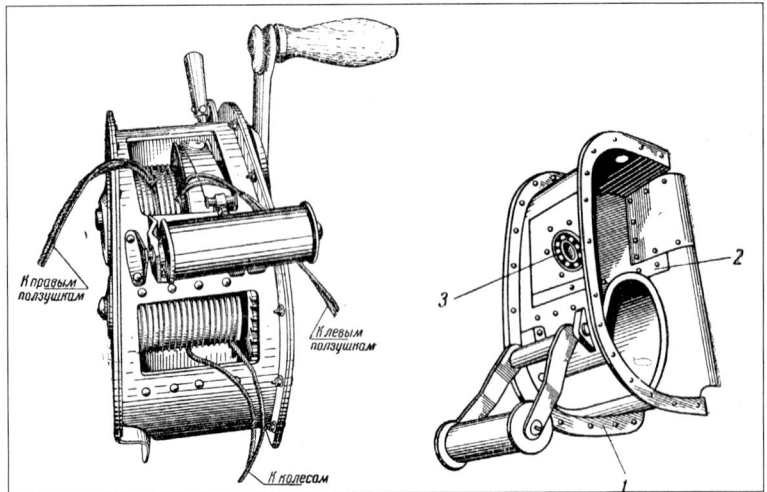

The landing gear retraction jack.

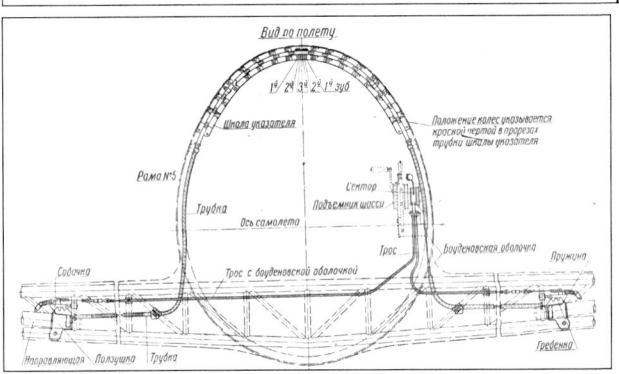

Mechanical indication system of the landing gear retraction.

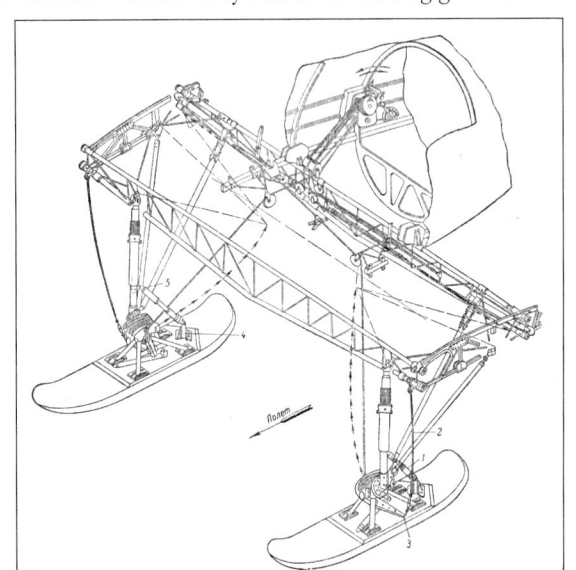

A retraction scheme of a ski landing gear.

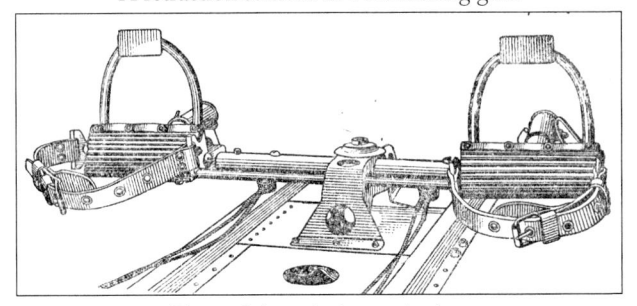

The pedals with the toe brakes.

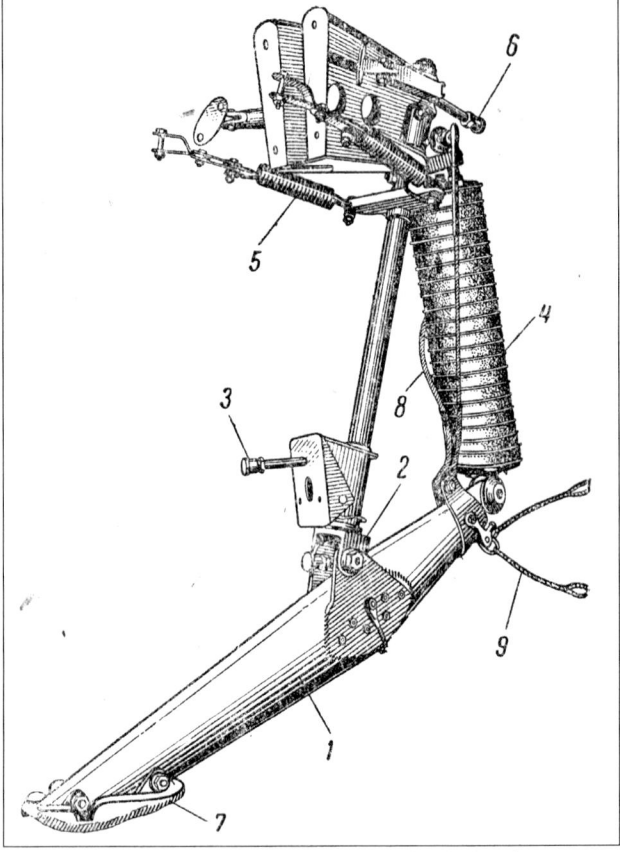

The tail skid with a rubber-ring shock absorber.

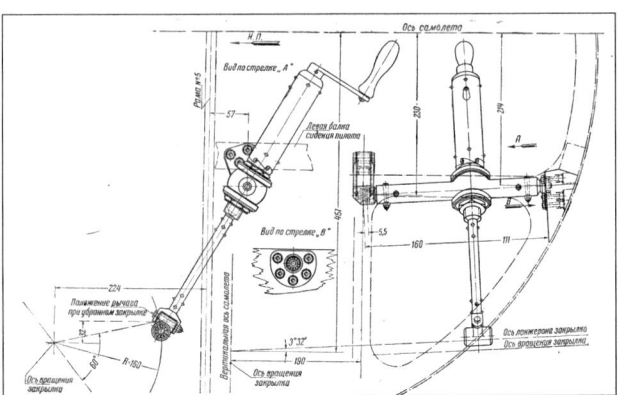

The screw mechanism for flaps control.

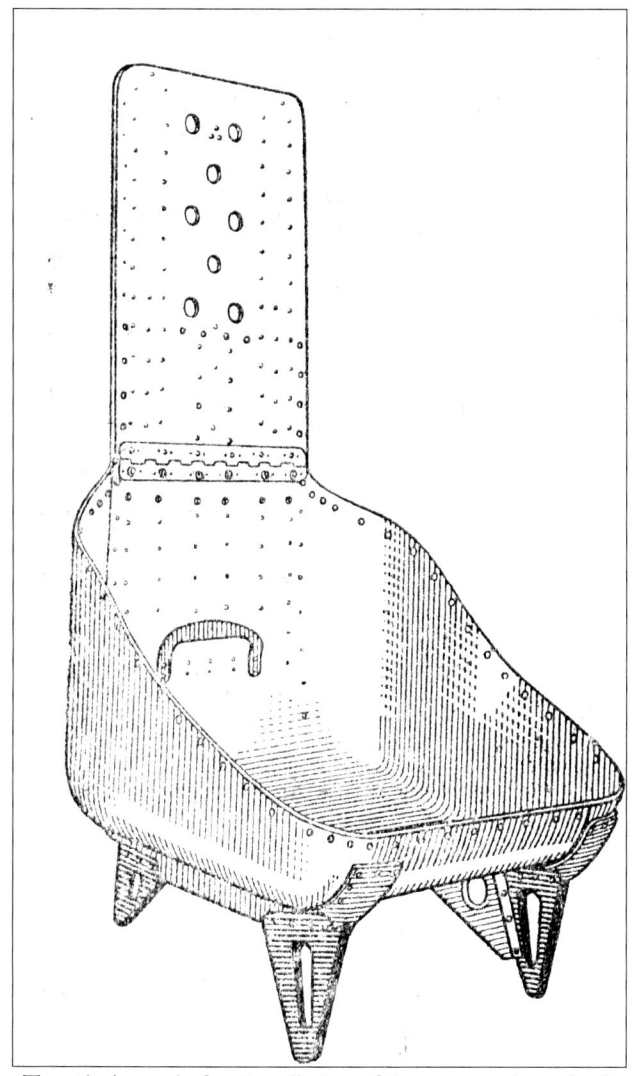

The pilot's seat before installation of the armoured seat back.

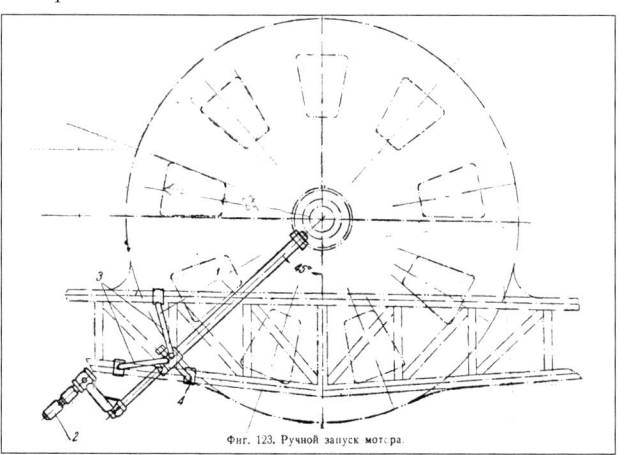

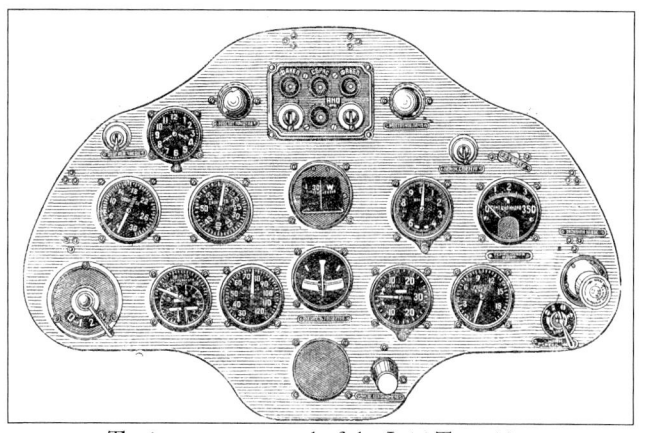

The instrument panel of the I-16 Type 10.

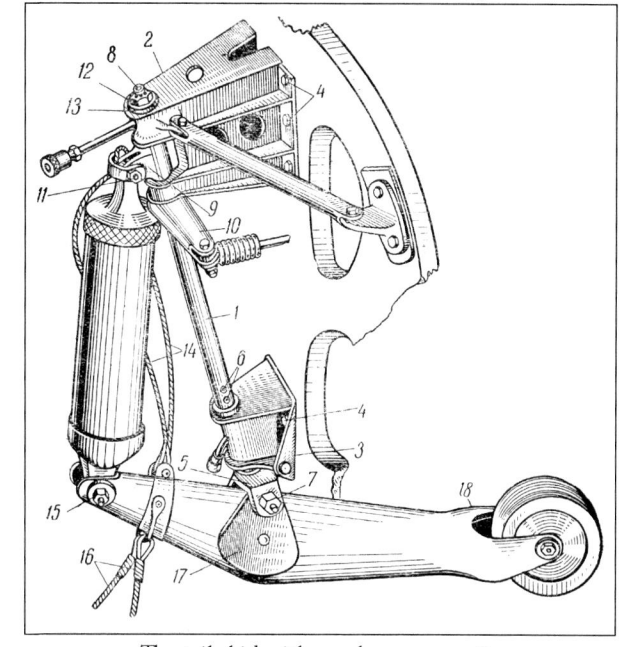

The tail skid with an oleo-pneumatic shock absorber and a metal wheel.

A plan of the inertia starter lever installation for engine starting.

The engine started with a motor-vehicle starter.

The I-16 Type 4 and Type 5 had a moving canopy with a hole for the OP-1 gunsight. To protect the front glass of the OP-1, it was covered with a movable panel which was opened by the pilot before firing.

Starting from the I-16 Type 10, the fighters were fitted with fixed Plexiglas windscreens with a stainless steel framework. The PAK-1 collimator gunsight was placed under the windscreen.

The M-22-powered I-16 was equipped with a cylindrical NACA cowling, which accommodated another (the so-called 'internal') cowling covering the engine crankcase. An original solution was employed for air supply to the engine

The right side of the cockpit in the first series of the I-16 Type 10. The slotted tube routed along the contour of the fourth frame is the mechanical indicator of the landing gear retraction.

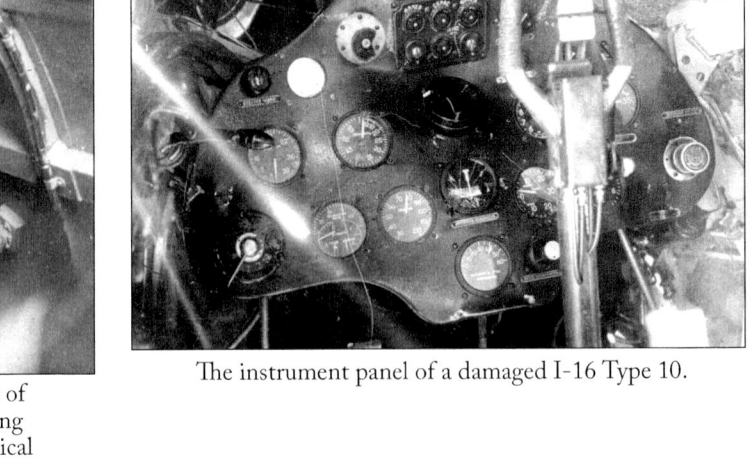

The instrument panel of a damaged I-16 Type 10.

Junior Lieutenant A. Kachanov standing in the cockpit of an I-16 Type 24 in 1941. A clipboard with deviation cards for compass setting is attached to the opened right panel.

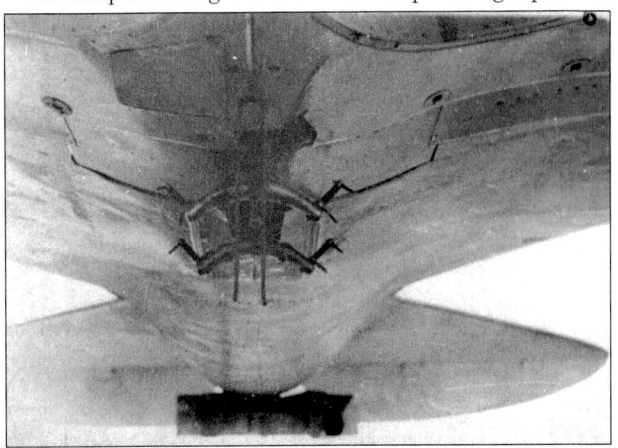

An I-16 Type 29 in the course of evaluation tests before acceptance for service with the Naval Air Force.

A pilot posing for a propaganda photo. Note the holes from the gun camera bracket in the upper portion of the I-16 fuselage (on which the pilot's right hand rests).

The lower portion of the aircraft with the bomb rack for a 100kg air bomb (Orlov's design). To the left of the aircraft centreline there is a hatch used for installation of a storage battery on the Type 5 and Type 10.

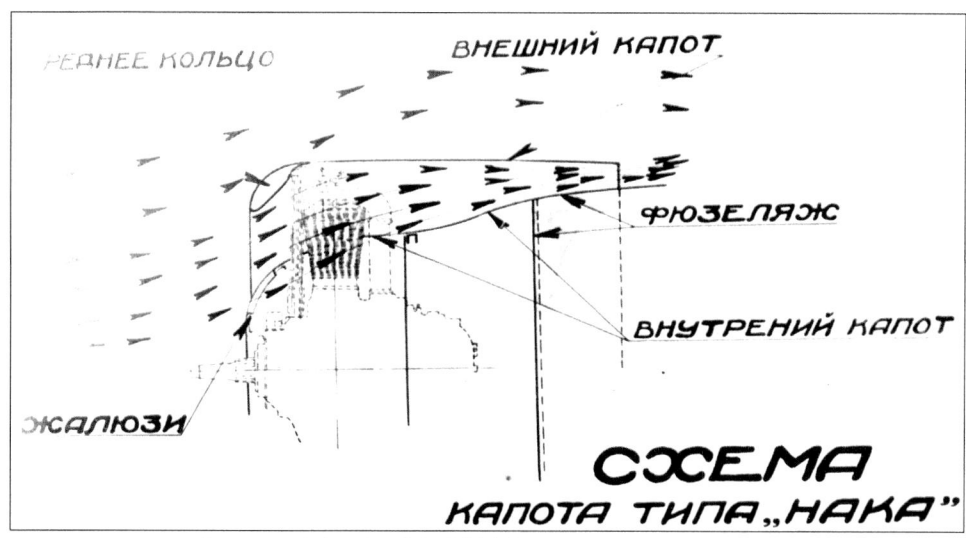

An original sketch of the NACA cowling with a schematic image of movement of the cooling air flow.

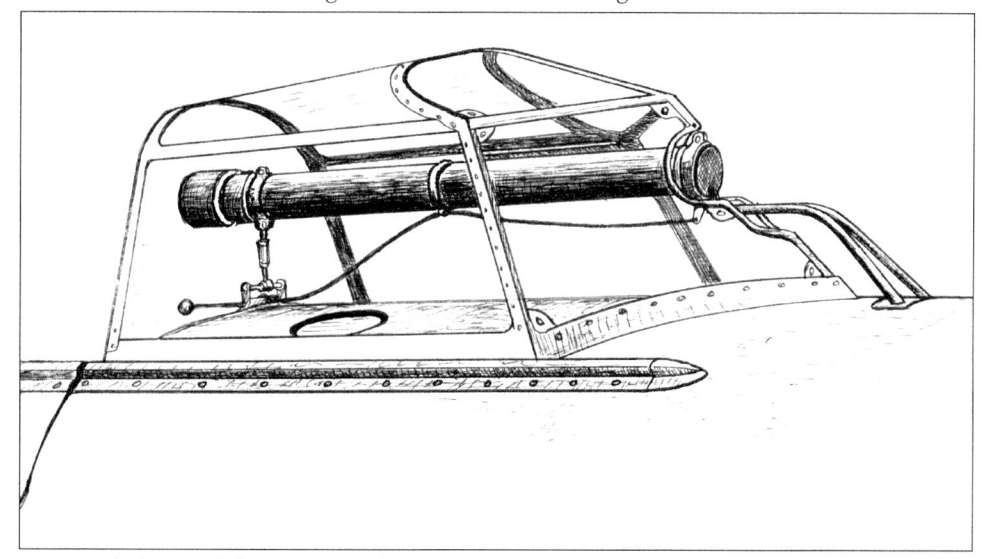

A sketch of the moving cockpit canopy shown in the extreme forward position.

carburetor. Initially, the air entered two openings in the upper frontal part of the cowling; then, moving inside a closed annular cavity, it went downwards. On its way, the air went around the hot exhaust pipes of the fifth and the sixth cylinders, and, in the heated state, entered the carburetor mixing chamber.

In the I-16s powered by the M-25, M-62 or M-63 engines, the cowling consisted of a 1,388mm frontal ring and six removable covers. The cowling was held together by retaining bars and Fairey locks. The interface of the covers' leading edges and the frontal ring was held together by a 0.5mm-wide stainless-steel band.

Starting from the Type 10, in the lower portion of the cowling side covers there were recesses to accommodate skis in the retracted position. In the summer season, the recesses were covered with special panels.

The air flow which cooled the engine cylinders passed through nine holes in the frontal portion of the cowling. On the side covers of the cowling there were eight (sometimes six) holes with tunnels (buckets) riveted inside them to allow the air to escape. The exhaust pipes were also run through these holes. Two exhaust pipes were connected to the upper left hole; in aircraft equipped with retractable skis, the lower pipes were also dual. To reduce fouling by soot, the pipe edge plane had to be level with the cowling line.

The propeller spinner (maximum diameter of 530mm) ended with a special ratchet for starting the engine with the help of a motor-vehicle starter.

The instrument panel, mounted on the third fuselage frame, had in its upper portion two rounded recesses for charging handles of the upper machine guns. The shape of the instrument panel remained almost unchanged on all types of the I-16s. The instrument panel was painted black using the 'moiré style' technique. To illuminate the instrument panel in daytime, there were two round windows arranged in the fuselage under the windscreen. At night, the instrument panel was lit by two lamps installed under the gunsight.

1.4. Camouflage and markings

The previous chapter briefly described the procedure of the fuselage preparation for painting. The last operation was coating with the silver-coloured APA nitro-dope. When outer wing panels complete with ailerons as well as the vertical and horizontal tail arrived for assembly, they were usually already coated with camouflage colours. Cowlings, hatches and fairings were, as a general rule, not painted at that stage. Assembled from such components, aircraft presented a rather motley picture; yet in such condition they usually set out for their first flight.

After being flown by an acceptance test pilot and upon rectification of the noted malfunctions and drawbacks, the newly hatched fighter aircraft was brought into the painting shop, where it was painted in dark-green on the top and grey-blue on the bottom. The I-16s built by Aviation Factory No.39 had black cowlings. Such liberty initially aroused disapproval on the part of Red Army officials; later, however, in some units, engine cowlings were painted black at the crews' own discretion.

In summer 1937, representatives of the Red Army Air Force, the GUAP and the All-Union Institute of Aviation Materials (*Vsesoyuzniy Institut Aviatsionnykh Materailov*, VIAM) made a joint decision that aircraft with monocoque fuselages should be painted matt silver. Indeed, such I-16s could sometimes be encountered later; however, they were not noticeably spread. In early 1938, a new instruction was distributed to factories which prescribed coating the upper surfaces of the wing, fuselage and tail unit with paint of khaki (dark green) colour, whereas the lower surfaces were to be painted in 'silver-aluminum matt colour'. Under Resolution of the Defence Committee No.220ss of 23 May 1940, all military aircraft were to be painted as follows: dark green on the upper surfaces and light blue on the lower surfaces.

Red five-pointed stars were painted on the upper and lower surfaces of the wings and on the fuselage sides. Tactical numbers were usually painted on the rudder. Because there was no unified standard, the quality of drawing the figures depended on the taste and diligence of those who applied them. Starting from 1939, fighter aviation units (first and foremost in the Naval Aviation) began to practice painting registrations in large figures on fuselage sides.

The only maintenance stencil, 'Take here', was painted above the red line encircling the fuselage near the ninth frame. In the centre of the red line, a canvas strap had to be positioned for hoisting the aircraft tail. After introduction of the PSB-21 drop tanks, another stencil appeared on the front portion of the tank, opposite the vent tube: 'Remove cap before flight'.

Serial numbers in 20–25mm-high figures were applied as follows: opposite the number on the vertical stabiliser there was the number on the rudder; opposite the number on the horizontal stabiliser was the number on the elevator; and opposite the number on the wing was the number on the aileron.

Among aircraft with unusual colouring, those from the 'Red Fives' stood out. There were completely red or two-coloured (silver and red) I-16s. In the aerobatic group led by the hero of the Spanish conflict Anatoly Serov, there was a single huge white letter on the lower surface of each aircraft. In flight, the aircraft flying close to each other formed the word 'LENIN', which was clearly visible from the ground. Before the war, aerobatic groups of five were formed in many military districts, and it is highly unlikely that details of their colour schemes can now be found.

The parade aircraft also had to take part in combat, and there are a large number of verbal reports confirming their participation in military operations in summer 1941. Some individual occasions are worth a more detailed description. For example, in late 1941, the 102nd Air Division of the Air Defence Forces was formed from crews of the Stalingrad Flying School and the Borisoglebsk Flying School in order to defend Stalingrad. Aircraft for two regiments (the 628th and 629th) were collected from all quarters; those were mostly I-16s and I-153s. According to recollections of former pilot of the 629th Fighter Air Regiment Alexander Popov, he received an *Ishachok* of Type 10 with the tactical number '9' on the rudder. Imagine the surprise of Sergeant Popov when, under the peeled-off protective paint, he found that the aircraft had earlier been painted red. When the young pilot consulted the aircraft log-book, he found out that he was given an aircraft which had previously belonged to Anatoly Serov. In this I-16, which had been flown before the war by Serov above Red Square, pilot Popov performed a ramming attack on a German Dornier Do-215 bomber on 23 July 1941 near Stalingrad.

Foreign insignia first appeared on the I-16s in autumn 1936. In Spain, wide red stripes were initially painted on the fuselage and wingtips, while the rudder had the colours of the national flag. Tactical numbers were painted in an arbitrary manner, usually on the vertical tail. Later, in May 1937, a uniform identification system was established for fighter aircraft, in accordance with which they were designated 'CM' (*Casa Mosca*). Registrations, from CM-001 through to CM-272, were painted in black against the background of the red stripe encircling the fuselage. There were numbers in white or two-coloured (black and white). The basic camouflage scheme remained unchanged in nearly all cases.

Among the nose art, the '6:6' domino tile was painted on the rudder of Jose Maria Bravo's CM-193 and Francisco Tarazona's CM-249. The 4th Squadron led by Antonio Arias was the only one that had an approved emblem in the form of the cartoon character Popeye the Sailor on the vertical tail. Unfortunately, the author has never seen any photo of the 'lame pelican' or 'kewpie doll' emblems, which are mentioned in several publications.

The I-16s which fell into the hands of the Spanish Nationalists featured a wide variety of colour schemes and insignia application variants. Initially, the aircraft were painted with small spots, in the same manner as was done on Italian aircraft. Black or white sidelong crosses were painted on the tail unit and on the wing panels, while sometimes the Falange emblem in a black circle was painted on the fuselage. Later, the sidelong crosses were applied only on the rudder, and the aircraft carried standard red-yellow-red Spanish cockades on the wings and the fuselage.

On the Chinese I-16s, insignia in the form of the white 12-pointed star on a blue disc were painted on the lower surface of the wing. Stripes on the rudder were an additional distinguishing feature.

During the period of the hostilities at Khalkhin Gol, Soviet I-16s of the 22nd Fighter Air Regiment received transverse light-grey stripes on the fuselage for quick identification in mid-air. On aircraft which were repainted from grey-silvery colouring, the insignia on the fuselage sides and on the wing upper surface were painted out.

The I-16 fighter 87

A totally unpainted I-16 Type 19 with wing-mounted SN machine guns at the airfield of Aviation Factory No.21 in 1939.

A UTI-4 with the Russian letter 'H' on the fuselage side in summer 1941. In training units, severely worn-out aircraft were sometimes marked with this letter on the fuselage or on the wing to indicate their limited capabilities. 'H' stood for *nepilotazhniy*, non-aerobatic.

Captain A. Sapozhnikov near an aircraft with a visible fragment of a broken arrow painted on the fuselage. It is known that a similar sign was painted on I. Krasnoyurchenko's I-16.

This I-16 Type 5 of the 13th Separate Fighter Air Squadron of the 61st Air Brigade of the Red Banner Baltic Fleet Air Force was flown by Senior Lieutenant Novikov. The inscription 'For the Constitution of the USSR!' was painted on 30 November 1939. Note a UTI-4 with covered cabins in the background.

The I-16 of Senior Lieutenant Sizov of the 13th Separate Fighter Air Squadron bearing the tactical number '1' and the slogan 'For the Motherland!'.

This I-16 was flown by Senior Lieutenant Baruzdin. An unknown poster designer who painted the slogan 'For Communism!# miscalculated the length of the inscription, and the last letter 'M' was placed on the engine cowling.

Aircraft being repaired on the North-western Front during the winter of 1942. The I-16 is painted with washable 'winter' white paint, among the ingredients of which were lime and casein glue.

An I-16 of the Baltic Fleet Air Force with the tactical number '13' ready for take-off in 1939 or 40.

Use of full-scale camouflage was not practiced by the Soviet Air Force up to 1941. Experiments with camouflage application in the 1930s had no effect whatsoever on the colour schemes of the airplanes in service.

In June 1941, a new painting system and insignia for Soviet aircraft were adopted. Two-colour black-and-green camouflage was introduced for upper surfaces, while stars were painted only on the lower surface of the wings, on the fuselage and on the vertical tail. In practice, many *Ishaks* took part in combat in summer 1941 in the same colours as they were at the outbreak of the war. However, it was during this period that a lot of I-16s appeared with makeshift spotted camouflage on the top surfaces.

The nose art and personal emblems on the I-16s were rare during the pre-war period. Cases are known when aircraft carried the Red Army Air Force emblem on the vertical tail, yet most often those were multifarious broken arrows or lightnings. Thus, before 1942, the *Ishachok* of Ivan Krasnoyurchenko – Commander of the 102nd Air Division of Air Defence Forces – was flying with a broken arrow painted on the fuselage and the Star of the Hero of the Soviet Union on the vertical tail.

During the initial period of the Winter War, patriotic slogans were painted on some of the fighter aircraft of the 13th Separate Fighter Air Squadron of the 61st Air Brigade. There were inscriptions such as 'For Communism!', 'For the All-Union Communist Party of Bolsheviks!', 'For Victory!', 'For the Constitution of the USSR!' and 'Freedom for the Oppressed!'. Judging by insufficient neatness of the painted letters, these were a hasty and, to a considerable extent, ostentatious addition, which did not reflect the actual mood of the pilots. Most likely, such inscriptions did not find a lot of followers and remained only isolated cases.

In summer 1941, slogan inscriptions again appeared on the naval fighters. From 20–29 June, they were painted on three I-16s which were, at that time, at the disposal of the 72nd Combined Air Regiment of the Northern Fleet Air Force. The inscriptions 'For the All-Union Communist Party of Bolsheviks!' and 'Death to Fascists!' appeared on Boris Safonov's

I-16s being repaired at Aviation Factory No.51 in Moscow in winter 1942. The aircraft are painted grey-silver and carry non-standard large red stars.

B.F. Safonov near an I-16 which carries the slogan 'For Stalin!'.

Five grey-silver I-16s in formation with a UTI-4.

Pilot of the 72nd Combined Air Regiment Surzhenko in the cockpit of an I-16 with the inscription 'For the USSR!'.

Senior Lieutenant Vasily Matsievich near his I-16 Type 5 with the tactical number '05'. The original photo has a caption which reads, 'Gorelovo.10.10.39 upon return from Poland'. In 1941, Matsievich continued to take part in military operations in the I-16 in service with the 26th Fighter Air Regiment near Leningrad. His total combat score throughout the Great Patriotic War amounted to 16 enemy aircraft shot down personally and six as part of a group. On 14 February 1943, Matsievich became a Hero of the Soviet Union.

An I-16 Type 10 of the 22nd Fighter Air Regiment made a forced belly landing due to failure of the landing gear to retract. The aircraft features a wide quick identification stripe painted across the fuselage. Judging by the fact that the hue of the stripe coincides with the colour of the aircraft's lower surface, the stripe is most probably of grey-blue or grey-silver colour. Stars and registrations are painted out. However, in the original photo, traces of large-size figures are discernible on the vertical stabiliser and the rudder.

aircraft, the slogans 'For Stalin!' and 'For Communism!' were painted on Senior Lieutenant A. Kovalenko's aircraft (tactical number 11), while Sergeant S. Surzhenko's fighter (tactical number 13) carried the inscription 'For the USSR!'.

This time, the slogans on the fuselages of the *Ishaks* proved to be more appropriate. Appearing during the initial period of struggle against a strong and unmerciful adversary, they could indeed boost the airmen's morale. It should be noted, however, that any unconventionally painted aircraft became a primary target and was the first to undergo the enemy's attacks. Under conditions of German air superiority, it was not advisable to paint anything unusual on the aircraft. For this reason, inscriptions and nose art on Soviet fighters only later began to appear in great numbers; by that time, the I-16s had almost completely been phased out of service.

Something else that manifested itself, again in naval aircraft, was the predilection for the number '13'. This was noted in peacetime, as well as during the Winter War and in the summer of 1941.

Vasily Golubev, who initially served with the 13th Separate Fighter Air Squadron and was No.13 on the list, also flew in an I-16 with the tactical number '13'. He described that period in his memoirs, where he emphasised his indifference to various superstitions, including the proverbial 'devil's dozen'. Later, however, several unpleasant incidents occurred which made Golubev move over to the side of the more cautious (or maybe even slightly superstitious) pilots.

On 13 July 1941, in his first air combat, a German fighter destroyed three engine cylinders in Golubev's *Ishachok* with a burst of cannon fire, compelling Golubev to make a forced landing.

On 13 August, Golubev was in two groups of I-16s which set out on a mission to cover the railway station of Veymarn near Narva. They were nearly at the end of their patrolling sortie when they were attacked by a group of up to 10 Messerschmitts. In the air engagement, Golubev's aircraft was hit and he was severely injured during a forced landing. He had to stay under medical treatment in hospital for almost a month. On 12 September, despite having hardly recovered from his injuries, he managed to obtain a discharge and returned to the squadron stationed at an airfield in Nizino. On the following day, in connection with the serious situation around Leningrad, Golubev was ferrying an I-16 after repair to an airfield in Novaya Ladoga. Near Shlisselburg, he and his wingman were subjected to fire from the ground. Just one bullet was enough to puncture the oil duct of his aircraft. Above Lake Ladoga, the engine stalled and the pilot had to make a ditching a kilometre or so from the lake's shore.

Having experienced yet another narrow escape, Golubev decided not to stretch his luck any more and abandoned the number '13'. On his next I-16, he had technician Bogdanov paint the tactical number '33'.

1.5. Types of I-16 aircraft built by Factory No.21 during the period of series production

Type 4
The I-16 with an M-22 engine. This was the first series production version of the I-16, the main distinguishing feature of which was the cylindrical NACA cowling. The term 'cylindrical' is rather figurative: the rear edge of the cowling skirted the fuselage with a steady exit slit, and the cowling was therefore slightly tapered.

Type 5
The I-16 powered by an M-25A engine. Series production lasted from 1936 until March 1938. The differences from the previous version consisted of a new power plant with a modified engine cowling and presence of a propeller spinner. At the final stage of production, the Type 5 was fitted with 700x150mm wheels, a fixed windshield and wing panels with closer rib spacing and smaller-span ailerons. These changes are explained by the fact that production of the Type 5 continued concurrently with later versions.

Type 6
The I-16 trainer version had the serial number 6211, which meant 'Type 6 built at Factory No.21, the first aircraft of the type'. After state tests in 1934, it was given the designation UTI-1. The produced series consisted of 20 aircraft.

Type 7
Fighter prototype s/n 7211 powered by the 800hp M-85 engine. It was designed by A. Borovkov and I. Florov, and built in 1937.

Type 8
The two-seater I-16 fighter trainer with the M-22 engine was built in 1935 under the designation UT-2 and had the s/n 8211. The aircraft featured a common canopy for the two cockpits. A total of three airplanes were built.

Type 9
The I-16 s/n 9211 prototype of ground-attack aircraft with six ShKAS machine guns was built in 1936. The machine guns could turn in the vertical plane downwards through 9° to fire at ground targets. The landing-gear was non-retractable.

Type 10

The I-16 powered by an M-25V engine was a cardinal modification of the fighter after three years of production. The armament was complemented with synchronised ShKAS machine guns mounted inside protruded fairings. The sliding canopy was replaced with a fixed windshield with stainless steel frame. The OP-1 Aldis optical gunsight was replaced with the PAK-1 collimator gunsight.

The structure was reinforced in accordance with strength standards for 1937. False ribs were added on the upper surface of the wing, while the duralumin skin on the outer wing was expanded to 44.5% on the upper surface and 14.5% on the lower surface. The aileron span was reduced and the aileron droop mechanism was removed. To reduce the landing speed, landing flaps were used, which were initially deployed using compressed air. In 1939, starting from the aircraft s/n 102175, the landing flaps were deployed mechanically by the pilot.

An oil cooler of 6-inch diameter was introduced, with an air intake arranged in the lower part of the cowling.

Type 11

The prototype of I-16 fighter trainer s/n 11211 with the M-28 engine. Only one aircraft was built in 1935 under the UTI-3 designation.

Type 12

The M-25A-powered I-16. The armament included two 20mm ShVAK cannons and two wing-mounted ShKAS machine guns. A total of 22 aircraft were built.

Type 13

No information could be found on this type. It is probable that the type number was omitted by reason of the number 13 being unlucky.

Type 14

The M-22-powered I-16 fighter trainer. It was in series production from 1935–36 under the designation UTI-2. A total of 45 aircraft were built.

Type 15

The M-25A or M-25V-powered I-16 fighter trainer. The type series production lasted from 1937–42 under the designation UTI-4. This is the most series-produced I-16 version, which was in service with the RKKA VVS until 1946.

Type 16

The I-16 with synchronised 12.7mm-calibre ShVAK machine guns. It is known that three aircraft (s/n 16211, 16212 and 16213) were built.

Type 17

The M-25V-powered I-16 was a further development of the Type 12 with wing-mounted ShVAK cannons and synchronised fuselage-mounted ShKAS machine guns. The design was similar to that of the I-16 Type 10. Ammunition was fed to the cannons via sleeves routed behind the first frame of the fuselage along the wing centre section forward spar. The wing centre section was additionally reinforced and the upper ammunition hatch was made longer (744mm instead of 650mm). Starting from 1939, the aircraft was fitted with retractable skis (including those for Type 10). In the lower portion of the cowling, recesses were made for ski tips stowage. Exhaust pipes of cylinders No.5 and No.6 were combined with exhaust pipes for cylinders No.4 and No.7.

Type 18

The M-62-powered I-16 was a modification of the four-machine-gun I-16 Type 10 with a more powerful engine. The engine mount was reinforced, a self-sealing fuel tank was installed and the oil system was modified. An additional 12-litre oil tank was introduced due to a reduction of the capacity of the main oil tank to 23 litres. The oil cooler diameter was increased to 8 inches and installed slightly lower; as a result, the cowling in the lower portion 'sagged' slightly. The oil cooler air supply pipe was enlarged. A carburetor air intake was installed in the upper frontal portion of the cowling.

The first series of the I-16 Type 18 were equipped with a fixed-pitch propeller; in such cases, propeller spinners from the Type 10 were used. Later, the AV-1 variable-pitch propeller with a standard spinner was installed.

The electrical equipment was of 24V double-wire type. The power source was the Type 12A-10 storage battery installed between the third and fourth rib of the wing centre section. Access to the battery was provided via hatches in the wing centre section lower skin.

Type 19
The I-16 with wing-mounted SN machine guns. The type designation was assigned on 21 January 1939. It is known that three aircraft (s/n 19211, 19212 and 19213) were built.

Type 20
The I-16 with synchronised SN machine guns. Three aircraft were under construction, bit no data about their tests could be found. In August 1939, the designation Type 20 was used for the I-16 with external fuel tanks. The designation Type 20 was never used for series production aircraft.

Type 21
The I-16 with four synchronised ShKAS machine guns. The aircraft was under construction in spring 1939 but was not developed any further. The designation Type 21 was also used for a short time for the IP-21 fighter prototype designed by Mikhail Pashinin.

Type 22
The I-16 with a combined installation of two ShKAS machine guns and two synchronised SN machine guns. The design was not developed any further.

Type 23
The I-16 with RS-82 rocket projectiles. In August 1939, the type designation was cancelled.

Type 24
The M-63-powered I-16 was a further modification of the Type 10 with four machine guns. The Type 24 was equipped with the AV-1 variable-pitch propeller and the R-2 regulator, which allowed the pilot to maintain constant engine rpms.

The landing gear strut with a torque link was installed; the shock strut travel was increased to 96mm (versus 30–36mm in the previous version). The tail skid had an oleo-pneumatic shock absorber and a small wheel. The second (right-hand) hinged door was installed in the cockpit. On the right side of the fuselage between the seventh and eighth frame, a hatch for a radio was arranged.

The aircraft was equipped with a system for manual starting from the RI starter handle. In the stowed position, the handle was positioned in the cockpit; for starting the engine, it was inserted into a special opening in the fuselage's right side.

Type 25
The M-88-powered I-180 fighter designed by Polikarpov.

Type 26
There is a lack of clarity in respect of the designation for this type. It is possible that the number 26 was assigned to the UPO-2 initial training aircraft designed by A.A. Smolin. This monoplane powered by an 85hp automobile engine was a further development of the earlier KSM-1 aircraft. Under the order of the NKAP No.201ss of 3 August 1939, the manufacturing of the UPO-1 was started at Factory No.21. The first prototype, powered by the Dodge 6 engine, crashed on 19 November 1940.

Type 27
The M-62-powered I-16 Type 27 was a further modification of the cannon-bearing Type 17, with the M-25V replaced by the M-62. All design changes were the same as in the I-16 Type 18.

Type 28
The M-63-powered I-16 Type 28 was a development of the I-16 Type 27, with general modifications as per Type 24. The armament comprised two 20mm ShVAK cannons and two fuselage-mounted synchronised ShKAS machine guns.

Type 29
The M-63-powered I-16 Type 29 had a 12.7mm synchronised BS machine gun installed in the fuselage; the aircraft had no wing-mounted armament. The oil cooler was installed in the space between the fourth and fifth engine cylinders. The air supply pipe was installed opposite the oil cooler. The aircraft of the later series had no air supply pipe; the air was supplied via cut-out windows in the frontal portion of the cowling. The landing gear legs were made 32mm shorter. The landing gear wells were moved apart, and the distance from the aircraft vertical axis to the wheels' axis in the retracted position increased from 380mm to 421mm. Radio-equipped aircraft had an aerial mast installed on the right side of the fuselage. The propeller diameter was reduced to 2.7m.

Type 30
The M-105-powered IP-21 fighter prototype designed by Mikhail Pashinin. Three aircraft were built in 1940.

Type 31
The M-105-powered LaGG-3 production fighter designed by Lavochkin, Gorbunov and Gudkov. The designation Type 30 was used in respect of the LaGG-3s of the early series.

Type 40
The designation Type 40 was used for the I-16 powered by the M-64 engine with an extension shaft. The M-64, uprated to 1,200–1,300hp, was the last single-row radial engine of this family. The M-64 was created at the Shvetsov Design Bureau in 1939–40, but due to numerous problems, the development never got to the final stage.

In January 1939, it was planned to build three M-63R- or M-64-powered I-16 Type 40s. According to calculations, the aircraft were expected to reach a maximum speed of 540km/h; for this reason, some of the specialists put forth an opinion that the I-180 was not needed.

In summer 1940, Pashinin was in charge of arranging the installation of the M-63R and the M-64. There were plans to move the wing forward by 70mm, shorten the engine mount by 65mm, modify the landing gear and reinforce structural components. In August 1940, it was decided that mounting the M-64 would require major design changes, and it was subsequently found unfeasible to continue the work. The actual reason was the abandonment of the M-64, a decision having been made to further develop the double-row radial engines.

Comparative table of parameters: M-25, M-25A, M-25V, M-62 and M-63 engines					
	M-25	M-25A	M-25V	M-62	M-63
Rated power on ground (hp)	635	650	700	830	930
RPM at rated power	1,950	2,100	2,100	2,100	2,200
Take-off power for 3 minutes max (hp)	635	715	775	1,000	1,100
RPM at take-off power	1,950	2,100	2,200	2,200	2,300
Rated power at design altitude (hp)	700	730	750	800	900
RPM at design altitude	1950	2,100	2,100	2,100	2,200
Design altitude (m)	2,000	2,500	2,900	4,200	4,500
Engine dry weight (kg)	435	435	453	520	515
Major diameter (mm)	1,365	1,375	1,375	1,375	1,375
Fuel octane number	87	87	87		

1.6. Combat use

1.6.1. The Spanish debut

The I-16s first took to the air on a combat mission in the skies above Madrid in autumn 1936. At that time, among other aircraft and equipment to render assistance to the Spanish Republic in their civil war with Franco's Nationalists, the Soviet Union sent 31 I-16 Type 5s. Together with the aircraft, pilots of the 83rd Air Brigade of the Byelorussian Military District arrived on 3 and 4 November 1936 on board the *Kursk* and *Blagoev* transport ships. The group of 31 pilots was under the command of Captain Sergey Tarkhov.

After the I-16s were assembled and test-flown, 16 aircraft led by Tarkhov set out from Alcantarilla to Madrid on 8 November. These were the groups of Vladimir Bocharov and Sergey Denisov. They arrived at the Madrid airfield of Alcala de Henares on 10 November. On the same day, the new fighters flew their first sortie to strafe enemy ground troops who had captured the Casa de Campo park in Madrid.

On 13 November, 12 I-16s led by Tarkhov and 12 I-15s under the command of Rychagov were scrambled to repel a raid by Francoist aircraft. The first air-to-air engagement of the I-16s was also a baptism of fire for the Soviet pilots, which probably accounted for its unfortunate outcome asthe grim reality of the civil war struck home. Bocharov's aircraft was hit, while group commander Tarkhov collided with another fighter and bailed out from his I-16.

Bocharov landed by mistake in enemy territory and was captured. On the following day, the Francoists dropped his body – hacked to pieces and placed in a box – by parachute above Madrid.

Tarkhov, meanwhile, while descending by parachute, had been mistaken for an enemy pilot and subjected to 'friendly' fire from ground; upon landing, he was severely beaten. Several days later, he died from his injuries in a hospital in Madrid.

Flight performance parameters of the main production I-16 types

Designation		Type 4	Type 5	Type 10	Type 12	Type 15	Type 17	Type 18	Type 24	Type 27	Type 28	Type 29
Year		1935	1936	1938	1937	1937	1938	1939	1939	1939	1939	1940
Wing span (m)		9,000	9,000	9,004	9,004	9,004	9,004	9,004	9,004	9,004	9,004	9,004
Height (m)		3,250	3,250	3,250	3,250	3,250	3,250	3,250	3,250	3,250	3,250	3,218
Length (m)		5,860	5,985	6,074	5,985	5,985	6,074	6,074	6,130	6,074	6,130	6,130
Engine		M-22	M-25A	M-25V	M-25A	M-25A	M-25V	M-62	M-63	M-62	M-63	M-63
Engine power (hp)		480	730	750	730	730	750	800	900	800	900	900
at altitude (m)		0	2,400	2,900	2,400	2,400	2,900	4,500	4,500	4,200	4,500	4,500
Wing load (kg/sq.m)		93.1	103.5	118	118	100	124	125.5	129	124.2	136.5	130
Gross weight (kg)		1,354	1,508	1,716	1,718	1,458,2	1,810	1,830	1,882	1,807.9	1,988	1,940
Empty weight (kg)		961	1,118.5	1,327	1,160	1,156.2	1,425.5	1,433.5	1,382.5	1,335.5	1,403.1	1,965
Speed (km/h) H=0		362	390	398	393	398	385	413	410	–	427	419
Calculated at H		346	445	448	431	450	425	461	462	–	463	470
		3,000	2,700	3,160	2,400	2,800	2,700	4,400	4,700	–	2,000	4,480
Landing		107	117	126	129	118	131	132	130.5	131	150	131
Time to climb to H=3,000m (mins)		4.4	4.0 (to 3,400m)	3.4	4.36	3.38	4.36	2.9	3.4	–	3.2	3.3
H=5,000m (mins)		9.9	7.7 (to 5,400m)	6.9	8.9	6.39	8.9	5.4	5.2	–	5.55	5.8
Service ceiling (m)		7,440	9,100	8,470	8,240	8,960	8,240	9,300	9,700	–	9,950	9,800
Range (km)		680	540	525	520	364	417	485	440	458	–	440
Time to turn (sec)		12–14	14–15	16–18	16–17	16–18	17–18	17	17–18	17–18	17–19	16–17
Armament		2xShKAS	2xShKAS	4xShKAS	2xShKAS 2xShVAK	–	2xShKAS 2xShVAK	4xShKAS	4xShKAS	2xShKAS 2xShVAK	2xShKAS 2xShVAK	2xShKAS 1xBS
Take-off run (m)		–	220	260	275	248	280	210	260	230	210	–
Landing run (m)		–	200	288	395*	278	405*	475*	300	405*	240	–

* Without using brakes and flaps.

The Nationalists also suffered losses in the combat on 13 November, with Republican pilots claiming four aerial victories. German pilots Eberhardt and Henrici, who were taking part in the engagement in Heinkel He 51s, were both killed. The former collided with another aircraft (probably Tarkhov's), while the latter was shot down by Sergey Chernykh.

On 14 November, a group of 13 I-16s under the command of Andrey Morozov arrived at Guadalajara airfield near Madrid. Another two fighters came to the front several days later. Starting from that time, Konstantin Kolesnikov took over as the I-16s' squadron leader. Alexander Negoreev, Denisov and Morozov became group commanders.

On the following day, a group of nine I-16s set out on a mission to intercept Junkers aircraft which were flying, under fighter escort, to bomb Madrid. In an aerial engagement, Denisov and Chernykh shot down one aircraft each.

On 17 November, Lieutenant Dmitry Pavlov was killed in an aerial combat against Italian Fiat aircraft. His I-16 came down in Republican territory.

On 19 November, Captain Dmitry Zhedanov was killed. His damaged aircraft burst into flames while approaching the airfield and crashed some 2km from Alcalá. According to Soviet pilots' reports, on that day they shot down three Fiat CR.32 fighters and one Junkers Ju 52.

After 20 November, there was a relative lull in the combat, which allowed for some summing up of the first clashes. The high-speed monoplane's debut in the skies over Spain had cost the squadron four I-16s plus one aircraft in repair. It had to be admitted that high speed did not automatically guarantee supremacy over the enemy; competent piloting, cautiousness and even cunning were required to achieve success in aerial combat. Overconfidence and haste only led to unfortunate consequences.

At the same time, the very appearance of the I-16s – together with the I-15s – had a considerable effect on the belligerents. The Republicans demonstrated high spirits and confidence in victory, whereas the Francoists for the first time became aware that the balance of forces had changed against them. It turned out that the German He 51s and Italian Fiat CR.32s were considerably inferior to the Soviet I-16s; the time of ease and impunity for the former had come to an end. It was probably for this reason that the fighter group of the Condor Legion began to be redeployed to the Northern Front, where the situation was estimated to be much less tense.

In November 1936, the I-16 was given several new nicknames. One of them, according to the widely circulated legend, was coined by pilots of Ju 52 bombers, which had previously been flying above Madrid without fear of opposition. Allegedly, at the sight of the impetuously attacking monoplanes of unknown design, the pilot shouted desperately over the radio desperately, "they are coming at us like rats from under the ground". The phrase determined the widely spread nickname *Rata* ('rat'), which was subsequently used by the enemy in respect of the I-16.

The amazingly high speed of the I-16s also needed some 'reasonable' European explanation. A number of Western experts doubted the Russian origin of the I-16, and therefore labelled it a 'Boeing, the assumption being that the aircraft was of American origin.

Soviet pilots originally dubbed the I-16 the 'Pike', and the I-15 the 'Crawfish'. These home-brewed nicknames did not catch on, and the name *Mosca* became more popular. From its spelling, it could well be understood as 'Moscow', but the most widely known interpretation of this nickname is instead connected with the Russian word *Moshka* ('housefly').

In early December 1936, the Nationalist aviation received up to 160 new aircraft, which were intended to reclaim their air superiority. Along with the already known Ju 52s, He 51s and Fiat CR.32s, there were 20 He 70 high-speed single-engine monoplanes.

The first He 70, which was used for aerial reconnaissance, was shot down by Sergey Chernykh on 13 December. On 7 January 1937, he downed another reconnaissance aircraft of this type. Chernykh, who stayed in Spain until early February, scored five personal victories and two shared throughout an almost three-month period. On 31 December 1936, he became one of the first pilots to be awarded the title of Hero of the Soviet Union.

In December 1936, on multiple occasions the air engagements were interrupted by bad weather. The I-16s flew reconnaissance and air patrol missions, and on several occasions they strafed ground troops.

On 20 December, according to Italian reports, three groups of five Fiat CR.32s assumed an echelon formation and approached Madrid. A group of four I-16s attempted to attack the middle group of five; however, it was intercepted by the upper five Fiats, which shot down three Republican fighters.

According to Soviet sources, the I-16s indeed flew a sortie on 20 December, but it was said they did not encounter any enemy aircraft. Furthermore, the competent tactics employed in using the fighters resulted in the absence of any losses for Kolesnikov's group that month. The total combat score of the I-16 pilots reached 15 air victories before the end of the year.

In January 1937, a new group of pilots arrived from the Soviet Union to gradually replace those who had already gained combat experience. Upon their return to Moscow, participants of the first 'business trip' were invited to the Air Force Administration to report on the use of their aircraft and the combat capabilities of German and Italian machines.

In spring 1937, during the course of such meetings (they were referred to in contemporary documents as 'interviews') with Air Force Commander Y. Alksnis, pilots spoke of the armament, equipment and peculiarities of the I-16. In particular, to Alksnis' question whether oxygen apparatus was used, pilot Chernykh replied as follows:

No, we had not been making use of oxygen units ... The canopy is not needed; it hinders the view ... If the tank is punctured and the fuel leaks out, even from the filling tank, the aircraft immediately catches fire. During climbing, it is not so heavy, but as soon as you keep a straight flight it burns actively because the fuel does not flow down the fuselage. The landing gear is good. As for armament, it should be enhanced.

His reply to a question regarding their machine guns' reliability was:

When firing ordinary rounds, they operate without delays. When incendiary rounds appeared – they are a little longer – the belts began to tear; sometimes, there were misalignments, and the machine gun failed; there were also incendiary armour-piercing rounds ... Was the ammunition allowance sufficient for a sortie? If you fire competently, there would even be something left. But if you fire like the Spanish do, from a distance of 1,000m, there would not be enough for the second attack ... Also, the rearward visibility needs some improvement.

To a comment by Nikolay Polikarpov, who was present at the interview, that the designers would install a mirror, Chernykh remarked, "Our pilots learned to look in such a manner that one is looking to the left and sees the right horizontal stabilizer."

A special mention was made of the insufficient efficiency of the I-16 armament, which consisted of two ShKAS machine guns. Sergey Denisov, who had personally shot down three enemy aircraft, concluded, "The firepower is not sufficient ... firing at close distances is not convenient; the distance between the wing-mounted machine guns is too large. It would be better to have two more machine guns firing through the propeller disc; in such a case, no enemy will escape. What we have now just allows us to fire at the wings."

On the whole, the pilots' comments had positive consequences, but it was only in 1938 that the results began to manifest themselves.

The arrival of the second group of pilots in Spain coincided with a period of bad weather. January 1937 saw few sorties. The major air combats which took place on 12, 14 and 18 February at the Central Front were characterised by the noticeable dominance of the I-16s. The pilots, who had by then acquired great experience, claimed to have shot down more than 10 enemy aircraft. However, the Soviet force suffered losses as well. In an aerial engagement on 18 February, Filipp Zamashansky was severely wounded when, in an attempt to make an emergency landing beyond the airfield, his aircraft crashed.

Between 14 and 28 March, there were 17 combat-worthy I-16s at the Central Front. Another seven aircraft were in repair; six had been lost in combat and one aircraft crashed in an accident. A month later, the balance of the aircraft remained the same: as of 25 April, there were still 17 combat-worthy aircraft in service plus seven I-16s in repair.

A study of aircraft survivability confirmed that the I-16 was up to the mark in this respect. Due to the high reliability of the airframe structure and the simplicity of rectifying combat and operational damage, some of the aircraft were able to withstand four or five overhauls and had a flying time of 350–400 hours. The percentage of aircraft becoming unserviceable was 34.5% per month; an average aircraft's life totalled 87 days.

On the other hand, there were problems with the M-25 engines. During taxiing on the ground, they tended to take in a lot of dust and quickly required service. When running at the maximum rpm, the engines became overheated; for this reason, there appeared a need to install oil coolers. Such radiators were first mounted in the later versions of the I-16s powered by the uprated M-25V engines.

In May 1937, another group of Soviet pilots (among them, 59 fighter pilots) arrived in Spain, together with 60 young Spaniards who had mastered the I-16 piloting technique at a Soviet flying school in Kirovabad.

At the same time, 62 I-16 Type 5s were delivered from the USSR. These were expected to tangibly increase the effectiveness of the Republican fighter aviation. In practice, however, the newly arrived aircraft were almost totally unsuitable for combat. The M-25A engines were of poor quality, while the wings had insufficient strength, which led to a number of accidents and a reduction of confidence in the aircraft. In their reports sent to Moscow, Soviet representatives alleged sabotage, pointing out that pilots Lesnikov, Moseyko, Burov and Orzhanov perished as a result of wing failures. The aircraft had to undergo improvements on-site, including wing reinforcement and full replacement of the fabric covering of outer wing panels.

Among those killed due to wing failure was the I-16 Squadron Leader Konstantin Kolesnikov. Before his death on 12 May 1937, he was credited with three personal aerial victories plus four shared. On 4 July that year, Kolesnikov was posthumously awarded the title of Hero of the Soviet Union.

In June and July, the formation of new units continued. During that period, even smaller-strength units were named 'squadrons'. In late June, five squadrons were raised, under the command of Ivan Lakeev, Anton Moseyko, Valentin Ukhov, Alexander Minayev and Grigory Pleshchenko. As well as Soviet pilots, the I-16s were also flown by Americans Frank Tinker and Albert Baumler. In early July, the first Spanish squadron was formed, originally under the command of Boris Smirnov.

In July 1937, the Republicans launched an offence at Brunete, aimed at encircling the Francoist troops near Madrid. The Republican fighter force mustered 15 combat-worthy I-15s and 38 I-16s. Against those, the Francoists fielded 140 fighter aircraft, including nine cutting-edge Messerschmitt Bf 109s. This provided a tangible quantitative supremacy for the Nationalists. One participant in the summer combats, Grigory Pleshchenko, wrote later, "I cannot remember a single occasion when we had to fight against an equal number of enemy combat aircraft." Such an imbalance and the unusual stress which the Republican pilots were experiencing perhaps accounted for the many summer losses. In late July, in spite of additional deliveries, there remained only 30 combat-worthy I-16s at the Central Front, whereas the number of those shot down from autumn 1936 had risen to 25.

On 12 July, a massive aerial combat took place near El Escorial. The I-16 squadrons under the command of Lakeev, Vinogradov and Shevtsov (a total of 29 fighters), and eight I-15s of Eryomenko's squadron, attacked a group of He 51s and CR.32s totalling 40 aircraft. Both sides claimed nine victories; later, however, each of the opponents confirmed only one lost fighter.

A short while later on the same day, another engagement occurred, with 'high-speed monoplanes' (the name Messerschmitt was not yet known at that time) attacking a squadron of R-Z biplanes. By all accounts, that was the first encounter of the I-16 with a German fighter. There were no losses among the I-16s, but one Bf 109 flown by German pilot G. Heness was shot down. The victory over the first aircraft of this type was ascribed to several pilots. The author believes, however, that it was I-16 pilot Pyotr Burtym whom luck favoured on that day.

On 17 and 18 July, two more Messerschmitts were shot down; one of them most likely by American pilot Frank Tinker, who flew an I-16. From that time on, claims of victories over the Bf 109s began to appear in pilots' reports on a regular basis (it is clear that confirmations were available only on rare occasions). The Messerschmitts usually carried out high-speed attacks without engaging in manoeuvring dogfights. Such tactics intrigued the Republicans and led to discussions about the new fighters each time they appeared: "[W]e took a keen interest in them. Rumours about the Messerschmitts annoyed us like unawareness usually does." These were the recollections of G. Zakharov, who was describing an episode, in which, as he believed, Sergey Chernykh shot down a Bf 109. In fact, Zakharov witnessed Chernykh's engagement with another modern aircraft, a Heinkel He 70. After many years, his recollections had become superimposed on other, stronger and less distant impressions resulting from discussions of the Bf 109's superiority over Soviet fighters. Despite this, in mid-1937, the Bf 109B powered by the 680hp Junkers Jumo 210 engine was in almost no respect superior to the I-16 Type 5 fitted with the 710hp M-25A engine. The performance comparison table below illustrates this quite well.

	Bf 109B	I-16 Type 5
Wing span (m)	9.85	9.00
Aircraft length (m)	8.55	5.985
Wing area (sq.m)	16.4	14.54
Empty weight (kg)	1,577	1,327
Gross weight (kg)	2,197	1,500
Wing load (kg/sq.m)	134	103
Flight range (km)	690	540
Maximum speed near ground level (km/h)	408	390
Maximum speed at 4,000m (km/h)	463	445 (at 2,700m)
Service ceiling (m)	8,200	9,000

The first versions of the Bf 109 flown by German pilots of *2./J88* had, among other things, design defects limiting the aircraft's capabilities. In particular, attachment of the horizontal stabiliser proved to be not strong enough, which sometimes led to crashes. In 1938, when improved Bf 109B-2s arrived, pilots of *3./J88* began to score quite convincing victories. The superiority of the German aircraft became much discussed in the final stages of the war, with the arrival of the Bf 109Es. It should be noted, however, that the situation had by that time already heated up to a sufficient extent, and 'Messerschmitt mania' had reached its climax. This concerned not only the events in Spain, but also the sentiments of the top Soviet leadership, who demanded, in spring 1939, that an equivalent Soviet fighter should be created.

One Bf 109B was captured by the Republicans in a nearly serviceable condition. On 4 December 1937, a group of five I-16s led by Alexander Gusev encountered 30 Francoist bombers and 11 Bf 109s of *1./J88* above the airfield in Bujaraloz. During the aerial combat, one of the Bf 109s was hit and came down in Nationalist territory. Another Messerschmitt's fuel system was damaged, and it was consequently unable to make it back across the front line. Gusev and his wingman accompanied the Bf 109 B until it landed, and then patrolled above the aircraft for a while until Republican ground forces arrived to capture it. Several sources later claimed that the pilot of the Bf 109, Otto Polenz, had lost his bearings and thus had to make a forced landing in Republican territory.

Vladimir Bocharov's I-16, captured near Madrid on 13 November 1936.

The I-16 Type 10 registration number CM-225 which belonged to the 7th Squadron.

The Messerschmitt, bearing the registration number '6-15', was first studied in Spain. During trials, it was flown by a French pilot of Russian origin, Konstantin Rozanov. The aircraft was then shipped to the Soviet Union to be tested at NII VVS.

Returning to the I-16 and its presence in Spain, a new batch of 62 I-16s arrived on 10 August 1937. These were apparently Type 6 aircraft (that is, the export version), which featured better workmanship and had been subjected to stricter acceptance inspection at Factory No.21. However, there is no information regarding the suggested additional third machine gun on these fighters, as none of the participants in Spain ever mentioned that any I-16s were fitted with one.

Another group of Soviet pilots also arrived in Spain in August and formed squadrons under the command of Alexander Gusev and Ivan Devotchenko. In early September, there were another two Soviet squadrons commanded by Pleshchenko and Starikov, and Spanish pilot squadrons led by Smirnov, Shipitov and Plygunov.

In mid-September, the total number of I-16s in all sectors of the civil war (in the north, in the central area and in the south) was estimated at 115.

The situation in the Northern Front during this period remained serious for the Soviet pilots. Starting from autumn 1936 and throughout that year, 45 I-15s were sent to the area around Bilbao and Santander. At the beginning of July 1937, only 13 I-15s flown by Spanish pilots were left there. On 2 July, eight I-16s of Valentin Ukhov's squadron redeployed to Santander as reinforcement, then in August, nine I-16 of Boris Smirnov's Spanish squadron arrived. Unfortunately, such a force was still not enough to cope with the more numerous Francoist fighters. In early September, there were only six I-16s and seven I-15s left on the Northern Front. Realising that the situation in this sector of the front was hopeless, the Soviet pilots were subsequently evacuated to France, although the Spanish Republican aviators fought almost to the last aircraft. A single I-16 and two I-15s were flown to France on 21 October. Among other captured Republican aircraft on the airfield in Gijón, the enemy found three relatively serviceable I-16s.

From late 1937 until early 1938, the Francoist aviation continued building up its strength, while at the same time upgrading the aircraft fleet. Meanwhile, the number of Republican aircraft was inexorably decreasing. In January 1938, out of the 155 I-16s that had been delivered to Spain, less than half (some 70 aircraft) remained in service. As of mid-March that year, there were hardly more than 35 combat-worthy aircraft. Furthermore, these 'old-timers' were seriously worn out, their engines having overrun their normal service life.

In April 1938, 31 M-25V-powered I-16 Type 10s were delivered to Spain. Once again, however, these I-16s' workmanship left much to be desired. The newly arrived group of Soviet pilots, who test-flew the aircraft, soon realised that fact after several flying accidents. Because of aircraft's engine and armament defects, some of the pilots even refused to fly combat sorties.

As of 21 May, the total number of combat-worthy *Moscas* in Spain was 43. Along with two Soviet squadrons (the 2nd and 5th), there were three actively operating Spanish squadrons (the 1st, 3rd and 4th).

In early August 1938, the Republicans received a large shipment of 90 new I-16 Type 10s. This delivery allowed the raising of new squadrons and greatly lessened the odds against them. In mid-August, the list of Republican units was as follows:

This is possibly one of the first I-16s assembled in Spain in 1939.

The Heinkel He 51 German fighter, which was captured in Spain, was given the designation I-25 during testing at NII VVS.

- 1st Squadron, led by Jose Redondo;
- 2nd Squadron, led by Pyotr Nedelin;
- 3rd Squadron, led by Francisco Tarazona;
- 4th Squadron, led by Antonio Arias;
- 5th Squadron, led by Sergey Gritsevets;
- 6th Squadron, led by Francisco Meroño;
- 7th Squadron, led by Jose Puig.

One of the I-16 Type 5s modified at Aviation Factory No.21 in 1937.

In spite of these numerical improvements, in practice there were still numerous complaints about the poor quality of the M-25 engines. Many pilots believed that the majority of combat failures were brought about by defective engines. The M-25's service period until the first overhaul, as specified by the manufacturer, was 250 hours. However, in the Spanish conditions of 1938, 142 M-25s which were sent in for the first major overhaul had flown, on average, just 37 hours each. It should be also noted that their operation had been accompanied by multiple failures and numerous repairs at the airfield.

The problem was partially solved by engine overhaul and repair, and there were some hopes for deliveries from abroad. During this period, 24 'contraband' Wright Cyclone F-54 high-altitude engines reached Spain. These American engines were mounted on the aircraft of the 4th Squadron, led by one of the highly scoring Spanish pilots, Antonio Arias. The F-54-powered I-16 offered noticeably better performance: the time to climb to 5,000 metres decreased to five minutes, whereas the speed at altitude, according to the pilots, reached 480km/h. Moreover, the F-54 regained its power nearly up to 5,000m, which allowed for combat superiority over the German-made Bf 109Bs.

A line of Republican fighters captured in 1939.

This aircraft displaying the registration number IW-6 was camouflaged in the style of Italian fighters. Note the Falange emblem painted on the fuselage and the designation '161' on the vertical stabiliser, which is probably part of this I-16's serial number.

A C.8-25, which was subjected to modifications in 1947, at the airfield of the flying school in Morón. The aircraft rudder was fitted with a duralumin plate for directional stability control. The fuselage fairing behind the pilot's head was raised by 12cm, while the windscreen was made of flat Plexiglas sheets.

The captured I-16 registration number CM-193, which had previously been flown by pilot Jose Maria Bravo, already carrying the Francoist insignia.

The I-16 Type 5 displaying the registration number 1W-1 was, in 1939, stationed at the Cuatro Vientos airfield near Madrid.

A lunch of 4th Squadron personnel at a temporary airfield during the summer of 1938. In the background is the I-16 Type 10 registration number CM-177, with 'Popeye the Sailor' painted on the vertical tail.

A Messerschmitt during tests at NII VVS in 1939. This Bf 109 had formerly been flown by German pilot Otto Polenz and had borne the registration number 6-15. The photograph shows no trace of the former insignia; instead, note the transverse red stripe painted by the Republicans. The cause of the tailwheel's absence is unclear.

After installation of the high-altitude engines on aircraft of the 4th Squadron, pilots began to fly with oxygen masks; for this reason, they were jokingly dubbed 'the squadron of suckers'. According to a report by Arias, on 18 September 1938, in an aerial combat above the Ebro River, two groups of six 'suckers' made a sudden attack on two groups of eight Messerschmitts, and shot down four of them.

In autumn 1938, it was Spanish pilots who were predominantly involved in air combats. In accordance with a statement by the Republican government, which ordered all military personnel of non-Spanish citizenship to be pulled out, the Soviet pilots were withdrawn to the USSR in late September. The war was steadily approaching its end.

However, events in 1938 had another unexpected turn. Early that year, France had expressed an interest in buying a batch of I-16s. In April that year, the French air attaché in Moscow, Colonel Donsue, and the French ambassador in the USSR, Coulondre, were checking out the situation in respect of purchasing the aircraft. Information regarding the I-16's performance, which was of interest to them, was provided on 17 May. Apparently, the Soviet government would not have denied France (which was, at that time, friendly to the USSR) the opportunity to purchase the aircraft, and the history of the I-16 could have become enriched by another episode. However, the French became hesitant, and remained so until the end of the year. In late 1938, the officials in Paris finally made a decision and, instead of opting for the I-16s, ordered 100 Curtiss Hawk Model 75 fighters from the USA.

In conditions of shortage of fighter aircraft, France also had an option of appropriating the aircraft which were accumulating at its border. However, the French did not hinder the aircraft – which proved to be too late for the war in Spain – from returning home.

During the period from 1936–38, a total of 276 I-16s and four UTI-4s were supplied to Spain. Of these, 31 I-16s were delivered in October 1936; 62 I-16s and four UTI-4s in May 1937; 62 I-16s in August 1937; 31 I-16s in March 1938; and 90 I-16s in August 1938. It is known that, in late 1938, the Republican government was making efforts to obtain an additional batch of the fighters, but the period from late 1938 untill early 1939 remains underinvestigated. It is possible that there were additional shipments which failed to reach their final destination. For example, according to documents of Aviation Factory No.21, in early 1939 the factory was working in a rush as it had received a special order to deliver a batch of aircraft in the quickest possible time. In total, 24 I-16 Type 10s and a UTI-4 were ordered (another list included 26 aircraft; the additional list specified 40 aircraft plus five in reserve). On the list, there were the I-16 aircraft s/n 448, 576, 578, 581, 582, 590, 596, 597, 598, 599, 600, 606, 609, 611, 612, 613, 616, 617, 618, 619, 621, 623, 633 and 646, and the UTI-4 s/n 441. Special attention had to be paid to shipping containers, which were to be provided with additional attachment points. The aircraft were fitted with armoured backrests, and the stars on the wings had to be painted over. The delivery set did not include retractable skis. Judging by the special attention to be given to shipping containers, which had to be secured in a special manner for transportation by sea, that was the last shipment to Spain. However, a later delivery from the Chinese factory cannot be ruled out.

In spring 1939, the war between the Republicans and the Francoist Nationalists ended with defeat for the Republican forces. Below is a breakdown of the I-16s losses in Spain throughout the conflict:

Shot down in aerial combat: 112
Shot down by fire from the ground: 1
Destroyed on the ground: 11
Accidents and crashes: 62
Landed on enemy territory: 1
Total: 187

The victors captured 22 relatively serviceable I-16s and two UTI-4s at various airfields around Spain. The combat aircraft were then given registration numbers from 1W-1 through to 1W-22. Furthermore, there was a possibility to add new Spanish-manufactured aircraft to that quantity.

Officially, the I-15 fighters were in series production in Spain during the Republican period. The manufacturers were provided with technical documentation, engines and materials. However, building the I-16 in series was deemed a more preferable option, due to its higher performance. The Soviets took no steps in this direction, so the Spanish began to manufacture the aircraft unofficially. For this purpose, the available aircraft and spare parts were used as models for making drawings and reverse-engineering. The intent to build the I-16s was also expressed by Spanish leaders, who had a plan for the manufacture of 1,000 such fighters.

In summer 1938, production of the I-16 Type 10 was launched at the SAF-15 factory in La Rabassa (Alicante). Until the end of the year, the factory almost completed manufacture of four aircraft, designated CH-001 through to CH-004. However, these aircraft never received Republican registrations. After the collapse of the Republic, they – together with the stock of materials and an unidentified quantity of engines and spare parts – fell into the hands of new owners, who continued building the aircraft.

Series production continued until 1941. A total of 30 aircraft were built, and were given registration numbers from 1W-23 through to 1W-52. The total number of I-16s put into service with the Francoist air forces was thus 52.

In autumn 1940, the majority of the airworthy I-16s joined the newly formed Group 26 stationed at Tablada airfield. During the Second World War, the unit conducted training flights to maintain piloting techniques. Due to wear and accidents, by December 1945, only 27 I-16s remained in Spain. Of them, 21 aircraft were operated by Group 26 at Tablada airfield, two I-16s were at the disposal of the flying school in Morón and another four fighters were in the repair shops in Seville.

In the same year, the aircraft was given the new Spanish Air Force designation 'C.8', and serviceable aircraft joined the renamed *Grupo 22*.

In 1947, when the number of the airworthy I-16s had dwindled to 15, the issue of upgrading the aircraft arose. After a feasibility assessment, the aircraft was modified by the repair shops in Seville. The modifications included a new windscreen consisting of flat Plexiglas sheets, a new annular gunsight and more efficient oil cooler. Special changes were made to the fuselage, with a crash pylon made of welded tubes installed into the fairing behind the pilot's head. After such modification, the I-16 'bristled up', with the upper fairing rising 12cm above the pilot's head.

The first modified aircraft (registration number C.8-4) was test-flown in mid-August 1947. Captain Tordesillas, who was the author of the modification and at the same time served as a test pilot, was happy with the work done. The upgraded C.8s (a total of 13 aircraft) were operated in such configuration until they were decommissioned.

As of late 1950, there were still two airworthy I-16s in Spain (one at the airfield in Tablada and another in Morón). The last serviceable I-16 (registration number C.8-25) was flown by the most experienced instructors of the flying school in Morón up to 15 August 1953.

1.6.2. In China

Starting from 1937, the I-16 fighters formed part of the military materiel and equipment supplied by the Soviet Union to China, which was fighting against Japanese aggression. During the first years of the war alone (from October 1937 to September 1939), China received 885 Soviet aircraft, among them 216 I-16 Type 5 and Type 10 fighters.

The aircraft allocated to the Chinese were gathered in Alma-Ata and then ferried to Lanzhou. The route was 2,400km long and passed through the mountain ranges of the Tian Shan and the deserts of north-west China. Flying along this route was an unprecedented phenomenon in itself, with poor visibility and dust storms making this risky activity considerably more difficult. Airfields, which were arranged hastily in mountain gorges and rocky valleys, greatly increased the risk. For this reason, in 1938, individual batches of the fighter aircraft were delivered by ZIS-5 trucks to Hami, where they were assembled and test-flown, and only then joined the 'air race' above the desert. Upon arrival in Lanzhou, the aircraft had the Kuomintang 'Blue Sky with White Sun' symbol painted on them, and from that moment on they were part of the Chinese Air Force. Pilots attached red silk patches with white hieroglyphs to their overalls – thenceforth, all Chinese were obliged to render every assistance to them in case of an accident.

The first group of 23 I-16s led by G.M. Prokofiev crossed the whole of China from west to east in one rush in the second half of November 1937. Some of the aircraft were handed over to Chinese pilots of the 4th Regiment. However, the shortened training course on this fighter type, which was not in the least intended for novice pilots, merely resulted in unjustifiable non-battle losses. It is known that eight I-16s flown by Soviet pilots arrived at the airfield near Nanking.

On 1 December 1937, Prokofiev's group was engaged in its first aerial combat while on a mission to provide air cover for Nanking – the new Chinese capital (the former capital, Shanghai, having been abandoned to the Japanese on 11 November). According to the pilots' reports, seven I-16s shot down three Japanese aircraft, suffering no losses of their own.

In China, the Soviet aircraft received new nicknames. The I-16s were dubbed 'swallows', while the I-15bis were known as 'siskin'. During the course of hostilities, the Japanese also found a nickname for the Soviet monoplane – they dubbed it *Abu* ('horsefly'). The aircraft did indeed turn out to be fast and agile like a horsefly; it was perseverant in reaching its goals and stung painfully.

In early December 1937, a new group of Soviet pilots arrived and joined in the defence of Nanking. At this phase of the confrontation, Chinese pilots also took part in combat in the I-16s. According to recollections of pilot Kudymov, who arrived in China at that time, pilot Tóng took over as commander of the fighter regiment with which Kudymov was flying. In total, the Nanking group mustered 30 fighter aircraft of various types.

Kudymov recalled this period in his memoirs:

> The first engagement proved not quite successful for us. Pilot Andreev was shot down, whereas pilot Remizov, at landing, got into a crater created by a Japanese bomb, and damaged his aircraft. However, the combat score was in our favour: we destroyed six enemy aircraft of the LB-92 (light bomber) type. In total, up to twenty Japanese bombers escorted by the Mitsubishi A5M (Type 96) fighters took part in the raid. The latter aircraft was not familiar to us – it first appeared in the sky above Nanking. In

the Soviet Union, we had studied the Kawasaki Ki-10 (Type 95) fighter, which was inferior to our 'swallows' in terms of main combat qualities …

Chinese pilots, from whom I endeavored to get any information about the aircraft, had an extremely vague idea of it. They said that it was the best fighter in the world … 'Fear makes the wolf look bigger', Zhukotsky (who had 'found out' the same) and I decided. All the more so, because Chinese pilots were constantly suffering losses in air combats. It was on rare occasions that a sortie ended with no losses on their part. And it should be noted that four to five sorties were flown every day: Japanese bombers were coming at the city wave after wave; the numerical advantage – [a] rather impressive one – was on their side. I must say, however, that Chinese pilots engaged in combats against the enemy courageously and fought stubbornly and fiercely, as if making thus up for other disadvantages. But a combat is a combat; courage alone is not enough to outfight the enemy, and the Chinese pilots evidently looked insufficiently skilled versus the well-trained Japanese fighter aces. Furthermore, the Japanese fighters behaved, in combats, not in the least cowardly; there was no denying that they were brave.

I learned that from my own experience – especially when I had a one-on-one encounter with a so-called 'king of the sky'. In the Imperial Japanese Army Air Force there were four of them – the renowned Japan's fighter aces, which were styled 'the invincible' or 'the lords of the sky'. We watched Chinese pilots pray before a combat sortie that they would not have an encounter with the 'kings' …

From early in the morning, our detachment was in full readiness for immediate take-off. We were whiling away the time in aircraft cockpits, which had already been heated up by the merciless sun. It should be noted, however, that the enemy usually did not appear so early. As a rule, the bombers tended to 'pay visits' around noon. Suddenly there was a piercing shriek from my aircraft technician, 'Japan, Japan! *Fēijī!*' ('A Japanese aircraft!') I took a close look in the direction where the technician was pointing and noticed a dot which was rapidly approaching. It was heading for the airfield. Was that the enemy? That was not likely; it did not look like a Japanese. A thought flitted through my mind: what if I was lucky and got a chance to engage one on one?

The technician had already begun to rotate the propeller. Without waiting for the red flare (the signals for departure were usually given with a delay due to poor operation of the air observation and warning service in Nanking; not infrequently, we had to take off with the enemy already above the city or even above the airfield), I took off.

That was a right thing to do. While my fighter was climbing – I still had to change to level flight in order to retract the landing gear by turning the drive mechanism drum handle 42 times – the enemy aircraft had already moved closer to the airfield and began to dive onto my clumsy aircraft from above. It occurred to me that he might shoot me down as if I were a partridge taking flight … I ceased fumbling with the drum, applied full power, and directed the nose of my fighter towards the Japanese. We were approaching each other head on! But the enemy had already managed to throw a burst of fire from a long distance – from about 300 metres – and I felt my fighter give a jump. It was clear that he was making a turn for a new attack, trying to get behind me, that is, to take me in the reverse. I immediately changed to level flight and began to turn the annoying handle with all my might. The main thing was to avoid being nervous and fussy. The Japanese was just finishing the turn, I had some seconds left before he rolls out on the attack heading … I nearly hoorayed when my fighter dashed forward like a horse unfettered. The landing gear was retracted! As a result of the abrupt vertical 'jump', the aircraft assumed an almost upright attitude and rushed headlong towards the attacking enemy …

Due to strain and acceleration, things were dancing before my eyes; everything around seemed painted yellow. I saw small air streams stretch along the outer wing panels; at some moment, in the course of performing one of the turns, I noticed the fabric, with which the wings were covered, swelling and instantly puckering. And there were red flashes flickering incessantly before my eyes. Those were the scarlet stripes on the enemy's fuselage, which had fused into a single fiery circle. There were red arrows of some sort, and big blood-red sun spots on the wings (the Japanese Air Force insignia). It was a mere 'merry-go-round'. The Type 96 was dashing to and fro before my eyes like mad, agile and uncatchable.

I cannot now recall all the 'twists and turns' of that air combat. It seemed to me that it lasted for ages; in fact, it was a matter of just ten minutes. Most probably, the Japanese pilot, being unable to withstand the accelerations any more, decided to leave the vertical plane; when I climbed away, he entered a normal inside loop, intending to dart to the side. Apparently, that triggered the 'fighter instinct' in me: I broke off the turn abruptly, dashed downward, and threw a long burst of fire on the 'belly' of the enemy fighter, which was flying upside down.

It fell to the ground at the outskirts of the airfield. The Chinese pilots, who had come running to the site of the crash, met me with exultant cries. Tóng, in a state of agitation, explained, that I had shot down one of the 'kings of the sky', which was evidenced by the menacing arrows and some other emblems on the mutilated fuselage of the Japanese fighter aircraft. Later, in February 1938, when we were already in Nanchang, senior military advisor at Chiang Kai-shek's headquarters Division Commander M.I. Dratvin mentioned their names while congratulating me on being awarded the Order of the Red Banner for the liquidation of the best two Japanese fighter aces. With time, they faded from my memory.

In January 1938, the fighters were redeployed to Nanchang. At that time, A.S. Blagoveshchensky took over as the commander of the group of Soviet pilots flying the I-16s. The load on the pilots during that period was extremely heavy, as he too recalled in his memoirs:

A Chinese I-16 Type 5. The wing-mounted ShKAS machine guns were replaced with Vickers machine guns.

Chinese I-16s on a temporary airfield.

An I-16 Type 5 bearing the registration number P2105.

A Chinese pilot near an I-16 Type 10 in 1941.

The captured A5M Japanese fighter during tests at NII VVS. In the USSR, this aircraft was referred to as I-96.

We flew two or three sorties per day to repel the enemy. Once again, death was walking beside us; yet, it passed us by. It was not a matter of sheer luck: we had gained certain experience (vertical air combat on had become our preferred technique; Japanese fighters, both aircraft and pilots, failed to withstand it for long); we had learned to make use of our aircraft advantages in speed and manoeuvrability to the maximum possible extent. However, neither aircraft nor pilots had unlimited capabilities: the metal, the nerves, and the muscles underwent fatigue. Personally I weighed slightly over fifty kilograms at that time. I had [a] jaded appetite; besides, our meals were miserable. Other volunteer pilots did not look very fit either. It was just one thing on top of another …

As if he were sensing our moods, senior military advisor for the Chinese Army, Division Commander Mikhail Ivanovich Dratvin arrived at the airfield in Nanchang. He gathered us Soviet volunteers together, and said, 'You are having a hard time, aren't you, guys? I see and know it for myself. I am not going to try to comfort you with what Chiang Kai-shek told me recently, that Chinese pilots began to fight much better after your arrival. That's all very fine; yet, there are people here who expressly take advantage of your courage, throwing the Soviet volunteers into the thick of the fighting.' …

We all were indignant at a circumstance that defied our understanding: the fact that other foreign volunteers who flew the Herculeses, the Hawks, and the Fiats, were invariably the second ones to engage in a combat, leaving it to Soviet pilots to pull the chestnuts out of the fire for them … At the same time, they were credited with air victories achieved by Soviet volunteers, for which they were to receive prize money. 'Let nothing be wasted, as you Russians say,' our interpreter smiled. 'You anyway refuse to take the prize money because you are told to risk your lives for the idea, not dollars.'

In early 1938, two more groups of the I-16s arrived. After the fall of Nanking, these aircraft, together with the I-15bis fighters, defended Wuhan, Nanchang and Hankou. Aerial combats at that time became fiercer. After a dogfight above Wuhan on 18 February, Soviet and Chinese fighter pilots claimed 12 enemy aircraft shot down.

On 29 April 1938 (the Emperor of Japan's birthday), 18 Japanese G3M bombers escorted by 27 A5M (Type 96) fighters took part in a raid on Wuhan. All the available I-16s flown by Soviet pilots, six I-16s of the 21st Chinese Squadron and 19 I-15bis of the 3rd and 4th Regiments were scrambled to intercept them. A violent aerial combat then took place above the confluence of the Yangtze River and the Han River. The Sino-Soviet aviators claimed to have brought down 20 Japanese aircraft, but the enemy later confirmed the loss of just two bombers and two fighters. Nine Chinese aircraft were lost in this encounter, along with two Soviet ones.

During the autumn of 1938, the Japanese reinforced their bomber aviation noticeably. In particular, they put into service the BR.20 bombers, which were purchased in Italy. Two regiments of these bombers (the 12th and 98th Regimens), with a total strength of 36 aircraft each, began to bomb Chongqing – China's provisional capital – in December that year. In January and February 1939, the BR.20s took part in raids on Lanzhou, which was the terminal point of the southern route for deliveries from the USSR. Cover for the repair facility and training centre was provided by Chinese squadrons and a special-purpose group of 10 I-16s led by F.F. Zherebchenko. Several such groups, which were not subordinated to the Chinese command, were placed along the entire aircraft delivery route.

The bombing raids on Lanzhou failed to yield the desired results: the repair facility kept functioning. During the course of a raid on 20 February, 20 Japanese bombers encountered 29 Chinese and Soviet fighters, which claimed nine aerial victories. In Zherebchenko's group, casualties comprised just one wounded pilot. On 26 February, the fighters intercepted 12 bombers approaching the target and made them turn back. Subsequently, bombing raids on Lanzhou were abandoned.

In mid-1939, China began to receive the more advanced I-16 Type 10s. Chinese regiments (the 3rd, 4th, 5th and 11th) were converted to these aircraft on a step-by-step basis. Usually, the aircraft were put into service by individual squadrons, one squadron after another. It should be noted that for the I-16s, which were deemed more valuable than the I-15bis, only experienced pilots were selected. The 5th Air Regiment took part in the defence of Hankou and Chengdu, and later, up until 1942, provided air cover for Lanzhou. The 4th Air Regiment, after conversion to the new aircraft, provided the defence of Chongqing. In a combat on 13 September 1940, six fighters from the 24th Squadron of the 4th Regiment, along with three I-16 and 19 I-15bis from other squadrons, were scrambled to repel a raid of 27 G3M bombers. The Japanese bombers were escorted by 13 new Mitsubishi A6M 'Zero' fighters. This was the first encounter of the Chinese with aircraft of this type, which was essentially a logical development of the A5M and the Ki-27 fighters. With a new 1,100hp engine, the Zero was capable of accelerating to a flight speed of 540km/h. Thanks to the low wing loading (for the first series, it was approximately 100kg/sq.m), the aircraft still ranked among the more manoeuvrable air combat fighters.

In the aerial encounter on 13 September, the Chinese lost nine pilots; another six men were wounded. It seems that with the introduction of Zero fighters, the air war in China entered a new phase, which demanded the finding of a worthy adversary for the new Japanese aircraft. In early 1941, the I-16s and the I-153s from the 3rd Regiment suffered heavy losses in combat near Chengdu. In summer 1941, the Soviets admitted that the Japanese air superiority was unquestionable, and the use of the I-16 was all but discontinued. However, small groups of the I-16s and some individual aircraft remained in service in China almost until 1944.

In much the same way as it was in Spain, the Chinese also attempted to build I-16s using their own resources. They planned to do so by using components of damaged aircraft, spare engines and repair kits, which were being supplied from the USSR. It is known that two such fighters were successfully built at an underground factory in the province of Chongqing in 1939. The aircraft were given the designation Chan-28. The accumulated experience was further used to build a two-seater version of the fighter. Between 1940 and 1944, approximately 30 UTI-4 trainers were manufactured in China.

The last Soviet pilots entered combat in this conflict during 1940. Until that point, famous fighter pilots such as A.Z. Dushin, S.P. Suprun, A.S. Blagoveshchensky, P.K. Kozachenko, G.N. Zakharov, A.A. Gubenko and K.K. Kokkinaki were participating in aerial combat over China. From late 1939 there was a serious cooling in relations between the USSR and Chiang Kai-shek's government. This resulted in the termination of military assistance and withdrawal of Soviet volunteers from China in the first half of 1940. According to incomplete data for the period (up to May 1940), Soviet pilots took part in over 50 major air combats, shot down 81 Japanese aircraft, achieved hits against 114 aircraft and damaged 14 large warships. From 1938–40, approximately 100 Soviet pilots were killed in battles for freedom of the Chinese people; with aerial crashes taken into account, this number totalled over 200.

1.6.3. Conflict in Mongolia in summer 1939

In mid-1939, the I-16s took part in the Soviet-Japanese conflict near the Khalkhin Gol river in Mongolia. This brief war became widely known due to large-scale use of aviation by both belligerents in order to gain air superiority.

At the time of the beginning of military operations, the Soviet aviation group (the Air Force of the LVII Special Corps) consisted of the 70th Fighter Air Regiment (24 I-16s and 14 I-15bis) and the 150th Mixed Air Regiment (29 Tupolev SBs and 15 Polikarpov R-5s). Service in Mongolia was not deemed as prestigious: it was a really godforsaken place. Accordingly, the level of pilot training and the condition of aircraft were poor. It is no wonder that the first encounters near the border river of Khalkhin Gol went in favour of Japanese pilots. On 21 May, the Japanese managed to catch by surprise and shoot down an R-5Sh liaison aircraft, which was on its way to the 6th Mongolian Cavalry Division. On the following day, at 12:20 p.m., three I-16s and two I-15bis set out on a mission to conduct air patrols along the border. Near the river, they were attacked by a group of five Japanese Ki-27 fighters, which shot down a straggler I-16 flown by pilot Lysenkov. This was the first time Soviet pilots met the Nakajima Ki-27 fighters, which explains why they initially mistook the aircraft for the earlier Mitsubishi A5Ms (Type 96).

On 23 May, the 22nd Fighter Air Regiment – comprising 28 I-16s and 35 I-15bis under the command of Major Glazykin – arrived at Bain-Tumen airfield in Mongolia from the Transbaikal region. The level of flight training in this regiment was not rated as high. Indeed, according to a combat operations report by the commander of the 23rd Air Brigade, Colonel Kutsevalov, the regiment's crews, for fear of accidents, had only limited flying experience and no skills in group operations. On 25 May, the 22nd Fighter Air Regiment flew to Tamtsak-Bulak airfield in expectation of combat operations. Thus, as of 25 May, the Soviet force had 51 I-16s and 49 I-15bis at its disposal.

The enemy was also building up strength in the region. On 24 May, 20 Ki-27s arrived at Hailar, increasing the strength of the Japanese fighter force to 52 aircraft. A group of fighters from this force, flying a patrol sortie on 26 May, reported an encounter with 18 I-16s near Lake Buin-Nuur and claimed nine of them destroyed. However, the Soviet fighters flew no sorties on that date; the unsuccessful combat took place the following day, 27 May.

Early that morning, a group of six I-16s under the command of Senior Lieutenant Cherenkov of the 22nd Fighter Air Regiment initially carried out three futile patrol sorties. During a fourth sortie, six I-16s were scrambled to intercept a group of nine Ki-27s detected by ground observers. Proceeding in a scattered manner towards the front line, the I-16s encountered the enemy at an altitude of 2,000–2,200m. In a brief combat, group commander Cherenkov was shot down, pilot Pyankov bailed out from his burning aircraft and pilot Savchenko was killed during a forced landing. The rest of the aircraft escaped, although two of them were noticeably damaged.

On 28 May, an order was received to make 10 I-16s and 10 I-15s (according to some reports, 20 I-15bis) combat-ready. A report later stated: "The ten I-16s which set out on the sortie encountered no enemy aircraft and returned to the airfield, whereas ten I-15s, which remained in mid-air, encountered 15 to 18 enemy aircraft and engaged them." According to other sources, a group of three I-15bis set out first at 7:00 a.m., and were attacked by the enemy near the river. All the I-15bis were shot down, with pilots Voznesensky, Ivanchenko and Chekmarev being killed.

At 10:00 a.m., 10 I-15bis of the 22nd Fighter Air Regiment, commanded by Captain Balashov, took off from Tamtsak-Bulak airfield. Above the Khalkhin Gol crossings, they were suddenly attacked and overcome by by 18 Ki-27s. In this brief combat, six Soviet pilots were killed, one bailed out and another made a forced landing. Balashov and Gavrilov managed to land safely on a neighbouring airfield.

According to another document describing the events on 28 May, 13 I-15bis flew in singles and groups towards the front line. After an encounter with 18 enemy fighters, only one aircraft returned; nine pilots were killed.

All the above data testifies to the fact that the I-16s did not take part in the combat on 28 May, whereas the I-15bis flew their sorties first in a group of three and then a group of 10 aircraft. However, Japanese reports claimed 42 I-16s and I-15s being shot down. Such a dramatic overstatement of achievements became characteristic of the Japanese throughout the entire period of hostilities. It should also be noted that although the Soviet pilots did not claim any aerial victories, the Japanese recorded that a Ki-27 was lost on 28 May.

In view of the frustrating results of the first air combats, further operations by the Soviet aviation were prohibited by a special order of the People's Commissar of Defence K. Voroshilov by reason of their poor preparedness.

On 26 May, the 70th Fighter Air Regiment, as the less combat-worthy of the Soviet aviation units, was redeployed to Bain-Tumen to be equipped with new aircraft and manned by new crews.

On 29 May, a group of experienced fighter pilots was delegated to be sent to the region of operations. The group included participants of the air war in Spain: Sergey Gritsevets, Nikolay Gerasimov, Alexander Gusev, Stepan Danilov, Sergey Denisov, Nikolay Zherdev, Alexander Zaitsev, Pavel Korobkov, Viktor Kustov, Ivan Lakeev, Viktor Matyunin, Boris Smirnov, Viktor Smirnov, Platon Smelyakov, Andrey Stepanov and Evgeny Stepanov. In total, there were 48 pilots in the group, led by Deputy Air Force Commander Y. Shmushkevich. They set out from Moscow in three Douglas DC-3 transports.

The lull in Mongolia lasted nearly a month, with no combat sorties flown up to 17 June. During that period, the strength of Soviet fighter aviation was considerably increased. The 70th Fighter Air Regiment by now mustered 60 I-16s and 24 I-15bis, whereas the 22nd Fighter Air Regiment had 35 I-16s and 32 I-15bis at its disposal. At that time, the Soviet air force in Mongolia began to be referred to as the Air Force of the 1st Army Group (1st AG).

After 20 June, aviation activity on the part of both of the belligerents grew abruptly. The Japanese strove to consolidate their progress, whereas the Soviets intended to make use of their numerical superiority (150 Soviet fighters versus 78 Japanese ones).

On 22 June, a major aerial combat lasting some two-and-a-half hours took place near the river of Khalkhin Gol. The considerable duration and successive entry of fresh fighter groups allows this engagement to be interpreted as three separate air combats. On the Soviet side, some 105 aircraft took part (56 I-16s and 49 I-15bis of the 22nd and 70th Fighter Air Regiments), whereas the Japanese was represented, according to Soviet data, by up to 120 aircraft. In fact, the Japanese took part in the battle with just 18 Ki-27s of the 24th Regiment stationed in Ganchzhur at an advance airfield 40km from the front line. According to Soviet pilots' reports, 25 Japanese fighters were shot down at the expense of 13 Soviet losses in the air and four on the ground. The main Soviet losses were suffered by the I-15bis fighters, whose combat capabilities were not rated highly at that time. The Japanese pilots confirmed the loss of only seven aircraft, while at the same time claiming nearly 50 victories.

The recollections of Arseniy Vorozheikin, who took part in his first aerial combat here, help clarify the confusing situation to a certain extent:

I started the engine and then saw aircraft take off from the neighboring airfield. We, too, took to the air.

The squadron flew to Khalkhin Gol in a tight formation. High above us, there was a group of Japanese fighters. Vasily Vasilyevich [Squadron Leader Captain Gugashin] decided to overtake the enemy at any cost. He rushed after the Japanese at full throttle, paying no attention to his wingmen. The formation broke and became stretched out.

The enemy group had an altitude margin and was thus already disappearing from sight. The commander probably abandoned the hope of catching up with them and darted to another side. But it was only another group of our fighters that was visible there. Gugashin was rushing towards them headlong, with great determination. I could not understand him. It could only be assumed that he had mistaken our aircraft for enemy ones.

Meanwhile, a whole pack of aircraft became discernible at a long distance on the left. Initially, I thought that those were our aircraft, which had taken off earlier. But the group was too large; there were about sixty aircraft. And there seemed to be something unusual, cold, and sinister in their flying … I could not determine what it was. They were moving with some defiant composure, confidently and steadily, like masters of the Mongolian sky.

I attempted to warn the leader by rocking my aircraft wings, but in vain! Without changing the course, he was approaching our group. 'He does not see the Japanese!' I thought with anxiety, and turned in the direction of the enemy together with several other pilots.

It would be wrong to say that my heart began to beat at a faster rate at that moment. It was not so. Instead, it missed a beat, contracted, and stood still. Then, it kind of flared up, wrathfully and acutely. The novice's worrying, the hatred and the ardour of youth – everything became intertangled. I saw nothing except the enemy aircraft.

Suddenly an unexpected thing happened: an avalanche of aircraft descended onto the Japanese group from somewhere above. The strike was so powerful and sudden that it seemed to me that a huge explosion demolished the enemy formation leaving the burning aircraft to hang in the air. Everything reeled before my eyes in a kind of a crazy dance.

Stupefied by this sudden attack, I was involuntarily viewing the new, unprecedented picture of the dogfight. And there I noticed other Japanese aircraft rushing to the rescue of the first group. We had to intercept them, and we rushed towards them.

A head-on attack! We must stay the course under any circumstances!

Despair seized me. How many publications were there about the head-on attack! How many legends were there about pilots who heroically rushed towards the enemy head-on! How skilled and strong-willed one had to be to come out victorious after it!

Everything in me stretched into a string; I could barely catch my breath. But the enemy aircraft arose so rapidly before me that I instinctively pulled the triggers without looking into the gunsight. Jets of fire flashed, and everything disappeared.

Not yet believing that the terrible head-on attack had just so ended, I was flying, for some fraction of a minute, in a state of tense expectation of a collision, because both my enemy and I had stayed the course. At least, it seemed to me that it had been so.

But what had happened to the rest? I recollected myself and took a look at the sky. There was nobody beside me, and something unimaginable was going on around me. The air was swarming with aircraft and streaming fire. It seemed to me that the sky itself was on fire, and the wind was blowing up that fire, overwhelming and whirling everything, never leaving anything alone. That was the sky of a combat; it was breathing out death.

I was at a loss and did not know what to do. All my notions of an air combat had nothing in common with what I saw. There was no formation. It was not clear where our aircraft were, and where the Japanese were. Everything was mixed up.

Apparently, everything indeed got mixed up in the encounter on 22 June. New groups of Soviet aircraft entering the action were mistaken for enemy formations and fired at, and this most probably brought about additional losses.

After 22 June, the Japanese side realised that a considerable number of Soviet aircraft had taken to the air simultaneously, and consequently made a decision to build up their forces too. All the 59 Ki-27s of the 1st Regiment and the 11th Regiment were relocated to advance airfields in Ganchzhur and Saendzho. This increased the total number of Japanese fighters at the front to between 80 and 90 aircraft. Violent air combats which took place during the following days usually involved several dozens of aircraft on each side. During clashes in late July, the belligerents fought nearly as equals; however, Japanese losses

An I-16 Type 5 with the tactical number '15', which made a full nose-over on a landing run. According to the pilots, landing gear failure followed by a nose-over due to groundlooping at the final stage of the I-16 landing was one of the aircraft's drawbacks.

There was a tacit understanding that playing dominoes was not gambling; for this reason, such a pastime was seen as quite fit for a front-line picture of "pilots having rest during a break between combat sorties".

Pilots of the 70th Fighter Air Regiment discussing an aerial combat. The I-16 Type 10 in the background, with the red cap and longitudinal white stripe on the vertical tail, was most probably flown by Viktor Rahov (second from the left), who was credited with eight aerial victories.

Pilots A. Murmylov, I. Sakharov and P. Mityagin, with an I-16 Type 10 in the background.

Grigory Kravchenko and Ivan Prachik demonstrating their ability to ride a motorcycle. The Douglas DC-3 with the spotty-and-wavy camouflage, in which they arrived at the air base in Bain-Tumen on 2 July 1939, also features the Douglas logo.

Heroes of Khalkhin Gol (left to right): Squadron Leader of the 70th Fighter Air Regiment S. Gritsevets, Chief Engineer I. Prachik, Commander of the 22nd Fighter Air Regiment G. Kravchenko, Squadron Leader of the 70th Fighter Air Regiment P. Korobkov and Piloting Technique Inspector of the 70th Fighter Air Regiment B. Smirnov.

Technicians G. Oleynik and I. Lebedev carrying out maintenance on an M-25 engine in field conditions.

Skobarikhin's I-16 Type 10 with visible signs of damage on the wing after an aerial ramming attack. Note the red star with white edge painted on the propeller spinner.

Hero of the 'Khalkhin Gol ramming attack' Senior Lieutenant Vitt Skobarikhin posing for a newspaper photographer.

A shot-down I-97 Japanese fighter with the pilot's personal hieroglyph on the black-painted rudder.

The instrument panel of a captured Ki-27. This photo was taken on 9 May 1940.

A rare picture of an aerial combat between an I-16 and a Ki-27.

A Ki-27 of an earlier series in mid-air. The aircraft is not fitted with a radio and has no central sliding portion of the canopy.

were lower, totalling 41 aircraft versus 79 on the Soviet side. The I-16s constituted the majority of the losses (41 aircraft) because they were used to the largest extent in all combat operations.

The higher efficiency of the Japanese was still rooted in involving only experienced pilots in aerial combat. The Soviets, in spite of the arrival of the 'Spanish fighter aces', continued using large groups of fighter aircraft manned by pilots with widely varying skills. In a combat on 21 July, 95 I-16s and 62 I-15bis opposed just 40 Japanese aircraft. It is inconceivable how such an armada' of 157 aircraft of different types could be commanded (without a radio). It is no wonder than that in such a large dogfight, not all of the Soviet pilots were able to find their targets, whereas the enemy were at liberty to choose their foes.

Nevertheless, the Soviet command was not disconcerted by the high level of aircraft losses. Indeed, the events that were taking place fitted into their planned rate of aircraft and personnel attrition, which was only allowable in a mass workers' and peasants' army. That was why the Soviet Union was building as many aircraft as possible without taking into account degradation of their quality, As for the losses of pilots, their number were deemed acceptable for a socialist country. It would be worthwhile to remember here the pithy phrase by Joseph Stalin to the effect that "the life of a Soviet pilot is more valuable than any aircraft".

Reserves were brought up to the front on a continuous basis. In July, the 56th Fighter Air Regiment arrived under Major Danilov. Before the beginning of August, the total number of Soviet fighter aircraft in the region was raised to 320 (including 194 I-16s).

In terms of external appearance, the Nakajima Ha-1 engine was little different from the M-25 Soviet engine.

During the same period, the first seven I-16 Type 17s arrived. A squadron of these aircraft under the command of Evgeny Stepanov joined the 22nd Fighter Air Regiment. On 29 July, the cannon-armed fighters, as part of a group of 20 I-16s, participated in an attack on an enemy airfield near Lake Uzur-Nuur. During the course of two sorties to the airfield, including strafing attacks and aerial combat, the Soviet fighters managed to destroy six Ki-27s and inflict noticeable damage on another five aircraft, suffering no losses of their own. An attack on 2 August against a Japanese airfield 18km from Jinjin-Sume proved no less successful. The Japanese confirmed the loss of six aircraft in this attack, along with a considerable number of damaged planes in parking areas.

Air combat in August saw significant success for Soviet aviation. From 20–31 August alone, the Japanese acknowledged the loss of 43 aircraft. Combat losses of the Soviet 1st AG throughout the month totalled 54 aircraft.

In September, the intensity of combat dwindled. On the last day of the conflict (15 September), over 200 Japanese fighters and bombers attacked the Soviet aviation hub in Tamtsak-Bulak. In the unfavorable conditions of the unexpected attack (a ceasefire had already been signed), the Soviets lost five I-153s. In spite of the enemy's treacherous actions, the I-16s of the 56th and 70th Fighter Air Regiments managed to reverse the situation in their favour, with nine Japanese aircraft shot down at the expense of one I-16.

The war in Mongolia ended with a convincing victory on the ground for the Red Army. Soviet aviation losses during the course of the conflict totalled 249 aircraft, of which 207 were lost in aerial combat. There were a total of 109 I-16 losses, with 87 of those through combat action. The Japanese lost 162 aircraft (88 in combat and 74 more written off due to combat damage).

Assessment of the combat results revealed that the outcome of the air battles against the Japanese Ki-27 fighters had in the main been determined by the I-16 Type 10s and the I-153 sesquiplanes. It was said, in respect of the I-16, that it had advantages over the Ki-27 at altitudes below 4,000m.

To obtain more reliable comparative evaluation data, NII VVS conducted tests of two captured Ki-27s. One of them, which had been flown by Leader of the 1st Squadron of the 11th Regiment Shintaro Kajima, made a forced landing in Mongolian territory due to a damaged fuel system. The pilot was rescued by his comrades, but the aircraft, upon the order of Smushkevich, commander of aerial forces in the 1st AG, was immediately sent to Moscow for investigation.

An interesting fact is that tests of the Ki-27 did not arouse any noticeable response. In 1939, discussing the German Bf 109 fighter was a more popular practice; that was an aircraft which came under closer attention. Moreover, there was an opinion that the USSR should further build similar fighters with liquid-cooled engines. However, in Mongolia, the Soviet pilots encountered an aerial adversary which was no less serious, and whose testing revealed numerous interesting points.

The Ki-27 proved to be a light and manoeuvrable fighter – in other words, it was just the type advocated by Nikolay Polikarpov. The all-metal aircraft offered good aerodynamic performance, which was ensured by its smooth contours and elaborate skin with flush riveting. The 650hp Nakajima Ha-1 geared radial engine had a diameter of 1,285mm, compared to 1,365mm for the Soviet M-25, which allowed a considerable reduction of the aircraft's mid-section. The high-quality wing with a thickness-chord ratio of 15–9.5% and the enclosed canopy added to the set of measures which helped achieve high speed in flight. In spite of the non-retractable landing gear, the Ki-27, during the tests at NII VVS, accelerated to 444km/h, which corresponded to the maximum speed of the I-16 with its more powerful engine. According to data from other sources, the Japanese fighter actually developed a maximum speed of 470km/h.

The weight of the Ki-27 was reduced to the maximum possible extent (the fighter was not even fitted with an armoured backrest). As a result, the aircraft had impressive manoeuvrability characteristics. With wing loading of below 90kg/sq.m, the aircraft was able to perform a turn in just 12 seconds, while the landing speed with extended flaps was 90km/h. The high flight stability and decent controllability allowed Japanese pilots to feel confident in almost any flight configuration.

Test pilot Stepan Suprun was already familiar with Japanese aircraft. During his tour of duty tin China, he encountered the Type 96s among his adversaries. In the course of training for air combat in 1940, he flew alternately the I-16 and the Ki-27 (in the Soviet Union, the latter was referred to as the I-97). His opinion was in favour of the Japanese aircraft:

> The tactical advantage of the I-97 is especially manifested at altitudes over 3,000m. The I-97 performs a turn in 12 seconds, versus 16 or 17 seconds in the I-16.
>
> In a turn, the I-16 is not stable enough; with the control stick pulled hard, it may either recover from the turn or fall into a spin, whereas the I-97 performs stably with the control stick pulled to the extreme position and does not demonstrate any tendency to falling into a spin. In a turning combat, the advantage will be on the side of the I-97.
>
> In a vertical manoeuvring combat, the advantage remains with the I-97, which climbs higher than the I-16 does, and is thus in a more advance position.
>
> The I-16 can disengage only by means of a prolonged vertical dive … The I-16 routine technique to conduct a battle has always consisted in making use of altitude and a higher vertical speed to accelerate and climb after the attack. Having delivered an attack, the I-16 disengaged with a descent, and, after making sure that there is no pursuit, climbed again for another attack.

After testing the second captured aircraft, Suprun wrote:

> All instruments in the cockpit are well arranged. The cockpit is spacious … The forward visibility is poor; however, it is better than that in the I-16.
>
> The aircraft demonstrates no tendency towards wing stall and allows high-altitude levelling off … it is very good in performing turns. With the pulled control stick, it does not fall into a spin.
>
> When the aircraft loses speed, it performs a strict nose-down and accelerates rapidly. It is stable in dive … When the aircraft is being pulled out from dive vigorously, some buffeting appears … There is no rocking from one wing to the other like in the I-16. In terms of stability, the aircraft resembles the Me-109.
>
> The aircraft is intolerant to low speeds with the engine running; it vibrates considerably. Tangible buffeting exists when the control stick is pulled vigorously or when the aircraft is performing a chandelle or a turn.

Among the Ki-27's drawbacks, low wing strength was mentioned. Test pilot Nikolayev, who took part in combat operations in summer 1939 in an I-153, wrote in his report:

> The I-97s avoided head-on attacks. If an I-153 got into a tight situation, it could easily escape in a prolonged dead leaf dive … The I-97s can do a steep dive for 700 to 1,000 metres maximum, and then abandon the pursuit.
>
> When the captive pilots were inquired about why they performed steep but not prolonged dives, they answered that their aircraft wings, especially outer wing panels, experienced considerable vibration; furthermore, the engine got cooled quickly, and could cut off after that.
>
> In the course of combat operations, there was an occasion when an outer wing panel separated from an I-97 in a dive as it was being pursued by an I-153 flown by Captain A.S. Nikolayev. The wing panel broke off after a 500m to 700m dive; it should be noted that the wing could not have been damaged during the pursuit, because Nikolayev was firing on the cockpit. According to eyewitnesses' accounts, the aircraft was new. Another similar case occurred during a combat near Tamtsak-Bulak.

The Ki-27's armament consisted of two 7.7mm Vickers machine guns, with ammunition allowance of 500–550 rounds per machine gun. One would think that such armament was noticeably inferior to that of the I-16 Type 10, yet the Japanese somehow managed to do well with the two machine guns and to hit their targets when firing. Most probably, this was brought about by the fact that the machine guns, having a lower rate of fire, provided for longer continuous bursts without the hazard of the barrel overheating (as was the case with the ShKAS). These additional seconds allowed the pilot to move the trace closer to the target and to ensure a higher probability of hitting it.

Comparison between the Ki-7 (I-97) and I-16 Type 10		
	Ki-27	I-16 Type 10
Wing span (m)	11.35	9.004
Aircraft length (m)	7.57	6.074
Wing area (sq.m)	18.61	14.54
Empty weight (kg)	1,174	1,327
Gross weight (kg)	1,600	1,716
Wing load (kg/sq.m)	85.9	118
Fuel (kg)	250	190
Maximum speed near ground level (km/h)	395	398
Maximum speed at 3,100m (km/h)	444	448
Time to climb to 5,000m (mins)	6.2	6.9
Service ceiling (m)	10,040	8,470
Time to perform a turn at an altitude of 1,000m (secs)	12	16 to 18
Landing speed (km/h)	90	126
Take-off run/Landing run (m)	120/256	260/288

1.6.4. The Winter War of 1939–40

By the beginning of combat operations against Finland on 30 November 1939, Soviet air forces concentrated near the border approximately 800 aircraft. The I-16s of all versions constituted slightly over a half of that number – some 410 in all. The Air Force of the 14th Army (Murmansk sector) mustered 18 I-16s, while the Air Force of the 8th Army (Petrozavodsk sector) had 33 I-16s.

The Air Force of the 7th Army, which provided cover for a 100km front at the Karelian Isthmus, mustered approximately 360 I-16s. These were in service with the 7th, 25th, 38th and 68th Fighter Air Regiments. Fighters of the 54th Air Brigade consisting of the 19th, 26th and 44th Fighter Air Regiments provided air defense for Leningrad. In the latter three regiments, 168 I-16s were fitted with M-25 engines, while a further 15 were powered by the M-62.

As matters developed, the aviation group near the Soviet–Finnish border kept increasing, with the front units receiving mostly bombers and the new I-153 fighters. The I-16s were coming in lesser quantities; their total number reached a maximum of 470–480 aircraft in January and February 1940. At the termination of hostilities in March, there remained 427 I-16s of all types in service.

In December 1939, combat sorties were flown in conditions of unfavourable weather and poor visibility. There were numerous cases when aircraft lost their bearings in flight. Fighters were not active at this stage, providing only limited cover for bombers during their sorties. In mid-December 1939, as soon as ice thickness on lakes reached 20cm, fighters began to be redeployed to the ice airfields. Near Leningrad, ice airfields began to operate in mid-January 1940.

The severe frost of that winter complicated flying in an open cockpit to a considerable extent. In spite of the fact that some of the I-16s could then be used with retractable skis instead of wheels, retracting the landing gear by means of a hand-operated winch was a rather difficult procedure for a pilot wearing fur coveralls. Sometimes, due to failure of hydraulic shock absorbers, the skis got jammed in an extended position and failed to retract.

Attacks on ground targets constituted a considerable share of the fighters' combat tasks. In the Air Force of the 8th, 9th and 14th Armies, such activities totalled up to 90% of all sorties flown. Since the top priority for aviation was initially described as blocking all kinds of supplies and destroying the Finnish system of communications, the main strikes were made on railways, rolling stock and rail station buildings.

It was later specially emphasised in reports that the cannon-armed I-16 Type 17s had been used for strafing attacks. In their final report, the commanders of the 19th and 44th Fighter Air Regiments claimed 82 destroyed steam locomotives and 32 liquidated trains respectively. The 68th Fighter Air Regiment flew 300 sorties in the sectors of Antrea, Hiitola, Pyhäjärvi, Kexholm and Hiitola. Considerable success was reported, with the pilots claiming to have damaged 50 steam locomotives. Later, indeed, numerous destroyed locomotives were found. However, the complete blocking of Finnish communications was never actually achieved. The Finns demonstrated high skills and competence in camouflaging both their vehicles and the railway lines themselves, Furthermore, the majority of their transport operations were carried out at nighttime.

During the Winter War, Senior Lieutenant F. Shinkarenko flew 46 combat sorties with the 7th Fighter Air Regiment and shot down three enemy aircraft. On 7 April 1940, he was awarded the title of Hero of the Soviet Union.

Pilots of the 7th Fighter Air Regiment near one of their I-16s. In the centre is F. Shinkarenko, with second from the left P. Pokryshev. At the time of the Winter War, the latter was credited with one air victory. During the later Great Patriotic War, his personal score rose to 38 victories. He was twice awarded the title of Hero of the Soviet Union.

The I-16 Type 5 with the tail number '2' from the 13th Separate Fighter Squadron of the 61st Air Brigade. The aircraft, flown by Senior Lieutenant Boruzdin, was damaged by anti-aircraft fire on 4 February 1940 above the island of Bjorko.

The I-16 Type 5 with the number '11' and the slogan 'Freedom for the Oppressed!' painted on the right side of the fuselage was assigned to Major Gubanov of the 13th Separate Fighter Squadron of the 61st Air Brigade.

On the left side of the fuselage of the aircraft with the tail number '11', note the slogan 'For the All-Union Communist Party of Bolsheviks!' and an image of the Order of the Red Banner. This I-16 was fitted with a radio and non-retractable skis.

Pilots of the 13th Separate Fighter Squadron had their picture taken near an I-16 Type 17 during the period of hostilities in the winter of 1939–40.

Probably the same personnel as in the previous photo. The war and its terrors are over as they pose for a newspaper photographer in summer 1940. The closest I-16 Type 17 has no modifications providing for installation of retractable skis; for this reason, it may be reckoned a series production aircraft of 1938. The muzzle ends of the ShVAK cannons are 'packed' in fabric covers to protect them against airfield dust until the first firing of the cannon.

A group of pilots of the 61st Air Brigade, Air Force of the Red Banner Baltic Fleet, together with their aircraft technicians. The pilots are wearing raglans and life vests, while the technical personnel have uniform berets. This is a photo taken to remember the moment and each other, not for a newspaper. This is testified to by the parachute lying on the ground. Newspaper photographers usually asked pilots to don a parachute to obtain a more presentable image of a 'Stalin's falcon'. The PAU-22 camera gun on the fuselage upper fairing adds to the non-standard composition of the picture.

According to information obtained from captives, the Finns spread an up to 1m-deep layer of sand onto the floor of railway cars, which provided reliable protection even from 20mm cannon projectiles. In case of air attacks, people hid under the railway cars and waited until the raids were over.

Throughout the entire period of combat operations on the North-western Front, six major and 65 minor aerial combats were recorded. Some of them are described in a report entitled 'Combat Operations of the Red Army Air Force during the War against Finland'.

On 2 February 1940, fighters of the 59th Air Brigade of the 7th Army Air Force became engaged in an aerial combat. Upon their return from a reconnaissance sortie, a Flight Commander reported that enemy fighters had been detected on a lake near Mattarila, north of Vuoksenniska station. A group of 15 fighters under Assistant Regiment Commander Captain Bushev was promptly gathered. It consisted of a striking force (three I-16s plus three I-153s) and a covering party of nine I-16s.

Near Imatra station, the entire group was subjected to heavy fire from the ground. As a result of an evasive manoeuvre, the striking force and the covering party lost sight of each other for some time. Furthermore, the Finnish fighters were not found at their expected location. At this stage of the sortie, the covering party of nine I-16s was subjected to an attack by a group of up to 20 Fokker D.XXI fighters. The encounter occurred at an altitude of 2,000m. The Soviet striking force of six aircraft approached the combatants and shot down two enemy fighters. The formations then became dispersed, and the combat continued in pairs. In total, 12 Finnish aircraft were claimed as shot down. The Soviet fighters suffered no losses.

A line of cannon-armed I-16s of the Red Banner Baltic Fleet Air Force before the beginning of flight operations in 1940.

On 25 February, two groups from the 149th Fighter Air Regiment were attacked by eight Fokker D.XXIs during the course of a raid on a train. The I-16 pilots claimed to have brought down four Finnish fighters, suffering no losses of their own.

On the same day, two I-16 groups from the 68th Fighter Air Regiment of the 13th Army Air Force engaged nine Bristol Bulldog fighters near Melkelya after escorting nine Tupolev SB bombers. In the course of a 12-minute aerial combat, the I-16s shot down five enemy aircraft without suffering any losses. However, the Soviet aviators had been fortunate, as upon their return to base, a total of 40 bullet holes were found in three I-16s.

On 26 February, escort fighters of the 149th Fighter Air Regiment, while accompanying a group of SBs for a bombing raid near the station at Kouvola, shot down three D.XXIs and a monoplane of unidentified type. It was reported that 12 enemy fighters took part in the encounter; the number of Soviet fighters was not specified.

On 29 February, a group of I-16s from the 68th Fighter Air Regiment of the 15th Air Brigade was flying a reconnaissance sortie along the Vuoksi River. Near the station at Vuoksenniska, Finnish fighters were detected beginning to take off from an ice airfield. The I-16s managed to shoot down one of them at take-off and another in mid-air before leaving the combat area.

Upon returning to their home airfield, it was decided to repeat the attack in the same area. A group of 23 aircraft commanded by Major Gil was immediately gathered, consisting of a striking force (nine I-16s plus three I-153s) and covering party of eight I-16s plus three I-153s. At a distance of some 10–12km from their target, the Soviet pilots saw Finnish fighters taking off from the ice airfield. Several more Finns began to take off from another airfield, some 2–3km from the other airfield. Senior Lieutenant Efimov, who was leading the covering party, attacked the second Finnish group. It was later reported that due to "sucking-in of the skis" (probably what was meant here was the tuck-under), his aircraft entered a negative dive and crashed to the ground.

After the first attack, the Finnish formations became dispersed, and the combat continued in pairs or in the form of one-on-one engagements. The enemy's strength in this encounter totalled 27 Fokker D.XXI and Bristol Bulldog fighters.

Upon their return, the Soviet aviators claimed 18 victories. Apart from Efimov, Lieutenant Volokhov was the only one not to return from the mission (in both cases, aircraft types are not specified). Later, the Finns confirmed the loss of just six Gloster Gladiators of the 26th Squadron and a Fokker D.XXI of the 24th Squadron.

Along with the Red Army Air Force, naval aviation of the Baltic Fleet took part in aerial combat during the Winter War. At the initial stage of hostilities, all 246 fighters of the Red Banner Baltic Fleet Air Force constituted part of the 61st Air Brigade and were stationed at airfields near the Gulf of Finland. The I-16s of different versions (a total of 129 aircraft) were in service with the 5th and 13th Air Regiments, as well as with the 11th and 13th Squadrons. Five I-16s (stationed at Paldiski) were, in March, part of the separate fighter group of the 10th Air Brigade. As was the case with the Red Army's I-16s, the naval fighters were, during the period of hostilities, actively involved in ground target strafing operations. Naval pilots also took part in several aerial combats and claimed numerous victories. According to a report by the operational department of the Red Banner Baltic Fleet Air Force, there were no combat losses of the I-16s up to 25 January. Five aircraft suffered accidents, and three of them were later written off. On 10 February, one I-16 of the 5th Regiment did not return from a mission.

Upon the termination of hostilities in March 1940, over 400 Finnish aircraft were reported destroyed; of them, 211 were claimed shot down in combat. However, the strength of the Finnish aviation in the winter of 1939–40 (even with replenishments taken into account) did not exceed 200 aircraft of all types. After the war, Finland acknowledged the loss of 67 aircraft, only 21 of them in aerial combats. Another 69 aircraft were reported as severely damaged.

The Winter War entailed no implications or consequences for the fate of the I-16. Listed below are some figures to complement the above brief account of the winter's events; it is up to the reader to draw conclusions. Shortly before the war, the Soviet Air Force strength near the Finnish border totalled approximately 2,000 aircraft. Throughout the entire period of the hostilities, an additional 1,535 aircraft arrived at the front line to reinforce the Soviet aviation. During the time of the force's build-up, six crashes, 18 accidents and 21 forced landings were reported. In the course of redeployment to rear airfields, which began on 17 March 1940, 23 air regiments and 10 separate squadrons and detachments (groups) – a total of 1,221 aircraft – were withdrawn in four days. This final action led to three crashes, three accidents and four forced landings.

1.6.5. The I-16s in service with the Finnish Air Force

This brief chapter owes its existence not to the significance of the events, but solely to their extraordinary nature and their detailed description in numerous Finnish aviation publications.

The Finnish command in Helsinki became keenly aware of the need for deliveries of military aircraft during the winter of 1939–40. At the same time, it was found out that there were a number of damaged Soviet aircraft left in Finland after the Winter War. After the evacuation from landing places and additional inspections, a decision was made to repair these Soviet aircraft at the aviation factory in Tampere and thereafter to continue their flight operations. Consequently, an additional 15 aircraft were successfully put in service with the Finnish Air Force.

After the German invasion of the Soviet Union, Finland also entered the war in the hope of regaining territories which it had lost in 1940. The Finns then succeeded in replenishing the fleet of captured Soviet aircraft – consisting of I-15bis, I-153s, SBs, DB-3s, Pe-2s and MBR-2s – to a still more considerable extent. The Germans rendered additional assistance by selling a number of aircraft captured in 1941. Thus, in total, the Finns managed to collect approximately 100 aircraft of various types, some of which were successfully operated up to 1944.

The most widely spread Soviet fighter left the least significant mark in the Finnish aviation history. There are no known examples of any damaged I-16s being restored after March 1940. The photograph of the aircraft with the number '228' shows one of the few captured aircraft.

However, the Finns unexpectedly found themselves lucky: on 10 April 1940, an intact I-16 with a ski landing gear landed on the ice on Lake Pyhäjärvi due to the failure of its M-62 engine. After a minor repair, the fighter was given the registration VH-201 and began flying with the blue *swastika* of the Finnish Air Force in April that year. The aircraft was at the time believed to be an I-16 Type 18. The aircraft had no wing-mounted armament; most probably, it was removed when the aircraft was already in Finland. Analysis of the known photographs of this aircraft, in which the large 'windows' for ejection of cannon ammunition belt links are seen, allows the assumption that the Finns had actually captured an I-16 Type 27. Later, this aircraft was fitted with wing-mounted Browning machine guns. After that, the airplane indeed bore greater resemblance to the Type 18.

In the course of further operation, the aircraft was given the registration VH-21 and joined the LLv 24 unit, with which it flew for a total of six hours and 20 minutes. On 15 April 1941, the aircraft was sent to Germany for evaluation.

During 1942 and 1943, the Finns captured another five I-16s, which were given registrations from IR-101 to IR-105. All of these were finally posted to LeLv 30 and remained part of this unit until November 1943. According to the available information, only one of them (the IR-101) was made airworthy. There is no data regarding participation of the I-16s in hostilities on the side of Finland.

On 8 September 1941, on the Svir River near Troitsankontu, the Finns captured a UTI-4 two-seater in almost perfect condition. The propeller spinner and blades were the only damaged components. By 17 October, the aircraft was repaired, given the registration VH-22 and prepared for flying. Later, the registration was changed to UT-1; on 10 April 1942, the aircraft was put in service with the LeLv 48 unit. On 10 August 1942, the UT-1 was handed over to the ⊠-LeLv 35 training

118 The King of Fighters Volume 2

The fuselage of the I-16 Type 5 with the tail number '228' was picked up at the site of its forced landing on 28 December 1939. It was probably one of the first damaged aircraft intended for further restoration.

This I-16 was captured by the Finns in April 1940 in an intact condition. In Finnish use, the aircraft was initially given the registration VH-201, which was later changed to VH-21.

This I-16 Type 5, with the tactical number '64' and four underwing RO-82 rocket projectile launchers, made a forced landing on Lake Ladoga outside Kakisalmi on 10 December 1941. The Finnish registration IR-104 was then allocated for the aircraft, but its repair was cancelled in June 1943 due to the lack of engine spare parts and the type's obsolescence.

unit, with which it flew a total of 43 hours and 25 minutes before 11 September that year. The aircraft was removed from the

This I-16 Type 5 with the tail number '15' of the 11th Fighter Air Regiment of the Red Banner Baltic Fleet Air Force made a forced landing on ice near Gogland on 28 March 1942. Pilot Captain Zharnikov walked away to reach friendly territory. The aircraft is equipped with four underwing RO-82 rocket projectile launchers and non-retractable skis of the same type as on the I-15bis.

After restoration, the Zharnikov's former aircraft was given the designation IR-101. It flew a total of six hours and 35 minutes with LeLv 30 until it crashed in an accident on 22 June 1943.

This UTI-4 was captured by the Finns on 8 September 1941 on the Svir River. Currently, it is on display at the Finnish Aviation Museum in Vantaa, near Helsinki Airport.

records on 9 August 1944 and stored for several decades. Currently, the well-preserved aircraft is on display at the Finnish Aviation Museum in Vantaa.

1.6.6. The Great Patriotic War of 1941–45

Shortly before the war started in June 1941, air forces of the Soviet Western border military districts mustered 4,226 fighter aircraft. Of them, the overall number of I-16s of all types was estimated at 1,635, constituting 26% of the total strength. The distribution of the I-16s over the military districts was as follows:

Air Force of the Leningrad Military District: 396
Air Force of the Baltic Military District: 142
Air Force of the Western Special Military District: 361 (according to some sources, 424)
Air Force of the Kiev Special Military District: 455
Air Force of the Odessa Military District: 143

In total, the border military districts comprised 57 regiments equipped with I-16s; some of them had a mixed fleet of aircraft at their disposal. There was also a considerable number of I-16s in flying schools, at repair shops and in reserve units.

In the western part of the Soviet Union, Naval Air Forces of the Northern, Baltic and Black Sea Fleets were concentrated. Those mustered 763 fighters, of which I-16s constituted nearly half (344 aircraft). The Pacific Fleet Air Force had 155 I-16s at their disposal, and 110 I-16s were in service with naval flying schools. The number of UTI-4 trainers was estimated at 145. Unlike Soviet Army records, naval ones provided a breakdown of the I-16s per versions:

	Air Force of the Red Banner Baltic Fleet	Air Force of the Black Sea Fleet	Air Force of the Northern Fleet	Air Force of the Pacific Fleet	Air Force of river flotillas	Flying schools	Other
I-16 M-22	–	–	–	–	–	26	–
I-16 Type 5	38	39	–	74	9	66	1
I-16 Type 10	10	9	–	16	–	16	1
I-16 Type 12	–	–	–	10	–	–	–
I-16 Type 17	28	5	–	15	–	–	–
I-16 Type 18	15	16	–	–	–	–	–
I-16 Type 24	33	43	16	33	10	4	–
I-16 Type 27	5	–	–	–	–	–	–
I-16 Type 28	6	21	–	7	1	–	–
I-16 Type 29	45	15	–	–	9	2	–
UTI-2	–	–	–	–	–	3	–
UTI-4	28	21	2	26	6	61	1

At dawn on Sunday, 22 June 1941, borders of the Soviet Union along their entire length from the Baltic Sea in the north to the Black Sea in the south were suddenly attacked by troops of Nazi Germany. An almost simultaneous strike was delivered on 66 airfields where the main forces of the Red Army aviation were stationed. The sudden nature of the attack allowed the Germans to destroy 900 Soviet aircraft while still on the ground. By the evening of 22 June, the losses had grown considerably, totalling over 1,200 aircraft.

The main strike of Army Group Centre, supported by *Luftflotte 2*, was directed against the Soviet forces of the Western Special Military District. Towards evening on the first day, the district's aviation had lost 738 aircraft (528 on the ground and 210 in aerial combat), which constituted approximately half of their initial strength. The main goal of the German plan for destroying Soviet airpower on the ground and gaining air superiority was thus successfully achieved.

During the following days, the Germans consolidated their success and the number of destroyed Soviet aircraft grew noticeably. It should be noted that the units equipped with I-16s were one of the primary targets for the *Luftwaffe*. After just two days of warfare, their number had decreased to 937, while as of 30 June, the front-line units had 873 I-16s, 99 of which required repairs.

In spite of the suddenness of the attack and the heavy losses on the ground, the I-16 pilots put up severe resistance to the German aviation on the first day of the invasion, codenamed Operation *Barbarossa*. As early as 3:30 a.m., the I-16s of the 33rd Fighter Air Regiment stationed in Pruzhany took to the air. In the dawn sky above Brest, they scored several victories, the pilots reporting that they shot down six enemy aircraft. In the Baltic Military District, pilots of the 15th and 21st Fighter Air Regiments were credited with nine victories per regiment, while seven 'kills' were achieved by the pilots of the 10th Fighter Air Regiment. In the Odessa Military District, the 55th Fighter Air Regiment, stationed in Beltsy, scored 10 victories before the end of the day, and the 67th Fighter Air Regiment in Bolgrad achieved a combat score of 15 German aircraft.

Aerial combat victories on 22 June also cost many I-16 pilots their lives. One pilot of the 67th Fighter Air Regiment, Lieutenant Moklyak, shot down up to four enemy aircraft during the morning battles but was then killed in a ramming attack on his fifth victim. Meanwhile, Lieutenant Gudimov of the 33rd Fighter Air Regiment destroyed his third enemy aircraft by aerial ramming at the expense of his life, and 19th Fighter Air Regiment pilot Vasily Loboda shot down two German aircraft in combat before ramming a third one with his *Ishachok*.

Aerial ramming was a last resort in combat, and was seen as a heroic deed. However, on the first day of the invasion, with aviators striving to fend off the aggressors, even at the cost of their own lives, it became a regular combat practice. Furthermore, pilots used ramming for the thrill of battle, in a desperate situation or when their armament failed. On 22 June, 15 Soviet pilots performed aerial ramming to destroy enemy aircraft, and ramming was also used during subsequent days. Given the Soviet military failures of 1941, a pilot's decision to resort to such dangerous last-ditch tactics was even encouraged.

Pilots who chose to use aerial ramming were also the first ones to be awarded the title of Hero of the Soviet Union in the summer of 1941. Pilot of the 158th Fighter Air Regiment Junior Lieutenant Petr Kharitonov rammed a Ju 88 bomber with his I-16 on 27 June, near Pskov. On 28 June, another two pilots of the 158th Fighter Air Regiment – Junior Lieutenant Stepan Zdorovtsev and Junior Lieutenant Mikhail Zhukov – destroyed one German bomber each in the same manner. In all the three cases, the young pilots were flying their first combat sorties, and performed the ramming after a failure of onboard armament or after running out of ammunition. In all three cases, the pilots made forced landings and survived.

The Commander of the Air Force of the Northern (Leningrad) Front, Alexander Novikov, later described subsequent events as follows:

> In a day or two after the ramming attacks by Zdorovtsev and Zhukov, I reported to Commander of the Northern Front M. Popov and to A. Zhdanov on the three heroic regimental comrades, and suggested nominating them for the title of Hero of the Soviet Union.
>
> Somewhat later on the same day, Zhdanov called Moscow in my presence, and reported to J.V. Stalin on the three heroes of the Leningrad Front. Stalin supported our suggestion to nominate the meritorious pilots for the award. No documents regarding such nomination are extant in the archives – there simply were none. The conversation between Stalin and Zhdanov and a telegram to Supreme High Command General Headquarters (*Stavka*) replaced standard award sheets.
>
> On 8 July 1941, a Decree of the Presidium of the Supreme Council of the USSR was issued to award the title of Hero of the Soviet Union to P. Kharitonov, S. Zdorovtsev and M. Zhukov. Thus, pilots of the Leningrad Front became the first recipients of this highest combat distinction at the time of the Great Patriotic War.

It has been already mentioned that the Air Force of the Western Special Military District lost a considerable number of its aircraft in the first bombing attacks of the invasion. However, several units located further to the east were not subjected to morning attacks on 22 June. That was the case with the 43rd Air Division was commanded by the hero of the air combat in Spain, Major General Zakharov. The division was stationed on airfields at Mogilev and Orsha, and had the following combat strength:

- the 160th Fighter Air Regiment, 60 (according to some sources, 66) I-153s and 72 pilots;
- the 161st Fighter Air Regiment, 62 (or 64) I-16s and 70 pilots;
- the 162nd Fighter Air Regiment, 54 I-16s and 75 pilots;
- the 163rd Fighter Air Regiment, 59 I-16s and 72 pilots.

The above listed 175 I-16s of the 43rd Air Division constituted its core power. Furthermore, after the massive losses suffered by the entire district during the morning, they turned out to be the backbone of Soviet fighter aviation in the path of the main German advance.

On the morning of 22 June, all four regiments were given their combat tasks and redeployed in the direction of the the German advance. On the same day, the division entered combat. The 163rd Fighter Air Regiment, which together with the 160th Regiment was tasked with covering the city of Minsk, operated highly effectively. On the first day, pilots of the 163rd Regiment scored several victories. Towards the evening, Division Commander Zakharov personally shot down two Ju 88s. Two days later, on 24 June, I-16s of the 163rd Fighter Air Regiment shot down 21 enemy aircraft. Zakharov later confessed that, during the subsequent years of the war, even a complete fighter division had never managed to bring down such a number of aircraft in a single day.

The well-organised actions paid off: in the majority of cases, the I-16s had more victories than losses in aerial combat. However, the seemingly never-ending bombing raids on airfields where these fighters were stationed resulted in a steady decrease of their number. It was to the destruction of aircraft on the ground that German aviation owed its unconditional success. Another cause of the heavy losses was the decision to send fighters to strafe *Wehrmacht* tank and motorised columns, which, as a rule, were well protected with mobile anti-aircraft defence.

After two weeks of active operations, there remained only some 15–20 serviceable fighters in each regiment of the 43rd Air Division. By that time, the combat performance of the division had been highly praised by the command of the Western Front Air Force (with the onset of the war, military districts began to be named as 'fronts'):

> The 43rd Fighter Division carried out missions to stave off and destroy enemy aircraft in mid-air on the approaches to Minsk, Pukhovichi, Bobruisk, Mogilev, Smolensk and Vyazma. The division forces escorted bombers, destroyed enemy aircraft on airfields and personnel at the front line, flew reconnaissance sorties and provided cover for ground troops. The 43rd Division flew 4,638 combat sorties with a total flying time of 5,965 hours. Throughout this period, the division shot down 167 enemy aircraft in air combats. The division's own losses totalled 63 aircraft destroyed on the ground, 26 shot down in air combats and three pilots killed in crashes.

In general, the invasion of the USSR proved far from painless for the *Luftwaffe*. During the period from 22 June until 5 July 1941, Germany lost 807 aircraft of all types, then from 6–19 July the losses increased by another 477. This number does not include aircraft losses by Germany's allies, for example Romania, which took part in the war against the USSR in the southern part of the Soviet western border.

The German and Romanian aviation in the southern sector of the front were opposed by the Air Forces of the Odessa Military District and the Black Sea Fleet. Fighters of the 20th and 21st Mixed Air Divisions, with a total strength of approximately 300 I-16s, were providing cover for the border. On the first day of the invasion, pilots of the 21st Mixed Air Division shot down over 20 enemy aircraft; a month of battles later, the total number of victories reached 150. By that time, the advance of the Romanian troops had been successfully brought to a halt on the approaches to Odessa.

The 69th Fighter Air Regiment, which entered the war with 70 I-16s and five MiG-3s, was the most combat-worthy air unit among those operating in the southern sector of the front. Throughout three months of the defence of Odessa, pilots of the 69th Fighter Air Regiment not only protected the skies over the city but also flew numerous sorties to counteract the enemy's advance. In aerial combat alone, pilots of the 69th Fighter Air Regiment shot down 94 German and Romanian aircraft during that period.

Regiment Commander Lev Shestakov converted to the I-16 in 1936. He had taken part in the combat in Spain, where he shot down two enemy aircraft personally and had one other shared victory. Around Odessa, Shestakov shot down three more aircraft personally and was involved in eight shared successes. Before he was killed on 12 March 1944, Shestakov had been credited with 21 personal victories and 14 shared.

After the surrender of Odessa, remnants of the 69th Regiment flew to the Crimea, where they continued operations against the Axis forces jointly with the fighters of the Black Sea Fleet Air Force.

The I-16s which were in service with the Black Sea Fleet Air Force were flown mostly by the 8th and 32nd Fighter Air Regiments of the 62nd Air Brigade. Fierce combats during the defence of Sevastopol resulted in a considerable reduction in the number of all types of fighters. After the fall of the fortress on the Black Sea, just four I-16s flew from the Crimea to airfields further east. In July 1942, the 62nd Air Brigade mustered only 11 I-16s and three UTI-4s. The aircraft were stationed at airfields in Anapa, Lazarevskoye, Myskhako and the settlement of Gaiduk. Eight I-16s were assigned to the 87th Air Squadron, which was initially stationed in Yeysk, and later in Olchinka and Anapa. In late 1942, the Black Sea Fleet Air Force had just seven I-16s and four UTI-4s remaining at its disposal.

The successful advance of the German troops and their allies deep into the territory of the Soviet Union allowed them to begin bombing raids on Moscow after only a month of hostilities. To provide for the air defence of the capital, the Soviet command established the VI Fighter Air Corps of Air Defence Forces. As of 31 July 1941, the VI Fighter Air Corps mustered 495 fighters, including approximately 110 I-16s. The *Ishaks* were stationed as follows: the 16th Fighter Air Regiment (eight I-16s) at Lyubertsy, the 34th Fighter Air Regiment (30 I-16s) at Vnukovo, the 27th Fighter Air Regiment (31 I-16s) at Klin, the 176th Fighter Air Regiment (15 I-16s) at Stepykhino, the 233rd Fighter Air Regiment (18 I-16s) at Tushino and the 2nd Separate Air Squadron (four I-16s) at Ramenskoye.

The first night raid on Moscow took place on 22 July 1941. According to Soviet sources, up to 150 bombers took part in it. The Germans were met on the distant approaches to Moscow above decoys simulating city blocks, while searchlight systems arranged in thick forests simulated airfields. During that night, Soviet fighters shot down 12 German bombers in 25 separate aerial combats, and anti-aircraft gunners were credited with another 10 enemy aircraft. Only some lone Axis aircraft managed to break through to the city.

A total of 18 night raids on Moscow were carried out before 15 August 1941. These failed to inflict the expected damage on the Soviet capital, thanks to the well-coordinated performance of the entire air defence system. During those tense

Fighter pilots of the 13th Fighter Air Regiment of the 61st Air Brigade, Air Force of the Red Banner Baltic Fleet.

Scrambled fighters taking off. The I-16 with the tactical number '2' is equipped with PSB-21 external fuel tanks.

Grigory Yakovenko, Commissar of an I-16 squadron, in April 1940.

An I-16 Type 29 in flight above the clouds.

The I-16 Type 5s which were hit during an aerial combat and performed a forced landing in summer 1941.

Another I-16 Type 5 in summer 1941 in a non-typical 'on-the-nose' position. The author suspects that the Germans set the aircraft in such position on purpose, in order to obtain a spectacular picture. How otherwise could they have stripped off the skin on the horizontal stabiliser?

This I-16 Type 5 tactical number '29' has been prepared for evacuation and placed onto the body of a ZIS truck.

Smoking cigarettes near a combat aircraft.

Captain V. Simanishin in the cockpit of his I-16. The pilot was awarded the Order of Lenin for successful performance in combat missions.

Pilot A. Chirkov (centre) giving details of a task for a combat mission to Junior Lieutenants S. Medvedev and N. Shioshvili. The aviators were with the 158th Fighter Air Regiment near Leningrad on 12 July 1941.

A cannon-armed I-16 Type 27 (or 28) getting ready for engine-start. Note the rare rail launchers for RS-82 rocket projectiles under the wing. The cannons are protected from penetration of dust in an original manner: the muzzle ends are covered with pieces of percale fabric glued to them by means of dope.

The I-16 Type 27 with the tactical number '58' being started using a motor vehicle starter.

An I-16 Type 18 taxiing to the take-off point. Judging by the flying helmet and goggles being worn by the accompanying person, the *Ishak* pilot is being seen off on a combat sortie by his comrade.

Pilot of the 191st Fighter Air Regiment Lieutenant G. Zhuikov in front of an I-16 Type 17 on the Leningrad Front in September 1941.

Pilots of the 191st Fighter Air Regiment who took part in combat near Ropsha (Leningrad Front) on 10 September 1941: Senior Lieutenant Zhuikov and Junior Lieutenants V. Plavsky, V. Dobrovolsky, A. Savchenko and G. Mamykin.

Pilot of the 158th Fighter Air Regiment Junior Lieutenant P. Kharitonov, who performed an aerial ramming near Pskov on 27 June 1941.

Pilot of the 158th Fighter Air Regiment Junior Lieutenant M. Zhukov, who also carried out an aerial ramming on 29 July 1941.

days, Soviet pilots continued to use aerial ramming. On the night of 6/7 August, 177th Fighter Air Regiment pilot Viktor Talalikhin, having run out of ammunition, rammed a He 111 bomber with his I-16 above Podolsk, near Moscow, and then bailed out from his disintegrating fighter. The following morning, Talalikhin became a national hero. Fragments of the Heinkel destroyed by him are still kept in the Central Museum of Armed Forces in Moscow.

By early September 1941, the activity of the German aviation was declining, with raids on Moscow becoming mostly only sporadic, and many Soviet air defence night fighters also began to be used in the daytime. At the time of the battle for Moscow, all the I-16s were extensively used in combat, but upon the termination of the winter campaign, they began to be handed over to front-line units. In autumn 1942, only 13 such aircraft were left with the Moscow Air Defence Forces. In spring 1943, the I-16s in the VI Fighter Air Corps were replaced by MiGs and Yaks.

Air units of the Baltic Fleet were among those who operated the I-16s with the highest efficiency. Shortly before the German invasion, some 1,500 *Ishaks* in the Baltic region were distributed as follows:

The 61st Fighter Air Brigade (airfields in Nizino, Lipovo, Kummelovo and Kuplya):

- 77 I-16s in the 5th Fighter Air Regiment;
- 12 I-16s in the 12th Separate Red Banner Squadron;
- 25 I-16s in the 13th Separate Red Banner Squadron.

The 10th Mixed Air Brigade (air bases in Tallinn and Hanko; airfields in Kerstovo and Pernov/Pärnu):

- 38 I-16s in the 13th Fighter Air Regiment.

The 13th Fighter Air Regiment, under the command of Lieutenant Colonel I.G. Romanenko (participant of the Winter War and Hero of the Soviet Union), comprised four squadrons:

- 1st Squadron equipped with I-16 Type 17s;
- 2nd Squadron equipped with I-16 Type 24s, Type 27s and Type 29s;
- 3rd Squadron equipped with I-16 Type 5s;
- 4th Squadron equipped with I-153s.

In spring 1941, it was announced that the 3rd Squadron of the 13th Regiment would undergo conversion training to fly the MiG-3. In May, nearly all flight crews were transferred to a summer camp near Narva, with the intention to convert three squadrons to the new fighters. After a short while, the command of the fleet decided that the 5th Fighter Air Regiment would be the first to receive the MiGs. For this reason, pilots of the 13th Fighter Air Regiment fully focused on preparing the I-16s for combat use (with aerial gunnery, bombing, air combats and formation flying in a group).

Pilots of the 13th Fighter Air Regiment saw the onset of the Great Patriotic War at different airfields. Some of the crews were stationed near Tallinn on Lagsberg airfield. On 25 June, an aerial victory was scored by Captain A. Antonenko, who, in front of the whole city, shot down the first Ju 88. Antonenko was an experienced pilot; before the Great Patriotic War, he had fought at Khalkhin Gol and taken part in the Winter War.

The 4th Squadron (flying the I-153s) of the 13th Fighter Air Regiment, commanded by Captain L. Belousov, was, during the early days of the war, stationed at the Hanko Peninsula, which had been leased to the Soviet Union for a period of 30 years as one of the trophies of the Winter War. It was a territory some 26km long and 6–12km wide, and a naval base was promptly set up there. Many of the facilities were built after the onset of the war, under fire from Finnish artillery. In particular, there were shelters for aircraft made of thick logs laid in six to eight layers which provided reliable protection even in the case of a direct hit by an enemy projectile. Due to its strategically favourable location, the naval base at Hanko controlled accesses to the Gulf of Finland and to southern regions of Finland. For the enemy, it was thus 'like a thorn in the flesh'. But neither was serving at Hanko a picnic for Soviet units. Almost all positions, airfields and shelters were known to the enemy (German reconnaissance aircraft had taken detailed photos of the peninsula), and were constantly being shelled by the Finns. Aircraft taking off from and landing on runways under artillery fire often suffered heavy losses.

On 2 July, two groups of I-16 Type 17s from the 13th Fighter Air Regiment, led by the Commander of the 1st Squadron, Captain Leonovich, were transferred to Hanko. Later, other fighters from the 13th and 71st Air Regiments and from the 13th Separate Squadron arrived at the peninsula. The defence of Hanko, which lasted for over five months, was rich in numerous combat episodes, with convincing victories and bitter losses.

Starting from 3 July, Hanko bore witness to effective operations by Soviet fighter aces Antonenko and Petr Brinko, who were the first to have obtained authorisation from the air force command to fly their sorties in a pair.

On the morning on 4 July, two biplanes appeared from the Finnish side of the front. Observers determined them to be Bristol Bulldog fighters, which attacked Soviet artillery positions and dropped bomblets. Two I-16s rapidly took off to pursue

The inscription across this photograph reads, "The hot days in June 1941. Hero of the Soviet Union Mikhail Zhukov has just returned from a combat sortie. He has driven a Ju-88 bomber into Lake Pskov. Nikolay Pilshikov has drawn the hero near the combat aircraft."

A comrade instructing Lieutenant Sergey Gusev before a combat sortie on the Leningrad Front. Gusev was killed in an aerial combat near the station of Malaya Vishera on 23 August 1941.

An I-16 Type 29 taxiing out of a protective shelter on the Hanko Peninsula in the summer of 1941.

An I-16 Type 29 of the 13th Fighter Air Regiment of the Air Force of the Red Banner Baltic Fleet taking off. This may be the aircraft flown by Baltic fighter ace Petr Brinko.

Another I-16 Type 17 with the tactical number '11' from the aircraft of the 13th Fighter Air Regiment, Air Force of the Red Banner Baltic Fleet.

A squadron of cannon-armed I-16s in the 'readiness line' before a combat sortie. In accordance with the table of organisation, three motor vehicle starters begin to start engines from the outermost aircraft on the right flank.

The original caption for this photograph reads, "Pilots of the air unit where Y.M. Zhuravlev is Commissar, shot down 38 enemy aircraft in air combats. 22 July 1941."

Damaged I-16s being restored in a repair shop in Kaluga in 1942.

Lunch at an airfield during a break between sorties. The I-16 Type 29 in the background features small black stripes painted on it, including on the propeller and the propeller spinner.

Squadron Leader of the 72nd Mixed Air Regiment, Air Force of the Northern Fleet, B. Safonov in the cockpit of an I-16.

Pilot Vasily Matsievich during the Winter War. In 1941, Senior Lieutenant Matsievich was a Squadron Leader with the 26th Fighter Air Regiment, which was part of the VII Fighter Air Corps of the Leningrad Air Defence Forces. On the night of 24/25 October 1941, he shot down a German Heinkel He 111 using RS-82 rocket projectiles. Matsievich's total score included 16 personal victories and six shared 'kills'. On 14 February 1943, he was awarded the title of Hero of the Soviet Union.

Lieutenant A.P. Vershinin shot down two Ju 88s and a Bf 109 in his I-16 in several aerial combats.

Nikolay Polikarpov and his Aircraft Designs

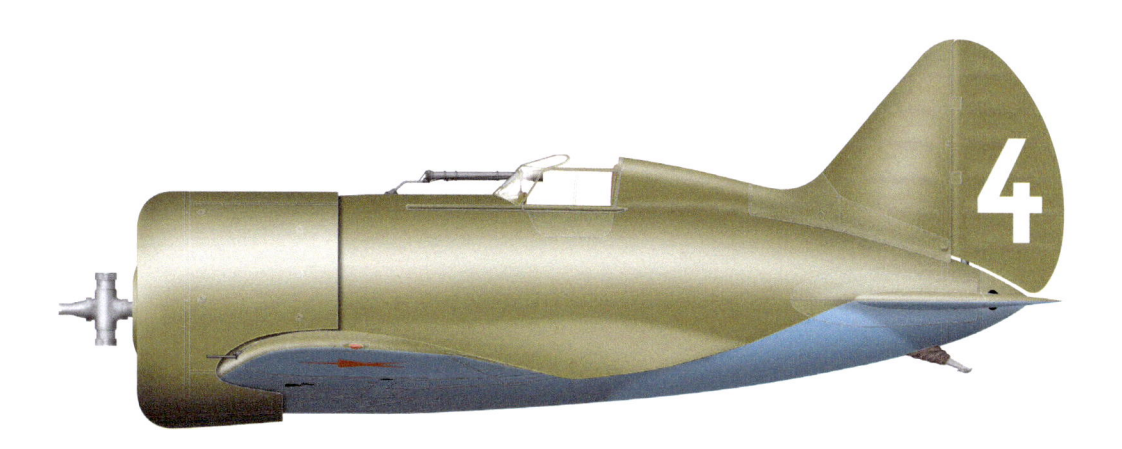

— *Not to scale* —

I-16 Type 4 of the 119th Fighter Squadron, 70th Separate Fighter Unit, at Baku in spring 1936. The airplane was flown by pilot I.T. Eremenko.

I-16 Type 5 of the 61st Air Brigade, Red Banner Baltic Fleet Air Force, in August 1937.

I-16 Type 5 (s/n 521A110) of the 2nd Air Squadron, 145th Fighter Air Regiment. The airplane was flown by Junior Lieutenant P.A. Khizhnyak at Murmashi airfield in February 1941.

(i)

— *Not to scale* —

I-16 Type 5 of the 3rd Air Squadon, 68th Fighter Air Regiment. The airplane was flown by pilot I.I. Kovalkov during the Winter War in December 1939.

I-16 Type 5 armed with Vickers machine guns, which belonged to the Chinese Air Force. It is possible that the airplane was flown by Chinese ace Liu Chi-Sheng.

I-16 Type 5 flown by Commander of the 1st Squadron of Moscas Captain Sergey Tarkhov, in November 1936.

Nikolay Polikarpov and his Aircraft Designs

— *Not to scale* —

I-16 Type 5 at Barajas airfield in November 1936.

I-16 Type 5 flown by Sergey Kuznetsov, who was taken as a prisoner of war by Francoists in Spain in 1937.

I-16 Type 5 which was demonstrated at the Milan Exhibition in summer 1935 under the ASB designation as a sporting aircraft.

The King of Fighters Volume 2

— Not to scale —

I-16 Type 5, which was a part of Zveno-SPB configuration, being tested at NII VVS in November 1938.

I-16 Type 10 of the 3a Escuadrilla, Grupo 21, at Vilajuiga airfield, Spain, in February 1939.

I-16 Type 10 of the 26th Grupo de Caza, Spanish Nationalist Air Force, in 1944–45.

— *Not to scale* —

-16 Type 10 of the 235th Fighter Air Division, flown by Major General I.A. Lakeev, in June 1941.

I-16 Type 10 of the 70th Fighter Air Regiment at Khalkhin Gol in July 1939. CS caption

I-16 Type 10 of the 3a Escuadrilla, flown by pilot Artiga, at Sabadell airfield, Spain, in 1938.

The King of Fighters Volume 2

— *Not to scale* —

I-16 Type 15 (UTI-4) of the 286th Fighter Air Regiment in October 1941.

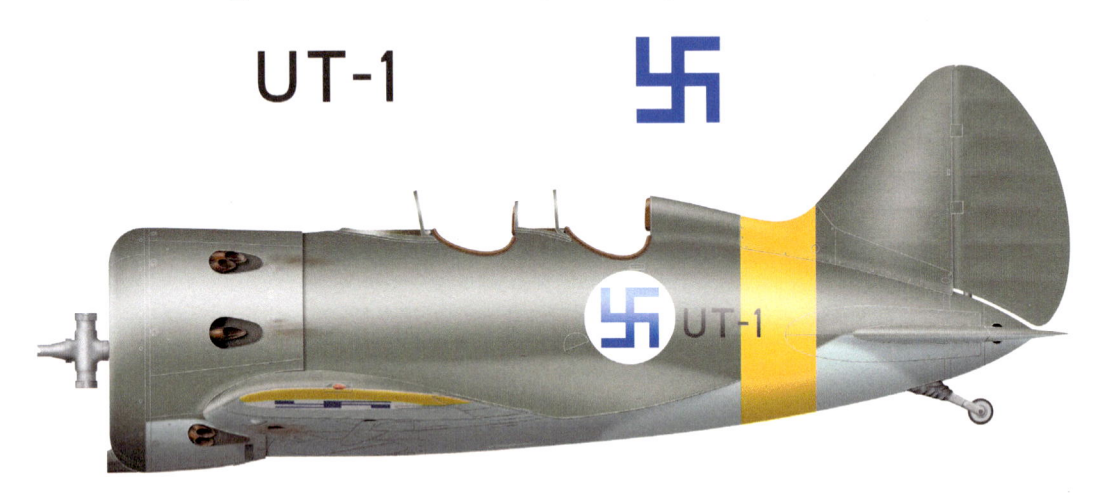

I-16 Type 15 (UTI-4) of the Finnish Air Force T-LLv 35 Supplement Squadron in 1942.

I-16 Type 17 flown by Lieutenant Vorozheykin at Khalkhin Gol in July 1939.

(vi)

Nikolay Polikarpov and his Aircraft Designs

— *Not to scale* —

I-16 Type 24 on tghe Southern Front during the summer of 1942.

I-16 Type 24 s/n 2421321 of the 4th Guards Fighter Air Regiment, Red Banner Baltic Fleet Air Force. The airplane was flown by Senior Sergeant G.D. Tsokolaev at Vystav airfield in the summer of 1942.

I-16 Type 29 during state tests in 1940.

(vii)

The King of Fighters Volume 2

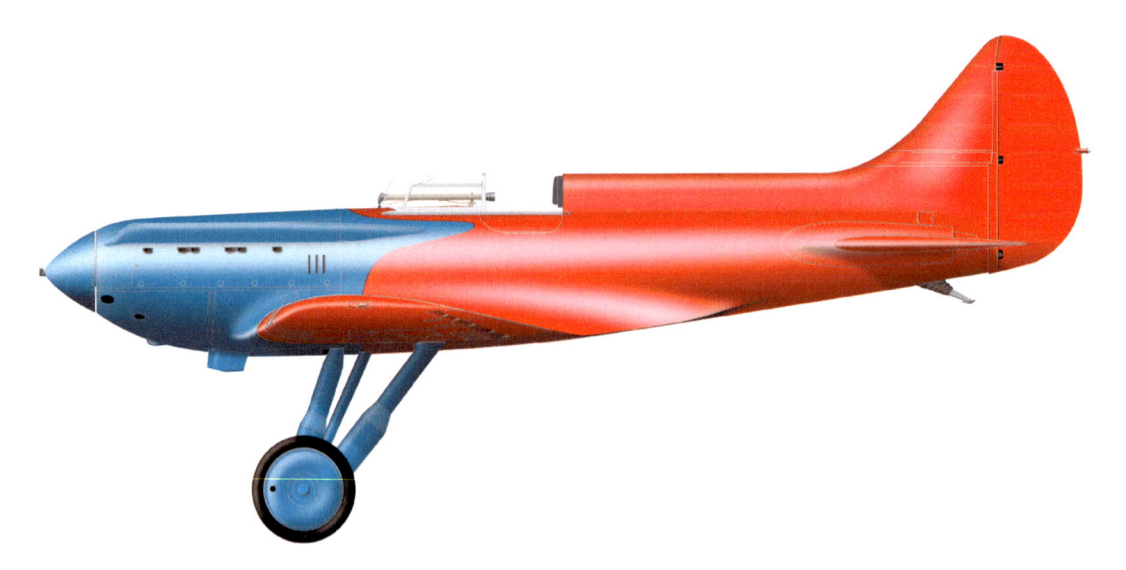

— *Not to scale* —

I-17 (TsKB-15) fighter prototype at Moscow Central Airfield in 1935.

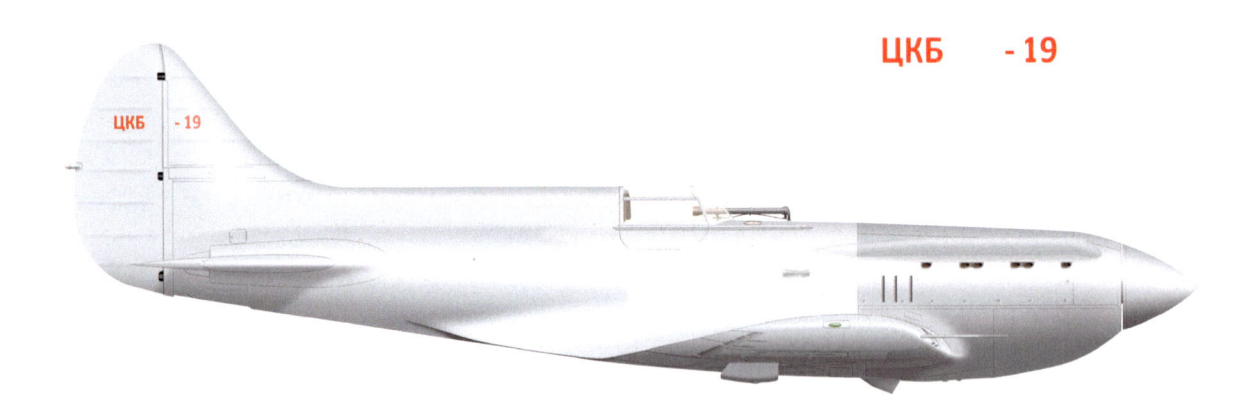

ЦКБ - 19

I-17 (TsKB-19) fighter prototype at the 15th Salon de l'Aviation in Paris in November 1936.

I-17bis (TsKB-19bis) fighter prototype during factory tests in November 1936.

(viii)

Nikolay Polikarpov and his Aircraft Designs

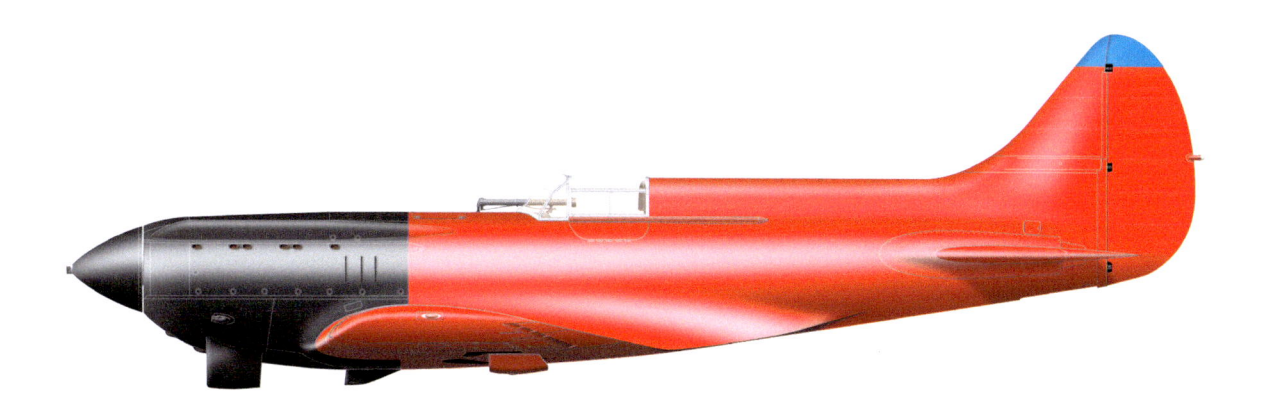

— *Not to scale* —

I-17bis (TsKB-19bis) fighter prototype during armament tests at the Noginsk range, in August 1938.

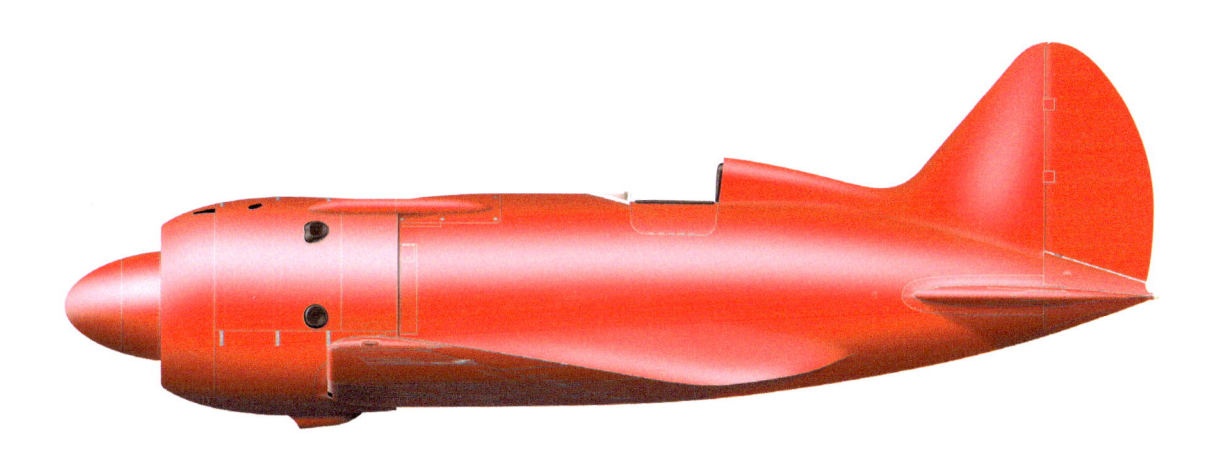

I-180-1 fighter prototype in December 1938.

I-180-2 fighter prototype during factory tests in April 1939.

(ix)

The King of Fighters Volume 2

— *Not to scale* —

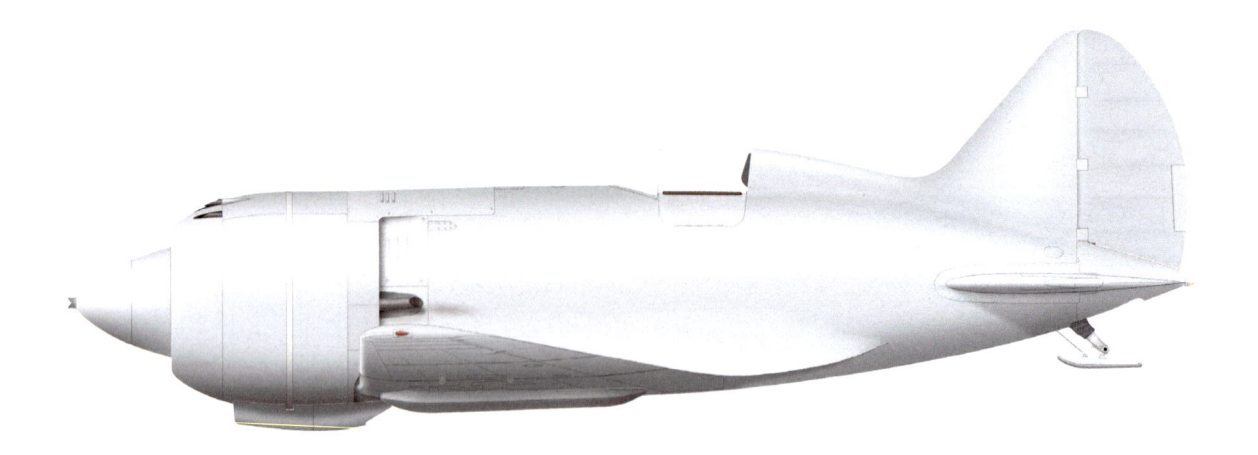

I-180-3 (E-3) fighter prototype during factory tests in February 1940.

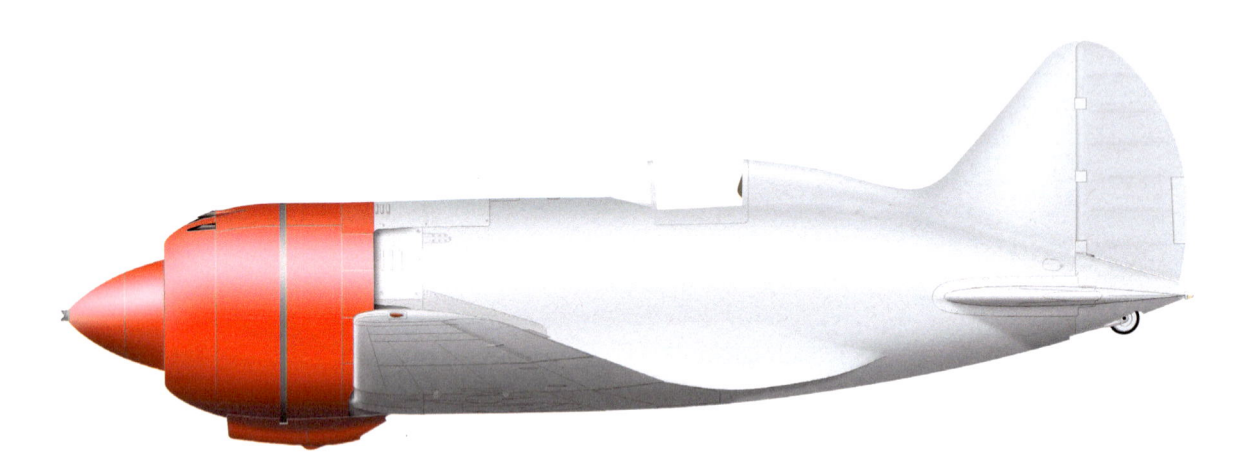

I-180-3 (E-3) fighter prototype during state tests in June 1940.

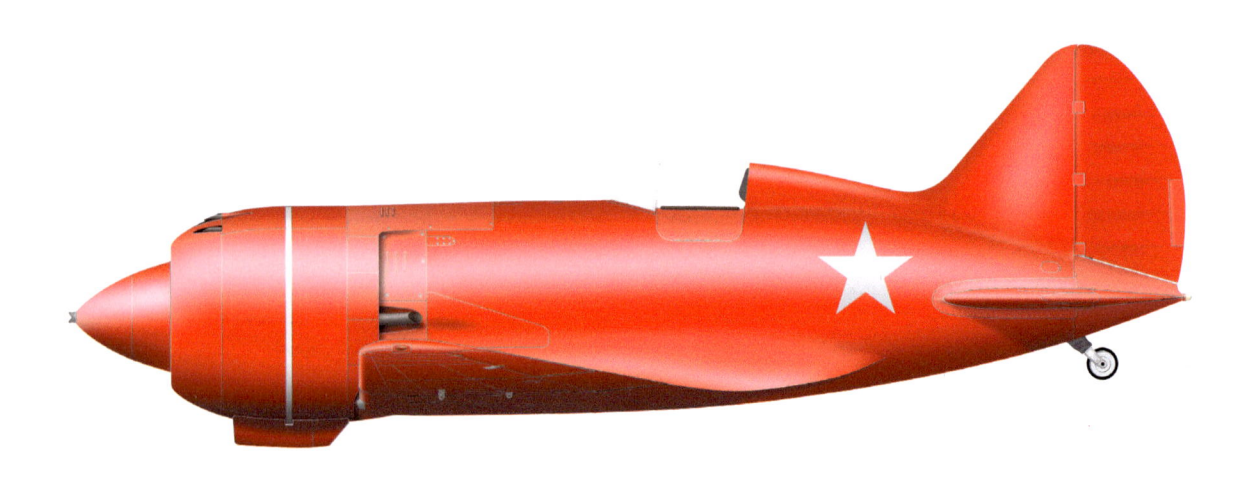

I-180S s/n 25212 during factory tests in May 1940.

(x)

— *Not to scale* —

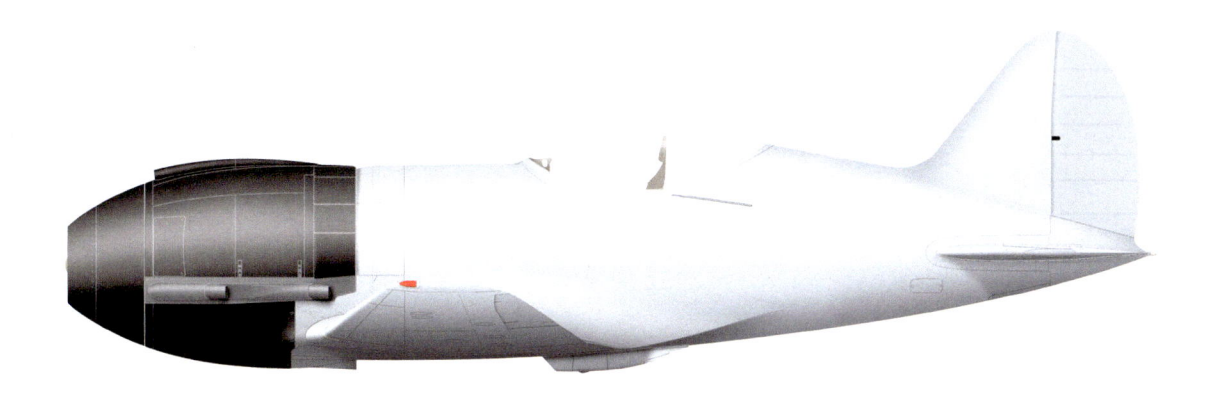

I-185 s/n 6201 fighter prototype with M-90 engine in the TsAGI T-101 wind tunnel in September 1940.

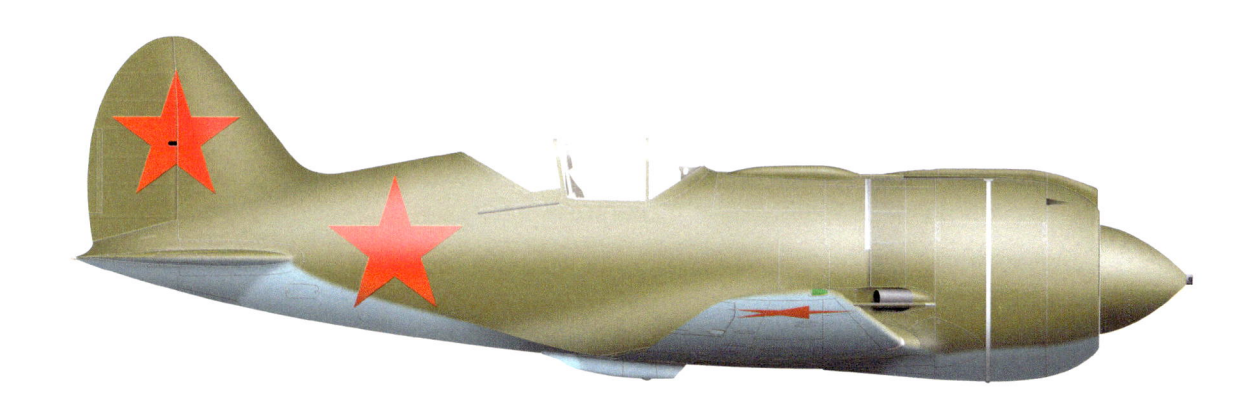

I-185 s/n 6202 fighter prototype with M-81 engine at Moscow in February 1941.

I-185 s/n 6202 fighter prototype with M-71 engine at Moscow in October 1941.

— *Not to scale* —

I-185 s/n 6204 fighter prototype with M-71 engine at Moscow in March 1941.

I-185 s/n 6204 fighter prototype with M-71 engine at Novosibirsk in January 1942.

I-185 s/n 6203 fighter prototype with M-82A engine at Novosibirsk in April 1942.

— *Not to scale* —

I-185 with M-71 engine (the first reference aircraft) at Novosibirsk in June 1942

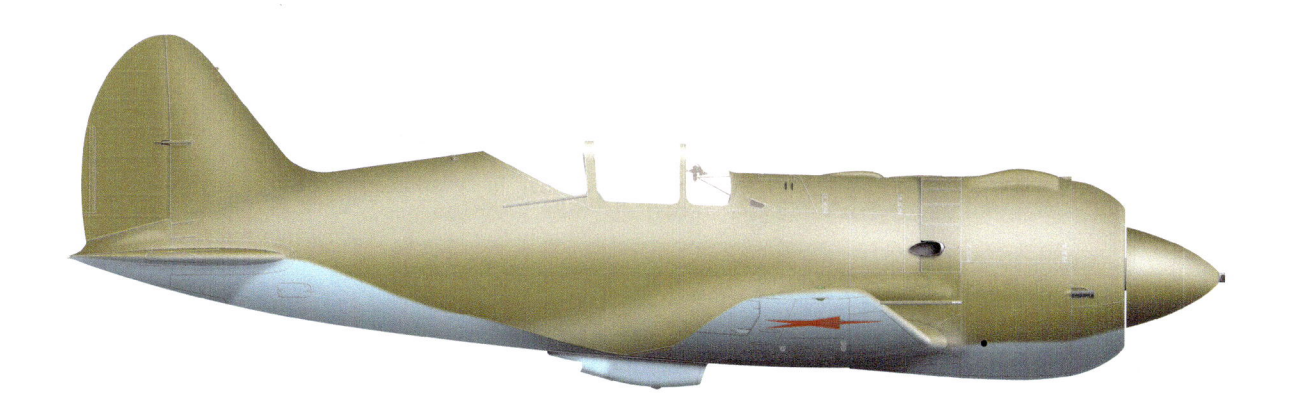

I-185 with M-71 engine (the second reference aircraft) at Novosibirsk in December 1942.

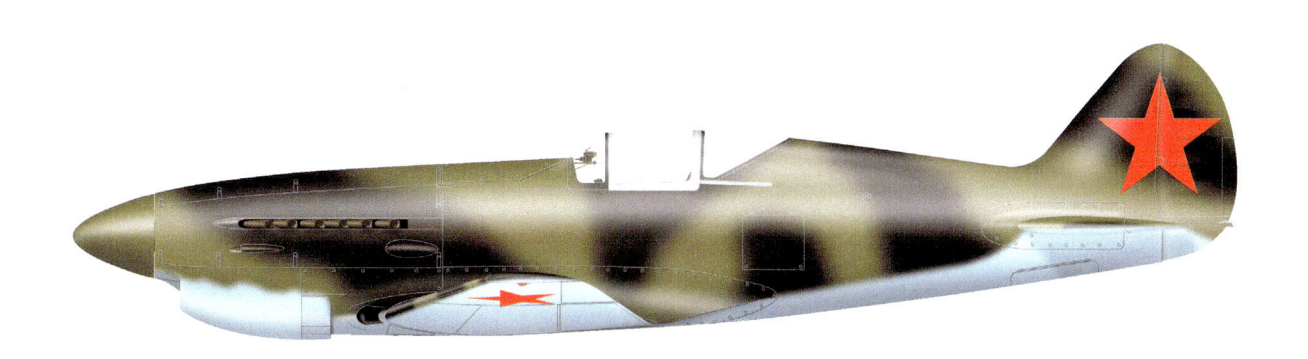

ITP (M-1) fighter prototype in late 1942.

The King of Fighters Volume 2

— *Not to scale* —

ITP (M-2) fighter prototype in the summer of 1943.

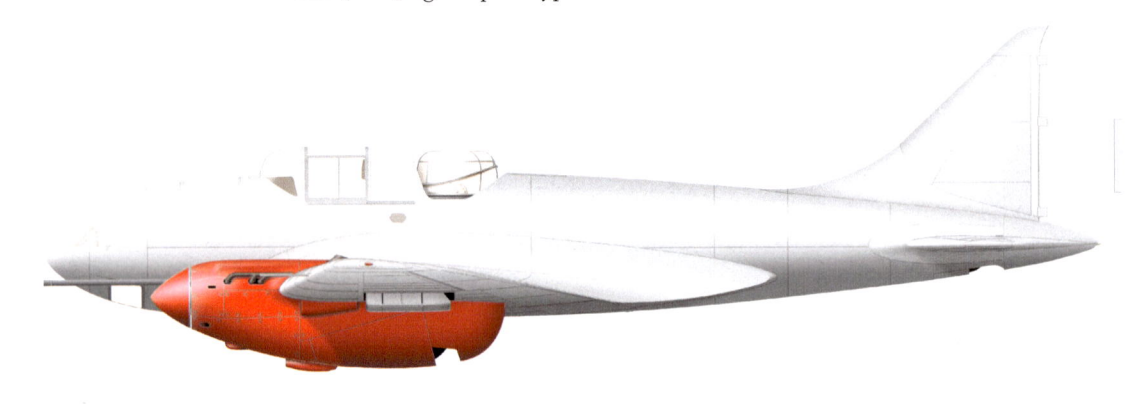

Prototype of VIT-1 (MPI) air destroyer of tanks at the Aviation Armament Research and Testing Range of the VVS RKKA in summer 1939.

VIT-2 with M-103 engines during factory tests in May 1939.

VIT-2 with M-105 engines during state tests at NII VVS in March 1939.

(xiv)

Nikolay Polikarpov and his Aircraft Designs

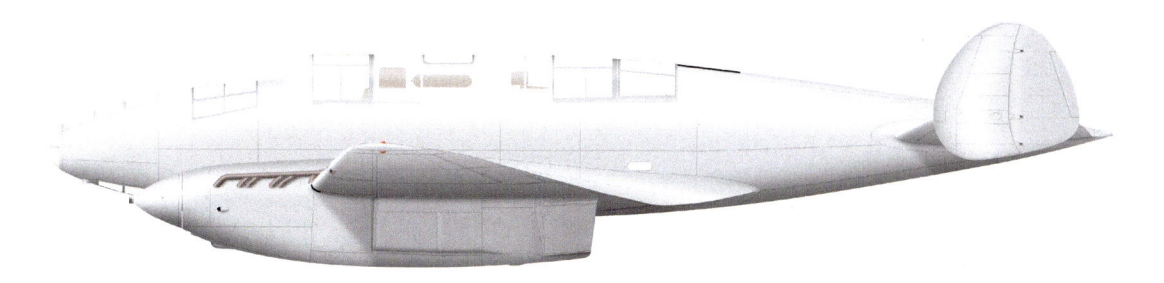

— *Not to scale* —

SPB high-speed dive-bomber prototype No.1/0 in January 1940.

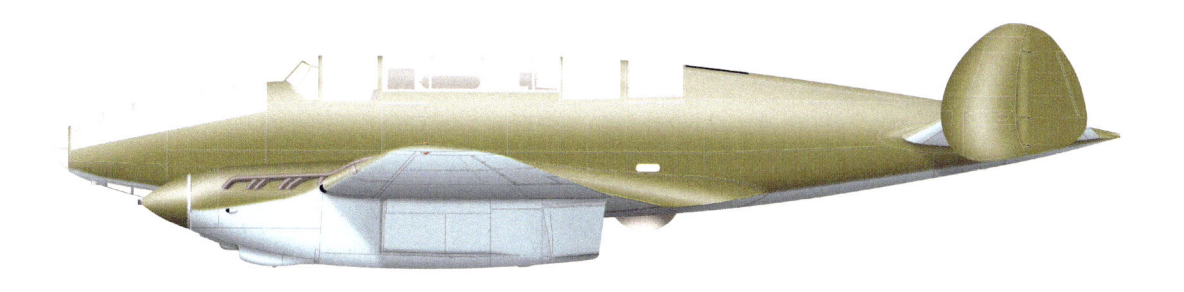

SPB high-speed dive-bomber prototype No.1/0 in November 1940.

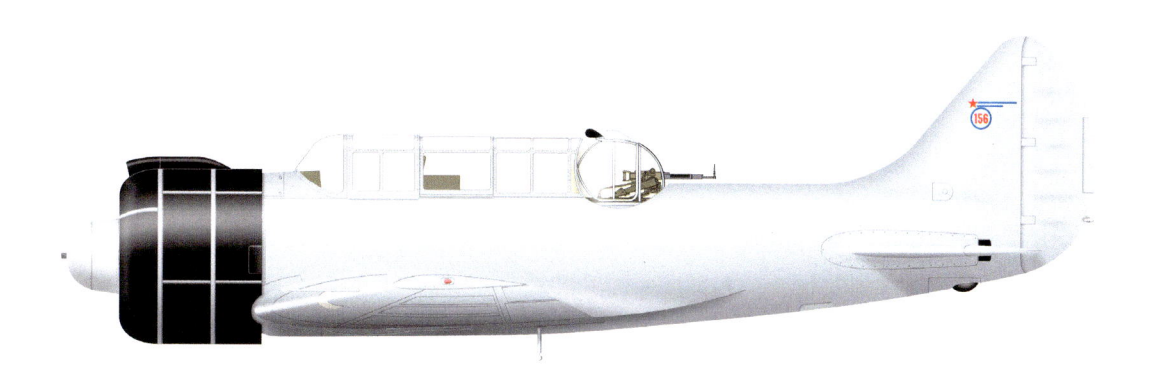

Ivánov single-engine bomber prototype at Moscow Central Airfield in August 1938.

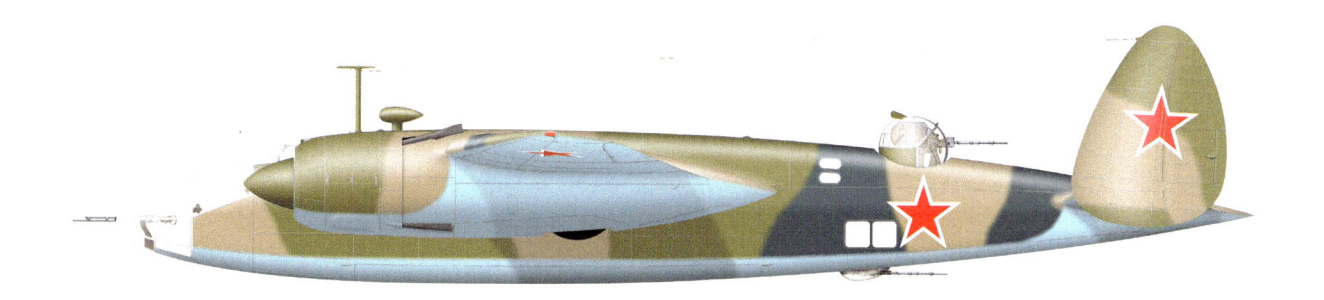

NB night bomber prototype during factory tests in August 1944.

(xv)

— Not to scale —

BDP combat troop-carrier glider prototype in September 1941.

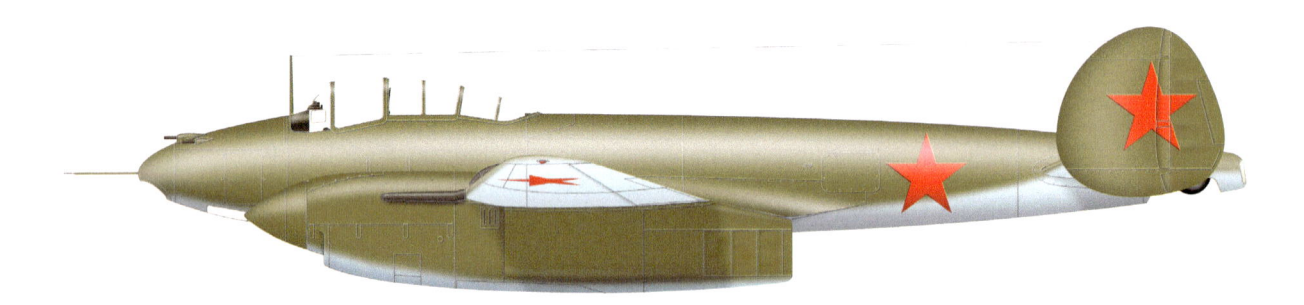

TIS 'A' heavy escort fighter prototype during factory tests in July 1941.

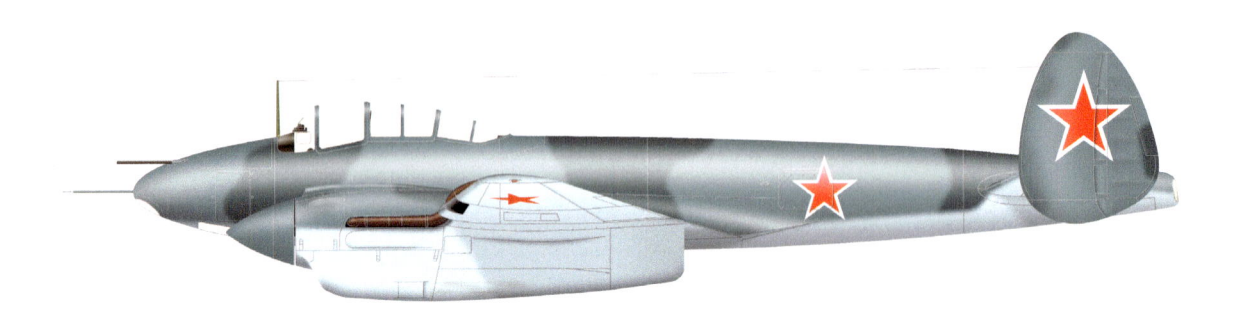

TIS 'MA' heavy escort fighter prototype in September 1944.

Artist's impression of the Malyutka rocket-propelled aircraft project.

An I-16 of the 27th Fighter Air Regiment in a snowy environment on an airfield near Klin in the autumn of 1941.

Young pilots Sergeants Slesarchuk, Gozin and Perevera near a camouflaged I-16 Type 29 of the Moscow Air Defence Forces in 1942. The aircraft with the tactical number '1' features an additional star on the propeller spinner and the slogan 'For the Motherland!' painted on its side.

Damaged aircraft being repaired at the facilities of Aviation Factory No.51 in Moscow during the winter of 1941–42. The factory was an experimental base for the Polikarpov Design Bureau. After returning from evacuation, the factory was involved in the refinement of Polikarpov airplanes the I-185, NB and TIS.

The I-16 Type 17 piloted by Sergeant M. Vasilyev of the 4th Guards Fighter Air Regiment, Air Force of the Red Banner Baltic Fleet, taxiing to the starting point at Novaya Ladoga airfield in the spring of 1942.

The original caption for this photograph reads, "Senior Lieutenant G. Shevtsov talking to Kronstadt delegates in 1942."

A pilot of the 3rd Guards Fighter Air Regiment stationed on Vystav airfield getting ready for a combat sortie. The original photograph bears a blurred inscription, which includes, "Guards Captain … v".

Fighters of the 4th Guards Fighter Air Regiment during the winter of 1942. Lieutenant G. Guryakov is reporting readiness for the sortie.

Fighters of the 3rd Squadron, 4th Guards Fighter Air Regiment, at Vystav airfield in autumn 1942.

G. Tsokolayev instructing young pilots. Tsokolayev's combat score totalled 26 personal victories and 11 shared successes. On 14 June 1942, he was awarded the title of Hero of the Soviet Union.

Pilots of the 3rd Guards Fighter Air Regiment at the naval base of Ostrovnaya, on the island of Lavansaari, in 1944. In the background, note the I-16 Type 5 with the tactical number '25'.

The I-16 fighter 131

Fighters of the 4th Guards Fighter Air Regiment at Novaya Ladoga airfield in spring 1942. The closest I-16 with the tactical number '21' and the 'Guards' emblem (s/n 2421321) was flown by Senior Sergeant G. Tsokolayev. The *Ishak* next to it has the tactical number '75'.

In this photo, the closest I-16 has the tactical number '96'.

Pilots of the 3rd Guards Fighter Air Regiment near the I-16 with the tactical number '96'.

I-16s with RS rocket projectiles attached under their wings are ready to go at an airfield near Mozdok on the Southern Front in 1942.

An Air Force of the Black Sea Fleet I-16 Type 5 in formation with Yak-7 fighters in 1942.

them, right from under their camouflage nets. One of the Finnish aircraft was shot down after being attacked by Brinko, while the other one, despite being attacked by Antonenko, escaped in the direction of the Finnish anti-aircraft defences.

During this period, the peninsula was subjected to intensive artillery fire from Finnish offshore and onshore batteries. On 6 July, an I-153 was shot down by a direct hit, and another three *Chaikas* were damaged.

On 8 July, Antonenko and Brinko flew to Tallinn (less than 100km across the gulf from Hanko). On their way, they encountered a lone two-engine German aircraft (a Ju 88 or Do 17) and shot it down. On 8 July, the lucky pair reported the destruction of two Finnish fighters, which had been attacking a torpedo boat base.

On 10 July, two I-153s (piloted by Alexey Lazukin and Konstantin Belorustsev) flew a sortie to strafe a Finnish airfield. Antonenko and Brinko in their I-16s provided an escort for them. In an aerial combat with Finnish fighters (depending on the source, these were either Fiats or Fokker D.XXIs), the Soviet pilots managed to shoot down five of them.

The higher command commended the Baltic pilots for successful combat operations, and on 14 July 1941, Antonenko and Brinko were awarded the titles of Hero of the Soviet Union.

Unfortunately, the combat activity of these two skilled pilots did not last long. On 25 July, an enemy projectile exploded on the Hanko runway in front of Antonenko's I-16, which was coming in to landing. The aircraft flipped over, throwing the pilot out of the cockpit. Before his tragic death, Antonenko had shot down 11 enemy aircraft.

During the following days, Brinko flew several sorties in Tallinn, and was then sent to Leningrad, where he flew in a pair with Lieutenant Maltsev. Here, Brinko raised his personal victory tally to 15.

On the evening of 14 September, the Germans launched an observation balloon near Ropsha, south of Leningrad. The Soviets decided to destroy it with their fighters, but the first attack failed. While a second group was being prepared for the task, Brinko insisted that he would perform the mission himself. Taking off, he accelerated his I-16 at low altitude, then soared up and fired six RS-82 rocket projectiles at the balloon. He hit the target, but his I-16 had by now become a target for fire from the ground. Brinko was wounded, but managed to fly his aircraft back to his home airfield. Nevertheless, he died later as a result of his injuries.

One of the most efficient pilots of the Baltic Fleet – Vasily Golubev – also fought at Hanko. In a relatively short period, he flew over 100 combat sorties, took part in 45 ground strafing operations and shot down 11 German and Finnish aircraft in aerial battles. After Soviet troops left Hanko on 2 December (five I-153 and eight I-16s flew to Kronstadt, but one of the I-16s crashed upon landing), Golubev fought near Leningrad and took part in aerial combat above what was known as the 'Road of Life'. This was the route across Lake Ladoga, which was used to transport supplies to the besieged city and was undergoing constant bomber attacks. In late 1941, pilots of the 13th Fighter Air Regiment joined in this not widely acknowledged air battle, which lasted with some minor breaks for nearly two years. Stationed at Vystav and Novaya Ladoga airfields, pilots of the regiment shot down 54 German aircraft between 12 March and 13 April 1942, at the expense of only two I-16s. The majority of victories were scored by the regiment in its new capacity: in mid-March it was renamed the 4th Guards Fighter Air Regiment.

These pilots deserved their distinguished new 'Guards' title, as before summer 1942, many of them were credited with 10 enemy aircraft 'kills'. Captain Golubev, who was appointed the regiment's Commander, personally destroyed 27 enemy aircraft in his I-16 before the end of 1943. These included the two Fw 190 downed by him on 10 and 15 January 1943. Later, the regiment converted to the La-5s, and Golubev subsequently raised his score to 39. As for the I-16s, aircraft of this type were still operated by the 3rd and 4th Guards Fighter Air Regiments up until 1944.

In the northern segment of the front, near Murmansk, the 145th Fighter Air Regiment of the 14th Army Air Force was the most powerful fighter unit. The regiment was equipped with 56 I-16s, some of which had been in service with it from the time of the Winter War. The I-16s of the 145th Fighter Air Regiment bore the main burden of combat in the region in this first stage of the war.

However, the 72nd Mixed Air Regiment of the Northern Fleet Air Force, which was stationed in the same area on Vaenga airfield, became even better known than the 145th. The most successful pilot in the region, Boris Feoktistovich Safonov, flew with the 72nd Regiment, the operations of which also involved use of the I-16s, and later became its commander (by when it was renamed as the 2nd Guards Mixed Air Regiment).

The 72nd Mixed Air Regiment received the first four I-16 Type 24s in April 1941. These aircraft were used for pilot training, and only three of them remained serviceable at the onset of the war. In one of them, Squadron Leader Senior Lieutenant Safonov shot down his first German aircraft (a Ju 88) on 24 June 1941. After the beginning of the war, another 22 I-16s arrived, but their number gradually decreasing until 1943.

In autumn, the 72nd Mixed Air Regiment converted to the British Hawker Hurricanes, and later to American-built Curtiss P-40 Kittihawks. Before Safonov began to fly fighters of other types in September 1941, his combat score in the I-16 had reached 14 enemy aircraft.

Flown by a skilful pilot, the I-16 remained a dangerous adversary in 1942. After a year of warfare, the *Ishak*'s combat loss rate remained lower than that of other aircraft types, including more modern ones. *Luftwaffe* pilots who fought on the Eastern Front by no means thought of it as easy prey. While the Germans were, on nearly all occasions, able to force their initiative on an I-16 pilot, they still tried to avoid a manoeuvring engagement with the Russian 'old-timer'. The

German pilots used to say that "one should avoid driving the rat into a corner", as the *Rata* pilot nearly always then had an opportunity to make use of the manoeuvring capabilities of his aircraft.

Hero of the Soviet Union Colonel N. Ignatyev fought in an I-16 in 1942 with the 728th Fighter Air Regiment on the Kalinin Front. In a conversation with aviation historian V. Ivanov, the elderly Ignatyev recalled that they were flying in the I-16 Type 5s, but claimed they never experienced fear when encountering German fighters. Furthermore, he said that in combat they always strove to act daringly and resolutely. Almost all of his fellow pilots had arrived at the front having flown a considerable number of hours as instructors, which meant they had excellent knowledge of the I-16. In particular, on combat patrol sorties, former instructors pre-deflected their ailerons through several degrees downwards, which helped to make the aircraft more stable and even allowed hands-off flying and increased their 'loiter' time. In encounters with the enemy, several I-16s would engage them while a pair of Soviet fighters were loitering at a higher altitude. As Ignatyev put it, "If the Germans attempted to disengage from a manoeuvring combat, the watching pair fired RS rocket projectiles at them, and made them return to their place."

In *Fighter Aviation Tactics*, a specially issued manual published in 1943, the following was stated:

The I-16 aircraft is, of course, inferior to the Me-109 in terms of speed; however, in terms of manoeuvrability it excels the Me-109. The I-16 is not able to force the air combat to a Messerschmitt if the latter is not willing to fight; but the I-16 is quite capable of doing away with an opponent which engages willingly. The I-16 can always dodge a Me-109's attack provided that the I-16 pilot notices the enemy early enough. Usually, the I-16 uses head-on attacks in a combat with the latter. For the I-16, just like for fighters of any type, altitude advantage is of high importance. When a Me-109 is being attacked from the upper front hemisphere, the latter's pilot is not protected in any way. An I-16, positioned above, may also attack the Me-109 at a descent from the rear. Therefore, for a group of the I-16, it is essential that they have altitude advantage and altitude separation, so that at least one pair is positioned above.

However, the number of the 'old-timers' in combat units was steadily decreasing. In the naval aviation, the presence of I-16s from 1942 until the end of the war was as follows:

	1 May 1942	1 July 1942	18 November 1942	1 July 1943	1 January 1944	1 June 1944	1 January 1945
Air Force of the Norther Fleet	12/3*	8/3	10/6	5/0	4/0	3/1	1/0
Air Force of the Red Banner Baltic Fleet	52/17	23/7	28/11	21/3	8/1	–	–
Air Force of the Black Sea Fleet	27/7	14/8	8/2	3/1	7/3	2/0	–
Total	91/27	45/18	46/19	29/4	19/4	5/1	1/0

* The first number shows the aircraft total, while the second shows the number unserviceable as of that date.

In spring 1942, the highest number of I-16s were in service with the Air Defence Forces, with 333 aircraft of this type providing protection for rear area objects and large cities. Apart from the already mentioned VI Fighter Air Corps of the Moscow Air Defence Forces and the VII Fighter Air Corps of the Leningrad Air Defence Forces, there were 118 I-16s in the VIII Fighter Air Corps of the Baku Air Defence Forces, while 13 I-16s of the 106th Fighter Air Division were protecting Bologoye, 24 I-16s of the 102nd Fighter Air Division of the Air Defence Forces were dealing with the protection of Stalingrad and eight I-16s of the 105th Fighter Air Division of the Air Defence Forces were providing cover for Rostov-on-Don. In summer 1942, the presence of I-16s in air defence units even grew, to 348, but from the autumn they began to dwindle, with the fighters being sent to the front. In mid-1943, the Air Defence Forces mustered 143 I-16s; by the end of the year, there remained just some 40 aircraft of the type. By 1944, the I-16s had bene completely ousted from the Air Defence Forces by more advanced aircraft.

Front-line units of the Red Army Air Force saw the most intensive attrition of the I-16s. In spite of the increased volume of newly arriving aircraft, there were 240 I-16s at the front in late 1941. Up until mid-1942, this number was more or less successfully maintained by means of repairs and replenishments arriving from rear units. Aircraft repairs were carried out in front-line repair shops and at certain factories. Thus, for example, after the evacuation of Aviation Factory No.51 to Novosibirsk, repair shops were arranged at factory facilities in Moscow. Before June 1943, 31 I-16s were repaired there.

In May 1942, the largest quantity of the *Ishaks* was concentrated on the South-western Front near Kharkov. In mid-May, Soviet aviation there totalled approximately 300 fighters of different types. The I-16s constituted slightly below a quarter of the total number. Up to 70 I-16s of all versions were in service with the following fighter air regiments: 40th, 43rd, 88th, 161st, 271st, 282nd, 446th, 581st and 762nd. There were also some with the 3rd Separate Air Squadron.

At that time, the *Ishaks* were used not only employed in the role of fighters, but also as ground-attack and reconnaissance aircraft. When night bomber regiments appeared at the front, some of the I-16s were handed to them and used in night operations, with their main task being the destruction of searchlights. However, the number of these fighters at the front decreased noticeably in 1942: at the end of the year, there remained only 75 combat-worthy I-16s. By mid-1943, just 42 I-16s were in operation near the front line.

According to the Record of Combat Losses in the Red Army Air Force, 1944 became the last official year of the I-16's service. The decommissioned aircraft included 538 I-16 M-25s and 65 I-16 M-62s and M-63s. The number of airplanes lost in accidents and crashes totalled 55. Other aircraft (a total of 549) were written off due to wear, being deemed unfit for further use.

Up Until August 1945, I-16s, together with I-15bis, were in service with the 888th Fighter Air Regiment stationed near Petropavlovsk-Kamchatsky at Ozernaya airfield. According to Kamchatka researcher S.A. Zakurdayev, the fuel tanker *Sakhalin* was sent to Kamchatka from Vladivostok in July/August 1943. The tanker was already approaching Petropavlovsk when it was attacked by Aichi D3A1 Val Japanese dive-bombers, which had taken off from Shumshu. I-16 fighters of the 888th Fighter Air Regiment attacked the Japanese aircraft and shot down four of them, thus saving the *Sakhalin* from destruction.

American aircraft were also being encountered by the I-16s over Kamchatka. Thus, on 12 September 1943, I-16s supported B-25 and B-24 bombers landing near Petropavlovsk. Then on 12 June 1944, they warded off Japanese fighters which were threatening a Lockheed Ventura of the USAAF and directed it to their home airfield. Cases are also known when the Americans assisted I-16s in combat with Japanese fighters.

Air operations around Kamchatka remained intensive right up to the end of the war. Pilots of the 888th Fighter Air Regiment were dealing with American aircraft until 1945: the known cases included landings by B-24s on 25 September 1944 and on 11 May 1945.

It was in the Far East that the *Ishaks* remained in service for longest of all. As of 9 August 1945, the Pacific Fleet Air Force still mustered 14 I-16s. However, when it came to hostilities, there was no need to disturb the 'distinguished veteran' – there were quite enough modern combat aircraft in 1945.

1.6.7. *'Vakhmistrov's Circus'*

'Vakhmistrov's Circus' was the name given to one of the most exotic ways of using the I-16s, suspended under the wing of a Tupolev TB-3 mothership. The original idea of airborne aircraft carriers was developed in the 1930s by engineer Vladimir Vakhmistrov. Originally, in 1931, he arranged two I-4 fighters on the wings of a TB-1 two-engine bomber, so that the fighters were able to disengage in mid-air to protect their mothership. The system was given the designation *Zveno-1* (the Russian word *Zveno* stood for 'chain link' or a military unit 'flight') and was successfully tested in 1931–32.

Vakhmistrov continued to improve the original design and suggested several new options on the platform of the TB-3 heavy four-engine bomber. The systems, designated *Zveno-2*, *-3*, *-4* and *-5*, utilised various combinations of the I-5, I-Z and I-16 fighters. In 1934, the most successful combination of the TB-3, with two I-16 fighters, was created. It was initially designated *Zveno-6*. The I-16 taxied in under the bomber's wing on its own and was positioned under the attachment mechanisms. Each fighter was attached using three locks, two of which were arranged on its wing, with the third one on the fuselage's rear behind the pilot's head. After the fighters were attached to the bomber, the I-16 pilots retracted the landing gear and the whole system was ready for take-off. The *Zveno-6* was tested for two years and fully met the designer's expectations: indeed, the results turned out to be brilliant.

The peculiar feature of the *Zveno-6* consisted in the provisions for feeding the fighters with fuel from the bomber's tanks. This component of the system was developed by the special-purpose Design Bureau No.1 of the Air Force Administration under the supervision of designer Zapanovanny. It was intended to further use this principle for inflight refuelling of other I-16s which were not components of the *Zveno* configuration. During the tests in spring 1936, the I-16 s/n 23915 was used for this purpose. The process, in essence, was rather simple. A hose was lowered from the TB-3 refuelling aircraft. The fighter pilot was expected to catch the tip of the hose and connect it to the filling socket on the left side of the I-16. As soon as the fuel tank was full, the hose tip automatically disconnected from the socket. Since the fighter aircraft pilot had to catch the hose with one hand, the throttle control lever was arranged on the control stick. In June 1936, pilots Sokolov, Suprun and Evseev test-flew the I-16, which had been subjected to the abovementioned modifications. On 22 June 1936, Senior Lieutenant Evseev, who was one of the most experienced aerobatic and military test pilots, successfully performed two inflight fuel transfers.

In 1935, another configuration was evaluated when five fighters (two I-5s, two I-16s and an I-Z) were attached to the TB-3 while the I-Z was attached under the fuselage of the mothership in mid-air. Vakhmistrov himself named this complex configuration *Aviamatka* (airborne mothership), and suggested the future attachment of up to eight I-16s to the

TB-3. It was intended that two fighters would be placed on top of the *Aviamatka* wing, while six I-16s were to dock with the TB-3 from below in shifts (three aircraft in each shift) in order to refuel. This extraordinary 'airborne stack' was expected to find application in air defense forces, with an estimated patrol time of 6.5 hours.

In practice, however, there were never more than two I-16s suspended under the TB-3's wing. As for in-flight docking of the fighters, such work never went further than several successful trials. In the *Zveno-7* system, a special-purpose lowering truss with a trapeze was arranged under the TB-3's right wing. On the I-16, a three-strut pyramid with a yoke and lock was mounted on top of the fuselage. The docking took place at a speed of 155–160km/h, after which the bomber crew pulled the fighter up until it touched special stops on the lower surface of the wing. In summer 1938, several mid-air dockings were performed successfully. The aircraft were flown by NII VVS test pilots Stepan Suprun and Petr Stefanovsky.

In 1938, Vakhmistrov changed the tasks for the suspended fighters and decided to use them as dive-bombers. Each of the I-16s could carry two FAB-250 bombs, and the radius of action of the fighters was increased by 80 percent due to inflight refuelling from the mothership. The maximum range of the entire system thus reached 2,500km.

On approach to the target, the pilot of the TB-3 gave a signal to disengage, whereupon a special annunciator panel lit up under the TB-3 wing and a horn sounded for the fighters to duplicate the light indication. Pilots of the I-16s released the aft locks on their aircraft and pulled the control stick; as a result, the angle of attack increased and, with the aircraft turned through 3°30', the wing locks released automatically. After disengagement, the dive-bombers hurtled towards the target.

With two FAB-250 bombs, the I-16 Type 5 had a maximum speed of 410km/h at an altitude of 2,500 metres, while the service ceiling reached 6,800m. The dive was performed at a speed of 650km/h. After the bombs were dropped, the I-16 remained a full-fledged fighter capable of conducting aerial combat. An advantage of the proposed technique consisted in the most efficient use of the obsolescent TB-3 bombers, a considerable number of which was still in service with the Red Army Air Force.

In summer 1938, the system designated *Zveno-SPB* (*Skorostnoy Pikiruyushiy Bombardirovshik*, or High-speed Dive Bomber) was successfully tested. Marshal Voroshilov and People's Commissar of the Navy Frinovsky supported the idea of accepting such airborne aircraft carriers for service. The following decree of the Defence Committee of the USSR was issued in October 1938:

1. *Zveno-SPB* shall be accepted for service by the VVS and Naval Aviation of RKKA.
2. The People's Commissariat of Defence Industry shall provide by 1 February 1939 the components for attaching the aircraft using Comrade Vakhmistrov's method:
- 20 TB-3 AM-34RN aircraft for the VVS RKKA;
- 20 TB-3 AM-34RN aircraft for the Naval Aviation;
- 40 I-16 aircraft for the VVS RKKA;
- 40 I-16 aircraft for the Naval Aviation.

It was suggested that Vakhmistrov should present a plan to the government for the further development of his designs. Inspired by the success, the designer promptly created several new projects involving the newest TB-7 bomber, MTB-2 and GST flying boats, I-16 fighter carrying a 500kg bomb and I-180 fighter. However, even introduction of the already tested *Zveno-SPB* system lagged. The initial order for 40 carriers was reduced to 12; aviation factories, being loaded with work, could not begin to manufacture them for a long time.

The first series production *Zveno-SPB* system consisting of a TB-3 AM-34RN and two I-16 Type 24s was built at Aviation Factory No.207 in June 1940. The factory manufactured a total of five *Zveno-SPB* sets, which were placed in service with the 2nd Squadron of the 32nd Fighter Air Regiment of the 62nd Air Brigade of the Black Sea Fleet Air Force, which was stationed in Evpatoriya in the Crimea. Until the end of the year, the squadron was practicing tactics of the new system application using battleship mock-ups. However, in January 1941, the command of the Black Sea Fleet found the *Zveno-SPB* equipment too burdensome, so their main components were dismantled and placed in storage.

With the onset of the war, the aviation of the Black Sea Fleet was tasked with reducing supplies of Romanian oil to Germany. The Fleet's command demanded that "air strikes should be used to destroy oil tanks, repair shops, ships, and railroad depots in Constanța and Sulina … as well as the enemy's onshore facilities on the Danube". The railroad bridge across the Danube near the station of Cernavodă, 60km west of Constanța, was deemed one of the most important targets for the bombing aviation. Some 1,662m long and 75 metres tall at its highest point, this was a major bridgework. The bridge carried the Ploiești–Constanța oil pipeline laid under its lower deck. Destruction of the bridge would block all railway transportation between Bucharest and other industrial centres, cut off the main transport communication with the port of Constanța and undermine delivery of supplies for Romanian troops. Multiple attempts by the 63rd Bomber Air Brigade of the Black Sea Fleet to destroy the bridge using SB and DB-3 bombers had failed.

At that time, a decision was made to promptly restore Vakhmistrov's systems for further combat use. On 22 July 1941, an order for use of the *Zveno-SPB* was received from Moscow, then on 26 July, the first combat raid on Constanța's port facilities took place. In broad daylight, a pair of the TB-3s approached the Romanian shore. The four fighters disconnected

An I-16 Type 4 being pulled up by BL-4 winch under the TB-3 4M-17 wing using the *Zveno-6* system in 1934.

View of the wing of an I-16 Type 4 attached to TB-3 4M-17 in the *Zveno-6* system. Note the intercom and fuel supply connections.

An *Aviamatka* with two I-5s, two I-16s and an I-Z mid-air in 1935.

The lowering truss for attaching the I-16 under the wing of a TB-3 4M-17 in the *Zveno-7* system.

An I-16 Type 5 fitted with a 'yoke'-type pyramid for docking with a TB-3 in flight in the *Zveno-7* system.

An I-16 Type 5 piloted by Stepan Suprun approaching a TB-3 wing from below to perform mid-air docking.

An I-16 Type 5 attached under the wing of a TB-3 using the *Zveno-7* system in 1938.

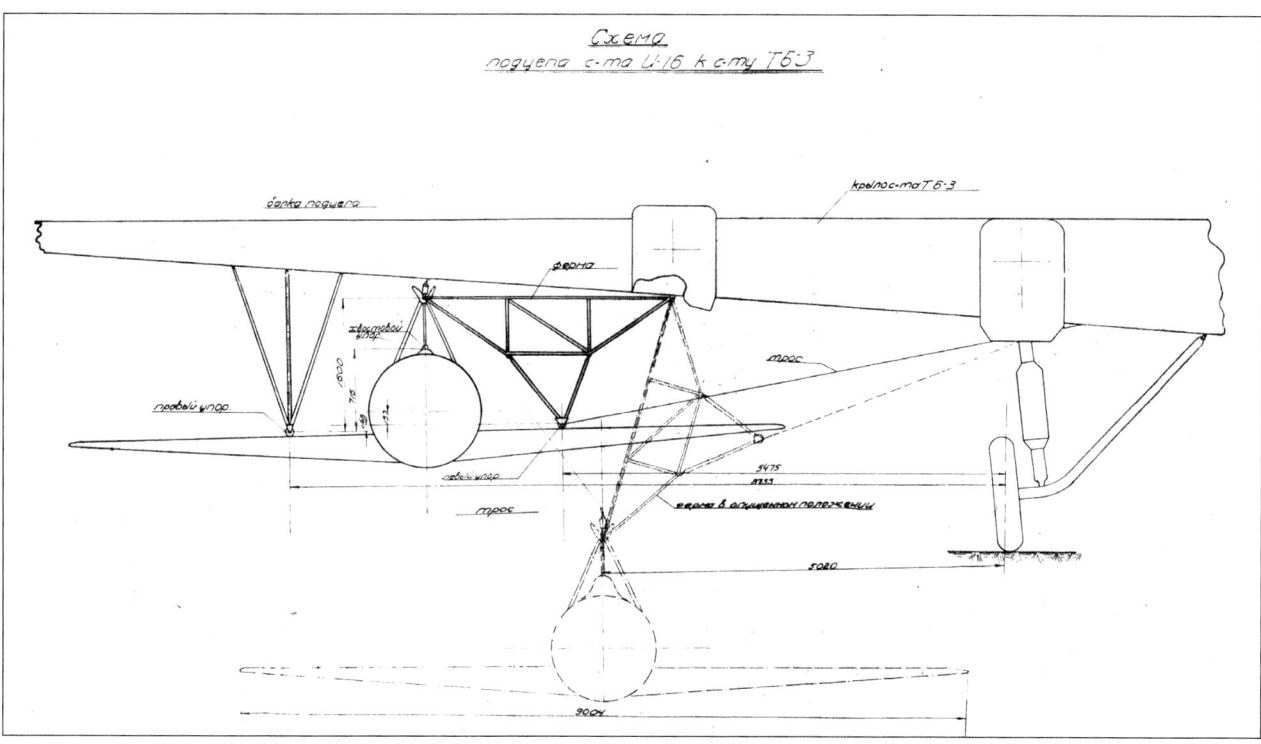

The I-16 fighter 137

The original scheme of attaching the I-16 under a TB-3 wing in the *Zveno-7* system.

A bent pyramid with a yoke on an I-16 after an attempted mid-air docking.

An I-16 Type 5 under a TB-3 wing before being attached on the ground in the *Zveno-SPB* 1938 version.

Fittings on the wing of an I-16 Type 5 for attachment to a TB-3 in the *Zveno-SPB* system.

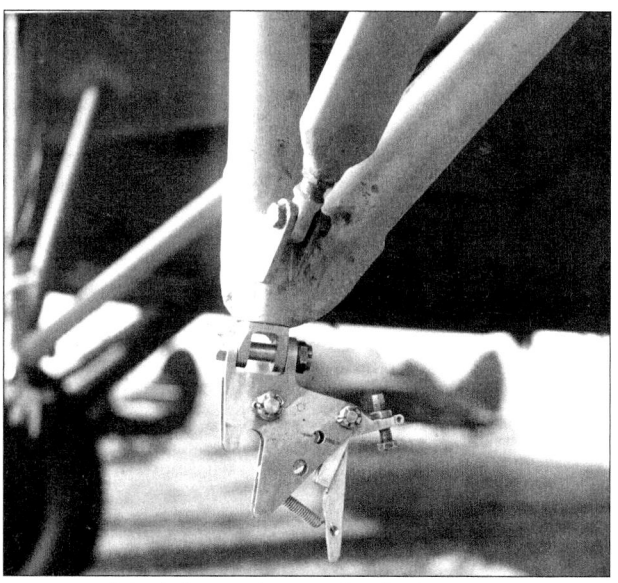

A lock for attachment of an I-16 wing to the pyramid arranged under the TB-3 wing, using the *Zveno-SPB* 1938 version.

Part of an I-16 wing centre section with visible elements for attachment of a FAB-250 bomb.

A FAB-250 under the right wing of an I-16 Type 5.

An I-16 of the *Zveno-SPB* 1938 version is fully prepared for flight.

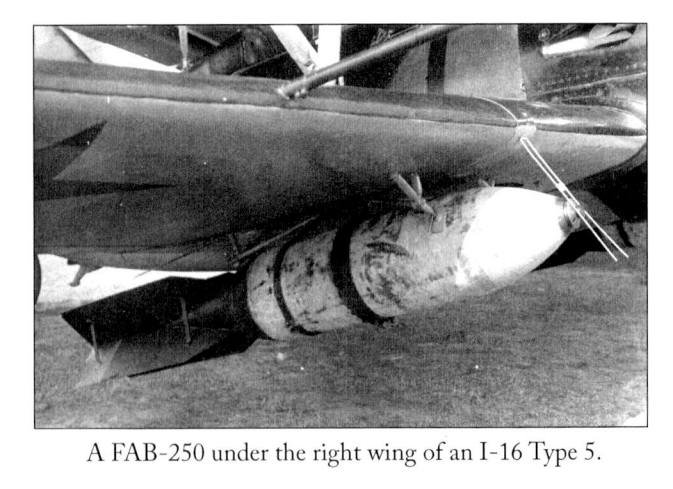

The TB-3 4M-34FRN with I-16s attached to it, using the *Zveno-SPB* 1938 version.

Disconnection of an I-16 carrying two FAB-250 bombs from a TB-3, using the *Zveno-SPB* 1938 version.

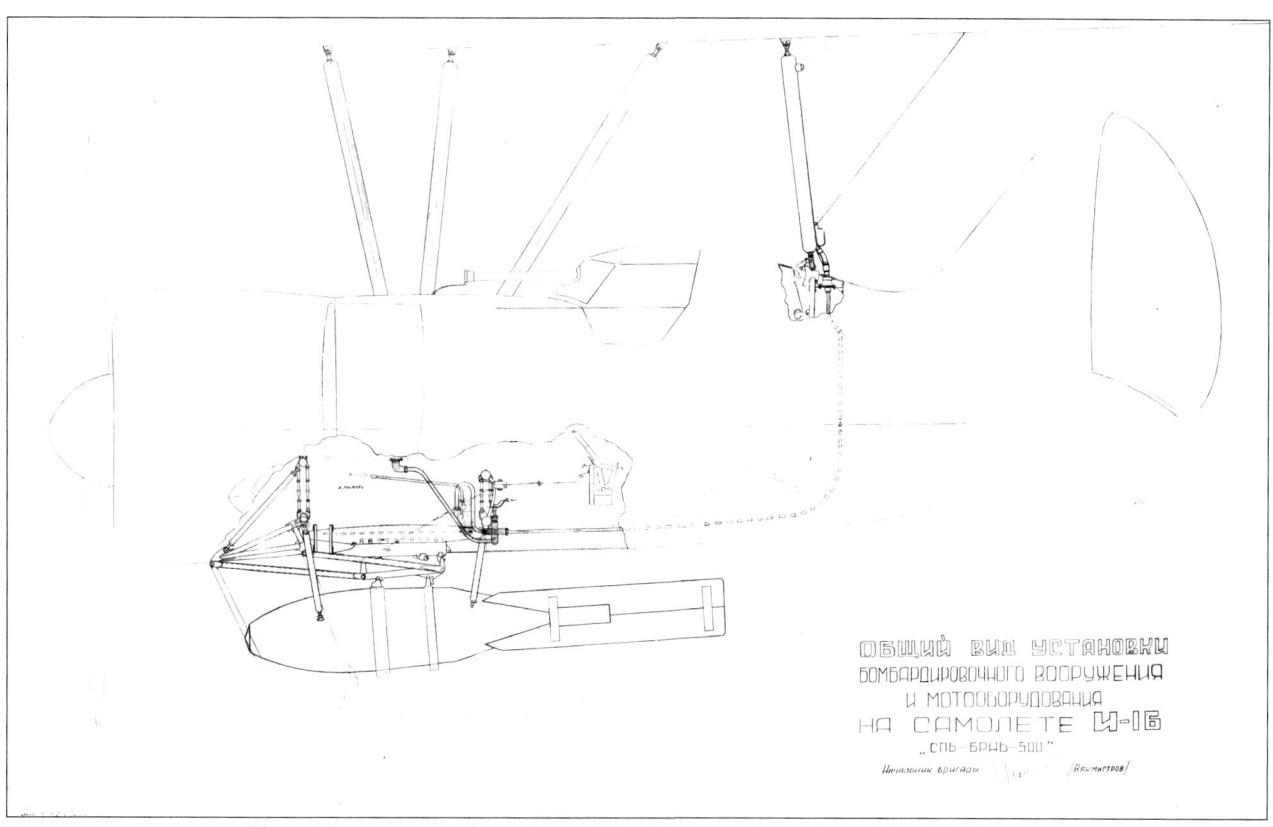

The original scheme of the *Zveno-SPB* with an I-16 carrying a FAB-250 bomb.

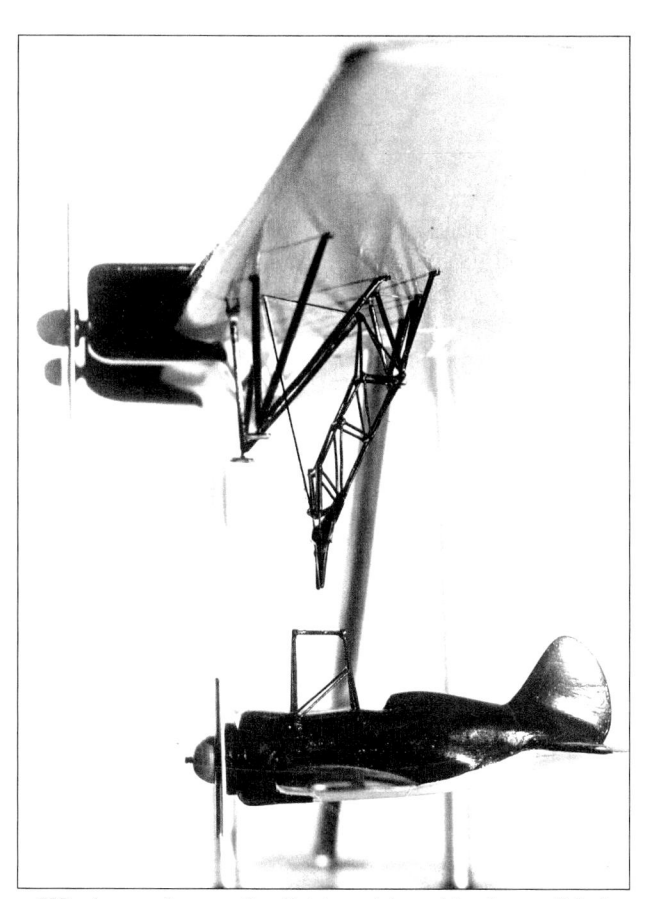

Wind-tunnel tests of an I-16 model used in the modified *Zveno-7* system in 1940–41. It was expected that three I-16s would dock with the mothership in mid-air in this version.

40km from the target. One pair of the I-16s successfully attacked the oil depot, while the other dropped their bombs on a floating dry dock. All four fighters then flew to their home airfield at high speed. An intermediate landing was made in Odessa, then, after refuelling, the aircraft flew to Evpatoriya.

For the attack on the Cernavodă bridge, three motherships and six fighters were prepared. The I-16s were fitted with additional 95-litre ventral tanks, providing an extra 35 minutes of flight. At 3:00 a.m. on 10 August, all three TB-3s took off from their Crimean airfield. One of them turned back halfway and returned to base due to a malfunction. However, the other two launched their fighters after a flight of two hours and 10 minutes, 310km from their home base and 15km from the enemy coastline. Fifteen minutes later, the four dive-bombers approached the target and were met with dense anti-aircraft fire. Having broken through the AA screen, the fighters dived from an altitude of 1,800m, dropping their bombs at a height of 300m. Thereafter, they left the area at high speed, landing at Odessa airfield for refuelling at 6:40 a.m.

The raid on the bridge was repeated on 13 August, this time with six dive bombers. Everything followed the same pattern as the previous sortie, but with the start time brought forward by half an hour. The attack took place this time at 5:50 a.m. The pilots scored five direct hits on the bridge and completely destroyed one of the spans. On the way back, all six fighters attacked enemy infantry with machine-gun fire near Sulina, then they landed in Odessa at 7:05 a.m.

This success restored interest in the *Zveno-SPB* system on the part of the Navy command. Consequently, a decision was made to bring the total number of airborne aircraft carriers up to the originally planned 12. However, further re-equipment was now limited by the lack of TB-3s with the M-34RN engine. The TB-3s of earlier series powered by M-17 engines were not fit for carrying aircraft due to their gross weight limitations. Out of 12 TB-3 4M-34RN bombers available with the Black Sea Fleet, five were duly modified as I-16 carriers, while the other seven were left for the performance of air transportation tasks. On 16 August 1941, Commander of the Navy Admiral Kuznetsov addressed Joseph Stalin with a request to transfer 10 such bombers from the RKKA Air Force to the Navy. However, losses of these low-speed giants during the first months of the war were rather heavy; for this reason, the request was denied.

Meanwhile, the use of the available carriers with suspended dive-bombers continued. On 17 August, six I-16s destroyed a floating dry dock in Constanța. At the end of the month, a *Zveno-SPB* group was tasked with destroying bridges across the Dnieper which were being used by the advancing German troops. On 28 August, two TB-3s took off from Evpatoriya airfield and headed for the area around Zaporozhye. At dawn, 30km from the city, the I-16s disconnected. The raid on the crossing was sudden and precise; all four I-16s returned, with no losses. On 8 September, *Zveno-SPB*s, in cooperation with Yak-1 air cover fighters, destroyed a crossing near Berislav. One Yak-1 and an I-16 did not return from this combat sortie. On the day after the bombing raid on the Dnieper crossings, four I-16s engaged German fighters and shot down two Bf 109s.

Further sorties were flown by the suspended I-16s in combat conditions which were worsening for the Red Army. In late September, German troops launched an offensive in the northern part of the Crimea. All available Soviet forces – even those designed for precision strikes in the enemy's rear – were involved in staving off the offensive. The TB-3s were at that time often used only to lift the loaded I-16s, the fighters being unable to take off under their own power with two 250kg bombs. Having dropped their bombs, the I-16s joined in aerial combat, which often resulted in heavy losses. On 2 October, Commander of the 32nd Squadron Captain Shubikov was killed in an engagement with German fighters.

There were no further reports on use of *Zveno-SPB*s. By October 1941, these airborne aircraft carriers had flown over 30 combat sorties carrying the I-16s.

1.6.8. The I-16s with rocket projectiles

The emergence of rocket armament in the USSR in the 1930s was preceded by a long process of improvement of the projectiles themselves and their launchers. The first experiments with installation of rocket projectiles on aircraft took place in 1934, but five years passed before 82mm RS-82s were first used in a combat environment.

In 1936–37, RS-82 rocket projectiles were tested on the I-5 and I-15 biplanes. As for the I-16, there were concerns that rocket gases would affect the skin of its wider wing and the aircraft ailerons in the process of firing. Eventually, however, the doubts were cast aside, and the I-16 Type 5 s/n 521253 was equipped with underwing rocket launchers in 1937. In view of the satisfactory results of firing from this fighter, it was planned to equip another 100 I-16s with rocket launchers in 1938. However, a year passed before they began to be installed in the *Ishak*s. During that period, certain changes occurred; in particular, new RO-82 launchers were designed. Made in the form of a beam with a tee rail, and known not only as 'rocket launchers' (RO, *raketnoye orudiye*) but also as a 'flute-type mount', they really took root in the I-16s. Compared with the initially used launchers (PS-82), the RO-82 offered noticeably lower air flow resistance. A set of eight such launchers (four under each wing, with a 200mm pitch) weighed only 20kg and brought about a 5–7km/h reduction in flight speed.

Production of the RO-82 was set up at Factory No.32 of the People's Commissariat of Defence Industry in Moscow. It was intended that 150 I-16s would be equipped with such launchers in 1939. However, practical implementation was, as usual, much more modest.

In April 1939, RO-82 launchers were mounted on two I-16 Type 10s, which were used not only for tests but also for pilot training. Simultaneously, an order was placed with Factory No.21 for equipping 35 series production aircraft with rocket launchers, to be completed in May 1939. The factory designation Type 23, which was introduced at that time for the rocket-armed I-16s, was in use for several months. As has been noted above, the designation was not introduced in practice.

During the period from 19 June to 15 July 1939, the Air Force conducted a special training course at the Aviation Armament Range (*Poligon Aviatsionnykh Voorazheniy*). Flight crews and technical personnel received theoretical training, familiarised themselves with maintenance of the RS-82 and took part in practice firing. After the training course, test pilot Captain Zvonarev was tasked with forming a group of experienced pilots to conduct tests in a combat environment – the conflict on Khalkhin Gol was in full swing.

Five I-16 Type 10s (s/ns 1021878, 1021879, 1021880, 1021881 and 1021882) were prepared first and sent by rail to Mongolia. The flight personnel of the group included Senior Lieutenant N. Tochkov, Senior Lieutenant S. Pimenov, Lieutenant V. Fedoseev, Lieutenant V.A. Mikhailenko and Lieutenant F. Makarov. The group's technical personnel consisted of Military Engineer Class 2 A. Popovich, Military Technician Class 1 A. Gubin and Military Technician Class 2 V. Popenko.

The I-16s, equipped with eight RO-82 underwing rail launchers each, were brought to the base of the Transbaikal Military District on 1 August 1939. At the same time, the RS-82 rocket projectiles, AGDT-A time fuses and AM-A detonating fuses arrived. Aircraft assembly and test flights were completed on 5 August.

On 7 August, the aircraft were flown to a front-line airfield; technical personnel and ammunition arrived on a TB-3 transport. Preparations for a combat sortie began almost immediately. By the morning of 8 August, one ammunition package (40 rocket projectiles) was attached to an I-16. Another package of RS-82s was kept near the aircraft.

Initially, Captain Zvonarev's group joined the 22nd Fighter Air Regiment under Major G. Kravchenko. As it was believed that aircraft of the group would not take part in manoeuvring air combat, wing-mounted machine guns were removed from them. Experience showed that such a decision was erroneous, and after the first combat sorties, ShKAS machine guns were reinstalled.

It was intended that air targets would be fired upon in four-rocket salvos at a distance of 1,500m in a head-on attack, and from 860m in a pursuit attack. The time fuses in the rocket projectiles were set within the limits of 2.8–4.2 seconds, which corresponded to an average firing distance of 1,000–1,500m at the aircraft's speed of 360km/h at an altitude of 4,000m.

During the period from 8–19 August, the I-16s flew sorties with RS-82s for purposes of familiarisation with the terrain and the position of home airfields. Flying across the front line was strictly forbidden; for this reason, the group did not take part in active aerial combats which occurred from 12–14 August.

The first use of the rocket projectiles in combat took place on 20 August. Five I-16s took off in response to a red flare signal when enemy fighters appeared in the sky. Four I-153s of the 22nd Fighter Air Regiment escorted the five I-16.

Before Zvonarev's group approached the front line, fighters scrambled from other airfields had also reached the area. The aerial combat involving several dozen aircraft almost immediately turned into a series of dogfights, so the possibility of firing the rocket projectiles on a group target was excluded.

Three aircraft from the group of five attacked the enemy together with fighters from other units with their machine-gun fire only. A pair of the I-16s flown by Zvonarev and Fedoseev detected a separate group of Ki-27s, upon which they fired a salvo of 12 rocket projectiles. Almost immediately they were attacked by enemy fighters and had to engage in a manoeuvring aerial combat. Zvonarev's aircraft disengaged riddled with nine bullet holes, while 14 holes were later found in Fedoseev's aircraft. Ground observers of the 22nd Fighter Air Regiment reported three Ki-27s shot down after the attack with the RS. Other eyewitnesses reported two crashed aircraft. Later, the RS-armed group was credited with a single valid victory. On the same day, RS-armed I-16s flew two more sorties but did not take part in any combats.

On 21 August, Zvonarev's group flew ahead of other units on a sortie towards the front line. They fired their RS-82s, then disengaged and returned to the airfield to replenish ammunition. Six combat sorties were flown on that day, in three of which the fighters took part in a manoeuvring combat. The group expended 102 rocket projectiles and shot down two SB-96 (Mitsubishi G3M) bombers and a Ki-27 fighter. On 22 August, the five I-16s took part in five combat sorties, shooting down another Ki-27.

Three days later, participants in the testinf decided that as their five aircraft were cumbersome and not manoeuvrable enough, they would subsequently act in groups of two and three aircraft. At the same time, they said the firing distance had to be reduced, which was achieved by setting the time fuses to 1,100m.

In further sorties, the I-16s still had no opportunity to meet large enemy forces, but did fire on small groups of three to five aircraft (in one case, on nine aircraft). In spite of the fact that the enemy airplanes usually had a more favourable position and were above the attackers, their formation always became dispersed regardless of the attack's outcome, proving the psychological impact of the rocket projectiles on the enemy's morale.

On 2 September 1939, the RS-82-armed I-16s were redeployed to a forward airfield near the Khamar-Daban mountains, 6km from the Khalkhin Gol river. They operated from this airfield until 16 September. The intensity of Japanese aerial operations in September became noticeably lower, so the I-16s had no opportunity of encountering a large aircraft formation. The enemy kept appearing in small groups at a considerably higher altitude than the I-16s, without displaying any willingness to engage. During the period from 8 August to 15 September, the I-16 group flew a total of 59 combat sorties, took part in 16 aerial combats involving RS firing and made use of the machine guns in six combats.

According to the records of the command post of the 22nd Fighter Air Regiment, during the course of combat operations, the RS-82-armed I-16s shot down 14 Ki-27s, two SB-96s and an LB-97 (Mitsubishi Ki-30). Among other results, hitting two Tupolev SB Soviet bombers was also noted. The final report made special mention of the fact that the SB-96 (Mitsubishi G3M) Japanese bomber was barely distinguishable from the Soviet Tupolev SB bomber at a distance of over 2km, especially in a head-on position.

Throughout the period of combat operations, Zvonarev's group expended 413 RS-82 rocket projectiles, with 16 failures occurring due to armament defects. The number of spent rounds for ShKAS machine guns turned out to be relatively low, totalling 21,690. Collective victories won by the group with the help of small-arms fire were not taken into account in the total score.

The first combat application of the RS-armed I-16s allowed the conclusion that they could be further used as a means of aerial combat to counteract fighters and bombers, and in strafing operations against personnel, cavalry, motorised columns and anti-aircraft and field artillery positions.

Salvo firing by a group of three aircraft from a distance of 1,000m was found to be the most efficient tactic. Further, there were suggestions that the PAK-1 gunsight should be modified, and the Pitot tube should be relocated along the wing span from the zone affected by firing gases of RS rocket projectiles being launched. Mounting a radio and more powerful M-62 engines was deemed mandatory. It was recommended that each fighter squadron should in future include an RS-armed group.

After the first use of RS-82 rocket projectiles in a combat environment in summer 1939, series production aircraft began to be equipped with such armament. Before the end of 1939, Factory No.21 supplied 31 RS-armed fighters to the military. However, there is no data confirming that Factory No.21 was equipping fighters with rocket armament on a large scale.

In early July 1940, the following note was prepared for the Head of the Chief Directorate of Aviation Supplies (*Glavnoye Upravleniye AviaSnabzheniya*, GUAS) of the Red Army Air Force, Division Engineer I. Sakrier: "Factory No.21: 150 I-16 fighters ordered to be equipped with RS during the first half-year. 78 aircraft ready. Of them, only 14 assembled and test-flown. Factory No.1: 126 I-153 fighters ordered to be equipped with RS during the first half-year. 106 aircraft ready."

Simultaneously, Factories Nos.70 and 12 of the People's Commissariat of Ammunition manufactured 11,230 RS-82 and 5,240 RS-132 rocket projectiles.

To evaluate the scale of production of aircraft with provisions for use of RS rocket projectiles, below are the summaries of I-16 manufacture for August and for 10 months of 1940.

Summary of the I-16 production by Aviation Factory No.21 in August 1940 (RSI stands for radio)	
I-16 Type 24 with rocket projectile launchers	5
I-16 Type 24 with RSI-3	11
I-16 Type 24 with rocket projectile launchers and RSI-3	11
I-16 Type 24 with RSI-4	5
I-16 Type 28 with external fuel tanks	6
I-16 Type 28 with RSI-3	5
I-16 Type 29 with external fuel tanks	1
I-16 Type 29 with RSI-3	9
I-16 Type 29 with rocket projectile launchers	1
I-180 Type 25 with external fuel tanks	1
UTI-4 Type 15	105
Total	160

Summary of the I-16 production by Aviation Factory No.21 as of 1 November 1940	
I-16 Type 24	586
I-16 Type 24 with rocket projectile launchers	86
I-16 Type 28	239
I-16 Type 29	57
I-16 Type 29 with rocket projectile launchers	44
UTI-4 Type 15	409
Total	1,421

In mid-1940, rocket projectiles were still rare equipment for the RKKA Air Force. At that time, only two I-16 units were equipped with them, namely the 22nd Fighter Air Regiment of the Transbaikal Military District (seven I-16s at the airfield in Bain-Tumen) and the 24th Fighter Air Regiment in Kubinka near Moscow. It should be noted that the aircraft flew with RO-82 launchers but never performed air firing. Under such conditions, the equipment tended to become loose and worn; some of the components already required replacement.

On 9 August 1940, the General Staff of the RKKA circulated an order for commanders of Air Forces of military districts and of the Far Eastern Front demanding the removal of all rocket armament from aircraft and to place it in storage. They were also prohibited from providing technical manuals and descriptions for RO rail launchers and RS rocket projectiles to pilots and officers until further orders.

However, manufacture of the rocket projectiles and rail launchers themselves continued. In accordance with the RKKA supply plans, by 1 January 1941, the factories had to supply 600 RS-32-armed I-16s for the Air Force against the main order. The total number of RS-32-armed I-16s actually supplied before the mentioned date was probably more modest and did not exceed 300. The exact figure of the equipped aircraft was determined on 14 April 1941 (in a report by the Chief Administration of Air Force addressed to Air Force Commander P.F. Zhigarev): 28 I-16s manufactured in 1939, 275 I-16s manufactured in 1940 and 38 I-16s manufactured in 1941. Afterwards, these figures underwent almost no changes due to discontinuation of the *Ishak*'s production.

However, up to the beginning of the war with Germany, pilots knew very little of the new armament. This is confirmed by numerous post-war recollections. Vasily Golubev, a pilot of the 13th Fighter Air Regiment of the Red Banner Baltic Fleet Air Force, later described training in the unit in spring 1941 as follows:

In the 2nd Squadron, the situation was easier: the pilots were simply extending their knowledge of the I-16s (Type 24, 27 and 29); their ground training programme was less extensive. They spent several days studying the electrical diagram for launching RS-82 rocket projectiles. The launcher was installed on the aircraft but it was prohibited to study it.

Then a three-sheet instruction on use of RS rocket projectiles in an air combat and for ground target strafing was received by the regiment. The wording was very concise and quite unclear. Even representatives of the Air Force Staff failed to explain why these weapons had to be used at distances of 800–1,600m, all the more so because pilots found difficulty in gauging such distances [by] eye. As for RS rocket projectiles themselves, nobody had ever seen them. People said that they were kept somewhere in the central depots under special guard. There was another instruction (an unclassified one) for use, on aircraft of these types, of external fuel tanks increasing the flight time by 40 to 45 minutes; but the tanks were not available either, and nobody knew whether the regiment was going to receive them. At any rate, there were none in the Naval Air Forces depots.

The example above is characteristic of the general state of things with installation of rocket armament on aircraft. As a result, in many cases the rocket launchers were installed by the units using their own resources. Sometimes it took place after several months of combat operations. In the course of the defense of Sevastopol, RS-82 rocket projectiles were recalled in November 1941 after the combined Black Sea Fleet aviation group had been redeployed to a new airfield in Nizhny Chorgun. A participant of the battle of Sevastopol, Hero of the Soviet Union Konstantin Denisov (at that time a pilot with the 8th Fighter Air Regiment) described the situation in his book *The Black Sea Below Us*: "In conclusion, General Ostryakov [Commander of the Black Sea Fleet Air Force] gave instructions that two or three pilots should be assigned to each aircraft, so that the load on each aircraft per day was 12 to 15 combat sorties. To enable this, maintenance of the fighters on a two-shift or three-shift basis had to be arranged. Furthermore, all the I-16s and I-153s had to be additionally equipped with special devices, each of which was intended to accommodate four RS-82 rocket projectiles for destroying airborne and ground targets." Indeed, within a short time, the majority of naval fighters were fitted with four rail launchers for RS-82 rocket projectiles.

Four (or in some cases only two) underwing RS-82 rocket projectiles were not an infrequent thing. In his book *In Pair with 'Number One Hundred'*, fighter pilot G. Golubev (a Hero of the Soviet Union who in 1941 was flying with the 40th Fighter Air Regiment of the 229th Air Division), described the following episode: "In accordance with an order issued in the unit, a combat aircraft was assigned to me. That was an already old I-16 fighter whose armament consisted of two wing-mounted normal-calibre ShKAS machine guns and two RS rocket projectiles. But I was happy to have at least such [an] aircraft."

There are a number of examples illustrating successful use of the rocket projectiles in aerial combat. K. Denisov continued to describe combat operations in 1941:

'Now we attack the bombers with RS salvo!' I heard the command of my deputy Captain G.I. Matveev in my headphones. I was staying nearby and saw G. Matveev, V. Borodin, N. Nikolayev, and N. Sikov firing a salvo of 16 rocket projectiles. A group of eight Ju 88s promptly dropped their bombs chaotically and began to leave with a turn to escape pursuit; one of the Junkers caught fire and crashed into water near the passage into the North Bay. After landing, the technicians just had time to attach new RS-82 rocket projectiles under the wing, to replenish ammunition for the machine guns, and to refuel the aircraft, and then we took off again. This time, we headed for the front-line. And during all those days it was six to eight or even more sorties per day.

Hero of the Soviet Union retired Colonel N. Ignatyev spoke quite respectfully of the efficiency of use of RS-82 rocket projectiles:

After completion of training in the Leningrad Flying Club in 1937, I was sent to Chuguyev Flying School. Having graduated from it in 1939, I was left there as an instructor on the I-16. At war time, instructors were gathered to form the 728th Fighter Air Regiments in the I-16 (Type 5) aircraft. Soon we were redeployed to the North-western Front (Vypolzovo airfield) where we saw action. In January 1942, we flew to the Kalinin Front and kept changing airfields depending on the front-line situation. Our regiment provided cover for ground troops against the fascists' air attacks.

In April 1942, we ferried two I-16s to Moscow for repair. That was where I had occasion to meet designer Polikarpov. He asked us how we were fighting in his I-16 aircraft. There were a lot [of] questions, and we gave definite answers to all of his questions. He was a pleasant, good-natured, and cultured person. At the end of our conversation he said that more advanced aircraft with powerful armament, in particular, the I-185 fighter, would enter service soon. [Ignatyev took part in front-line tests of the I-185 – *Author's note.*]

Having received the repaired I-16s, we returned to our regiment on Selizharovo airfield. Soon we were redeployed to a temporary airfield near Rzhev. Rzhev at that time was occupied by the Germans.

In July 1942, our troops initiated the offensive to liberate Rzhev. We, in a group of six I-16s, met six groups of Ju 88 bombers, nine aircraft in each group, escorted by 16 Me-109s. All the six of us assumed a position for an upsun attack and, on command (the rocking of the wings), fired 24 RS-82 rocket projectiles with time fuses set to different distances. As a result of the sudden attack, six Junkers were shot down; the bombers' formation became dispersed. We engaged the Junkers and then the fighters; as a result, three Me-109 fighters were shot down. We suffered no losses of our own.

On the next day, all the six of us received the Orders of the Red Banner from a Member of the Military Council.

Hero of the Soviet Union Vasily Golubev provides the most complete account of the number of combat episodes involving use of the rocket projectiles in the I-16s. Undoubtedly, use of these weapons helped him to become one of the most efficient I-16 pilots.

On 24 October 1941, at the time of defence of the Hanko Peninsula, Golubev was flying a combat sortie in a pair with pilot Tatarenko when he encountered Finnish pilots flying captured Soviet I-153 *Chaika* aircraft.

The *Chaikas* did not accept battle: they were leaving in the eastward direction to be protected by their anti-aircraft artillery. I was approaching them but slowly. In two or three minutes they would enter the zone of their artillery defensive fire from the ground. I was pursuing the enemy tail-on. Then I fired two RS-82 rocket projectiles. One of them exploded between the upper and the lower wing; the other one, at a distance of some five metres behind. The *Chaika* burst into pieces. Overtaking me, Tatarenko was firing from machine guns upon the leading aircraft. The latter slowed down and began to descend. Probably, his engine had been damaged. In front of Tatarenko's aircraft, over a dozen anti-aircraft projectiles exploded at once; traces of two-barreled and four-barreled Oerlikons were stretching. Tatarenko ceased the pursuit. While they were transferring their fire onto me, I had time to throw a long burst from a distance of 200m. The triple trace pierced the enemy aircraft; at the same time, however, an explosion of an anti-aircraft projectile shook my aircraft as well. I pulled the control stick fiercely, depressed the pedal, and the *Ishak* began to turn in an ascending roll. That was what saved me. I went into [a] dive; the anti-aircraft gunners saw as if I were falling and ceased fire, while I pulled out, levelled off, and left the firing area. After that battle and up to the end of our stay on Hanko, we never met the enemy's *Chaikas* anymore.

Later, the fact of destruction of these aircraft was not confirmed. However, the Finnish *Chaika* VH-19 was heavily damaged, and the wounded pilot made a forced landing. Damage to the aircraft turned out to be severe; it was in repair for nearly a year, and returned to service only in September 1942.

Golubev conducted another successful combat in March 1942. Shortly before that, he had been appointed Commander of the 3rd Squadron of the 4th Guards Fighter Air Regiment (the former 13th Fighter Air Regiment). At 5:00 a.m. on 12 March, the command was given an urgent combat mission: all crews of the regiment had to deliver a strafing attack on the station at Mga. In this sortie, Golubev decided to 'get even' with the German aerial hunters of JG54 *Grunherz*, which was operating in this sector of the front. He wrote:

The striking force consisted of the 1st and 2nd Squadrons, six aircraft in each, led by Mikhail Vasilyev. I was expected to lead the covering party consisting of the six aircraft of the 3rd Squadron. However, I, without reporting to the regimental commander, appointed Alim Baisultanov the leading pilot, whereas Vladimir Dmitriyev and I took the place of the trail pair.

Before take-off, I ordered my wingman to save half of the ammunition allowance for the way back, and emphasised that I would, in the course of the strafing, mostly perform fake attacks, trying to keep my ammunition intact. The enemy was not likely to forgive us for the massed strike on such an important location as the station of Mga, and the hunters would not fail to attack us near the front line or would wait for us near the airfield.

The eighteen I-16s carried out an evasive action and approached the target from the south, which was not expected by the enemy. With rocket projectiles and cannon and machine-gun fire, we descended upon the enemy from two directions. Railway cars and platforms with troops and military vehicles, with which all the railway tracks were literally crammed, caught fire.

"Fortunately, there were no enemy fighters above the target; breaking through the heavy anti-aircraft fire, we repeated the attack with all our aircraft from three directions. According to reconnaissance reports, which came later, fire and explosions persisted for several hours.

The I-16 fighter 145

State tests of the I-16 Type 29 s/n 292116 in the 'Six RO-82 + Two PSB-21' configuration, in August 1940.

A close-up of RO-82 launchers under the right wing of an I-16 Type 29. Due to the installation of the rocket armament, the star insignia was relocated closer to the wing tip.

Tests of an I-16 Type 29 equipped with modified bomb racks designed by Military Engineer Class 3 Bykov. The aircraft in the photograph, taken in summer 1941, is fitted with six RO-82 rail launchers and carries two FAB-100 bombs on the bomb racks. In another version, PLBG-100 teardrop-shaped external tanks could be suspended under the wing.

In summer 1941, the I-16 Type 29 was equipped with RS-132 rocket projectiles. Two rocket projectiles were carried under each wing. The configuration was tested from 18–26 June 1941.

Adjustment of fire is being conducted for synchronised ShKAS machine guns in this I-16 Type 29 of the 71st Fighter Air Regiment. In the cockpit is Sergeant V. Segalayev; the adjustment is being carried out by armament specialist I. Belokon. Judging by the fact that the aircraft is fitted with RS-82 rocket projectiles, these were going to be tested as well.

An I-16 Type 24 being prepared for a combat sortie. Six RS-82 rocket projectiles are already mounted, while a mechanic is refilling oil. The aircraft is placed in a permanent shelter; on the wall of the shelter, note the slogan 'We'll Make Every Effort to Destroy the Enemy!'

An I-16 Type 29 armed with four RS-82 rocket projectiles taxiing to the starting position.

The I-16 Type 29 with the 'unlucky' tactical number '13' taxiing to take-off position. The aircraft features a correct camouflage applied in accordance with instructions of 1941, and is armed with six RS-82 rocket projectiles.

This I-16 Type 5 with the tactical number '64' was captured by the Finns on 10 December 1941 on Lake Ladoga. The aircraft is armed with four RO-82 launchers, which were installed by the field repair shops.

The I-16 Type 29s of the 156th Fighter Air Regiment at an airfield near Leningrad (in the city of Pushkin) in autumn 1941. Each aircraft is armed with six factory-installed RO-82 launchers. The pilots are discussing combat operations, with Lieutenant Alexander Zhirnov speaking. Zhirnov failed to return from a combat sortie near Spasskaya Polist on 26 January 1942.

Vasily Golubev was one of the most successful Baltic pilots who used RS-82 rocket projectiles in aerial combat.

Lieutenant Krichevsky in the cockpit of an aged but rather interesting I-16 Type 24 of the 254th Fighter Air Regiment at Budogoshch airfield on the Leningrad Front in 1943. The main landing gear legs have no doors; an RS-82 is mounted under each wing; and wing-mounted ShKAS machine guns have noticeably longer barrels. The aircraft carries five stars indicating aerial victories; it has two tactical numbers ('1' on the rudder and '27' on the fuselage); and the earlier-type red star insignia on the vertical tail is complemented with a later type (with white outline) on the fuselage. Another star is painted on the propeller spinner. Note a radio antenna and – on the fuselage side – traces of an overpainted arrow whose head reached the edge of the cowling.

It was wise of Vasilyev not to take a short cut for leading the group back to the home airfield; instead, he flew over the enemy's rear to Maluksinskie Swamps and crossed the front-line there. On the way back, the observation point reported that a large group of Messerschmitts was waiting for us. I was almost sure that the enemy, having failed to intercept us above the target and above the front-line, would certainly send the hunters to the area near the airfield to attack straggling aircraft or those which might have been damaged in the course of the strafing.

"All right, let's see who will be the smarter one ...' I said to myself and began to trail behind the entire group at a height of two hundred metres. Some fifteen kilometres before the airfield, anti-aircraft projectile bursts appeared near our group at a low altitude; this meant that the Messerschmitts were hanging around somewhere above the forest.

"I put on speed and looked around. Aha, here they are! Above the tops of the trees, as I had expected, there was a pair of the Me-109Fs. Vladimir Dmitriyev also noticed the enemy and rocked the wings. I responded with the same signal. I had prohibited radio communications in such situations.

Our main group began to land when I was at a distance of some five kilometres from the airfield. The enemy kept at the extremely low altitude without drawing closer. Thus, the Germans had swallowed the bait. Believing our pair to be disabled, they decided to shoot us down 'in style' above our home airfield with a simultaneous attack by their pair. Well, I had been waiting for this moment for a long time.

I accelerated and climbed higher. I saw the Messerchmitts' engines emitting smoke, operating at augmented power for rapid approach and attack. Having reached the centre of the airfield, I made an abrupt left combat turn to get on [a] head-on course ... I completed the turn at approximately 500 metres, with the enemy at a considerably lower height. They did not expect such a manoeuvre and found themselves in a head-on attack. Both Messers, with their yellow noses up, began to advance on me. Probably, they believed that I had run out of ammunition, and that I [was] attempting a fake attack. The dark traces from the two Me-109Fs were stretching out precisely towards my engine. Through the gunsight, I saw the leading 'hunter'; the distance was approximately five hundred metres; I had only a second and a half left for everything – maybe, even for my life. Fingers of my right hand pulled the common trigger of the machine guns mechanically, and three fiery traces pierced, like lightning, the thin body of the Messerschmitt, which flickered some five metres below me.

Without thinking of the outcome, I made the second combat turn. And here I saw the single remaining Messer above and ahead of me, climbing higher. Mechanically, I took the control stick, determined the lead at a rough guess, and fired all the four RS rocket projectiles right after the Messerschmitt. Four black explosion 'caps' appeared behind the enemy's tail but the Messer continued the steep climb. Catching up with it was not possible.

But then, at approximately fifteen hundred metres, the enemy performed a loop and rushed downward while keeping firing. What was it? Had he decided to offer battle on his own? Or, maybe, he wanted to see the burning aircraft of his leading pilot? No; he pulled out and began, for some reason, to perform another loop. That was when every second counted. I ordered Dmitriyev over the radio to attack him from below, and threw my aircraft abruptly into a climb. At the highest point in the third loop, I fired on the German from a distance of fifty metres. But the aircraft did not fall; again it went down and was once more climbing up. What was all that strange manoeuvring about? And suddenly I understood: the enemy is in a deadlock; fragments of the RS rocket projectiles had caused a jamming of the elevators in his aircraft at the time when he had been trying to escape by climbing after the head-on attack.

Upon recovery from the fourth loop, the Messer got caught by the tops of the fir-trees near the parking area of the 3rd Squadron, and, having lost his wings, began to crawl over the snow near the airfield. I saw the pilot jump out of the cockpit. Tumbling down every now and then, he was running towards the forest – right to the parking area of my squadron. Now the German had no chances of going far away. I reported to the regiment's command post over the radio, gave a command to the wingman to land, and myself made a landing as close as possible to our squadron's parking area. The combat had been taking place in the presence of the entire garrison, and a loud 'Hurray!' had [run] over the airfield when the first Messer exploded. The same was the case with the second one ... In a quarter of an hour, the mechanics brought the dead fascist pilot. Having run away from the aircraft in a fever, he died from wounds received in mid-air.

Vasily Golubev's victims in this air combat were the pilots of JG54. They were the Soviet fighter ace's 11th and 12th German aircraft shot down. In an aerial combat above Lake Ladoga on 12 May 1942, Squadron Leader Golubev scored another two victories, after which he was awarded the title of Hero of the Soviet Union.

Comparisons

As early as 1939, there already was a general understanding that the era of the I-16 was coming to an end. Additional flight tests showed that further improvements of the aircraft would be inexpedient. One such test was dedicated to aircraft entering a dive (tuck-under) with the horizontal stabiliser set to positive angles of attack. Several crashes forced the performing of meticulous testing in order to determine the causes of this phenomenon.

It was found out that the I-16s of later series were especially sensitive to changes in the stabiliser setting. At the same time, with the stabiliser set to neutral and with the aft centre of gravity position of the aircraft, pilots experienced extremely high pressure on the control stick. The fact that the tuck-under had not occurred earlier was connected with gradual, from series to series, relocation of the aircraft centre of gravity position in the aft direction due to installation of the storage battery, flaps, armoured backrest and radio. In some aircraft, the CG position had already reached 35 percent MAC. The non-retractable skis accounted for an additional pitch-down moment.

Tests performed in early 1939 showed that, with a CG position of 32–33 percent MAC, an aircraft in dive with the landing gear retracted entered the so-called 'zone of complete instability'. The phenomenon turned out to be dangerous; the I-16 became almost incontrollable. Test pilot Captain Taborovsky, who was involved in these risky flights, was killed. His aircraft s/n 1021101, with a CG position of 33.6 percent MAC and horizontal stabiliser setting of +2°, crashed into the ground.

Afterwards, the CG position for all aircraft in service was limited to 33 percent MAC. This instability of the I-16 was thereafter recognised as a shortcoming. The pilots' opinion was unanimous: the aircraft had better flight performance with a more forward CG position.

Another study, 'Determination of Rudder and Aileron Control Stick Pressures and Elevator Control Pedal Pressures in the I-16', was undertaken in summer 1939 in TsAGI. Test pilot Stankevich, who conducted the flight test, wrote the following:

Due to the aircraft instability, even small longitudinal forward pressures of 4–5 kilograms in steady flight mode are uncomfortable for the pilot (his hand gets tired). During performance of aerobatic manoeuvres, abrupt control stick pressure variations occur, which are uncomfortable for the pilot. Extending the flaps affects the longitudinal stability and increases the forward pressure on the control stick. During extension of the flaps, the aircraft noses up; during their retraction, it sinks down abruptly, with a tendency to dive ... When a high angle of attack is reached, the instability increases abruptly ... During take-off run, the aircraft is reluctant to lift its tail; the pilot has to push the control stick with great pressure ... During high-altitude levelling-off, the aircraft drops the right wing; aileron effect is not sufficient to counteract the stalling.

The issue of increasing the aircraft's maximum speed became another stumbling block. In spite of the fact that the M-62 and M-63 engines were much more powerful than the M-25, it seemed that the I-16 had run into some unsurmountable obstacle. Indeed, the fabric-covered wing, open cockpit and various projections on the fuselage prevented the aircraft from accelerating to a higher speed. The flat front part of the engine cowling, nearly a metre-and-a-half in diameter, also reduced the propeller efficiency. Engineer I. Rabkin, who participated in tests of the latest, M-63-powered versions of the I-16, described some episodes that took place at the NII VVS airfield in 1940:

Once there was a dispute regarding the maximum speed. Representatives of the Design Bureau were not happy with the fact that the speed measured by us at the altitude of 5,000 metres was only 488 kilometres per hour. 'How come?' they exclaimed in indignation. 'Only 24 kilometres per hour higher than with the M-62? That could not be true! You should have obtained at least 500 kilometres per hour.'

And, in spite of the fact that they found nothing out-of-the-way in the materials that I provided to them, they addressed my superiors and wrung a promise out of them to perform several additional flights. However, we did not obtain better results. It was clear that the I-16 had exhausted all its capabilities for improvement, and that higher performance might be obtained in another aircraft but not the I-16.

The I-16 had a rather vast history, and the lessons learned should not be wasted. When I was studying the test reports which had accumulated throughout the time of the I-16's existence, I made a most interesting discovery for myself. It turned out that some of the aircraft defects migrated from one report to another. Among them, there were some 'veterans', which had been able to withstand the pressure of any and all reports. They, of course, did not affect the safety of flight; however, they made piloting more difficult, and had an adverse effect on some of the aircraft performance parameters. I made a report with the list of all defects detected in the aircraft (so as not to break with the established tradition), though I was not quite sure that the industry would attend to them. If the people from the industry had not done it before, it was hardly likely that they would do it now that production of the I-16 was about to be discontinued.

In 1940, performance parameters of Soviet aircraft were compared with those of aircraft purchased in Germany. The intention was to determine the most efficient structural elements and flight performance parameters in order to use them in design of new aircraft. The I-16 data was also included in this evaluation sheet. The assessment of flying qualities of different aircraft performed by TsAGI pilots (starting from March 1941, the TsAGI flight department was renamed the Flight Research Institute – *Lyotno-Issledovatelskiy Institut*, LII) gave interesting results, which are combined in the table below.

The alphabetical symbols in the table stands for:

A – longitudinal stability;
B – lateral stability;
C – directional stability;
D – elevator efficiency;
E – aileron efficiency;
F – rudder efficiency;
G – control lever pressures from elevator;
H – control lever pressures from ailerons;
K – handling properties which the pilots found positive;
L – handling properties which the pilots found negative.

Grades in each individual parameter were allotted on a scale from one to five, where five stands for 'good', three stands for 'satisfactory' and one stands for 'poor'; four and two are intermediate grades. The asterisk (*) indicates that pressure on the control lever from rudder and elevator is extremely high.

No.	Type	A	B	C	D	E	F	G	H	I	J	K	L
1.	Bf 109	5	5	5	4	3	4	3	3	3	5	Ease of piloting in a straight flight, at take-off and at landing.	Insufficient manoeuvrability. The aircraft sluggishly responds to rudder and elevator controls during manoeuvres.
2.	He 100	2	4	5	5	5	5	2	4	3	3	Excellent behaviour of the structure in flight. Good controllability of the aircraft.	
3.	I-16	1	2	4	5	4	5	2*	3	3	2	Good efficiency of the control surfaces and manoeuvrability of the aircraft.	The aircraft is unforgiving in piloting. High instability at low speeds. The elevator is not provided with a trim tab.

The above results demonstrated by the I-16 just confirmed everything that had been known before. Nevertheless, it was the I-16 fighter that bore the main burden of air combat in 1941. Some sources indicate that the critical situation in Soviet aviation during the first months of the war was brought about by shortage of advanced aircraft at the front. However, it should be noted that the heaviest losses were suffered, first and foremost, by regiments equipped with the Yak-1s, LaGG-3s and MiG-3s. Indeed, this is not so surprising, as the flying time in these aircraft for the average Soviet pilot totalled not more than 10–20 hours, whereas the I-16 had been extensively studied by flight crews and technicians. The vertical speed of M-62-powered and M-63-powered I-16s at altitudes below 3,000m exceeded that of the LaGG-3 and MiG-3 (see Figure

1). At the same time, at low altitudes (below 1,500m), the I-16 was almost on a par with the German Bf 109E f[...] terms of speed and rate of climb (see Figure 2). All this also translated into the results of aerial combat. It is not b[...] that the first regiments, which were granted the honour of being named a 'Guards Regiment', were equipped with t[...]

To confirm the above, note the following abstracts from a report of Air Force Staffs of fronts and fleets ('A[...] during a Year of the War: 22 June 1941 till 22 June 1942'):

> Throughout the reporting period, fighter aircraft (along with performance of their main tasks) were extensively used in st[...] operations against enemy troops. The I-16s and I-153s proved to be more suitable for this purpose. They have sufficien[...] power and are more robust that the LaGG-3s, MiG-3s, and Yak-1s, which were often shot down, since damaging the [...] cooling system of the engine with a single bullet was enough for a need of a forced landing ... Armament effectiveness in st[...] operations is high: a medium tank catches fire after a direct hit by RS-82 rocket projectile; a large motor boat, after a direct [...] a single RS-82, sinks in approximately three minutes; after a hit by two RS-82s on an infantry column, approximately 40 so[...] were found dead. BS and ShKAS machine-gun fire destroys motor vehicles and damages tankettes.
>
> ... Reconnaissance missions were performed using the I-16 aircraft carrying photographic equipment providing for both [...] and area air photography.
>
> The I-16s quite coped with the reconnaissance tasks assigned to them, and were used in the role of main reconnais[...] aircraft for obtaining information on front-line situation and enemy troops.
>
> ... The Yak-1s and the cannon-armed I-16s may prove to be the most efficient aircraft for repelling the enemy's bombing [...] since they have sufficient fire power and speed for approaching the enemy and delivering a decisive blow on it within limited [...] in an area lit by searchlights.
>
> ... The Yak-1 and the I-16 fighters are the best aircraft for escorting bombers.

Figure 1. Time to climb to 5,000m f[...] production fighters of the first half o[...]

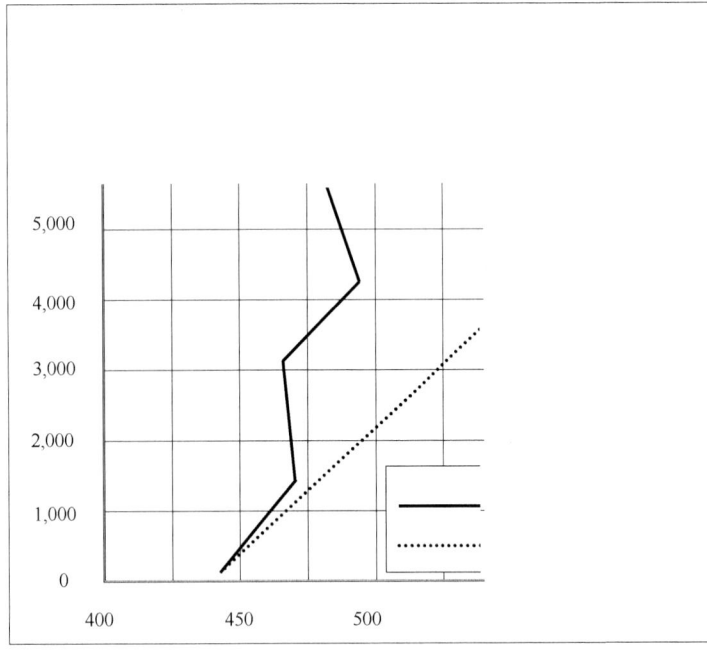

Figure 2. Maximum speeds of the I-16 [...] and Bf 109E-4 fighters at altitude.

The I-16 prototype – the first TsKB-12 M-22 prototype. Many Soviet pilots remembered it after the tests in Kacha in spring 1934.

The TsKB-12 s/n 123954 was a prototype for the series production I-16 Type 5s which were still in operation in 1943–44.

Evaluation tests of the I-16 s/n 2421274 before confirmation of acceptance of these aircraft for service with the Naval Air Force in 1940.

Alerted pilots and technicians of the 13th Regiment of the Baltic Fleet Air Force hurrying to their I-16 Type 24s in 1940.

Pilots of the Red Banner Baltic Fleet Air Force at the parking area of the I-16 fighters.

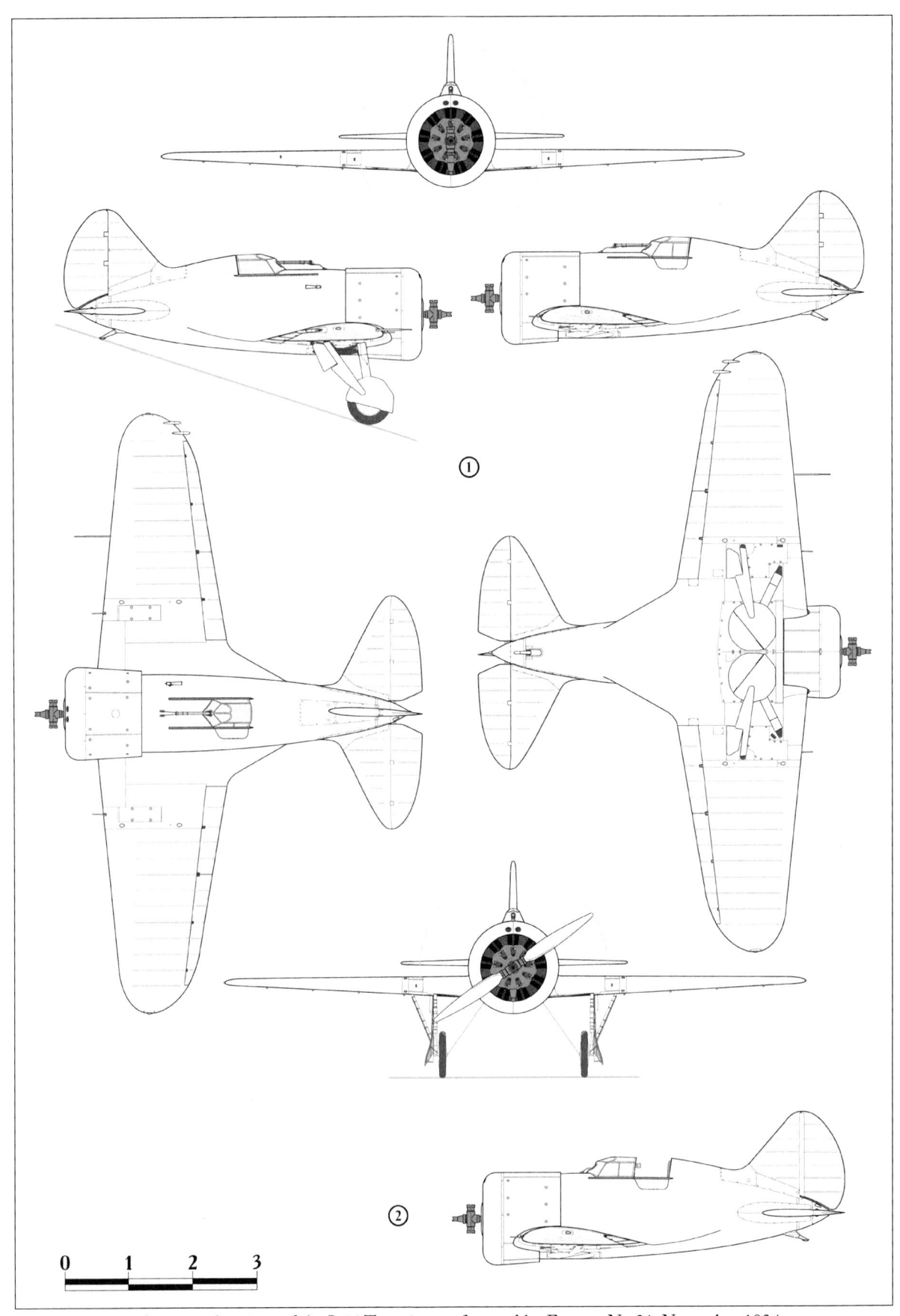

1. Six-view drawings of the I-16 Type 4 manufactured by Factory No.21, November 1934.
2. Side view drawing of the I-16 with M-22 engine, s/n 123903 or 123914 manufactured by Factory No. 39.

The I-16 fighter 153

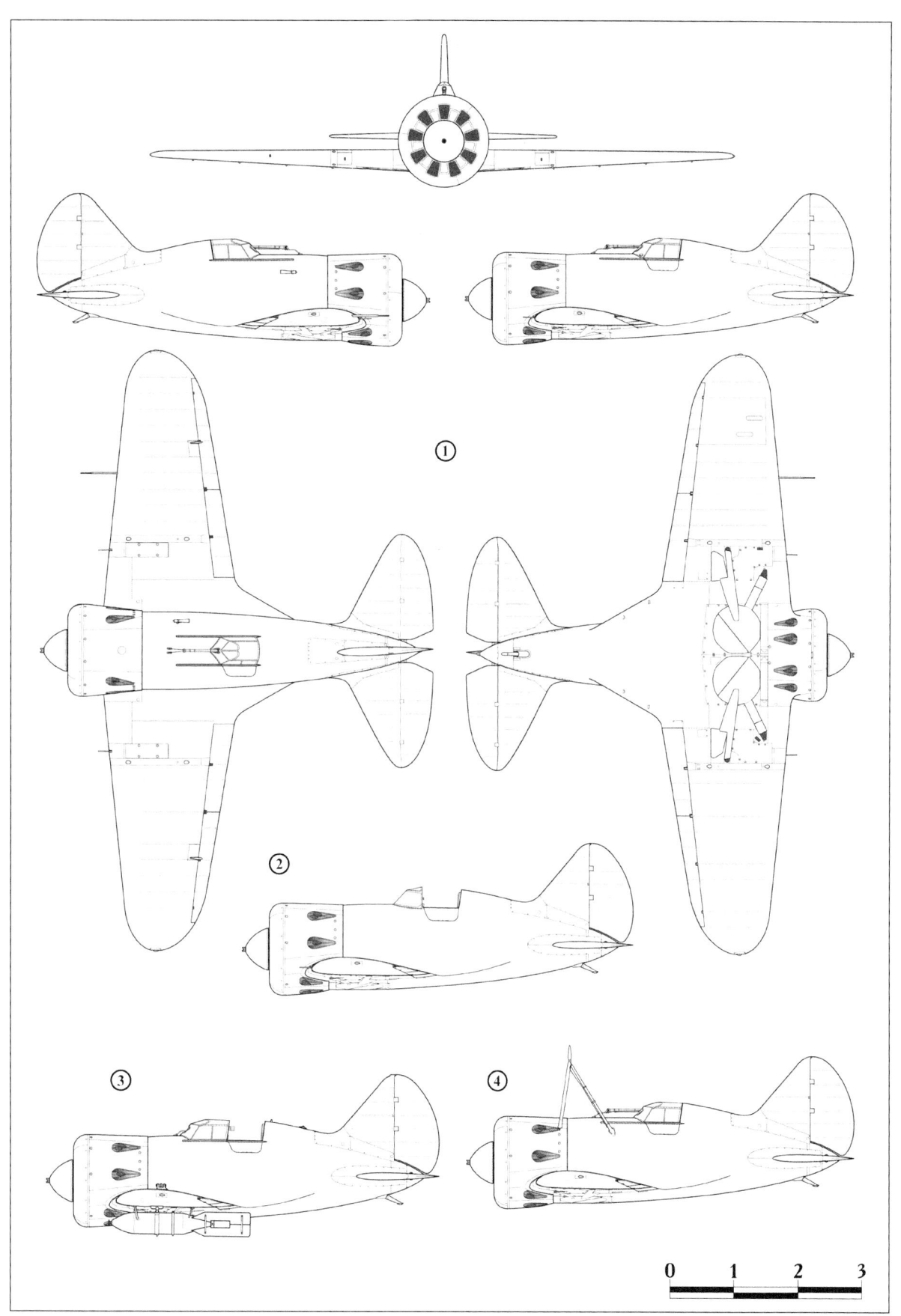

1. Five-view drawings of the I-16 Type 5, 1937.
2. Side view drawing of the I-16 Type 5, 1938.
3. Side view drawing of the I-16 Type 5 manufactured in 1938, s/n 521502 or 521507, which was used in the Zveno-SPB system.
4. Side view drawing of the I-16 Type 5 which was used in the Zveno-7 system.

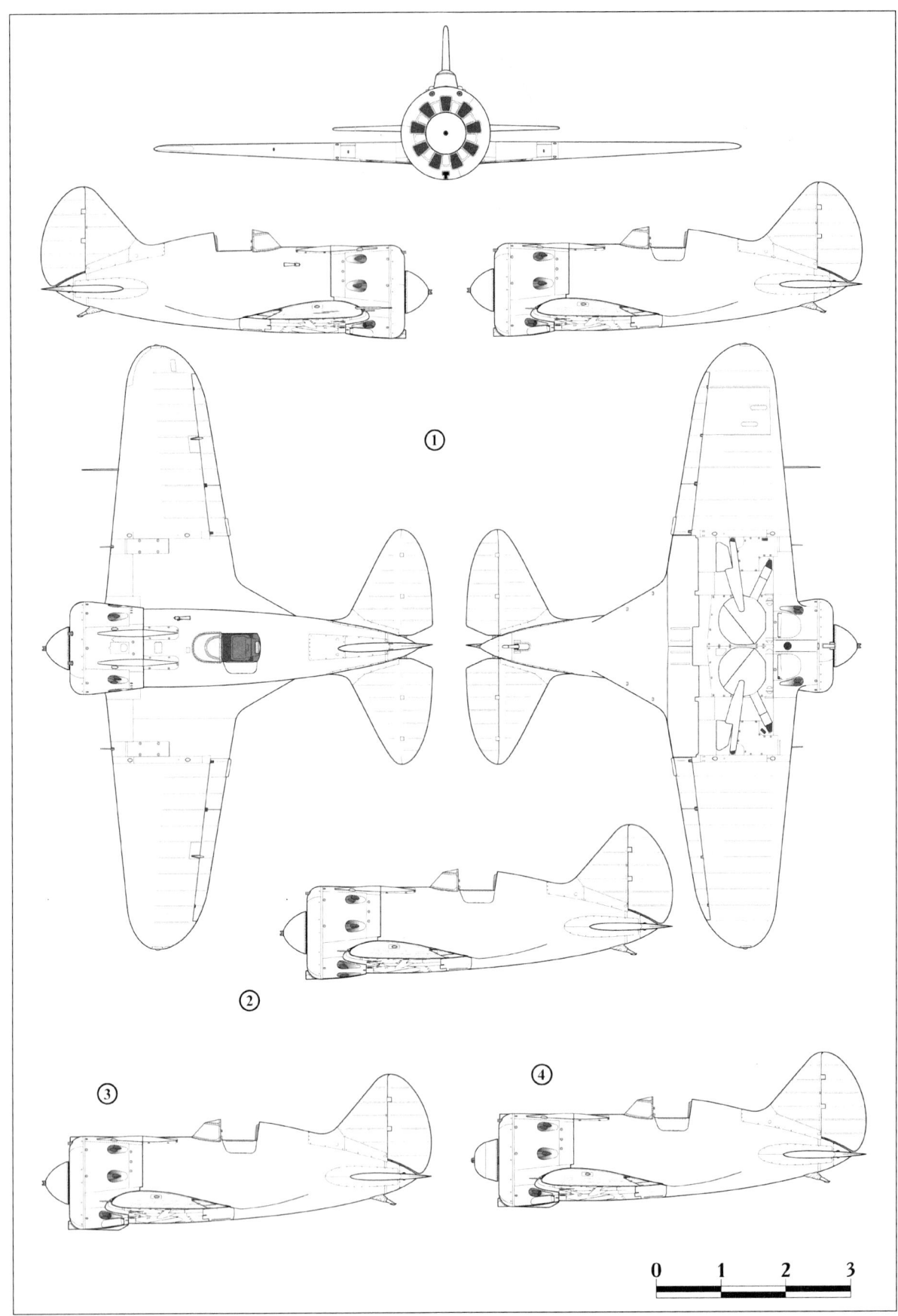

1. Five-view drawings of the I-16 Type 10 of the 27th series, manufactured by Factory No.21, 1938.
2. Side view drawing of the I-16 Type 10 of the 1st to 26th series, manufactured by Factory No.21.
3. Side view drawing of the I-16 Type 18 of early series.
4. Side view drawing of the I-16 Type 18 of later series

The I-16 fighter 155

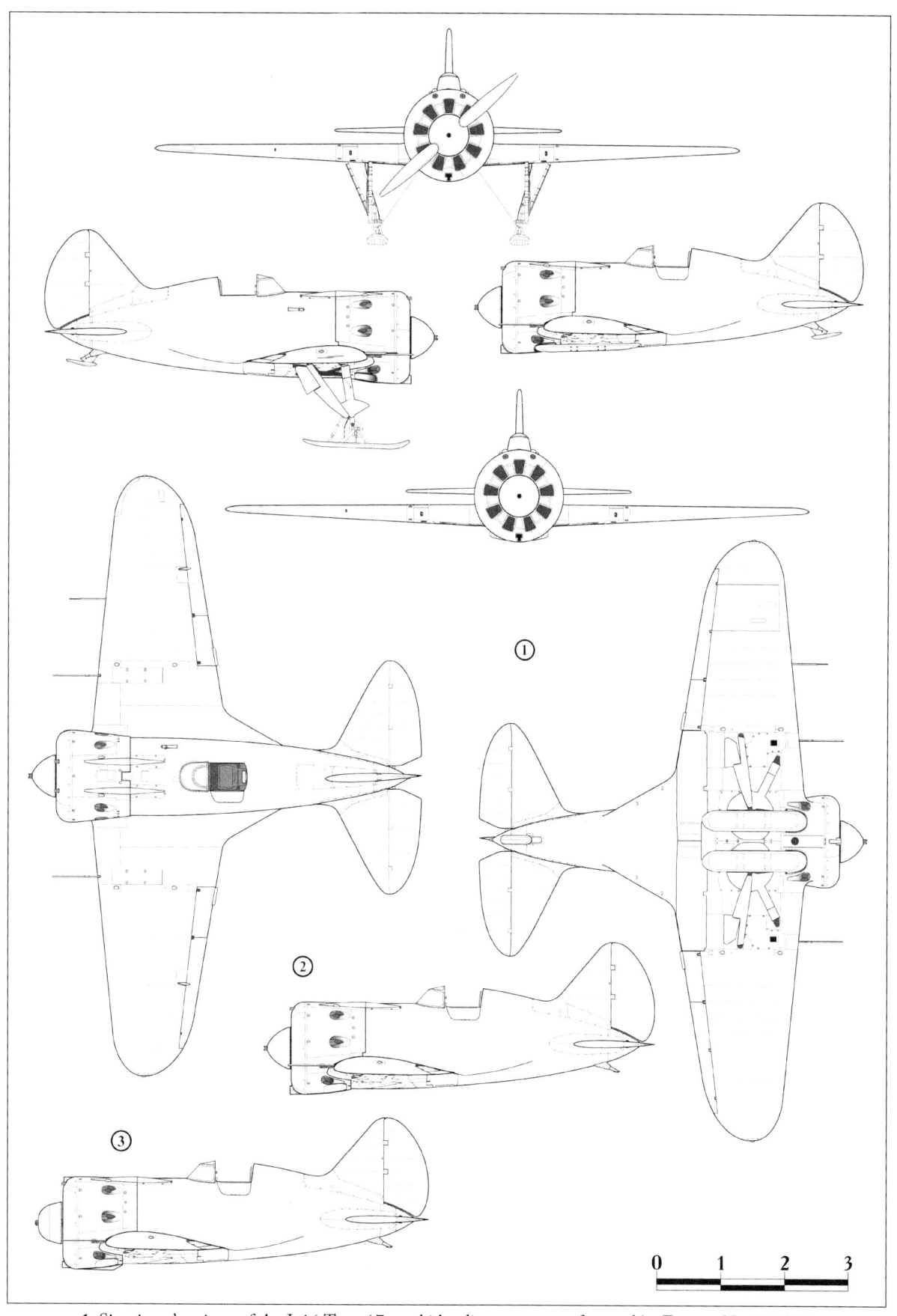

1. Six-view drawings of the I-16 Type 17 on ski landing gear, manufactured by Factory No.21, 1938.
2. Side view drawing of the I-16 Type 17 on wheel landing gear, manufactured by Factory No.21, 1938.
3. Side view drawing of the I-16 Type 27.

1. Six-view drawings of the I-16 Type 29.
2. Lower and side-view drawings of the I-16 Type 24.

The I-16 fighter 157

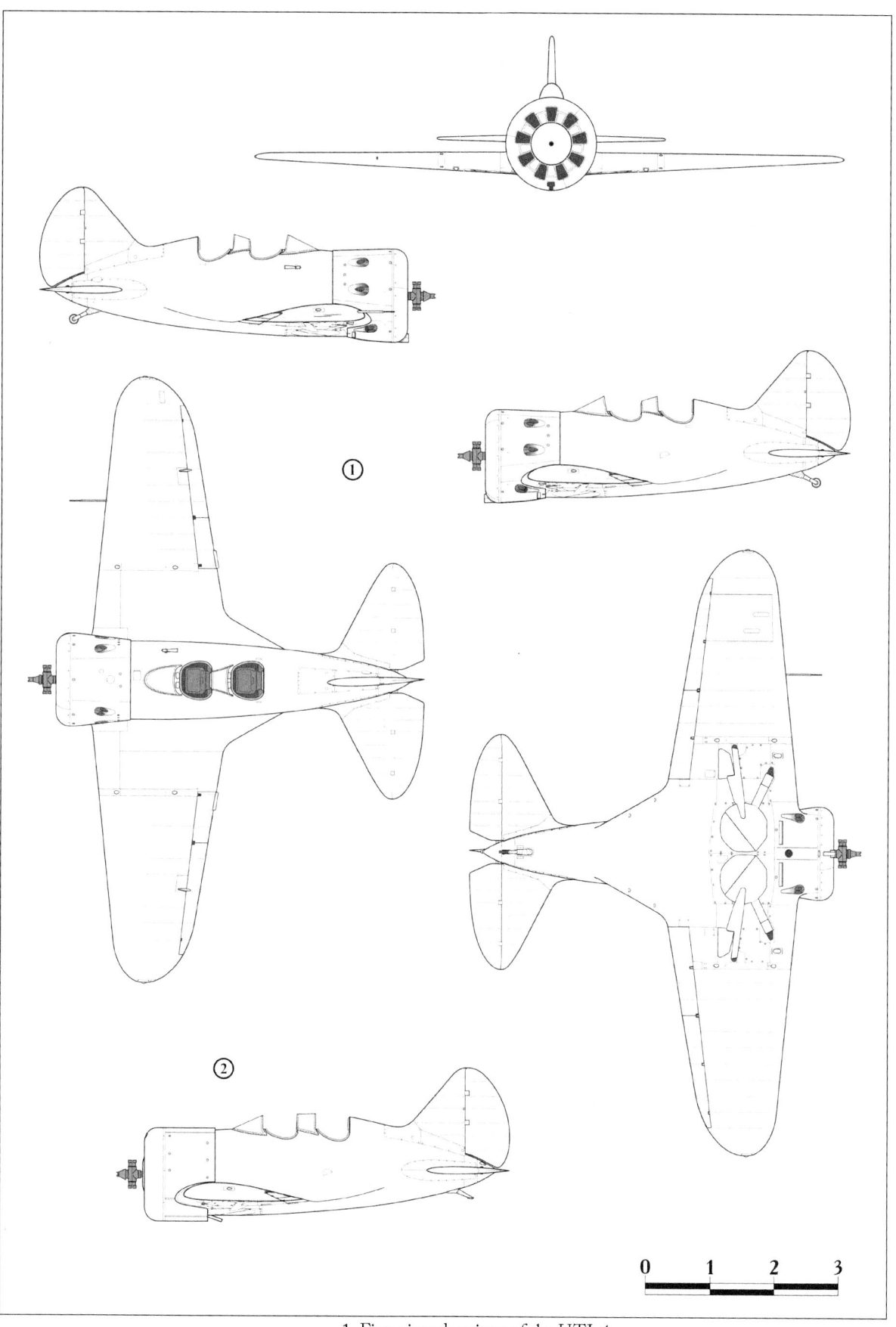

1. Five-view drawings of the UTI-4.
2. Side view drawing of the I-16 Type 14 (UTI-2).

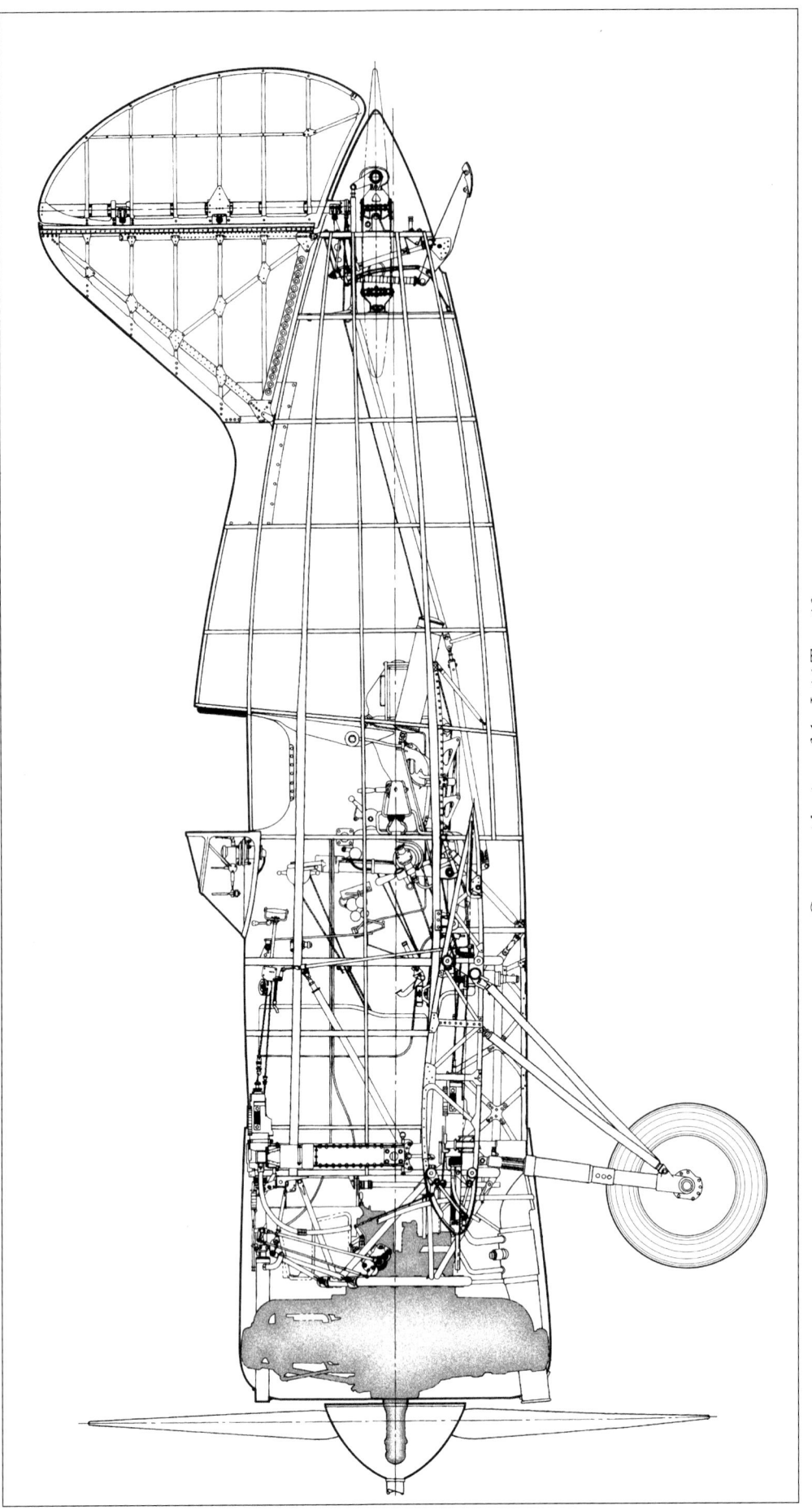

Cutaway side view of the I-16 Type 10.

2

The I-17 fighter

At the time of the war, the service pilots often wondered simple-heartedly: why had not it occurred to Nikolay Polikarpov to modify his successful I-16 to be powered by an inline liquid-cooled engine, for example, the M-105? That is, why did he not adapt the available airframe to the new engine without making efforts to develop a totally new design. To begin with, a new fuselage would have been required; then, most probably, in the course of a gradual development, further changes might have taken place. Finally, after all the improvements, such an aircraft might have become compatible, in terms of its specifications and combat performance, with its main opponent, the German Messerschmitt Bf 109 fighter.

In fact, very few Soviet combat pilots were aware of the existence of the I-17 prototype, which was essentially the above-described version of the I-16 with an inline liquid-cooled engine. The I-17 was designed approximately a year after the *Ishak*, and its initial development went on at approximately the same pace. With time, however, the gap between the fates of the two aircraft began to increase progressively. The I-16 entered production and was undergoing extensive improvements, whereas the I-17 forever remained a prototype.

So why was the I-17 not released into production? There is no clear answer to this question. In fact, there were numerous causes and circumstances which influenced the fate of this interesting aircraft. Let us piece together all the fragments and documentary evidence relating to it, and try to understand what happened.

The inline engine and the first TsKB-15 prototype

The period 1929–34 was, for the Soviet aviation industry, marked with noticeable qualitative and quantitative changes. New factories and additional facilities at those already running were built; new technologies and materials were introduced; and new employees and workers were hired in their tens of thousands. At some locations, changes were gradually translating into qualitative successes, with full-fledged combat aircraft (first and foremost, fighters) being intensively developed and put into production. It should be noted that the majority of such aircraft were powered by radial air-cooled engines. It appears that such lop-sidedness was rooted in the somewhat cyclical nature of improvements in any area of engineering: from the late 1920s to the early 1930s, the greatest progress was achieved in development of radial engines. Such engines offered a lower weight-to-developed-power ratio, had no 'capricious' cooling systems and were easier to maintain during the winter.

Further to obtaining the license to build American 600hp Wright Cyclone radial engine in the USSR, the Polikarpov I-15 and I-16 fighters began to be fitted with such power plants. These fighters satisfied the requirements and expectations of the Soviet Air Force, so it seemed that the purchase of another license for a liquid-cooled engine would pass unnoticed by the designers. However, Polikarpov, who was constantly tackling the problem of creating a modern fighter, was the first to pay attention to the purchase of a license for production of French 850hp Hispano-Suiza 12Ybrs engine in 1934. Back in 1931, Polikarpov took an interest in the lightweight and compact Hispano-Suiza engine of the new 12th series, which he believed to be the most suitable engine for a fighter aircraft. For several reasons, there turned out to be no possibility to purchase the license for the 12th series engine at that time. It was only three years later that representatives of the USSR and France came to a mutual agreement and the Soviets purchased the license for building the Hispano-Suiza 12Ybrs.

In the Soviet Union, licensed production of the Hispano-Suiza under the M-100 designation was launched in 1935 at Engine Factory No.26 in Rybinsk. The first M-100, which developed 750hp, was built in May 1935; before the end of the year, 100 such engines were supplied to the end user. Starting from 1936, production of the M-100 kept steadily increasing. The engines were installed mostly on Tupolev SB bombers. Fighter prototypes, which were being designed and built at that time, for the most part used French-made Hispano-Suiza 12Ybrs and Hispano-Suiza 12Ycrs (cannon version) engines.

By mid-1933, the TsKB Design Brigade No.2 led by Polikarpov had largely completed the engineering development of the TsKB-12 (I-16) monoplane fighter. Based on the experience gained with this aircraft, the Brigade proceeded with the implementation of the next project – the TsKB-15 monoplane fighter with an inline liquid-cooled engine. In much the same way as was the case with the TsKB-12, the engineers had been taking into account both the awaited American Wright-Cyclone engine and the already mastered Soviet M-22, with calculations in the new project also based on the

Soviet M-17 (BMW-VI), just to be on the safe side. In the final version, due to considerable incompatibility between the M-17 and Hispano-Suiza, the TsKB-15 was designed solely on the basis of the 12Ybrs.

Since Polikarpov reasonably expected to reach a maximum speed of 500km/h for the new aircraft, the fighter's external contours were made as slim as possible and the fuselage aerodynamics were refined. Due to the reduced fuselage cross-section and the resulting narrowness of the cockpit, the designers had to position the pilot at a considerable inclination to the vertical, with the pilot seat inclined at an angle of 22 degrees. To avoid the negative effect of the higher weight of the power plant together with the cooling systems on the aircraft's manoeuvrability, the wing span and wing area were made larger compared with the TsKB-12, totalling 10.0m and 17.7sq.m, respectively. The wing loading of 102kg/sq.m was nearly equal to that on the I-16 Type 5 (100kg/sq.m).

Concurrently with the design of the TsKB-15, which was given the formal designation I-17 by the Soviet Air Force, development works on its two-seater version named the DI-7 was going on in the second half of 1933. Intense discussions on the specifications and expected combat capabilities of the two aircraft began in December 1933. Commander of the VVS RKKA Yakov Alksnis personally took part in working out the tactical requirements: "On 7 December at 20:00, a meeting on the subject of these tactical requirements will be held in my office. We would like to have more powerful and long-range armament on both aircraft."

An interesting fact is that there are no further mentions of the DI-7 two-seat fighter. At a certain stage in the course of events, there emerged a variant of the DI-7 fitted with two coupled engines arranged in tandem and rotating two propellers in opposite directions. Such a power plant was termed a 'mechanical twin'. Interest towards this topic grew in early 1935 in connection with the launch of development works aimed at creating a record-setting high-speed aircraft. As a result, Engine Factory No.26 was tasked with development of a 'mechanical twin' consisting of the M-100 (afterwards, M-103) engines. Later, the work continued and resulted in creation of the Bolkhovitinov 'S' experimental aircraft. This, however, had nothing to do with the history of the I-17.

Tactical requirements for the I-17 single-seat fighter were approved by Y. Alksnis on 9 December, and on 13 December they were provided by NII VVS to TsKB. The main performance parameters of the I-17 fighter as specified in these requirements were as follows :

Maximum speed at an altitude of 5,000m	425km/h
Time to climb to 5,000m	6–7 minutes
Service ceiling	10,000m
Maximum landing speed	100–105km/h
Range at economic speed	600km

In accordance with the flight performance parameters required, the I-17 design underwent final modification. Signed by Head of TsKB S. Ilyushin, on 28 December 1934 the design was sent to NII VVS and GUAP for approval. In the presented document, the I-17 was determined as a high-speed fighter, which, along with a high maximum speed, provided for high manoeuvrability, "especially in the vertical plane".

Under the designation TsKB-15, the aircraft was being built throughout 1934. In terms of construction, it was in many aspects identical to the I-16; like in the latter, the I-17 wing featured spars made of chrome-molybdenum steel alloy tubes, duralumin ribs and fabric covering. The ailerons were split, of the differential type, able to operate as flaps by drooping at landing. Two extending wing-mounted water coolers, which had been specified in the preliminary project, were replaced with a single extending belly-mounted one. Such an arrangement led to an outward-retracting landing gear configuration. Fuel tanks having a total capacity of 360 litres were placed in the wing centre section leading edge, which helped lessen the load on the wing to a certain extent and contributed to a more efficient use of internal volumes of the space behind the engine in the fuselage. Such a solution was indicative of the initial intention to mount, in the fuselage, a high-rate-of-fire aircraft cannon firing through the hollow shaft of the propeller hub. However, armament of the first prototype (and, by the way, of the second one as well) consisted of four ShKAS machine guns mounted in the outer wing panels.

Tests of the TsKB-15 began in the second half of 1934. In September, test pilot V. Chkalov reached a speed of 424km/h near ground level and 455km/h at an altitude of 3,380m. In spite of the obtained flight performance parameters, which were quite decent, further work on the prototype slowed. In attempts to ensure an acceptable static ground angle (the propeller diameter of 3.4m turned out to be too large for such a compact aircraft), the designers had arranged the landing gear at a high angle to the vertical. This complicated the functioning of the shock absorbers, and as a result, further operation of the prototype. The landing gear retraction mechanism also proved to be unreliable. For this reason, the aircraft was later fitted with non-retractable 'pyramid' legs with rubber block shock absorbers.

For a long time, the TsKB-15 stayed abandoned at Factory No.39. Trying to prolong the aircraft's life, Polikarpov suggested, in particular, converting it into a suspended fighter (to be attached to a TB-3); this, however, was never implemented in practice. After the war, the TsKB-15 was on display in the Central Air Force Museum in Moscow. It hung under the showroom ceiling with its landing gear retracted. Later, the aircraft was again fitted with a fixed landing gear, in which configuration it survives until today in the small Museum of V. Chkalov near Nizhny Novgorod.

A bunch of projects

It should be noted that the TsKB-15 prototype was built subsequent to the I-16 in a rather short period of time, literally in the following year. It was later on that the history of the I-17 family stretched over more than five years, finally running into an unsurmountable obstacle. Initially, however, everything appeared rather promising, and the concept of a fighter powered by a liquid-cooled inline engine gave rise to various projects and variations on the theme.

According to the plans of Polikarpov's design brigade in 1935, further improvements of the TsKB-15 were as follows:

1. The TsKB-19 (I-17) second prototype with the Hispano-Suiza 12Ybrs engine. This aircraft was actually built, and is explained in more detail below.
2. The TsKB-25 (I-19) of April 1935, with a radial Gnome-Rhône engine. The design was never worked out in detail, but is mentioned in the general list due to similarity of designations.
3. The TsKB-25 (I-19), a project of December 1935, with the M-34 (uprated) glycol-cooled engine.
4. The TsKB-25 (I-19), a project of 1935. Powered by the Hispano-Suiza 12Ycrs engine combined with the ShKAS-2 magazine-fed cannon firing through the propeller hub, the aircraft was built under the designation TsKB-19bis.
5. The TsKB-28 (I-20), one of the variants powered by the Hispano-Suiza 12Ybrs engine. Judging by unavailability of any additional information, the project went no further than allocation of the mentioned designations.
6. The TsKB-33 (I-18), initially a preliminary project of September 1935, intended as a development of the TsKB-15 and the TsKB-19, with the Hispano-Suiza 12Ycrs engine, cannon mounted in the engine Vee and a steam-evaporation cooling system. The project documentation specified a maximum design speed of 500km/h at an altitude of 3,000m. In several documents, the project was named as the TsKB-19 with evaporative cooling. The main distinctive feature of this aircraft consisted in the use of an evaporative water cooling system arranged in the wing skin. The area of wing-mounted water condensers under a stainless steel skin totalled 7.0sq.m. In the project of 1935, the aircraft was designed as cannon-armed, but it was later converted into an unarmed record-setting version.
7. The TsKB-43 (I-17 or I-18) prototype with the Hispano-Suiza 12Ycrs engine. The project was never implemented.

This list of 1935 developments should be complemented with the I-17MP -multiple-machine-gun fighter', also known as the 'Sh' (*Shturmovik*, ground-attack aircraft) project. This variant was worked out under an assignment given by Tukhachevsky, and it was intended that some of the machine guns would be arranged in suspended streamlined containers.

In 1936, the above projects were still under development; three aircraft – the TsKB-19, TsKB-19bis and TsKB-25 (I-19) powered by the AM-34FRN – were being built. Among new proposals, a suspended fighter project emerged in 1936.

The I-17 (TsKB-19) suspended fighter

This project, dated 30 April 1936, was not given any additional designations (at least the author of this text knows none). It was defined as a TsKB-19 version to be carried by the TB-3 heavy bomber; hence the name 'suspended fighter'. The main difference between this version and the ordinary TsKB-19 consisted of a reduced wing area (from 17.65sq.m to 9.13sq.m), which allowed enhancing the speed performance considerably (up to 550km/h). The aircraft had no landing gear: landing on the ground was considered as an emergency. The 'suspended fighter' was expected to disconnect in mid-air and, upon completion of the combat mission (which was providing escort for bombers), dock again with the mother ship. According to calculations, docking in mid-air was intended to occur at speeds of 180–200km/h.

The 'suspended fighter' was planned to be powered by the water-cooled or glycol-cooled Hispano-Suiza 12Ybrs engine and armed with two ShVAK cannons or a ShVAK cannon plus two ShKAS machine guns.

For implementation of the project, Polikarpov suggested using the first I-17 (TsKB-15) prototype, which was, at that time, still out of demand at the base of Factory No.39. In the designer's opinion, only a new wing and a new tail unit were needed; manufacturing them would have required minimum labour and time input. However, the suggestion aroused no interest and was never considered in detail.

The speed record episode

According to Nikolay Polikarpov's personal correspondence, the possibility of setting a world speed record began to be discussed in the USSR in 1930. However, it was only on 2 May 1935 that a start was made for launching the respective activities on a large scale. On that day, the suggestion that record-setting aircraft (both seaplanes and land-based aircraft) should be built came from Joseph Stalin, who attended the Central Airfield in Moscow, where an informal demonstration of Soviet aviation industry achievements was held. The words spoken by the leader were taken as a directive for action.

Consequently, on 5 May 1935, Deputy Head of the GUAP Margolin sent a formal task to TsKB to study a possibility of creating record-setting aircraft – a landplane developing a speed of 600km/h and a seaplane capable of flying at 800km/h. As a result of the issuance of this document, Polikarpov's Design Brigade No.2 and Ilyushin's Design Brigade No.3 began to work on the projects.

The main advantage of Polikarpov's suggestions for a record-setting land-based aircraft was the possibility to utilise the experience gained during the development of I-17 prototypes. At the same time, solving the problem of record-breaking high-speed aircraft was also related to the prospects of creating high-speed fighters in the near future.

Polikarpov's proposals, outlined by the designer in summer 1935 in his report notes and during meetings in the GUAP, envisaged an aircraft powered by the Hispano-Suiza 12Ybrs and another airplane with the AM-34FRN. Both engines needed to be uprated so that their power could be twice the original figure, while aircraft aerodynamics had to be brought to perfection by using wings with a smaller area and higher loading. Evaporation cooling also had to be employed. Before the end of the year, preliminary projects of record-setting aircraft (the I-19 and the I-18, both with a speed of 600km/h) were prepared. It was planned that the TsKB-25 (I-19), which was being built at that time, would be converted into the I-18 (TsKB-43).

In 1936, work on the record-setting aircraft was still going on at the Polikarpov Design Bureau. However, in view of the withdrawal of such work from the plan and the subsequent relocation of the Design Bureau itself, it was soon cancelled. Polikarpov himself hoped to continue the activities. In particular, in June 1936, he appealed to Head of the GUAP Kaganovich:

> Under an assignment given by Stalin, we have developed record aircraft: the I-18 (powered by the M-100 or the M-103) having a design speed of 530km/h and the I-19 (powered by the M-34FRN) having a design speed of 600km/h. Engineering drawings for the aircraft had been completed at Factory No.39, and the aircraft manufacturing had been started; however, the GUAP did not include them in the plan for 1936, and the manufacturing process was ceased ... We have to resume working on the I-19; this guarantees us breaking the record and fulfilling the task set personally by Comrade Stalin.

This was probably Polikarpov's last request to give him a chance to continue working on the high-speed theme. However, the assignment for the record-breaking aircraft and its military version designated the I-21 was allotted to S. Ilyushin.

In May 1936, under a resolution of the government to allocate certain design groups with their own production facilities, the Polikarpov Design Bureau (into which Design Brigade No.2 was reorganised in September 1935) was transferred to Aviation Factories No.21 and No.84. In July that year, Polikarpov was appointed Chief Designer for the two factories. Part of the design team moved to Gorky, while the rest stayed in Moscow. Meanwhile, the topics were divided between the two newly formed design groups. Aviation Factory No.21 was to deal with fighters; therefore, the TsKB-15, TsKB-19, TsKB-19bis and TsKB-43 (I-18) were relocated there. All other aircraft of this family were withdrawn from the plan. In practice, only the former three airplanes were completed; the TsKB-43 was never made airworthy. The fate of the TsKB-19 and TsKB-19bis is described below.

The I-17 (TsKB-19) second prototype

This aircraft was built taking into account the results of the TsKB-15 tests performed in 1935. According to documents accompanying the process of building the TsKB-19, the aircraft was fitted with the Hispano-Suiza 12Ybrs engine, having a propeller of 3.0m in diameter. However, there is some confusion as at the stage of preparations for the tests, documentation of the TsKB Weight-calculations Brigade No.6 indicates the M-100 engine. It might well be that the engine had been replaced; at the same time, for several known reasons (the fact that production of the engine had been launched at the factory, manufacturing of the first series production engines, the desire to use Soviet designations, etc.), the French Hispano-Suiza engine could be referred to as the M-100. Whatever the case, in all later documents, the designation M-100 was used.

As for the propeller diameter of 3.0m, there is no absolute clarity in this respect. This diameter seemed the most favourable option for a fighter with a wing span of 10.0m. However, the Hispano-Suiza 12Ybrs, as well as the M-100 – which by that time had entered production – and taking into account the availability of a gearbox, were fit for operation with a two-blade propeller of 3.4m in diameter (just what was needed for the SB bomber). That was why the landing gear of the TsKB-19 was of such height, providing for the installation of a 3.4m-diameter propeller with the minimum safe clearance between the blade tip and the ground.

Unlike the first prototype, the TsKB-19 had a retractable landing gear of a different design – the landing gear legs retracted towards the aircraft centreline. Due to the new configuration, the wheel track in the static ground position was 2.868m. Extendable water coolers were arranged in the root portion of the wing centre section. The ailerons had a reduced span and were not capable of differential deflection; the role of landing high-lift devices was now taken by deflectable flaps with an area of 1.75sq.m. The aircraft armament consisted of four ShKAS machine guns arranged in the outer wing sections, beyond the propeller disc area.

The TsKB-19 was completed in the late summer of 1935. After final adjustments, determination of weight and balance parameters, engine run-up, taxiing and ground runs, the aircraft first took to the air. On 16 September 1935, at two o'clock sharp, factory pilot Valery Chkalov made the first eight-minute flight in the aircraft. In his usual laconic manner, the test pilot recorded his opinion: "Flight completed. The flight performance is good. No vibrations detected."

Then, up to mid-November, several more flights were performed, followed by adjustment of the cooling system, fine tuning of the landing gear and other activities.

There is no available data on any winter tests of the aircraft. It is most probable that full-fledged flying resumed towards the following summer. On 1 May 1936, the TsKB-19 was demonstrated in flight above Red Square. In the course of tests during the summer season, a maximum speed of 485km/h and a ceiling of 9,700m were reached.

During the period from 13–30 November 1936, the TsKB-19 – along with Tupolev's ANT-25 and ANT-35 – was displayed at the XV Paris Aviation Exhibition. In its coverage of the exhibition, *Samolyot* (Airplane) magazine wrote about the TsKB-19 as follows:

> The liquid-cooled engine provides for a considerable reduction of the undesired drag due to a lesser fuselage cross-section.
>
> There has been substantial interest in such designs lately. It is enough to mention the British Spitfire-1 fighter powered by a liquid-cooled Rolls-Royce engine developing a speed of 500km/h.
>
> The modern configuration and the streamlined contours of the TsKB-19, along with the powerful high-altitude engine, account for the aircraft high speed. The airplane has high stability and manoeuvrability.
>
> The displayed series production [? – *Author's note*] aircraft was built at the Aviation Factory named after Menzhinsky. It has the following performance parameters: maximum speed of 493km/h; service ceiling of 11,350m; flight duration of 2.5 hours.

The performance data mentioned was obviously copied from the placard accompanying the exhibit. This encouraged a certain overstatement of the flight performance parameters, so they should be taken into consideration with some corrections. It is doubtful that the I-17 prototypes reached a speed of 500km/h. Furthermore, the obtained results varied from 480–495km/h.

To complement the TsKB-19 'exhibition story', it is of interest to turn to the memoirs of Russian military diplomat General A.A. Ignatyev in his book *Fifty Years in the Ranks*. In the capacity of Commissar of the Soviet stand at the Paris Aviation Exhibition, Ignatyev, on a November day, met Marshal of France Louis Franchet, with whom he had been well acquainted since the time of the First World War. Ignatyev wrote of the occasion:

> Marshal of France honoured us with his visit, and I had to welcome him at the entrance, with my trilby hat taken off respectfully.
>
> 'Good afternoon, *monsieur*,' Franchet addressed me, without mentioning not only my former title but even the last name, in order to emphasise his contemptuous attitude to me. This left me untouched; the final provocation on the part of the marshal did not embarrass me either.
>
> 'Tell me, is it such aircraft that you send to Spain?' he asked me, having listened to the explanation regarding the little silver-coloured fighter placed at the corner of the stand.
>
> 'No, *monsieur* Marshal,' I replied. 'We are displaying such aircraft only for the *Parisiennes*.' (At that moment, we were surrounded by a throng of festively dressed ladies.) 'As for Spain, we supply much more advanced aircraft to them.'
>
> The public began to applaud: that was an era of the Popular Front.

The above episode contains a number of interesting points. First, the appearance of the I-15 and I-16 Soviet fighters in Spain became the main news in the aviation community during the period of the XV Paris Aviation Exhibition. It was those aircraft that were meant by the Marshal of France when he mentioned Soviet assistance to the Republicans. At the same time, Ignatyev himself speaks of the TsKB as if it were obsolescent. Most probably, the phrase was neither an expression of his personal opinion nor a smart joke; what the Russian count implied was the lukewarm attitude towards the aircraft on the part of the Soviet personnel who were servicing the exhibit.

The next fact to be noted is that, during the period of the exhibition, a Dewoitine D.510 monoplane fighter powered by a Hispano-Suiza 12Ybrs engine arrived in the Soviet Union from France and was handed over to NII VVS to be tested. During the course of the tests, the French fighter demonstrated mediocre performance, including insufficient lateral and directional stability and shortcomings in the engine cooling system. In spite of the three-blade propeller and excellent French-built engine, the Dewoitine D.510 turned out unable to exceed a speed of 400km/h. It should be noted that it was the future installation of a three-blade propeller with which Soviet specialists connected further opportunities to increase the TsKB-19's maximum speed. After completion of the D.510 tests, it was stated that "the Dewoitine aircraft, in terms of its flight performance parameters, proved to be of no interest for the VVS RKKA". Who knows, maybe the French-built Dewoitine, along with the I-16's successes in Spain, added up to the general understanding that, over time, the Polikarpov I-17 had ceased to be 'of interest' as well.

After the exhibition in Paris, the TsKB-19 returned to the Soviet Union, but there were no further mentions of it as an airworthy prototype. There were rumours that the aircraft had been considerably damaged during transportation. According to archive materials, the second I-17 prototype (TsKB-19) was, in early 1939, at the facilities of Factory No.21 in Gorky (Nizhny Novgorod). Its further fate is not known.

The I-17 (TsKB-19bis) third prototype

This aircraft was sometimes referred to as the I-17bis, so this designation will be used to simplify the further narration. Dmitry Tomashevich was Leading Designer for the I-17bis project.

On the third prototype, it was planned to perform installation of a high-rate-of-fire aircraft cannon arranged in the engine Vee and firing through the hollow shaft of the propeller. The entire assembly was briefly named as an 'engine cannon'.

In 1934, along with purchasing French aircraft engines, the Soviet party was also considering the question of buying aircraft cannons (a French variant of the license-built Oerlikons) with ammunition feed kinematics, attachment systems, etc. The Soviet variant of such a cannon was developed by designers Shpitalny and Komaritsky. It was based on the design of the ShKAS machine guns, which had already entered production, and was initially designated the ShKAS-2; later, it became known as the 20mm ShVAK cannon. It is this cannon that was mounted on the third prototype of the I-17.

The I-17bis was, on the whole, similar to the second prototype (TsKB-19), but had a modified cockpit canopy, which featured a backward-sliding middle portion and a fixed forward windscreen. In addition to the engine cannon, two ShKAS machine guns were mounted in the outer wing panels, while provisions were made for attachment of up to 100kg of bombs. In terms of the exterior, the aircraft's differences from the predecessor included the upper fuselage hatch for cannon mounting and the oil cooler arranged in the left lower portion of the engine cowling.

The I-17bis, powered by the M-100A engine s/n 601, first flew in early November 1936. It took to the air with test pilot K.K. Popov at the controls. Upon completion of brief factory tests, on 16 November, Popov ferried the aircraft to NII VVS in Shchelkovo. The I-17bis became the first aircraft of its family to undergo state tests, which began on 27 December. Eight flights were performed by pilot V.A. Stepanchonok, and two by P.M. Stefanovsky. The pilots noted reliable operation of the engine, although several forced landings at the airfield took place. On the whole, the pilots had a positive opinion of the aircraft. They commented that the visibility from the cockpit was better than in the I-16, and found the aircraft easy and comfortable to control, stating that it was "flying smoothly in all flight modes, without the need for any excessive motions". As for the cockpit, the test pilots unanimously found it too narrow. They suggested making it some 10–12cm wider and raising the pilot seat by 5–6cm so that the pilot could sit up higher.

In early 1937, tests of the cannon armament began at a gunnery range near Noginsk. The engine cannon operated flawlessly. On 10 February 1937, on the way back from the gunnery range to Schelkovo, the engine unexpectedly stalled. Stepanchonok, who was at the aircraft controls, made a forced landing on the outskirts of the village of Elino. The pilot himself commented on what happened as follows: "I decided to land on the edge of the village with the landing gear down because, in case of a nose-over, local people might help me out of the aircraft."

Upon landing, the right landing gear leg collapsed; as a result, the right wing was damaged. The aircraft was sent for repair to Aviation Factory No.84, where it stayed until summer 1938. After the aircraft was checked in flight in June 1938, the I-17bis' armament tests were resumed. From 7–10 August, the aircraft was flown by Tomas Susi, who fired 661 shots in mid-air at an average rate of fire of 963 shots per minute. It was noted that operation of the system involved no difficulties; all components functioned without fault and did not affect the power plant performance. Among disadvantages, Susi mentioned certain problems with the case ejection chute: empty cartridge cases were striking against the right wing with a considerable force.

It was expected that the state tests would continue, but meanwhile, the aircraft stayed at the facilities of Aviation Factory No.84. In early November, a crew from NII VVS arrived. On 10 November, a check flight was performed (it is not known who was piloting the aircraft). During the following days, the weather abruptly worsened and the tests were suspended. After the crash of the I-180 prototype piloted by Valery Chkalov on 15 December, all flights of aircraft designed by Polikarpov were ceased for some time. The I-17bis remained grounded at the base of Aviation Factory No.84 up to March 1939. Its further fate is not traceable.

After completion of the range tests of the I-17bis in autumn 1938, according to a report of the Aviation Armament Research and Testing Range of the VVS RKKA, it was suggested that a series of three such aircraft should be built for final refinement of the cannon armament. An order for three engine cannons was placed with the manufacturer. However, the story was not destined to continue – the I-17 was unexpectedly withdrawn from the aviation industry plan for 1939.

Dimensions and flight performance parameters of the I-17 prototypes			
Parameter	TsKB-15	TsKB-19	TsKB-19bis
Length (m)	7.4	7.365	7.425

Dimensions and flight performance parameters of the I-17 prototypes			
Wing span (m)	10.0	10.0	10.0
Wing area (sq.m)	17.7	17.65	17.65
Empty weight (kg)	1,350	1,560	1,465
Gross weight (kg)	1,823.29	1,916.92	1,950
Load on wing (kg/sq.m)	103.0	108.5	110.5–115.0
Maximum speed at design altitude (km/h)	456 (at 3,380m)	485 (at 9,700m)	No data available
Armament	4xShKAS	2xShKAS	1x20mm ShVAK 2xShKAS

The I-172 and I-173 projects

In early 1937, the 960hp M-103 engine underwent state tests. It was planned that series production of the engine would be launched in the following year at Engine Factory No.26 in Rybinsk. With the M-103 in mind, Polikarpov prepared a project of the I-172 fighter in 1938 which was a further development of the I-17. According to the designer's calculations, the aircraft powered by the M-103 could reach a maximum speed of approximately 550km/h at an altitude of 4,000m.

While a fighter with a liquid-cooled engine was in the prospective plan of the Soviet Air Force, one powered by an air-cooled engine was, at that time, deemed the most prospective option. It was for that reason that the Polikarpov Design Bureau focused mainly on development of the I-180 fighter. The hope to finally receive the M-105 engine, which had been waited for since 1937, was viewed an additional excuse for suspending work on the I-172. The M-105-powered aircraft was given the designation I-173, and certain design activities relating to it took place in early 1939. Due to various circumstances, full-fledged design work on it never began. Several months later, the entire accumulated experience in creating a fighter with a liquid-cooled engine was implemented in the I-200 project, and afterwards in the ITP prototype.

It might have become the third one

In the history of the I-17 there are certain parallels with two famous fighter aircraft of that period – the German Messerschmitt Bf 109 and British Supermarine Spitfire. Being contemporaries, they had rather similar layouts and nearly equal initial flight performance parameters. Among the similarities should be noted the multistep process of design, manufacturing and testing, and the presence of rivals. There were also some differences: for example, the I-17 was created in conditions of the rather limited capabilities of the Soviet aviation industry in terms of technologies and materials used. On the other hand, the higher technical level of the aviation industry in Germany and Great Britain enabled Willy Messerschmitt and Reginald Mitchell to create designs which remained modern in the years that followed.

To compare these three fighters, below is a table detailing the steps in the aircraft's histories and their specifics.

Description	I-17	Bf 109	Spitfire
Release of the task and beginning of development	The tactical requirements were approved in December 1933. The fighter was included in the experimental aircraft building plan of VVS RKKA for 1934–35. The I-17 had been proactively developed since mid-1933.	The technical task for the single-seat fighter to replace the He 51 was prepared in early 1934. The work had been proactively conducted since 1933 as part of the Bf.108 four-seat sports/leisure aircraft development.	Specification No. F7/30 for developing a modern fighter aircraft was approved by the Air Ministry on 1 October 1931. Supermarine Type 224, designed to these specifications, failed to overcome the speed limit of 400km/h. As a result, work on a high-speed fighter, which was afterwards designated the Spitfire, began in 1934 – first under Specification F5/34, then under Specification F37/34.
Earlier projects which allowed the designers to gain considerable experience	Over 10 types of created fighters. The TsKB-12 (I-16) monoplane, which was built before the end of 1933, could be viewed as the I-17 predecessor.	A range of developed sports and passenger aircraft. The Bf 108, on which the majority of structural components were tested, was a pinnacle of design work.	Racing seaplanes. The world speed record of 655km/h was set by Supermarine S.6B in 1931. The Supermarine-244 monoplane prototype was built per Specification No. F7/30.

Description	I-17	Bf 109	Spitfire
Construction features	Mixed construction employed by Polikarpov since the late 1920s; optimum weight-to-wing area ratios; a special focus on aerodynamics in order to obtain high speed. Outward retracting landing gear; narrow track in the first prototype (1,800mm); cooling radiators positioned under the wing.	All-metal construction, which had been tried out, stage by stage, in earlier aircraft in order to obtain high manufacturability and ease of maintenance during operation. Outward retracting landing gear; narrow track (approximately 2,000mm); oil cooler under the wing (later, water coolers were relocated and arranged under the wing in the same position as in the I-17).	All-metal construction; focus on good aerodynamics, high strength and optimum lifting surfaces-to-control surfaces ratios rather than on use of technologies. Outward retracting landing gear; narrow track (1,730mm); cooling radiator positioned under the right wing; oil cooler under the left wing.
Wing parameters	Two-spar fabric-covered wing. Span – 10.0m; wing area – 17.65sq.m; wing loading – up to 115kg/sq.m for the TsKB-19bis.	Single-spar wing with smooth metal skin. Span – 9.90m; wing area – 16.4sq.m; wing loading – from 119.3kg/sq.m in the earlier series to 152.7kg/sq.m in the E series	Single-spar wing with smooth metal skin. Span – 11.23m; wing area: 22.48sq.m; wing loading: 115.6kg/sq.m; approximately 150kg/sq.m in later series.
Engine and speed	According to specifications, the Hispano-Suiza 12Ybrs engine had power of 800hp near ground level; the M-100 engine, of 1935–36, had specified power of 750hp. During tests, none of the I-17 prototypes overcame the speed limit of 500km/h.	The prototype began to fly with the 695hp Rolls-Royce Kestrel engine, with which it developed a speed of 465km/h in 1935. With the Junkers Jumo 210 having take-off power of 680hp, the Bf 109 speed still did not exceed 500km/h. In 1938, manufacture of the E series began. These aircraft, powered by the Daimler-Benz DB-601 engine having take-off power of 1,050hp, developed a speed of 540–570km/h.	With the Rolls-Royce Merlin developing 790hp at an altitude of 3,660m, the prototype reached 560km/h in 1936. With the Merlin II engine having rated power of 900hp at an altitude of 3,730m (and maximum power of 1,050hp), the Supermarine Spitfire Mk.I developed a maximum speed of 582km/h at an altitude of 5,640m (according to the company's pre-war data).
Date of the first flight	The TsKB-15 began to fly in the first half of 1934; the TsKB-19 first flew on 16 September 1935. The third prototype (TsKB-19bis) first took to the air in November 1936.	On 28 May 1935 under the designation Bf 109V1.	On 5 March 1936 under the designation Supermarine F37/34.
The first public display	Demonstration of the TsKB-19 at the Paris Aviation Exhibition in 1936.	A demonstration flight of the Bf 109V-2 in August 1936 during the course of the Olympics in Berlin. During subsequent years, the aircraft needed no additional demonstration, due to the fact that it was taking part in combat operations in Spain.	The process of aircraft creation was going on in conditions of secrecy. However, after the aircraft reached a maximum speed of 560km/h, it began to be widely advertised. In November 1938, the aircraft was demonstrated in flight at the Paris Aviation Exhibition.

Description	I-17	Bf 109	Spitfire
Armament	4xShKAS machine guns in the TsKB-15; a ShVAK engine cannon in the Vee of the engine plus two wing-mounted ShKAS in the TsKB-19. Neither of the variants was fitted or intended to be fitted with synchronised machine guns.	Nearly from the very beginning, the aircraft was fitted with machine guns and, later, cannons in all versions (synchronised, wing-mounted and firing through the hollow shaft of the engine).	Initially, only machine guns (up to eight) were mounted; later, the aircraft was fitted with wing-mounted cannons.
State of affairs in 1938	The intended operational testing series was never built; all experimental work on the I-17 was discontinued. However, there was a fighter with a liquid-cooled engine indicated in the experimental aircraft building plan for 1938.	Before mid-1937, the first 30 production aircraft were built. The Bf 109 successfully took part in the Spanish Civil War from 1937–39. In 1938, the Bf 109s were in service with six fighter groups in the territory of Germany.	An order for 310 Spitfires was placed with the manufacturer even before completion of the prototype tests. The order was completed in August 1939. The first series production aircraft was rolled out on 15 May 1938. Before the end of the year, the aircraft began to be supplied to squadrons.
Attitude to speed records	Development and manufacturing process was started with a view to setting a speed record. In 1936, S.V. Ilyushin took over the topic.	On 11 July 1938, the world speed record of 610km/h was set in a Bf 109D powered by an uprated DB 601 engine. In April 1939, the world speed record of 755.138km/h was set in a Bf 109R powered by a 1,800hp DB 601A engine.	At the 1939 aviation exhibition in Brussels, the aircraft was displayed as the Spitfire 17 racing version. With the Merlin engine uprated to 2,000hp, reaching a maximum speed of approximately 800km/h was planned.
Installation of steam-evaporation cooling system.	Steam-evaporation cooling system was planned for both the record-setting and combat versions. It was never implemented in practice.	There were no provisions for the steam-evaporation cooling system in the combat version.	A mixed system utilising a wing-mounted steam condenser was used in the Supermarine-224 prototype. It was intended to be used for speed record setting purposes.

Comparison of the I-17, Bf 109 and Spitfire in the table above expressly highlights several points. The British designers were focused on refining the wing as the main structural component influencing the aerodynamics. Their efforts paid off – the Spitfire, with not a very high wing loading and an engine power comparable to that of the I-17, was the first to come close to a speed of 600km/h. No wonder that the British drew a veil of secrecy over the aircraft. The Messerschmitt also overcame the 500km/h speed limit confidently (though it took the aircraft some time to reach it). There was one common point for both these aircraft – there was a need for them, so they entered production promptly. In the case of the I-17, the situation was the other way around. In 1936–37, the I-16 was at the height of its fame, and Polikarpov promised to achieve a maximum speed of 520km/h in this aircraft. The inevitable question was, why create another new fighter, which did not offer any noticeable advantage at that time? Thus, there was no heightened interest in the I-17 in the Soviet aviation industry. Otherwise, the new aircraft would not have been sent in 1936 to the Paris exhibition, which was open to the public.

During the period from 1934–36, all the improvements of the I-17 consisted in the preparation of new projects. The prototypes had almost no differences from each other (except for landing gear design, canopy opening variants and some minor variations). It could be stated that the type was almost not being developed at all, and up to 1937 remained in the same condition as it was back in 1933. The aircraft's shortcomings, which 'ruined' it at the design stage, included the two-spar fabric-covered wing, the outdated pyramidal landing gear and the narrow cockpit, the width of which was adapted to suit the engine's dimensions. The latter feature was noted in the documents as the main cause of Soviet Air Force dissatisfaction with the I-17 prototypes.

On the other hand, the official documents do not mention the wing as the primary reason for insufficient flight speed. Indeed, the metal wing with more than half of its area covered with fabric was efficient solely at speeds up to 400km/h. To reach higher speeds, an all-metal wing of better workmanship and with accurately followed airfoil parameters was needed. Unfortunately, this problem was neglected in the Soviet Union. Most probably, with a more advanced wing, the I-17 would have come closer to flight speeds of 550km/h, and thus would have got a chance to enter production in a short time.

When viewing the aircraft's fate through the prism of its individual advantages and disadvantages, it is also relevant to review the status of its engine development.

As early as 1936, the M-100P engine (a variant of the license-built Hispano-Suiza engine) was designed. Three such cannon engines (s/n 601, 602 and 603) were built. The engine s/n 602 was subjected to fatigue tests; the other two entered test operation on the I-17bis.

In late 1937, development of the 960hp M-103P (M-103AP) engine was started. According to the plans, 12 such engines were intended to be built, but in practice, only seven (six serviceable engines and a mock-up) were completed. At least four of them (s/n 605, 606, 608 and 609) were sent to Aviation Factory No.84, where they were, most probably, used on the VIT-2 two-engine aircraft. The engine s/n 606 underwent fatigue tests, while the s/n 604 was handed over to TsKB No.2 for armament testing. Thus, the engines for the potential improvement of the I-17 were available in 1938, but it was only in 1939 that the necessity to create a fighter with higher performances was realised.

The first I-17 (TsKB-15) prototype at the Central Airfield in Moscow in summer 1934.

The second I-17 (TsKB-19) prototype at the XV Paris Aviation Exhibition in November 1936.

The third I-17 (TsKB-19bis) prototype at the beginning of its tests in 1936.

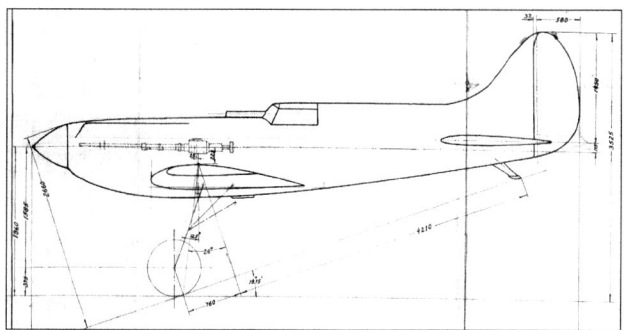

Side view drawing of the I-17 (TsKB-19bis).

The cover of the September 1938 issue of *Model Airplane News* magazine with a picture of the I-17.

General views of the M-100 engine with mounted cannon.

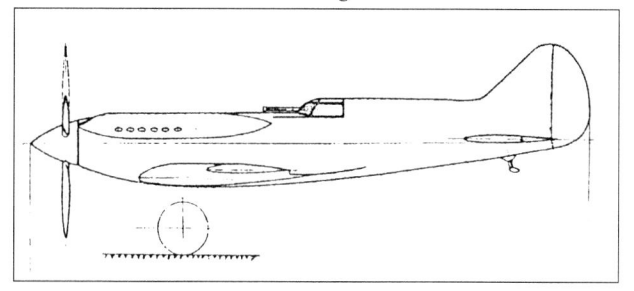

Side view drawing of the I-21 fighter developed by S.V. Ilyushin.

170   The King of Fighters Volume 2

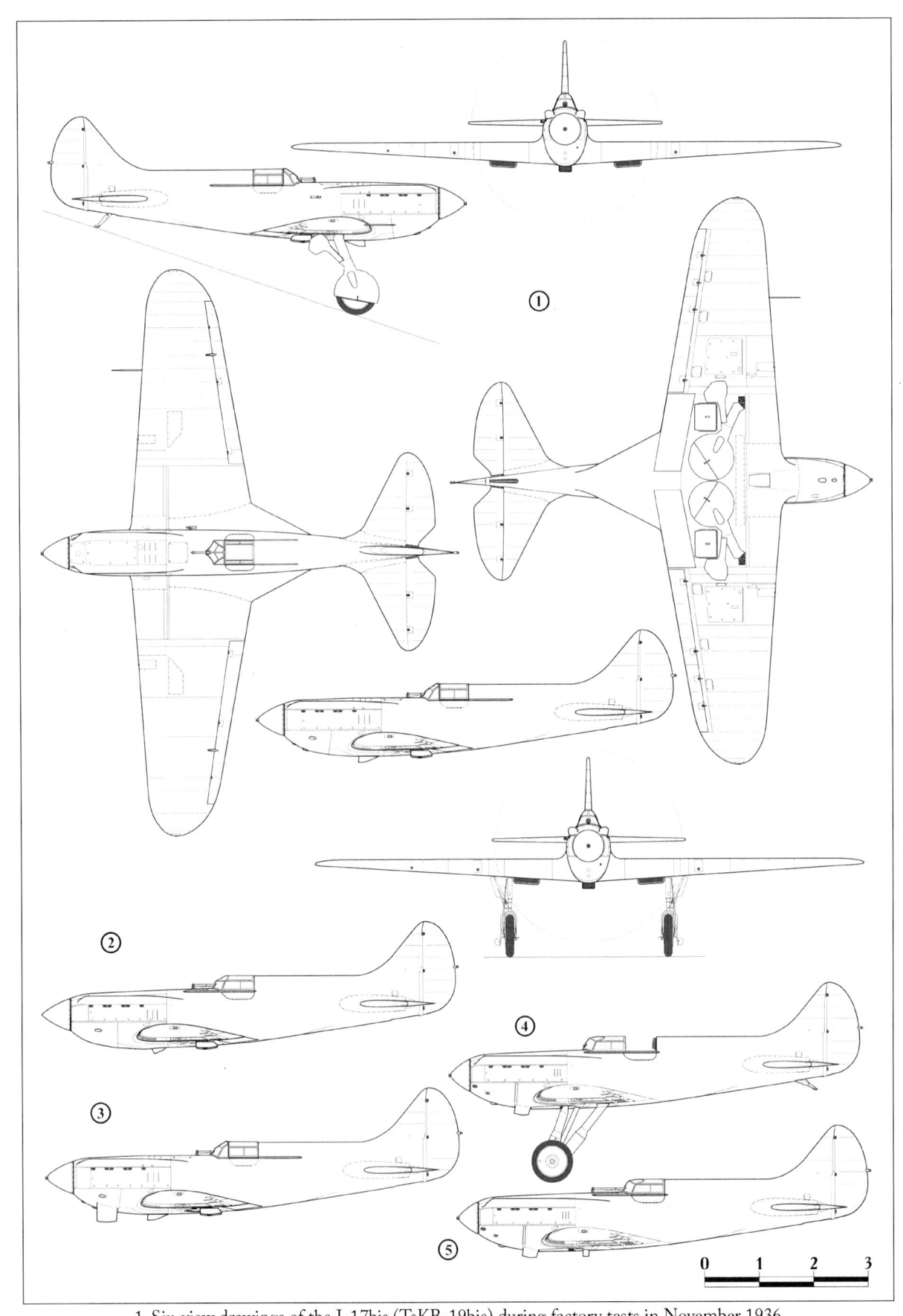

1. Six-view drawings of the I-17bis (TsKB-19bis) during factory tests in November 1936.
2. Side view drawing of the I-17 (TsKB-19) at Paris in November 1936.
3. Side view drawing of the I-17bis (TsKB-19bis) during armament tests at the range in Noginsk in August 1938.
4. Side view drawing of the I-17 (TsKB-15) at Moscow Central Airfield in 1935.
5. Side view drawing of the I-17 (TsKB-15) in September 1934

3

The I-180 fighter

In the mid-1930s, the I-16 fighter established itself as part of the Soviet Air Force. After over two years of series production and service with military forces, it was time to consider enhancing its flight performance and technical specifications drastically. Improvements to the aircraft in terms of armament, structural strength and reliability of systems and equipment had been made throughout all those years. Introduction of the M-25V uprated engine gave rise to hopes for an abrupt growth of the maximum speed (up to 520km/h). However, those hopes failed: given the higher gross weight, the slight growth of power resulted in a negligible increase of the maximum speed. To improve all flight performance parameters, the I-16's engine power had to be increased considerably. In Polikarpov's opinion, the best solution to the problem consisted in utilising double-row radial engines descending from the French-built Gnome-Rhône 14K Mistral Major series. The licensed version of the French engine entered production in Zaporozhye at Aviation Factory No.29 in 1934–35 under the M-85 designation. Throughout the two years that followed, the factory design bureau under A. Nazarov developed more advanced and powerful versions, namely, the M-86, M-87 and M-88. It was the M-88, with a declared take-off power of 1,100hp, that Polikarpov finally selected for the new fighter. Initially, the M-88-powered I-16 version was given the temporary designation I-161. It seemed to be as simple as that: the new engine had a lesser diameter, and adapting it to the *Ishak*'s airframe should not have been a tremendous task. However, being heavier, the M-88 shifted the centre of gravity to a considerably more forward position, so a noticeable rearrangement of the aircraft's entire nose portion was required. To solve the problem at the expense of minimum possible changes, Polikarpov for the first time suggested, as a trade-off, to utilise a wing with a straight leading edge. The I-161 was followed by the I-162, I-163, I-164, I-165, I-166 and I-167 projects. The aircraft variants were used to test new cowlings and engine cooling systems, new landing gear configurations, wing skin and fuel tank arrangements. All those works might prove helpful in creating a new fighter in the near future, and it was already known that the Soviet Air Force command wished to order such a fighter from the manufacturers.

Throughout 1937, senior officials of the aviation industry and the Air Force command were under the influence of two contradictory feelings brought about by reports from Spain. On the one hand, the authorities were happy to receive enthusiastic comments on combat operations of the I-15 and I-16 fighters. On the other, it was not clear in what direction to move on in terms of design, and what to improve. Take, for instance, the I-15. Criticised and discontinued in the Soviet Union, the aircraft did well in Spain. Consequently, a decision was made to meticulously collect all information on combat activity of Soviet aircraft, to determine advantages and shortcomings of various types, and to finally give new tasks to designers and manufacturers.

At that time, there existed a practice of sending pilots and technicians from the Soviet Union to Spain on a so-called 'Voroshilov's duty trip'. The first group left for Spain between October and December 1936, and returned, for the most part, by May or June 1937. Upon their return, the specialists who had seen action were summoned to the Air Force Directorate of Material-Technical Support, where they wrote detailed reports on advantages and shortcomings of aircraft, both Soviet and enemy ones. It was felt that such activity might prove useful in working out tactical requirements for ordering new aircraft types. It was expected that the work would be completed before autumn 1937. Indeed, numerous points related to combat tactics and trends in improvement of flight performance parameters, engines, equipment and armament became clear by the autumn. In particular, new fighter types, among which the German Bf 109 stood out, saw service on the Nationalist side.

In spite of the efforts taken, no orders for a new fighter aircraft development was issued in 1937. The cause of this was the arrest of many Air Force and aviation industry senior officials – all those directly involved in the rearmament plans. Furthermore, the already conducted extensive work on preparation of technical requirements remained hidden, and its results emerged only in early 1938.

Polikarpov was also affected by the reshuffles in the army and the aviation industry that took place in 1937. In late 1937, he was appointed Chief Designer of Aviation Factory No.156 (formerly known as the TsAGI Factory of Experimental Designs). The Polikarpov Design Bureau moved from Factory No.84 to the new location in late December 1937 and early January 1938. On 7 January, the relocated team received a most interesting document containing specifications of aircraft engines and due dates for their manufacture and supply to aircraft developers (see Table 1). The list of the document's recipients was no less interesting: Polikarpov, Sukhoi, Arkhangelsky, Kocherigin, Beriev, Bolkhovitinov, Chetverikov and Neman. The list was nothing but a kind of 'table of ranks', where Polikarpov was allocated the honourable top position.

A day later, a notification was received from the Soviet Air Force with the list of aircraft types requested for development, including their performance parameters. The request was accompanied by the following message from Head of the PGU NKOP Sergey Ilyushin: "I suggest to perform a check and to respond, in a five-day period, on the practicability of obtaining the flight performance data and on the due dates for presenting the aircraft for state tests as per the VVS RKKA requirements attached hereto, as well as on the conditions for creating such aircraft in accordance with the prescribed schedule." (see Table 2)

On 14 January 1938, Polikarpov sent a reply to Ilyushin stating that, judging by the parameters of available and planned engines, the Air Force requirements could not be complied with in full. In a table attached to the reply (see Table 3), some of the required data was confirmed as practicable and accomplishable, whereas others (primarily the maximum speed values) were reduced in accordance with performed calculations. In an explanatory note, Polikarpov, assessing the capabilities of the aviation industry, suggested that reducing an aircraft's gross weight should be reckoned among the top priority tasks:

> The Air Force requirements are at considerable contradiction with performance parameters of the engines; it is essentially the engines that limit further progress fighter aviation. Calculation and practical experience show that reducing the weight of the aircraft (and, accordingly, the weight of the engine) is a much more important factor for obtaining a manoeuvrable fighter. It is more important than the minor increase in power that we get. Decreasing size of the engines and reducing their weight to 400kg should be regarded as a top priority task.

As for the entire development programme of six new aircraft, Polikarpov found it unachievable for his design bureau because of a lack of human resources (according to his estimate, to perform the entire amount of required work, the number of personnel would have had to be increased more than two-fold). As for individual aircraft projects, their status was as follows:

- A single-engine bomber was already being built at Factory No.156 under the codename *Ivánov* and could further be converted into a ground-attack aircraft.
- A parasol-wing artillery spotter aircraft had already been discussed for a year. Preliminary projects for the AM-34FRNT and M-62 engines were developed.
- A long-range reconnaissance aircraft was intended to be built, based on the VIT-2 multipurpose aircraft platform.
- A manoeuvrable fighter intended to be powered by an air-cooled engine (initially by the M-25V and later by the M-62) was already being developed under the I-153 designation.
- The issue of a high-speed fighter to be powered by an inline engine was sidestepped by Polikarpov. The designer believed that the story of the I-17 was not over yet, and that it was the I-17 that deserved to be developed further. The Air Force, however, ordered another aircraft of the same type, since a decision had already been made in respect of the I-17 to withdraw it from the experimental work plan.

Thus, there was a need for a modern high-speed fighter powered by a radial air-cooled engine. While not being singled out from the list of required types, development of such a fighter was deemed to be the most pressing and urgent task. It is no wonder, then, that activities in this direction were launched immediately. Polikarpov, using the experience gained during the improvements of the I-16, promptly presented the design of a new fighter, which was designated the I-180.

The explanatory note, prepared in late January 1938, read: "The aircraft being designed is a further development of a fighter with air-cooled engine, based on the I-16 technology … the development goal is to create a high-speed fighter with powerful armament, with the possibility to introduce it promptly into series production at Aviation Factory No.21 to replace the I-16." The I-180 was indeed very close to the I-16, and could even be considered as its further development with a more powerful engine. The structural arrangement and layout, and design of the fuselage, wing, tail unit and landing gear were nearly identical. The primary dimensions were also identical or similar:

Parameter	I-16	I-180
Wing span (m)	9.00	9.00
Wing area (sq.m)	14.54	14.7
Aircraft length (m)	6.004	6.487
Horizontal stabilizer span (m)	3.500	3.500

The most noticeable difference of the I-180 was the wing with a straight leading edge, without sweepback in plan view. It is known that Polikarpov had already chosen this wing configuration in 1937, when attempting to combine the I-16 and the M-88 engine. Moving forward the mean aerodynamic chord allowed, with a heavier engine, the retaining of the same range of CG positions almost without any increase in the aircraft length, and also keeping the arm of the horizontal tail. Theoretically, such wing had a slight reverse sweep along the quarter-chord line, which allowed the expectation of some positive qualities such as improved performance in stall conditions.

The aforementioned M-88 engine should have provided the new fighter with high flight performance parameters and, first and foremost, a maximum flight speed of 600km/h. This promising double-row 14-cylinder radial air-cooled engine did not exist 'in metal' at the time of the I-180's development. Furthermore, Engine Factory No.29 oriented its product for bombers rather than fighters. With a rotation speed of 1,600–1,700rpm, the M-88 was designed for a propeller diameter of 3,150–3,200mm. For a small fighter aircraft, the propeller diameter had to be a maximum of 2,800–2,900mm, and the rotation speed, accordingly, had to be increased to 2,100–2,200rpm. The latter requirement meant that the engine factory had, within a short time, not only to build and test the engine, but also to equip it with a new gearbox. Obviously, it would take a certain amount of time to complete this work, and it was not worthwhile counting on the M-88 in the coming months. Therefore, it was decided that the first prototype would be fitted with the M-87 engine of the same family, which had a slightly lower power but was very close to the M-88 in terms of weight and size.

The preliminary project of the new aircraft was ready in late February 1938, and further development of the engineering documentation was in full swing. Work on the I-180's development was carried out by a team led by Mikhail Gurevich; shortly after, Dmitry Tomashevich was appointed the Leading Designer for the aircraft and Polikarpov's deputy. The first meeting of an evaluation commission was held on 10 April, at which a full-scale wooden mock-up of the fighter was examined. The main results were a positive assessment of the project and setting a state-defined deadline for the first prototype readiness – 'by the end of the year'.

Manufacturing of the I-180 began in summer 1938 in the workshops of Aviation Factory No.156. While difficulties in manufacturing were initially not expected, they nevertheless appeared during the course of the work. The manufacture schedule was tight, despite the fact that the manufacturing team had still to settle down at the new factory and figure out how to work together. Their superiors were driving the team to build the aircraft faster; Stalin personally made inquiries about the progress of the work. This was quite enough for superiors of all ranks further down the line to show their own interest in the prompt completion of the work. Indeed, they put pressure on the director of the factory, Usachev, and kept bothering Polikarpov.

There was nothing unusual about such a rush, as the desire to meet a certain deadline – even an unrealistic one – was a common matter in the Soviet aviation industry. It was believed important to carry out the first flight and report to the authorities, and then to proceed with months-long work on completion and refinement of the aircraft. This was also the case with the I-180. When the first prototype was taken to the airfield in early December 1938, the total number of defects that had to be fixed in the near future reached 30. Some of them were rectified during the first few days of the month. Things were done in a hurry, since there was pressure that the aircraft should take to the air before the end of the year. Head of the PGU NKOP S. Belyaykin came up with the following initiative: "Let us meet the upcoming party congress with labour successes – for this purpose, we should present the I-180 for flight tests ahead of the schedule." Polikarpov was against this as he believed that the prototype would be ready for flight tests only in February 1939. He even refused to sign the act of aircraft readiness for the first flight. As it turned out, this was a thoughtful step: on 12 December, during the first taxiing run at the airfield with the engine on, one of the most important parts in the engine control system – the power control rod – failed. Although the defect was eliminated, many others remained. The ground test programme was not completed, and frontal shutters which regulated engine cooling air flow were not installed. Despite this, on 14 December, the act of the I-180's readiness for the first flight was signed. The act read: "Defects … do not present an obstacle for the first flight … The aircraft is ready for the first flight without landing gear retraction, with limitations on the g-load and speed, according to instructions given by Chief Designer of the factory, comrade Polikarpov." The act was signed without Polikarpov's approval; indeed, he had been sidelined and excluded from taking part in the aircraft tests, and could only give recommendations.

The date of the first flight was set for 15 December 1938. Valery Chkalov – the most renowned Soviet test pilot – was to be at the controls of the aircraft during its maiden flight. Some time before, Chkalov had been the first to fly the I-16, and he had done a lot for the type in order to put it in service. Five years later, history was repeating itself with the I-180, and there were hopes for a favourable outcome. The task to be accomplished by Chkalov on 15 December was as follows: "To perform the first flight without landing gear retraction, with limited speed … along the route above the Central Airfield, at an altitude of 600 metres." It seemed that the task would not present any difficulty: a short flight in the airfield zone, then Chkalov could accept congratulations. Nevertheless, the first flight of the I-180 ended in a crash and the death of Chkalov.

The death of the most renowned and publicly loved pilot of the time has to date been accompanied by surmises and conjecture, some of which are based on the idea that everything had been fabricated, and enemies (whether saboteurs, agents of imperialism or NKVD head Lavrentiy Beria) had got to Chkalov. Furthermore, it is hypothesised that Chkalov violated the flight task and flew far beyond the boundaries of the airfield. In particular, test pilot Kokkinaki recalled that he had met Chkalov in mid-air at an altitude of 2,000–2,500 metres on the outskirts of Moscow.

As for possible attempts to eliminate Chkalov, they of course cannot be denied. The frank and straightforward pilot was becoming very popular in the USSR and may have been seen as a potential competitor or threat to the country's leaders. However, on the day of the disaster, none of participants of the events noted any signs of sabotage or extraneous interference. Furthermore, the events of the day were for the most part random in nature.

The established rules for performance of a prototype's first flight took into account any malfunctions which could take place, including an engine stall in mid-air. That is why the flight had to be carried out within the zone of the airfield, in order to provide for its safe completion in almost any situation. So what made Chkalov commit such a critical violation as flying beyond the boundaries of the airfield? According to one disputable version, which explains the haste in arranging the I-180's readiness, Chkalov's flight was a birthday present for Stalin; the pilot (either by arrangement or on his own initiative) left the airfield to fly over the Soviet leader's residence in Kuntsevo, located just 8km from the base. There is now no one left to be asked whether this was really the case. Whatever the truth, this off-airfield flight was not the direct cause of the crash and Chkalov's death.

The problem occurred in the final stage of the flight during the approach to the airfield. The day of 15 December was extremely frosty, with the air cooled down to 25 degrees below zero. The M-87 engine, which was not fitted with adjustable frontal shutters, cooled down when gliding and stalled unexpectedly during the pilot's attempt to change its power setting. Was this brought about by a design shortcoming or by the pilot's mistake? Perhaps this situation could have been dealt with; it is clear that the experienced pilot had a sufficient altitude margin when he was slowing the engine down. However, he miscalculated; but why? It appears that Chkalov made the landing approach like he would in the I-16, which was equipped with a fixed-pitch propeller. The I-180, however, was fitted with a VISh-3E variable-pitch propeller, which had two positions: low pitch for take-off and landing, and high pitch for maximum speed. Since, in this case, the blade rotation mechanism had not been refined, the blades for a single flight were set to one of the two available positions – to low pitch. If the engine stalled at the low pitch, the propeller blades, with their frontal plane towards the air flow, would turn into efficient air brakes. Chkalov might not have known this; it is hardly likely that he had come across a similar situation, as variable-pitch propellers had only just begun to be introduced in the Soviet aviation. As a result, his estimate for the landing approach turned out to be erroneous. The aircraft thus failed to reach the airfield, and instead landed beyond its boundaries in some wasteland. In the collision, the pilot was thrown out of the cockpit and struck his head on a protruding rail. An ambulance rushed to the crash site and Chkalov was taken to the nearby Botkin Hospital, but he died there two hours later without regaining consciousness.

Assessing the results of this crash, the further course of history changed from that moment on. There were terrifying consequences for many participants in the event. Head of the PGU NKOP Belyaykin, Leading Designer of the I-180 Tomashevich, Director of Factory No.156 Usachev and Head of the Flight Test Station Colonel Porai were all promptly arrested. Polikarpov was also mentioned as being among those guilty of causing the tragedy.

The death of Valery Chkalov and the loss of the first I-180 prototype had a negative impact on the continuation of the development and improvement of the fighter. Worst of all, Polikarpov lost Stalin's support, and consequently the support of other leaders who could influence events. This was not openly spoken of; however, another failure would have been enough to make the non-confidence in the designer and his aircraft quite tangible.

The second I-180 prototype, work on which was launched in January 1939, had some differences compared to the lost first aircraft. The wing span was increased to 10.09 meters, and the wing area thus became larger. The aircraft was also equipped with armament, consisting of two wing-mounted and two synchronised ShKAS machine guns. The I-180-2 was powered by an M-87A engine developing a maximum power of 1,000hp. Alexander Trostyansky was appointed Leading Designer of the aircraft, and was also to supervise introduction of the type into series production.

The I-180-2 was completed in April 1939. In the middle of the month, it was brought to the NII VVS airfield in Shchelkovo for testing. This time, especially thorough preparations were carried out before the first flight, with all systems and units checked and tried more than once. However, again there was a hurry, this time due to a willingness to demonstrate the new fighter at the traditional May Day flypast over Red Square. Major Stepan Suprun was appointed leading test pilot for the I-180-2. On 19 and 21 April, he performed the first taxiing runs and take-off hops. On the evening on 27 April, at 8:07 p.m., shortly before dark, the aircraft first took to the air with Suprun at the controls. This short flight over the airfield within the framework of a strictly set task lasted for just eight minutes. Nothing unusual was noted; the pilot was quite happy with the aircraft. More flights were performed on the following day, as well as on 29 and 30 April. In total, before the May Day holiday, the second I-180 prototype made 10 flights, the last of them being one from Shchelkovo to the Central Airfield in Moscow.

On 1 May 1939, at the due time, Suprun made a normal take-off, climbed to 1,200 metres and then flew along the route of Gorky (Tverskaya) Street. Over the Central Telegraph building, the pilot entered a dive at an angle of 30°, and by the time he was flying over Red Square, the maximum speed had exceeded 500km/h. Over Saint Basil's Cathedral, Suprun performed an energetic zoom climb, then climbed to 1,200 metres again, turned and flew back to the Central Airfield along the shortest possible route.

In the course of the post-flight examination of the I-180, traces of wing deformation and skin swelling were noted. Suprun had obviously been flying the aircraft over Red Square in a more intense manner than he had thought. It was clear that its wing strength had proved to be insufficient.

At the time of manufacture of the first I-180 prototype, a static test airframe had also been built. Tests with alternating loads, up to structural failure, were conducted at TsAGI in the second half of March. Everything was consistent with calculations and assumptions. The results obtained, however, were applicable to an aircraft with a wingspan of 9 metres. The enlarged wing had not yet been tested. After Suprun's flight, there arose a need to urgently reinforce the structure of the new wing and to conduct additional bench tests.

During May 1939, all further work on the I-180 was transferred to Aviation Factory No.1; the Polikarpov Design Bureau moved there as well. The aircraft arrived there on 16 May and underwent modifications and structural reinforcements over the following month. New outer wing panels were manufactured, which were reinforced and featured smooth metal skin (initially, prototypes had outer wing panels partly covered in percale). To obtain a more forward CG position, an elongated engine mount was installed, and a brand-new – just from the factory – M-87B engine developing 950hp at an altitude of 4,000 metres was secured on it. At the same time, the engine was equipped with an annular radiator to cool the engine oil. The radiator consisted of several concentric rings of a special shape, located immediately behind the plane of the rotating propeller in the inlet of the engine cowling. The 'fashion' for such a sophisticated design had come from abroad – in the Soviet Union, it was used on several prototypes (the DI-6, R-9, I-180 and I-28), but it shortly turned out to be a disappointment for everybody and was abandoned.

On 15 June, the I-180-2 resumed flying. Initially, Suprun was performing flights, but from 28 June he was joined by Petr Stefanovsky. On 8 July, Tuomas Susi took his seat at the controls for the first time. Shortly before, Colonel Susi had taken over as Head of the Flight Test Station at Aviation Factory No.21. Aged 38, he was reckoned among the most experienced and respected Soviet test pilots. The new appointment was for him, in fact, a demotion, since his duties were those of an acceptance test pilot at a series production factory. Such disfavour was connected with the pilot's previous activities. Until 1937, Brigade Commander Susi had headed a secret air brigade, which flew fighters equipped with Kurchevsky's dynamo-reactive DRP cannons. After the experiments with the recoilless cannons failed, there were attempts to blame sabotage by foreign agents or enemies of the people, rather than mistakes or lack of knowledge, and Susi had to look for new employment.

A flypast to celebrate Air Fleet Day was planned to be held in Tushino on 18 August 1939. Participation of the I-180 in the flypast was taken for granted. Preparations were made, with all systems and assemblies repeatedly rechecked. Despite all this, there was a major failing on 17 August, the day of the full rehearsal, after Susi departed from Chkalovskaya (the NII VVS airfield in Shchelkovo was given this name after Chkalov's death), heading for Tushino. Near the station of Losinoostrovskaya (north-west of Moscow), his oil pressure suddenly dropped. The pilot was forcedto return and and had to perform a landing with a dead engine. This had happened before – the oil system had not yet been refined well enough. Nevertheless, the holiday flight was not cancelled.

The flypast over Tushino Airfield on 18 August was completed successfully. Susi smoothly accelerated in a shallow descent to a speed of 450km/h, carefully entered into a climb, then turned and flew back to the base. Thankfully, everything went without any surprises or emergencies.

Test flights then continued, lasting until September. These were largely flights under the NII VVS state test programme.

On 5 September, there was a crash in which Susi perished. On that day, the test pilot was expected to fly to the maximum ceiling, with steps to be performed after climbing to each successive 1,000 metres. Twenty-one minutes after take-off, at 9:19 a.m., observers on the ground spotted a spinning aircraft at an altitude of 3,000 metres. The aircraft then went into a nosedive and crashed to the ground. The pilot abandoned the aircraft at a height of 200–250 metres, but was unable to use his parachute and perished. An accident board found the cause of the crash to be "a failure of the equipment". It was concluded that the annular oil cooler had burst while the pilot had been performing a step at an altitude close to the maximum ceiling. Blinded by the hot oil, the pilot lost consciousness and the aircraft entered an uncontrolled dive. Because of the intense heavy haze, the aircraft only became visible when it was at an altitude of 3,000 metres. The pilot had regained consciousness and made an attempt to use his parachute, but he did not have enough time. Susi's face and his light-coloured coveralls were found to be spattered with engine oil.

In spite of the conclusions made by the accident board, there were many who disagreed with them. For example, Head of Design Brigade No.3 Kostenko believed that the crash had most probably been brought about by a failure of the oxygen equipment. The oxygen system of the I-180-2 had been criticised before. In Kostenko's opinion, the pilot lost consciousness after he connected to the oxygen apparatus. His head had then leaned against the left side of the cockpit, and was partially protruding beyond the windscreen. At the same time, the engine was running at maximum speed; Kostenko believed the oil cooler failed a short while later, and the hot oil began to leak from under the cowling and spread over the fuselage. When this oil hit face of Susi, who had been unconscious, the pain caused him to come back round and he attempted to regain control of the aircraft. However, unable to see anything, the pilot was unable to do so and the aircraft fell into a spin. Kostenko felt that Susi had tried to bail out, but lost consciousness again and perished.

Nikolay Polikarpov was inclined to agree with this opinion. However, there was no substantial evidence. No matter what the truth was, what happened was a disaster in every sense. Another outstanding man was killed, and another aircraft, on which so many hopes had been pinned, crashed. Confidence in the correctness of the aircraft and its Chief Designer was badly shaken. However, the history of the I-180 continued.

Although the second prototype no longer existed, a detailed report was drawn up based on the results of its tests. It was concluded that the M-87B-powered I-180-2 was, in terms of its performance parameters, at the level of modern fighters. During the tests, the aircraft had developed a speed of 408km/h near ground level, and 540km/h at an altitude of 5,800 metres. The service ceiling, which was reached in 22½ minutes, was 10,250 metres. On the whole, the I-180-2 seemed to suite the Air Force, who intended to use it in the role of an interceptor, escort fighter and ground-attack aircraft.

At the same time, the test report noted that the aircraft which had been provided for the tests needed to be improved in terms of longitudinal and lateral stability, was unforgiving at landing (being sensitive to excessive pulling efforts on the control stick) and had several design defects and operational shortcomings. The notorious annular radiator was found to be poorly designed and unreliable from a combat point of view, while the carburettor intake, which was arranged in the lower portion of the cowling, collected a lot of airfield dust. Furthermore, the landing gear was too complex in service; it had a number of hinges and doors which required constant adjustments. There were also numerous minor complaints regarding cockpit equipment, controls and operation of certain units. It was suggested that all these issues should be resolved in the course of building a third prototype.

The third prototype was given the designation I-180-3, I-180 E-3 or simply the E-3. In June 1939, the aircraft began to be built at Aviation Factory No.1. However, the process was going on at an unhurried pace because the design brigade was waiting for the results of the second prototype tests in order to introduce appropriate changes. In total, in the summer of 1939, manufacturing of six I-180s was started. It was expected that four of them would be equipped with turbosuperchargers in accordance with the trend of increasing altitude performance of fighter aircraft. There was also a version designated the I-180Sh (I-180-4, I-184 or I-180 E-4), which was intended to have an innovative single-strut landing gear. Choosing the retraction configuration (for example, it was suggested that the landing gear should be retracted in the aft direction with a turn) took some time, and the I-180Sh was never completed by Aviation Factory No.1.

The I-180-3 had a smooth, all-metal wing, the design of which was entirely new compared to previous prototypes. Spar booms, which had earlier been made of tubes, were in the new aircraft replaced with open T-sections made of 30KhGSA steel. In order to improve lateral stability, the dihedral was increased to 6°30'. The third prototype was, at last, fitted with the long-awaited M-88 engine. The engine cowling was made more durable, and cooling control was arranged by special movable shutters (the so-called 'skirt'). A small air intake in the lower part of the cowling remained, but it now covered a honeycomb cylindrical oil cooler, with the air fed to the engine carburettor via openings in the root portion of the centre wing section. Major changes were made to the aircraft's armament, which now consisted of two large-calibre synchronised Berezin TKB-150 (later BS) machine guns and two synchronised ShKAS machine guns. All four machine guns were combined into a single battery and arranged densely in the upper part of the fuselage. Such an armament configuration had initially been tested on the I-16 prototypes.

There was also to be a bomb armament installed, consisting of four bomb carriers arranged under the outer wing panels. The aircraft was capable of carrying a maximum of 200kg of bombs.

It was initially intended that the I-180-3 would become a reference aircraft for series production at Aviation Factory No.21 in Gorky, under the designation Type 25. The transfer of technical documentation began in June 1939. Furthermore, specialists from Gorky arrived in Moscow in order to get acquainted with manufacturing peculiarities and techniques. The first series was expected to consist of 10 aircraft; the factory promised to build the first five in November that year. In practice, however, almost no work was done, Aviation Factory No.21 being fully occupied with manufacture of the I-16s.

To speed up work, Polikarpov sent his special representative Mikhail Yangel to Gorky. Yangel, who later became an academician and spacecraft designer, was at that time a very young man who had only recently graduated from an aviation university. He could hardly have expedited the development of events; a well-connected person with a good knowledge of the subtle mechanisms of the Soviet aviation industry was needed. However, such persons – who would also have to be loyal to Polikarpov – either were not available at the time or there were very few of them.

Meanwhile, the formal order of the NKAP for production of the I-180 was delayed. It was as if the crash of the second prototype served as an excuse for the factory to the effect that they should 'make haste slowly'. The management of Aviation Factory No.21 was quite aware of the rules of the game, and reasonably believed that work on the I-180 was going to be wound up. Such sentiments did not arise from nowhere; it was known that Stalin had decided to focus on young aviation specialists and to sideline old experienced designers. In Gorky, for example, work on the IP-21 fighter prototype designed by M. Pashinin was already under way, with much support from People's Commissar of Aviation Industry Mikhail Kaganovich. According to the available documents, Kaganovich repeatedly visited Factory No.21 to expedite manufacturing of the I-180 series. However, it is hard to say now whom he was pushing to a larger extent; perhaps it was Pashinin. Kaganovich's own position in the leadership hierarchy in late 1939 was rather insecure. Ultimately, he was removed from the post of People's Commissar of Aviation Industry and sent to Kazan to work as Director of Aviation Factory No.124.

Meanwhile, the situation around Polikarpov continued to deteriorate. While the designer was on a business trip in Germany (until the end of 1939), he was deprived of a significant part of the design bureau, and it was proposed that the rest of the staff should move to an old hangar on the outskirts of Khodynka airfield. The hangar had previously belonged to TsAGI and accommodated the Department of Operation, Flight Tests and Refinements. Now Polikarpov, together with the 'remnants' of his design bureau, was transferred to this location, and the hangar was derisively renamed Aviation Factory No.51. It was believed that the 'King of Fighters' would soon be arrested anyway, so it did not matter where he had to wait for his fate to come. Such rumours, however, did not come true. Polikarpov continued to work, and in early 1940, funds were even allocated for expanding and equipping Factory No.51.

Yet Stalin's focus on young specialists in the aviation industry persisted. He appointed Alexey Shakhurin as People's Commissar of Aviation Industry, and Alexander Yakovlev his deputy for experimental aircraft construction. Both aged thirtysomething, they were cautious in making independent decisions. In particular, when the question of the first flight of the third I-180 prototype arose, a special broadened commission had to be convened. Nobody was willing to assume responsibility, fearing that the ill-fated fighter would pull some new trick. The general mood is illustrated with clarity by Yakovlev's vague and woolly resolution on the I-180's act of readiness for the first flight: "In respect of this aircraft, if everything is in good order, I have no objections against the flight."

In late January 1940, the I-180-3 was rolled out to the airfield. On 21 January, taxiing over the airfield using a ski landing gear began. On 10 February, the aircraft first took to the air, with test pilot Evgeny Ulyakhin at the controls. According to the pilot, everything was fine. Ten days later, on 20 February, during the first inflight retraction of the landing gear, the right leg failed to fully extend. Ulyakhin decided to perform a landing on the left ski, with a roll to the left. During the landing run, the right leg finally locked down, and the flight ended safely. The incident again gave rise to criticism in respect of the aircraft, primarily regarding the landing gear configuration. It has already been noted above that variants of a single-strut landing gear were being developed throughout 1939. Eventually, the configuration of retraction along the wing span towards the aircraft's centre line was chosen (at that time it was named the 'He-100-type' layout). On 26 January 1940, the preliminary project commission finally approved this variant. The main external feature of the aircraft equipped with this landing gear was the presence of the fairings in the root portion of the centre wing section to accommodate the retracted wheels. The commission resolved that the type with such landing gear should be built, starting from the 31st series production aircraft. On 30 January, additional decisions were made in respect of the I-180 series. Aviation Factory No.21 was tasked with completing the first series of 10 aircraft (which was essentially an operational testing series, manufacture of which was launched back in June 1939) in February, and the second series of 20 aircraft in March. However, virtually none of these plans were accomplished. The factory received a written instruction to increase output of I-16s; the menacing oral statements were taken as nothing but empty talk.

Perhaps the most important factor that brought about delays in building the I-180 series was the absence of the M-88 engines. In spring 1940, the factory in Gorky had only three such engines available. These had been manufactured in the previous year, and their reliability was found low. The first three aircraft – s/n 25211, 25212 and 25213, sometimes named the I-180S (S for *Seriyniy* – series production) – were ready in late April. Their main difference from the third prototype was the wing structure – the wing spars were made of steel tubes and more resembled the wing of the second I-180 prototype.

Shortly before the May Day holidays, all three I-180S were delivered by rail to Moscow. It was planned that they would perform a flypast over Red Square. After some thought, it was decided that only one airplane would fly. On 1 May, Stepan Suprun, just like a year before, was sitting in the cockpit of a prepared aircraft awaiting take-off; but the command to start was never given.

Test flying of the aircraft from Gorky eventually began around mid-May. An extensive test programme was envisaged, with the participation of factory and NII VVS test pilots. On 26 May, at 3:00 p.m., Suprun took off from the Central Airfield in the aircraft s/n 25212 to perform an inspection flight. During his landing run, the fulcrum (a torque link connecting the strut and the shock absorber rod) of the landing gear's right leg failed. As a result, the strut and the wheel turned across the direction of travel, and the aircraft nosed over. According to the pilot, this happened spontaneously. Yet according to eyewitnesses, a Stal-3 passenger carrier had barred the path of the I-180, which was performing its landing, and Suprun thus had to apply brakes. The brake application occurred at the moment when the left wheel bounced on a bump and was lifted from the ground. Thus, the right wheel braked and, accordingly, turned around. However, there was another version of the accident which had it that as the brakes were applied at high speed, the aircraft lowered its nose and touched the ground with its propeller. As a result, the I-180 turned in the direction opposite to rotation. This was enough for the right leg to operate in torsion, and for the shock absorber fulcrum to collapse.

Whatever the cause, the aircraft was severely damaged in the accident; pilot Suprun escaped with just bruising. According to the official report of the accident, it had been caused by a failure of the manufacturer plant to comply with the production technology (bolts of unequal strength – both unhardened and hardened ones – had been installed in the torque link).

Suprun was as disappointed by the accident as others were. Assessing what had happened, he wrote: "I believe that the airplane should be thoroughly checked and cleared for series production. The airplane is very similar to the I-16; pilots who have mastered the I-16 would easily convert to the I-180. The aircraft is much better than the I-28."

An important circumstance that influenced the positive opinion of the I-180 was that just a week before the accident with aircraft s/n 25212, on 18 May, factory tests of the third prototype were completed. Although the M-88 failed to provide enough power, and the flights were performed with the tail skid extended, a maximum speed of 575km/h was achieved at an altitude of 6,900 metres. After elimination of the revealed defects, and with a higher-quality propeller and more carefully applied paint coating, it was felt the aircraft might be able to reach a maximum speed of 600km/h or even higher. Pilot Ulyakhin, who conducted the tests, compared the new aircraft with the I-16, and found the former more stable in all flight modes. At the same time, there were some comments and suggestions. In particular, during the course of winter flights, it was suggested that a closing cockpit canopy should be installed.

A transparent canopy protecting the pilot from external air flow was first suggested by Polikarpov back in 1932–33. Operation of the I-16 aircraft equipped with sliding canopies revealed a number of shortcomings. First, the canopy was small in size; it covered only the pilot's head, impaired visibility and was a nuisance for pilots. There was also the fact that the canopy was made of celluloid (there was a shortage of organic glass as it was purchased abroad), which tended to quickly lose transparency, and it was difficult – sometimes, even impossible – to open the canopy in flight due to insufficient rigidity. The majority of pilots secured canopies in the extreme open position – they preferred to feel chilly but more confident. In 1937, an attempt was made to fit an I-16 with a small canopy which slid backwards, but that too was rejected.

The suggested stationary windscreens for the I-16 Type 10 and I-15bis were also criticised by crews, who reported that due to smooth curvature, the transparencies distorted the view and created a glare. As a result, in 1938, a decision was made to fit new Polikarpov fighters with windscreens consisting of flat sheets. Several options were considered for the I-180, with four of them studied in detail. All these windscreen versions were installed on a mock-up and evaluated by invited pilots. The latest windscreen model was finally approved, and all prototypes were subsequently fitted with it.

In spring 1940, during the second phase of flight tests of the I-180-3, a single windscreen on the aircraft appeared an anachronism. Almost all new airplanes had already been fitted with enclosed canopies with a considerable area of transparency. The problem was fixed promptly: the windscreen was slightly modified and moved forward, then the central part was installed, which could be slid backwards on rollers. The solution was not characterised by much elegance, but it was believed that the design of the canopy would later be refined. On series production aircraft manufactured by Factory No.21, windscreens were left unchanged.

Factory tests of the I-180-3 consisted of two stages. The first stage was conducted from 10 February until mid-March 1940 with ski landing gear. During the second stage (between 23 April and 18 May) the aircraft was tested with a wheel landing gear and an enclosed canopy. Due to the grievous events which had taken place earlier, the factory tests were aimed, in the first place, at "verifying safety of flying the aircraft of this design", and only in then at determining flight performance and manoeuvrability parameters. In the course of factory tests, the mechanism for retracting the skis and tail skid was refined, a new cylindrical oil cooler with a diameter of 9-in (228mm) was installed, the efficiency of the carburettor air intake was improved (as a result, the engine's critical altitude increased by 750 metres), armament was adjusted and heat-resistant steel sheets were mounted on the fuselage sides near the exhaust manifold. During the tests, two M-88 engines were replaced; the third engine was installed on 11 May during the final stage (an engine manufactured in 1940 was mounted). When transferring the airplane to NII VVS for testing, pilot Ulyakhin noted: "Longitudinal stability with CG position of 58 percent MAC is neutral. With a more forward CG position, it is good. Lateral stability and directional stability are good. Wing sweep needs to be introduced." With the latter comment, Ulyakhin meant that the wing should have been angled backwards to obtain a more forward centre of gravity position.

Upon completion of the modifications, the I-180-3 was handed over for the performance of the state test programme in early June. Initially everything went well and within the scope of the approved programme. Then, towards evening on 5 July (at 7:15 p.m.), NII VVS test pilot Captain Afanasiy Proshakov took off in the aircraft to practice aerobatics. It was the 45th flight of the E-3, and Proshakov's 10th flight in an aircraft of this type. At an altitude of 3,500 metres, when the pilot was performing a right roll, the aircraft broke off from the manoeuvre and, after several somersaults, fell into an inverted spin. The pilot was unable to right the spinning aircraft, and bailed out at 1,000 metres. The spinning E-3 crashed into the ground, landing upside-down in the vicinity of the airfield. Proshakov landed safely by parachute.

The exact cause of the accident were never established, although an accident board assumed a jamming of the elevators or deformation of the horizontal stabiliser leading edge. Polikarpov, along with Ulyakhin, believed the accident was Proshakov's fault. In their opinion, the pilot had lost control and created a situation that had ended in an inverted spin. However, this was considered unlikely because Proshakov was ranked among the best aerobatic pilots of NII VVS, well respected for his outstanding flying skills.

Whatever the reasons, the I-180's reputation was once again ruined. It was as if an ill fate had befallen the unlucky aircraft. In a year and a half, out of the six aircraft built, four had been lost, and two of the best test pilots had perished. There was also a lack of confidence in other Polikarpov aircraft. In April 1940, a Polikarpov SPB two-engine dive bomber crashed, killing pilot Golovin and his crew; while on 20 July, two weeks after the loss of the E-3, an SPB flown by Mikhail Lipkin also crashed.

On 22 July, at a special meeting of the Air Force Directorate, a decision was made that one of the remaining series production I-180s (s/n 25211) should be handed over to TsAGI for stability tests. The other aircraft (s/n 25213) had shortly before been delivered to the service regiment for armament tests.

As for series production, this was still impeded not only by the negative attitude to the aircraft but also by the lack of M-88 engines. The engines already received were found to be unserviceable due to their low reliability. In August 1940, rumours were circulating on the sidelines of the NKAP that production of the M-88 was about to be discontinued, with the I-180 consequently withdrawn from the plan. It looked like this was the end for Polikarpov's 'super' *Ishak*. Other fighter prototypes created by other designers had already been flying for a long time, and there were plenty willing to get the aviation factory in Gorky to be used as a production facility to manufacture their own aircraft.

In September 1940, under an order of NKAP head Shakhurin, the production of the I-180 was cancelled and superseded by the Pashinin IP-21 fighter. A short while later, the Pashinin fighter was also withdrawn from the plan and replaced by the I-200 (MiG-1). Later still, a decision – this time a final one – was made to launch production of the LaGG fighter in Gorky. However, an argument can be made that continuing the production of the I-180 would have been the correct decision. In late 1940, it was the only fighter powered by an air-cooled engine, which had been well prepared for series reproduction. The still more advanced I-185, which was following hard on the heels of the I-180, was a consistent development of the previous design. As for the air-cooled engines, the period of difficulties associated with their development and improvement seemed to be coming to an end. If adhering to the theory of a cyclical nature in the process of aircraft engine development (initially, air-cooled engines prevailed, then the inline liquid-cooled engines took over, etc.), a new era of radial air-cooled engines was approaching.

The development of the M-88 engine in 1938 slowed down primarily due to the arrest of its Chief Designer, A. Nazarov, after the crash of the M-85-powered aircraft s/n 7211. Sergey Tumansky, who was then appointed to the post, attempted to complete the M-88 by rushing and overloading the personnel, but with no success. In autumn 1940, another change of management occurred at Engine Factory No.29 in Zaporozhye. Evgeny Urmin, who was appointed Head of the Design Bureau, finally completed the M-88, with a significant (up to 1,375hp) increase in power. This took place as late as 1941 during the period of evacuation of factory facilities due to the German invasion, when the I-180 had already been almost totally forgotten.

The final phase in the history of the I-180 aircraft at Aviation Factory No.21 was as follows. After the first three series production aircraft (s/n 25211, 25212 and 25213) were sent to Moscow, another I-180 with external fuel tanks was completed in late summer. Below is a breakdown of the factory output for August 1940 as per the official report:

- I-16 Type 24 RO: five aircraft
- I-16 Type 24 RSI-3: 11 aircraft
- I-16 Type 24 RO, RSI-3: 11 aircraft
- I-16 Type 24 RSI-4: five aircraft
- I-16 Type 28 PB: six aircraft
- I-16 Type 28 RSI-3: five aircraft
- I-16 Type 29 PB: one aircraft
- I-16 Type 29 RSI-3: nine aircraft
- I-16 Type 29 RO: one aircraft
- I-180 Type 25 PB: one aircraft
- UTI-4 Type 15: 105 aircraft

Total: 160 aircraft

N.B.: RO – version with the launchers for the RS-82 rocket projectiles
RSI-3 and RSI-4 – versions with RSI radios
PB – version with external fuel tanks

Apart from the I-180 Type 25 with external fuel tanks which was indicated in the report the aircraft s/n 25214 was rolled out from the final assembly shop on 17 August. In this airplane, over 100 defects were detected during inspection, and due to the numerous faults in workmanship it was not accepted. It was noted that airplanes s/n 25215, 25216 and 25217 would be ready before September.

Two fuselages from among the operational testing series (10 aircraft) were in the assembly shop at that time; however, their further fate is not known. Senior Military Representative at Aviation Factory No.21 Belousov reported, "There is lack of attention on the part of the factory management in respect of the Type 25 aircraft … The most competent workers have been withdrawn from this project and transferred to the I-21 … Voronin [Director of the factory] rarely visits the work areas of the I-180 assembly; on the other hand, he attends the I-21 assembly areas several times per day."

In September 1940, when work on the I-180 was ceased, there were six completed airframes (without engines) of the operational testing series in Gorky. In October, in spite of prohibitions (because the situation had not yet become quite clear), work on the second and third series continued. A production reserve of materials and parts was being prepared for a 100-aircraft series, and considerable work was carried out to prepare sets of production tooling. Subcontractors received orders for materials and semi-finished items for the I-180 production – the factory in Dnepropetrovsk was preparing a stock of chromansil T-sections, while the *Serp i Molot* factory in Moscow was fabricating 25KhGSA sheet metal stock. However, the most important point was that the two-year-long effort by Polikarpov's team and the desire to bring the work to a positive result finally began to pay off. In October, the design brigade of the factory in Gorky completed modification of the I-180 – a reference aircraft for production in 1941. The airplane, also known as the I-180 E-5, had a more forward CG position of 21.8 percent MAC (versus 24 percent MAC in earlier aircraft), which was achieved by rearranging the single-strut landing gear and making the wing panels backwards-angled. The wing area was slightly larger, totalling 16.3sq.m. The cockpit was closed with a sliding canopy, and the windscreen included reinforced glass. The airframe structure underwent a number of reinforcements: a landing light was installed on the wing and the tail skid was fitted with a 300mm-diameter wheel. All specialists involved in the I-180 programme worked for it to the last. They reasonably believed that, in a few months, it would be possible to ensure a daily output of three or four such fighters. The Chief Designer was also fighting for the I-180 – Polikarpov repeatedly appealed to the government to resume production of the fighter, but he never received a positive response.

The last I-180 prototype, designated the E-7, was being built in Moscow at the facilities of Aviation Factory No.51 in 1941. The aircraft had all the modifications for the 1941-series such as the transparent sliding canopy, the single-strut retractable landing gear and the redesigned wing. There is an opinion that in summer 1941, the aircraft performed several flights. At least, there was a single I-180, covered, in the parking area of Factory No.51 in Moscow at that time. It was in October 1941 that a decision was made to evacuate the aircraft eastward; however, a railway platform for it was not found. Then the Chief Designer decided that the last prototype should be ferried by air. The headquarters of Moscow Air Defence was contacted, and a pilot arrived from there. After a short preflight briefing, the pilot, who had not even sat in the I-180 cockpit before, took off safely, made a farewell circle over the airfield, and flew away. Several hours later, in his report over the phone upon completion of the task, he spoke with enthusiasm and surprise about the previously unfamiliar aircraft.

That was the end of the story. Traces of the last evacuated I-180 were lost. Later, however, a story was circulating – which may have been legend or the truth – that pilots had seen the I-180 at a front-line airfield.

The I-180 variants – differences and details

Some time ago, the author was haunted by Vadim Shavrov's lines concerning the I-180 from his book *The History of Aircraft Designs in the USSR in 1938–50*: "A more advanced design was also envisaged, which was innovative for 1938 and resembled that of the Polikarpov *Ivánov* monoplane, with extensive use of extruded sections, castings and forgings. With these considerations in mind, the I-180 with M-87A engine was designed at the prototype-building factory. However, yielding to the specifics of the series production factory, the customary mixed structure was adopted for it." What concessions are meant here? The I-180 was being created based on the capabilities of the Soviet aviation industry. Initially the new aircraft was no different from the I-16 either in terms of technology or its design; except that it was, perhaps, a bit more complicated. Take, for example, the landing gear – it was a different mechanism, but in terms of configuration it remained the same torsional pyramid. In 1939, such landing gear was an anachronism; on the other hand, it could be quickly mastered by a series production factory.

However, in 1939, there came a time to introduce more modern technologies. For the I-180-3, a decision was made to replace the tubular wing spar booms with advanced T-bars. Since Soviet industry was not yet capable of supplying suitable workpieces, it took the prototype-building division of Aviation Factory No.1 a considerable time to perform machining of these bars (their cross-section was reducing along the wing span). Obviously, such techniques were not suitable for a series production factory. That is why Polikarpov indeed yielded the requirements of the series production factory and agreed to use the old technology of the wing spars manufacturing for the first series of the fighter. For this reason, series production aircraft remained with the 'old' wing dihedral (it is known that, in the third prototype, the dihedral was increased to 6° 30' minutes in order to improve lateral stability).

In the course of flight tests of the second prototype, it was suggested that the tail unit span should be increased to 4.3 metres. An enlarged horizontal stabilizer was indeed manufactured; however, there are no documentary facts confirming that it was mounted on the aircraft.

The dimensions and weight differences between various versions of the I-180 are shown in the table below.

Parameter	I-180 project	I-180-1	I-180-2	I-180-3	I-180-5
Power plant	M-88	M-87	M-87	M-88R	M-88R
Wing span (m)	9.000	9.000	10.09	10.09	10.09
Length (m)	6.487	6.900	6.900	6.880	7.000
Height (m)	3.250	–	3.235	3.305	3.300
Wing area (sq.m)	14.7	14.7	16.11	16.11	16.3
Wheel track (m)	1.880	2.200	2.200	2.200	–
Empty weight (kg)	1,330	–	1,685	1,794	–
Gross weight (kg)	2,005	–	2,240	2,409	–
Armament	4xShKAS	4xShKAS	4xShKAS	2xShKAS 2xBS	2xShKAS 2xBS

A short note should be made about the aircraft colours. For the first prototype, since there was an unwritten tradition not to take photos of an aircraft before its first flight, we can judge about its appearance only by recollections. Most probably it was painted red, with the engine cowling in black. The second prototype, the I-180-2, was in silver overall, with red stars painted on the fuselage side and the lower surfaces of the wings. The third prototype was in silver as well, but the tone of the colour had a reddish tint. According to some eyewitnesses, the aircraft was a romantic colour of "pink seagull". During tests and refinements, the cowling was painted in a different colour, most likely black. Series production airplanes built at the factory in Gorky were painted bright red, with silver stars.

Comparison of performance parameters of the I-180, I-16 and I-153 fighters							
Type	Gross weight (kg)	Engine power (hp) at altitude (m)	Maximum speed near ground (km/h)	Speed (km/h) at critical altitude (m)	Time to climb to 5,000m (secs)	Service ceiling (m)	Armament
I-153 M-62	1,762	800/ 4,200	364	443/ 4,600	6.7	9,800	4xShKAS
I-16 M-25V	1,716	750/ 2,900	389	437/ 3,200	7	8,470	4xShKAS
I-16 M-63	1,879	900	440	489	5.15	10,800	2xShKAS 1xBS (12.7mm)
I-180-2 M-87B	2,175	960/ 4,700	408	540/ 5,850	6.25	10,250	4xShKAS
I-180-3 M-88	2,440	1,030/ 6,000	439	571/ 7,150	5.5 (5.6)	11,050	2xShKAS 2xBS (12.7mm)

Table 1: Technical parameters and specifications of aircraft engines produced by Soviet aviation factories (as of January 1938)					
Engine type	Take-off power (hp)	Rated power (hp) at altitude (m)	Dry weight (kg)	Scheduled date of readiness for mounting on aircraft
M-103A	1,000	950/4,000	495	April 1938
M-103 (glycol-cooled)	900	930/4,000	495	October 1938
M-105s (with two-speed supercharger)	1,100	1,050/4,000	510	November 1938
M-103P (with engine cannon)	1,000	950/4,000	510	fourth quarter 1938
M-110A (air/glycol cooling)	900	960/4,000	510	1939
M-103 ATK-1	1,000	875/9,500	565	first quarter 1939
M-103 with two-speed supercharger	1,000	900/6,000	530	first quarter 1939
M-105 with two-speed supercharger	1,100	1,050/4,000	550	1939
AM-34FRN	1,200	1,050/3,500	740	second quarter 1938

182 The King of Fighters Volume 2

Table 1: Technical parameters and specifications of aircraft engines produced by Soviet aviation factories (as of January 1938)				
Engine type	Take-off power (hp)	Rated power (hp) at altitude (m)	Dry weight (kg)	Scheduled date of readiness for mounting on aircraft
AM-35 with two-speed supercharger	1,350–1,400	1,250/4,500	720	second quarter 1939
AM-34 NRV TK-1	850	700/10,000	810	fourth quarter 1938
AM-34 FRN TK-1	1200	750/10,000	810	first quarter 1938
AM-35 RS	1,800–2,000	1,600/6,500	690	experimental
M-87	950	950/4,250	617	ready
M-88	1,100	1,000/4,250	615	third quarter 1938
M-89 with two-speed supercharger	1,200–1,300	1,100/4,500	650	first quarter 1939
M-62	1,000	800/4,000	495	ready
M-63 with two-speed supercharger	1,100	900/4,500	650	?
M-63R (geared)	1,100	900/4,500	575	fourth quarter 1938
M-62TK	1,000	760/9,000	565	fourth quarter 1938
M-70 (18-cylinder double-row radial engine)	1,400	1,400/4,000	800	fourth quarter 1938
MV-6 (Renault)	240	220/2,000	253	fourth quarter 1938

The I-180-2 second prototype with the M-87 engine.

Table 2: The VVS RKKA operational requirements for new aircraft, January 1938

Parameter	Single-seat manoeuvrable fighter with air-cooled engine	Single-seat high-speed fighter with air-cooled engine	Single-seat high-speed fighter with liquid-cooled engine	Ground-attack aircraft and single-engine bomber	Artillery spotter	Two-engine fighter and long-range reconnaissance aircraft
Speed (km/h) at altitude (m)	550/5,000 500/3,000	650/6–7,000 510/3,000	680/6–7,000 600/3,000	500/5–6,000	500/5,000 550/6,000	600/6–7,000
Normal range (km)	1,000	1,000	1,000	1,500 (500kg of bombs)	1,500 (200kg of bombs)	2,500 (300kg of bombs)
Range with overload (km)	1,500	1,500	1,500	2,000 (500kg of bombs)	2,000 (250kg of bombs)	3,500 (w/o bomb load)
Bomb capacity	100	100	100	500	250	400
Time to climb (mins) to combat altitude (m)	8/8,000	10.8/8,000	10.5/8,000	Service ceiling 9–10,000	Service ceiling 10,000	10.5/8,000
Armament	4xShKAS	2xShKAS 2xShVAK	1xShVAK 2xShKAS	4xShKAS (bomber) 6xShKAS (ground-attack aircraft)	3–4xShKAS	2xShVAK 2xShKAS
To be presented for state tests by	1 October 1938	1 December 1938	1 November 1938	1 August 1938	–	1 December 1938

Table 3: Polikarpov's assessment of the VVS RKKA requirement for the new aircraft, January 1938

Parameter	Single-seat manoeuvrable fighter with air-cooled engine	Single-seat high-speed fighter with air-cooled engine	Single-seat high-speed fighter with liquid-cooled engine	Ground-attack aircraft and single-engine bomber	Artillery spotter	Two-engine fighter and long-range reconnaissance aircraft
Engine type Speed (km/h) at altitude (m)	M-62 425/4,200 M-88 470/4,250	M-88 538/ 6,000	M-103P 540/ 4,000	M-70 satisfactory M-88 473/4,250	M-88 460/ 4,250	M-103 (TK) 585/9,500 M-70 541/4,000
Range	Overestimated	Overestimated	overestimated	satisfactory	satisfactory	satisfactory
Range with overloading	possible with external tanks	possible with external tanks	possible with external tanks	satisfactory	satisfactory	satisfactory
Bomb capacity	satisfactory	Satisfactory	satisfactory	400	satisfactory	satisfactory
Time to climb to altitude	satisfactory	Satisfactory	satisfactory	satisfactory	satisfactory	satisfactory
Armament	satisfactory	Satisfactory	satisfactory	satisfactory	satisfactory	satisfactory
To be presented for state tests before	satisfactory	1 November 1938	1 January 1939	1 October 1938	33 percent in 1938; completion by 1 April 1939	1 January 1939

The I-180 airframe, which fully corresponded to the first prototype (wing span of 9.0m, wing covered with fabric) during static tests at TsAGI in spring 1939.

An outer wing panel of the I-180 first prototype without the fabric cover.

The fuselage of the I-180-2 before final assembly of the aircraft.

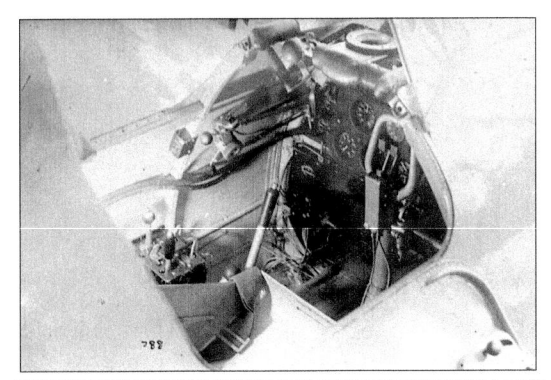

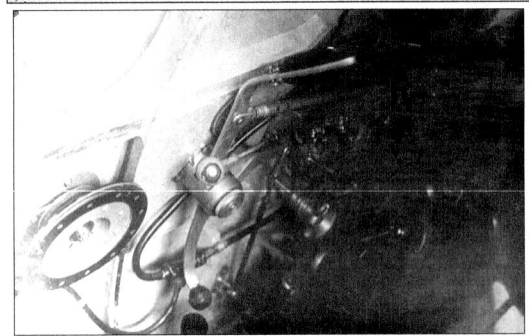

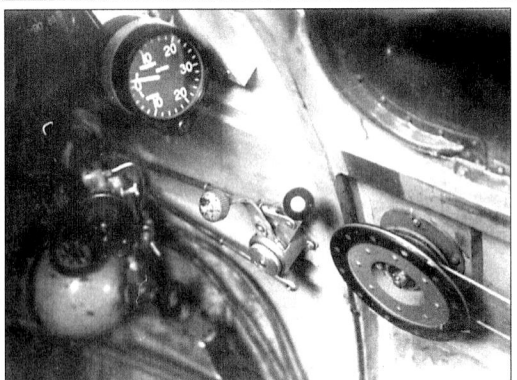

Views of the I-180-2 cockpit.

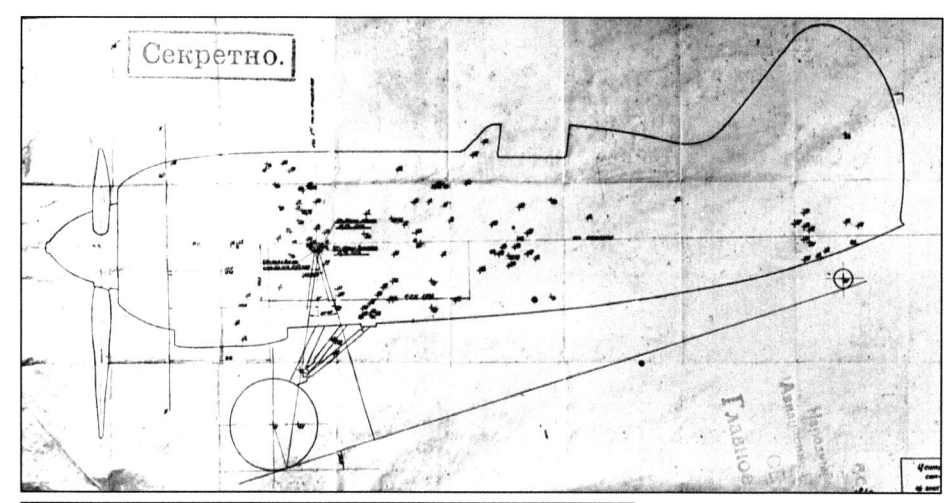

The scheme of the equipment layout indicating coordinates for calculating the CG position for the second I-180-2 prototype.

The M-87B engine mounted on the I-180-2.

The I-180-3 third prototype with the M-88 engine during tests with skis, in spring 1940.

Top-rear view of the I-180-3 demonstrating the unconventional shape of the wing with the straight leading edge.

The I-180-3 cockpit canopy.

Part of the I-180-3 cockpit.

The I-180-3 third prototype upon completion of modifications and with the cockpit canopy installed.

A view of the tail of the I-180-3.

The remains of the I-180-3 which crashed after entering into an inverted flat spin on 5 July 1940. Pilot Proshakov bailed out safely.

The wing of the I-180 used at the armament test range.

An outer wing panel of a series production I-180.

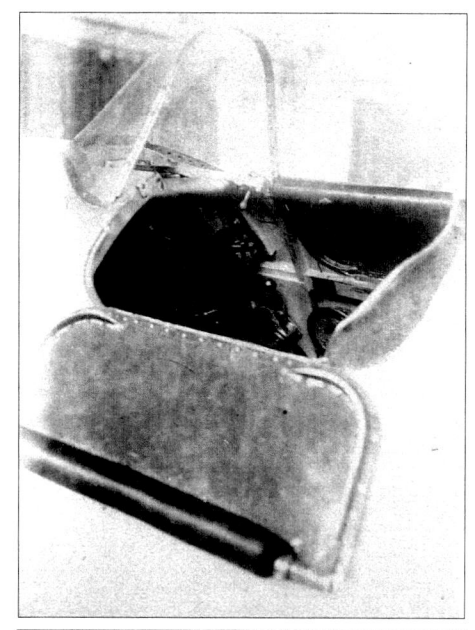

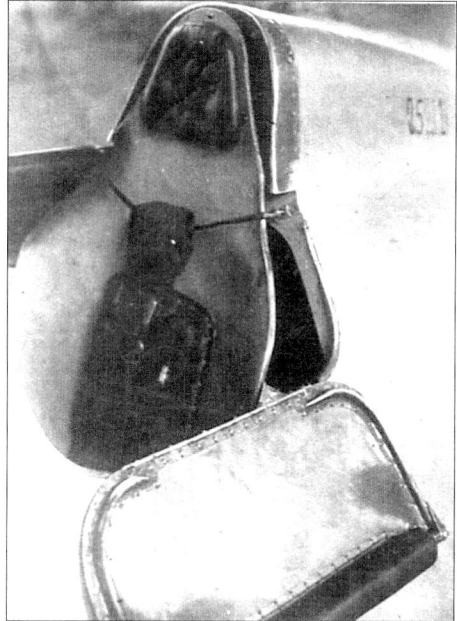

Cockpit door and windscreen of the series production I-180, s/n 21212.

Cockpit of the series production I-180, s/n 21212.

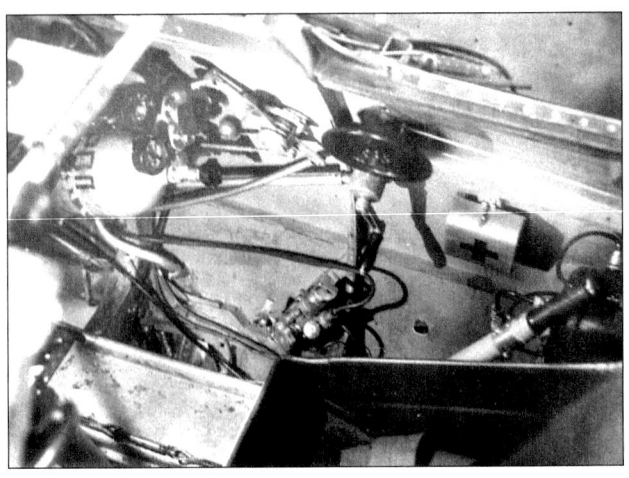

Views of wing root and fuselage of the series production I-180, s/n 21212, with the skin partially removed.

The I-180 s/n 25212 after an accident with pilot Suprun at the controls at Central Airfield in Moscow on 26 May 1940. During the landing run, the torque link of the right landing gear leg failed, the wheel turned against the direction of travel and the aircraft nosed over.

Test pilot Valery Pavlovich Chkalov.

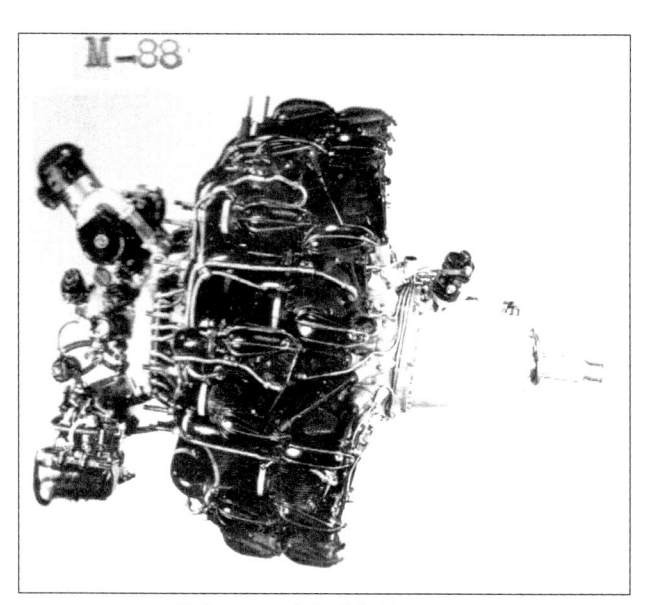

Side view of the M-88 engine.

Side view of the M-88BRL gearless engine.

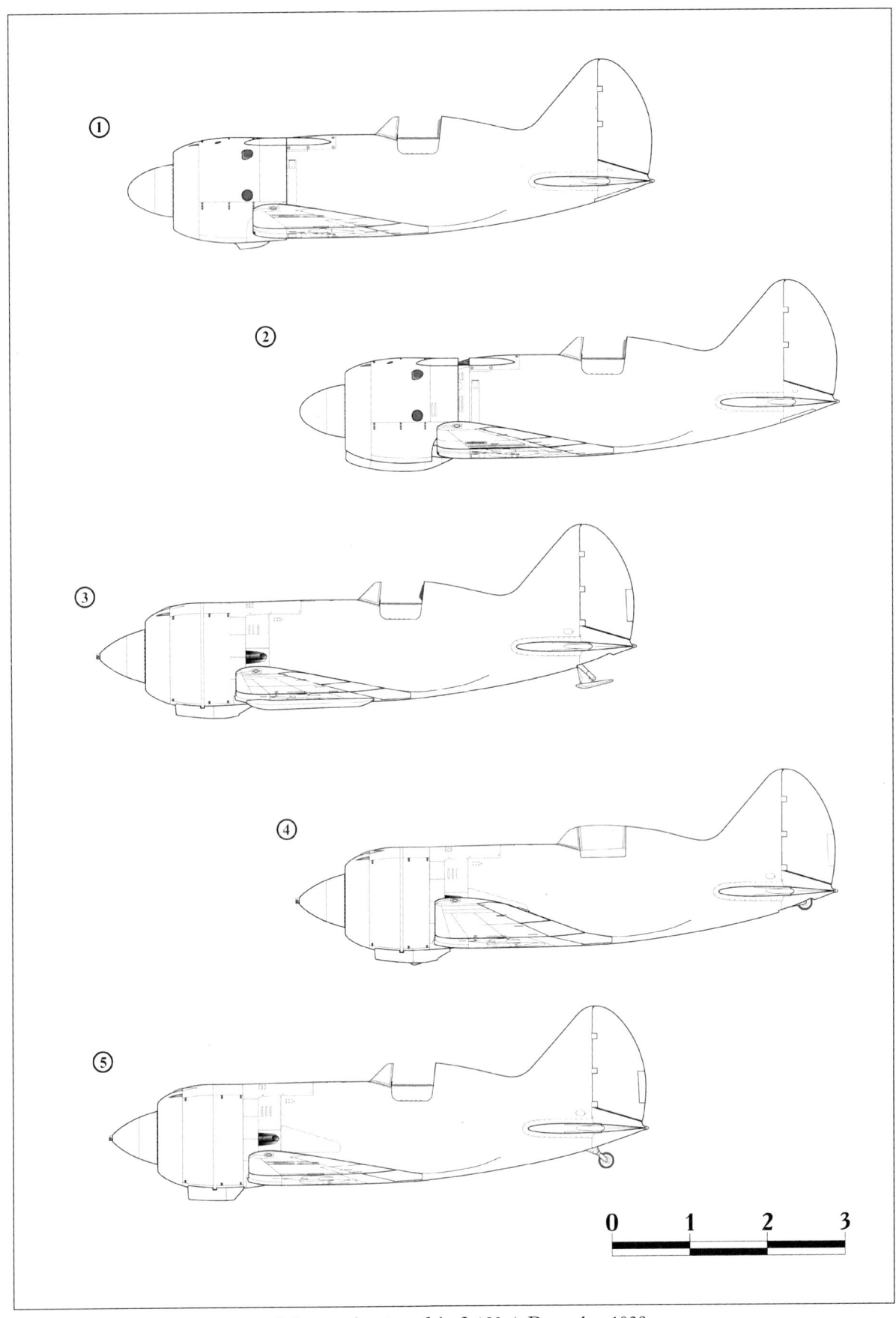

1. Side view drawing of the I-180-1, December 1938.
2. Side view drawing of the I-180-2, factory tests, April 1939.
3. Side view drawing of the I-180-3 (E-3), factory tests, February 1940.
4. Side view drawing of the I-180-3 (E-3), state tests, June 1940.
5. Side view drawing of the I-180S s/n 25212, May 1940.

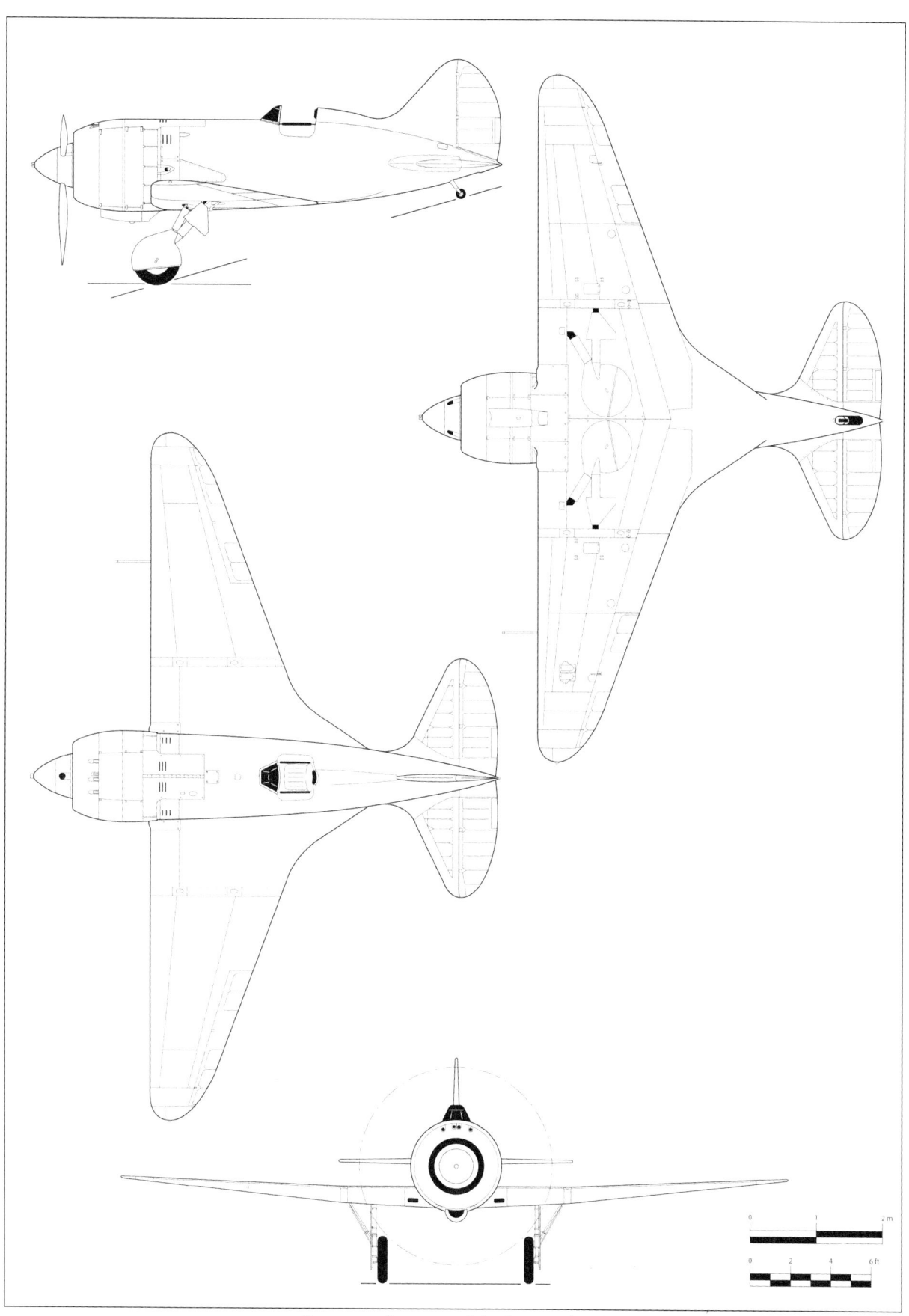

Four-view drawings of the I-180-3 (E-3).

4

The I-185 – the best fighter of designer Polikarpov

Beloved work is the best remedy for all kinds of failures and disappointments. Apparently, this simple worldly rule can, to a considerable extent, explain the unexpected emergence of a new fighter project created by Nikolay Polikarpov in January 1940. It was a kind of a retaliatory act on the part of the merited and experienced engineer for having been unfairly deprived of the majority of his design bureau personnel and manufacturing facilities.

On 6 November 1939, Polikarpov, as part of a Soviet delegation, departed to Germany for familiarisation with the German aviation industry. According to the Order of People's Commissar M. Kaganovich of 6 October 1939, N. Zhemchuzhin (in the capacity of acting Deputy Chief Designer for Aviation Factory No.22) and M. Tetivkin (as acting Deputy Chief Designer for Aviation Factory No.1) stayed in Moscow to take care of ongoing projects. The Polikarpov Design Bureau was located at the facilities of Factory No.1, while the materials related to the most recent developments were kept at the same location. There were two such advanced projects: the I-170 manoeuvrable biplane powered by the M-106 engine and the I-200 high-altitude fighter fitted with the AM-37 engine. For the biplane, A. Karev was appointed Leading Engineer in September. However, the final fate of the aircraft was not clear; for this reason, no further significant progress was observed in its development. The monoplane, being developed by Polikarpov jointly with Tetivkin for the role of a fighter with a maximum flight speed of 670km/h, was almost ready but had not yet been finalised and approved by the Chief Designer.

In the autumn of 1939 there was a certain nervousness among the management of the Soviet aviation industry. Such tension was brought about by the general sentiment that the country was lagging behind in aviation and there were no modern combat aircraft types in production. In particular, Aviation Factory No.1 kept manufacturing the I-153 manoeuvrable biplane, which was deemed obsolescent and unpromising. In November, in the absence of Polikarpov, a special commission began work at the factory with the purpose of launching production of new, modern aircraft. At a meeting of the commission, designer Alexander Yakovlev reported on his M-105-powered I-26 fighter project. The materials presented by Yakovlev aroused interest and the aircraft was recommended for series production.

It should be noted that as early as during the summer, in accordance with Decree of the Defense Committee No.171ss of 20 June 1939, it was decided that production of the Yakovlev BB-22 two-engine short-range bomber would be launched at Factory No.1. On 17 July 1939, a respective order was issued by NKAP to set up the KB-70 design bureau at the factory, manned by 70 engineers, in order to carry out preparations for series production of the BB-22. The newly appointed Head of the KB-70, engineer Strongin, and his deputy Kurbala were ordered to immediately get down to preparing engineering drawings. whereas Director of the Factory P. Voronin and his deputy P. Dementyev were tasked with finding, in a three-day period, working premises for the new team. This was followed by an order to immediately gather all the best specialists of wooden construction to work on the BB-22, and to set wage rates for workers to be 20–30 percent higher than for those involved in manufacture of the I-153 *Chaika*. It was required that the armament, landing gear and power plant of the new two-engine aircraft be refined before August 1939. All these measures were taken in order to build 1,000 BB-22s in 1940 in accordance with the adopted plans.

Thus, Yakovlev's 'advance' on the production facilities of the oldest Moscow aviation factory appeared quite tangible, while the launch of production of another Yakovlev aircraft there proved to be somewhat painful. It was against the background of such sentiment that, according to one version of how events were developing, engineer A. Karev informed members of the commission that the factory had been working on the I-200 fighter project, with its speed being significantly higher than that of the Yakovlev I-26. As a result, members of the commission decided to familiarise themselves with the project and became interested in it, and that got the ball rolling.

The commission found the I-200 project worthy of attention. After a report to and approval by the Central Committee of the All-Union Communist Party of Bolsheviks and the Soviet Air Force command, a decision was made to build the aircraft promptly. On 8 December 1940, Director of Aviation Factory No.1 P. Voronin issued an order to create an experimental design bureau to be manned by leading employees of the Polikarpov Design Bureau, with A. Mikoyan appointed head of the new unit and M. Gurevich his deputy. Thus, the project began to live its own 'life' separately from its original designer, and subsequently emerged as the famous MiG-3 fighter.

Upon his return from the German business trip in late December 1939, Polikarpov was naturally astounded. The situation was a painful hit for him; however, whatever had happened had happened. Life went on, and the designer continued his creative research, which in a short period of time translated into the I-185 project.

In January 1940, the noticeably depleted Polikarpov Design Bureau moved to the former hangar of the TsAGI Department of Operation, Flight Tests and Refinements, where facilities for building prototype aircraft were to be arranged. Formerly, the hangar had accommodated TsAGI Departments No.8 and 5, which had dealt mostly with flight testing. After TsAGI specialists moved to a new location in Ramenskoye (currently the city of Zhukovsky), the hangar had been vacant from summer 1939 and was ready for new occupants to arrive. It was there that Experimental Aviation Factory No.51, accommodating the Polikarpov Design Bureau, was arranged in February 1940. Of course, it took some time for the new production facilities to begin operation; gradually, however, the new factory received everything necessary for creating prototype aircraft. In particular, during 1941, mould lofts and a templates workshop and static test laboratory were set up at Factory No.51.

The engines

In early November 1939, just a few days before Polikarpov left for the business trip to Germany, his design bureau received specifications of aircraft engines which Soviet industry could offer to aircraft designers in the near future. The prospective air-cooled engines were as follows:

Engine type	Manufacturer	Maximum power (hp)	Diameter (mm)	Dry weight (kg)	Specific weight
M-90 (double-row; 18 cylinders)	Zaporozhye; Factory No.29	1,600 Take-off power – 1,700 Power at an altitude of 6,000m – 1,500	1,298 (1,296)	850	0.567
M-64 (single-row; nine cylinders)	Perm; Factory No.19	Up to 1,050	1,375	510	0.53
M-71 (double-row; 18 cylinders)	Perm; Factory No.19	Up to 2,000	1,375	970	-
M-81 (double-row; 14 cylinders)	Perm; Factory No.19	Up to 1,500	1,375	-	-

From among the above engines, the M-90 (sometimes also designated the 2M) – with the initially stated power of 1,600hp – appeared the most interesting and promising. It was noted that this engine had been designed in record time – between 15 May and 15 August 1939. On 29 November that year, the first M-90 was placed onto the test bench. Several months later, design and refinement work on the engine was being carried out in accordance with the set schedule; in view of this, it was planned that state tests would begin in May 1940.

In spite of this optimistic sentiment, Polikarpov felt ambivalent about Soviet-built aircraft engines. He understood that they might fail to be built in due time, and had hopes for procuring powerful engines from other sources. In particular, the designer repeatedly addressed senior officials of the aviation industry with a request to purchase the license for the American Pratt & Whitney or German BMW 801 engines. There is a hypothesis that Polikarpov's trip to Germany was connected, to a considerable extent, with the hope to procure the BMW 801.

In January 1940, the designer finally realised that the chances of purchasing a foreign-built aircraft engine were extremely remote. Therefore, he pinned all his hopes on the M-90 and began to design a new fighter to be powered by this power plant.

Design period

On 28 January 1940, a combat layout and explanatory note for the preliminary project of a high-speed fighter to be powered by the M-90 engine were presented to the NKAP. Apart from the M-90, it was expected that the AM-37, M-120 and M-71 engines would be used. It was specified that the aircraft was based on the I-16 and I-180 designs, and had a wooden fuselage and a metal wing with duralumin skin. The engine cooling was arranged through a special fan installed inside the propeller spinner. To enhance manoeuvrability and ensure more precise aiming, the armament was mounted in the fuselage and initially consisted of two BS and two ShKAS machine guns. The wing had a NACA-230 profile (14 percent thickness in the wing root and 8 percent at the wing tip).

The fighter project, not yet given any designation, had the following design parameters:

Length in the flight line (m)	7.250
Wing span (m)	9.800
Wing area (sq.m)	15.6
Gross weight (kg)	2,708
Wing load (kg/sq.m)	173

On 8 February, the NKAP expert commission reviewed the new Polikarpov fighter project (by now designated the I-185), finding it promising and its further implementation practicable. After several corrections to the project specifications, the Defence Committee issued Resolution No.102ss of 4 March 1940 'On Building a Single-Seat Fighter with the M-90 Engine (by Designer Polikarpov)' with the following parameters and schedule for creation of the aircraft:

Maximum speed (km/h)	680
Landing speed (km/h)	130
Range (km)	600
Service ceiling (m)	10,250
First prototype to be handed over for flight tests by	1 September 1940
Second and third prototypes to be handed over by	1 October 1940

In accordance with updated plans of the NKAP, the entire work on creating the I-185 was split into three stages:

Stage 1: Design, manufacturing and approval of the mock-up; preparation of engineering drawings – by April 1940.
Stage 2: Completion of manufacturing; preparation for the first flight – by 1 July 1940.
Stage 3: Performance of state tests – November 1940.

In practice, however, events developed as follows.

Engineering development of the I-185 'Item 62' with the M-90 engine was basically completed by 10 March 1940 (initially, the aircraft was given the designation as per the numeration system as adopted at Aviation Factory No.1, since Polikarpov remained Chief Designer with the factory). Almost immediately afterwards, four (this number later grew to five) flight prototypes and a static test airframe began to be built. The first two I-185s were oriented on receiving the M-90 engine and were built in the workshops of Aviation Factory No.1. As for other prototypes, the issue of power plant selection remained, for some time, unclear; they began to be built at the facilities of the newly arranged Factory No.51.

In March, negotiations with Chief Designer of Integrated Plant No.150 Zhdanov (on supply of propellers) and Chief Designer of Engine Factory No.29 Tumansky (on urgent preparation of a serviceable M-90 engine) continued. The engine manufacturers promised to prepare an engine with a lifetime of 20 hours within the shortest time possible. Polikarpov Design Bureau engineers Ionov and Sigayev were delegated to Zaporozhye to wait for the first run of the M-90 in early April. In May, the engine was actually started and ran for 10 hours on the test bench. However, numerous difficulties accompanying creation of any new equipment left no room for hopes to receive the M-90 on schedule.

In late May, when the first M-90-powered prototype was nearly ready, People's Commissar of NKAP Shakhurin suggested that Polikarpov should focus on the aircraft fitted with the M-71 engine. However, that was just an oral suggestion; even two months later, no written confirmation of the due dates for supply of the engine followed. Yet Polikarpov promptly revised the design – the aircraft with the M-71 was given the designation I-186 (in practice, neither this designation nor the subsequent I-187 were commonly used). The length of the M-71-powered aircraft increased, totalling 7.680m; the normal gross weight, according to calculations, amounted to 2,984kg, with the maximum gross weight being 3,189kg. Since TsAGI tests of the cowling with a central air intake and a centrifugal fan lagged behind, the I-186 was designed with the widely used NACA cowling. Performance characteristics of the I-185 and I-186 were as follows:

	Maximum speed (km/h) at altitude (m)	Time to climb to 5,000m (minutes)	Service ceiling (m)	Landing speed (km/h)
I-185M-90	680/6,000	4.6	12,100	125–130
I-186M-71	655/5,000	4.3	12,350	127–132

Despite the delay with the engines, the story of the I-185 continued to evolve. Test pilots were appointed – Stepan Suprun as the leading pilot for the first prototype and Evgeny Ulyakhin for the second prototype. Under a resolution of A. Shakhurin for a successful conduct of the first flight in the I-185s, the pilots could expect a one-off remuneration of 80,000 roubles.

In May 1940, a report on the I-185's spinning characteristics was prepared, which read: "Calculation results for the I-185 aircraft are comparable with the same results for the I-16 aircraft, which has an exceptionally good spin recovery performance." At the same time, it was noted that the wing loading of the I-185 was 1.85 times higher than that of the I-16, and there was a noticeable distribution of mass along the centreline. For this reason, an undesirable nose-up pitching moment due to centrifugal forces could take place. According to Professor Zhuravchenko – the chief specialist on the spin – a noticeable delay in spin recovery was expected.

Jumping somewhat ahead, it should be noted that a project for the DIT-185 M-90 two-seat fighter was prepared by October 1940. The aircraft was intended for conversion and training of the I-16, I-180 and I-185 pilots. In the course of a project review, it was pointed out that there already existed the DIT-26 (UTI-26) two-seat fighter based on the Yakovlev I-26 fighter (renamed Yak-1 from December 1940). Therefore, the issue of the expediency of building the DIT-185 was postponed until the appearance of the production I-185s.

It took some time to clear up the question regarding the use of the cowling with a central air intake on the I-185 M-90. The I-185 mock-up ('Item 62') with M-90 engine was tested in the TsAGI T-101 and T-104 wind tunnels from September 1940. The tests were carried out with various cowling versions, with the central air intake having a diameter of 380mm, 450mm and 500mm. Two intake pipe options (external and internal) also underwent testing. The aerodynamic parameters of the cowling and engine were defined, as well as distribution of air pressure at various parts of the power plant.

The tests showed that the use of the cowling with a central air intake was expedient at speeds of 700–850km/h. The cowling was characterised by high air pressure losses in the intake portion, and created excessive drag at the maximum flight speed. Also, adequate engine cooling was not possible on the ground during taxiing and take-off. To a certain extent, use of a centrifugal fan could solve the problem of cooling at take-off and help avoid losses at the intake in flight. According to calculations, the optimum size of the opening was 0.24sq.m.

All these results of the TsAGI studies were complete by February 1941. However, interest in this original invention had already dwindled, and cowlings with the central air intake were never used in practice.

The first flights

Shortly after the first I-185 prototype, which was oriented on the installation of the M-90 engine, the second prototype – designated the I-187 'Item 62-02' (s/n 6202) – was built at the workshops of Aviation Factory No.1. Development of the airplane, powered by the M-81 engine with a take-off power of 1,500hp, NACA cowling and well-established shutter-type engine cooling mechanism, began in July 1940. It featured an increased diameter of the engine cowling and the following dimensions and weight characteristics:

length – 7.765m;
normal gross weight – 3,119kg;
wing loading – 201kg/sq.m.

Compared to the initial version which was intended to fly with the M-90 engine, the flight performance parameters of the I-187 were to be much lower:

maximum speed – 611km/h (at an altitude of 6,400m);
service ceiling – 9,900m.

According to initial plans, the aircraft was to have been completed in late 1940. On 10 December 1940, the first engine test run took place. On 21 December, the reduction gear shaft was replaced, and another test run was conducted. On 25 December, a full-scale test run of the M-81 engine was carried out.

On 30 December, a meeting of the commission related to the I-187's first flight was held. After the meeting, the aircraft was cleared for testing.

On 9 January 1941, test pilot Ulyakhin performed trial taxiing, and the first flight was carried out on 11 January. The second and third flight with Ulyakhin at the controls took place on 12 January and 6 February. In the pilot's opinion, the aircraft behaved normally in flight, no signs of vibration were noted, while the speed reached 600km/h in a dive. Ulyakhin reported: "The aircraft lands very smoothly; I did not have to apply the brakes. The landing run is short. The aircraft is OK."

Factory test pilot Petr Loginov performed his first flight in the I-185 on 30 January 1941, and stated: "At landing, the plane behaves in an extremely simple manner. The overall impression of the aircraft is good."

On 28 February, when Loginov was taxiing to take off after an Ilyushin DB-3F at Moscow Central Airfield, the first disappointing mishap occurred. Colonel Stepanchonok, who was piloting the DB-3F, applied power too abruptly at take-off. As a result, the air stream from the bomber caused the I-187 to nose down, damaging the propeller. The damage, however, was promptly rectified, and flights continued until 18 March 1941, when the M-81 engine failed. By that time, the aircraft had made 16 flights. Full flight performance data had not been recorded, but turned out to be very close to the design figures. In particular, the maximum speed near ground level reached 495km/h instead of the expected 500km/h. Afterwards, the aircraft flight testing was stopped because it became known that the M-81 was to be discontinued as being not promising enough, and would undergo no further refinements.

By this time, two M-71 engines had already been received. One of them was mounted in place of the M-81. The aircraft was given the designation I-185 M-71 s/n 6202, and its first flight in the new configuration took place on 29 May that year.

Somewhat earlier, on 8 April, the I-185 M-71 s/n 6204 first took to the air. In two months, the aircraft made 23 flights from Moscow Central Airfield. Afterwards, on 28 June, test pilot Loginov ferried it to the LII airfield at Ramenskoye, where the tests continued. The obtained results inspired confidence and optimism – even with the M-71 engine not yet finalised, the aircraft demonstrated a speed of 620km/h.

At the LII airfield, the aircraft s/n 6204 underwent, *inter alia*, spin tests. Since, in accordance with Zhuravchenko's conclusions, there were certain concerns regarding safe recovery from a spin, the I-185 was modified appropriately. The tail fairing near the empennage was replaced by a box-type cone with attachment fittings for a spin recovery parachute. However, the need to use the parachute never arose, as it turned out that a spin up to two turns in the I-185 was absolutely safe.

The firing armament of the first two prototypes consisted of two synchronised 12.7mm BS machine guns and two synchronised 7.62mm ShKAS machine guns. Bombing armament was refined in the aircraft s/n 6204, and tests were conducted between 20 August and 23 September 1941.

During the course of the tests, the payload was attached to underwing racks in the following configurations: 4x100kg bomb, 2x250kg bomb, eight RS-82 rocket projectiles and VAP-6M spray tanks. Lifting and mounting of the load was carried out using a standard BL-4 winch installed on a special frame. It turned out that the FAB-250 bombs, which were made from old artillery shells, had a considerable length. With such bombs attached to the racks, it was not possible to fully deploy the flaps. During tests of VAP-6M spray tanks, there were fears that the sprayed liquid would splatter the empennage. For this reason, the horizontal stabiliser was pasted over with strips of white cloth. The subsequent inspection of the aircraft on the ground revealed no signs of spattering, which again testified to the aerodynamic perfection of the aircraft.

In summer 1941, two more aircraft, powered by the M-82 engines, joined the family of the flying I-185 prototypes. The Shvetsov M-82 was a new 14-cylinder double-row air-cooled radial engine developing 1,700hp and having a small overall diameter of 1,260mm.

As far as is known, Polikarpov began to study the variants of modifying the I-185 for the M-82 power plant in late 1940, immediately upon completion of the engine bench tests. However, the introduction of the M-82 lagged – the decision to conduct state tests and to further launch series production of the engine was taken only in May 1941.

When the fate of the M-82 finally became clear, the Polikarpov Design Bureau promptly redesigned the I-185 to be powered by this engine. The aircraft was given the designation I-185 M-82 'I', and featured the most powerful offensive armament, consisting of three fuselage-mounted synchronised 20mm ShVAK cannons. To build the aircraft, the fourth I-185 M-71 prototype (which was then under construction; but not the aircraft s/n 6204) was used. This allowed completing the manufacture of the first M-82-powered I-185 on 19 July 1941. The second I-185 M-82 prototype was built in late summer 1941, and was also handed over to the LII for testing in September, together with the I-185 M-71.

Thus, the pre-evacuation period in the history of the I-185 creation came to an end. According to official data, the approved plan of works for Aviation Factory No.51 for 1941 was as follows:

TIS 2 AM-37 – three airplanes;
ITP M-107 – two airplanes;
I-185 M-90 – one airplane;
I-185 M-71 – two airplanes;
I-185 M-81 – one airplane;
I-185 M-82 – two airplanes;
I-190 M-88 – one airplane;
S glider – two each;
ODB – two airplanes.

Initiative-based developments

The above list demonstrates that the working plan of the Experimental Design Bureau and Experimental Factory No. 51 was rather extensive, with the I-185s (four positions, six prototypes) holding a major place in it. However, the list also contained certain inconsistencies – one of the M-71-powered aircraft was not completed and later converted into an aircraft fitted with the M-82 engine, whereas another M-71-powered prototype emerged from an aircraft originally equipped with the M-81. Thus, before the evacuation, five I-185s were built, four of which were flown.

Due to the aggravation of the situation at the front, the equipment of Aviation Factory No.51 began to be dismantled on 9 October 1941 and prepared for transportation to Siberia. On 2 November, the first train with the factory equipment arrived at Novosibirsk, where the premises of the city circus and the airfield of the local flying club were allocated for Polikarpov's team. Until the end of the year, in the difficult conditions of a particularly cold winter, work on equipping the production facilities was conducted. As a result, starting from early 1942, the prototypes' preparations for flight testing were finally resumed.

Additional facts from the history of the I-185 are contained in the report of Aviation Factory No.51 on its production activities for 1941. According to the document, all five airplanes had been designed at the Experimental Design Bureau in accordance with the government's order; the prototypes were developed for installation of the M-90 engines, and were planned to be completed in 1940. Under an order of A. Shakhurin issued in 1940, four aircraft were modified – two to fly with the M-71 engine, one to be fitted with the M-81 engine and one to be powered by the M-90 with new engine cowling without central air intake.

The I-185 M-90 (s/n 6201) was assembled in early 1941 with a mock-up engine and mock-up cowlings. Apparently, the engine was regarded as an operational but not airworthy one. It is pointed out that the aircraft in such configuration was taken to the airfield, where trial starts and taxiing were conducted. An airworthy M-90 was received on 16 June. With this engine and new cowlings, the aircraft was assembled in evacuation conditions in Novosibirsk. The aircraft was rolled out to the airfield, but due to a lack of specialists, the refinements and further testing were suspended. Later, the I-185 M-90 s/n 6201 was dismantled and the M-90 engine was sent to Factory No.29.

The I-185 M-71 (s/n 6202) was modified from the one powered by the M-81, with adaptations including replacement of the power plant and engine cowling. After a test flight, the aircraft was transferred to the LII NKAP for performance of joint tests. The I-185 M-71 (s/n 6202), with an AV5-119 propeller, underwent joint tests during the period from 26 September to 2 October. The aircraft was flown by pilot Popelnushenko, with the engine running at the first speed of the gear-driven centrifugal-type supercharger. With rated power applied, the aircraft achieved a speed of 503km/h near ground level; with augmented power, the speed reached 520km/h. At an altitude of 3,300m, the speed was 582 km/h. It was hoped that 620km/h would be obtained at the supercharger second speed at an altitude of 6,150m. At the time of the evacuation, in October 1941, it was decided to ferry this I-185 to Kazan. but the aircraft made a forced landing along the route and was left in the open until January 1942. After Polikarpov's numerous requests, the aircraft was finally brought to Factory No.482 in Moscow, while on 12 May 1942 it was handed over to the Moscow branch of Factory No.51. As a result, the aircraft repairs took a relatively long time, until 18 March 1943.

The I-185 M-71 third prototype (the aircraft was given the s/n 6204, but it was referred to as 'the third prototype', which keeps causing some confusion to this day). In September 1941, the LII NKAP conducted spin tests, firearms-proof shooting and bombing armament testing. The factory tests were interrupted due to evacuation.

The I-185 M-71 fourth prototype had the increased radius of action in accordance with updated operational requirements (the capacity of fuel tanks was increased). The engineering drawings were prepared, and the parts and assemblies were manufactured with a level of readiness of 50 percent. This prototype was later used for installation of the M-82 engine.

The I-185 M-82 (first aircraft) was built under the NKAP Order No.438/ss of 13 May 1941 as a fighter with enhanced armament. The fuselage and its mounting points, canopy, tail skid, power plant and armament installation were redesigned and built anew. The rest was taken from the fourth prototype.

The aircraft was completed in a short period of time and handed over to the LII NKAP for joint tests on 20 July 1941. The first flight took place on 21 July. During the tests, the M-82 engine was replaced four times.

The I-185 M-82 (second aircraft) was built in accordance with an oral order of Deputy People's Commissar A. Yakovlev of 22 June 1941. It was tested at the LII in Moscow in September 1941.

The continuation of the I-185 'epic' in early 1942 was solely a Siberian one. In January, the I-185 M-71 s/n 6204 arrived in Novosibirsk. Joint tests of the aircraft, during which a maximum speed of 630km/h at the design altitude was reached, took place in February and March. It was noted that the aircraft, in terms of flight performance, was superior to all Soviet and foreign fighters. In the final report of NII VVS, it was recommended that the I-185 M-71 should be introduced into service, while in respect of the I-185 M-82A it was stated that the aircraft also excelled all production fighters, being inferior only to the M-71-powered version.

In the course of test flights of the I-185 M-71 conducted by front-line pilots in March 1942, Commander of the 18th Guards Fighter Air Regiment Major Chertov and his deputy Captain Tsvetkov expressed the following opinion of the I-185 as a fighter: "The advantages of this aircraft over other existing ones are obvious. Any pilot of average skill, especially one flying an I-16, can easily fly this aircraft. The take-off run and landing run are especially good for combat operations … Unlike in other existing aircraft, the cockpit is comfortable."

In March 1942, range tests of synchronised cannons installed in the I-185 M-82A 'T' were conducted in Novosibirsk.

Joint factory and state tests of the I-185 M-82A 'T' took place in Novosibirsk at the airfield of the Civil Air Fleet (GVF, *Grazhdanskiy Vozdushniy Flot*) from 13 April to 5 July 1942. A total of 42 flights were performed, with the total flying time amounting to 31 hours and 58 minutes. The aircraft was flown by pilot Loginov, who represented Aviation Factory No.51, and pilot Nikashin of NII VVS.

The maximum speed achieved was 549km/h near ground level with augmented power, and 615km/h at an altitude of 6,470m. It was noted that the I-185 M-82A, in terms of its flight performance, basically met the up-to-date requirements of the Red Army Air Force and could be recommended for production of an operational testing series. It was suggested that defects should be rectified, and that the aircraft should be made combat-worthy along with the I-185 M-71 s/n 6204 before 15 August 1942.

Before May 1942, the fifth airworthy I-185 M-71 (the so-called 'reference' version), built at Factory No.51, was ready for flight tests. This aircraft was made in accordance with drawings which were prepared for series production based on experience in building earlier aircraft of this type. The reference I-185 M-71 took into account all the previously revealed defects and shortcomings; its perfection had grown noticeably due to improvements in the external and internal aerodynamics of the engine cowling. During factory tests between 28 May and 12 October 1942, the aircraft made 21 flights, with a total flying time of 10 hours and 35 minutes. The maximum speed reached was 577km/h near the ground with augmented power, and 667 km/h at an altitude of 6,100m.

Front-line tests of the I-185

The appearance of four I-185s in the air above the front line was one of the most significant events in the history of the aircraft. However, it should be noted that it was not the only case when a small group of aircraft was tested in combat conditions. For example, in early June 1942, three MiG-9 fighters (the first aircraft with such designation, which was a version of the MiG-3 powered by the M-82 engine) were sent to the 34th Fighter Air Regiment of the VI Air Defence Fighter Air Corps for operational testing. These airplanes were essentially prototypes with a range of corresponding shortcomings, so in October 1941 they were returned for refinements and never entered the production phase. In the case of the I-185, the opinions were solely positive but the end result was the same.

The decision to test the I-185 in combat conditions was made in late August 1942. The 728th Guards Fighter Air Regiment operating on the Kalinin Front was tasked with conducting the tests. On 4 September, Deputy People's Commissar of NKAP for Experimental Aircraft Building A. Yakovlev ordered Polikarpov to prepare four I-185s for sending to the front. Polikarpov called and then telegraphed Factory No.51 in Novosibirsk with a request to immediately ship three I-185s to the factory branch in Moscow, together with a service team. The I-185 M-71 s/n 6204, the I-185 M-71 (reference aircraft) and the I-185 M-82A (second aircraft) were consequently shipped to Moscow. The fourth I-185 (I-185 M-82 'T') was being repaired at the Moscow branch of the factory after the incident of 5 July 1942 when NII VVS pilot Nikashin landed outside the airfield, destroying the landing gear.

It was not by chance that the Kalinin Front was selected for conducting operational tests. The 3rd Air Army was under the command of the famous test pilot, Hero of the Soviet Union Major General M. Gromov, former Head of the LII NKAP, who knew and understood the peculiarities of test activities perfectly well. It was also not surprising that Gromov appointed the 728th Guards Fighter Air Regiment to conduct the tests. The regiment was formed in late 1941 from instructor pilots of the Chuguev Aviation Flight School. Twice Heroes of the Soviet Union A. Borovykh and A. Vorozheykin and Heroes of the Soviet Union N. Ignatyev, A. Novikov and I. Kustov, among others, flew with the regiment.

In late September 1942, pilots of the 728th Guards Fighter Air Regiment Captain D. Kupin, Senior Lieutenant N. Ignatyev, Sergeants A. Borovykh and A. Tomilchenko and a team of technicians were sent on a duty trip to Moscow. There, they were told that they would have to take part in operational tests of the Polikarpov I-185 fighter. All of them were very skillful pilots, had front-line experience and fearlessly engaged the enemy even in conditions of the latter's numerical superiority. In July 1942, six (according to other sources, eight) I-16s led by Ignatyev attacked, near Rzhev, a large group of Ju 88 bombers escorted by Bf 109 fighters (according to the Soviet pilots' estimates, there were up to 70 aircraft). In the aerial combat, Soviet pilots shot down six bombers and three fighters without suffering any losses of their own. For this, every participant in the combat was awarded the Order of the Red Star.

In Moscow, the front-line pilots studied the aircraft and carried out preparation and acceptance of the I-185s under the supervision of Polikarpov Design Bureau engineers. Factory test pilot P. Loginov consulted pilots on the specifics of flying this aircraft type. Some design features were personally explained by Polikarpov.

In the course of the training, each of the pilots performed several flights to practice aerobatics and perform cannon proof firing. In late November, preparations for ferrying the aircraft to the front began. On 3 December, Polikarpov bid a warm farewell to every pilot, and blessed them by saying "God be with you!" and making the sign of the cross over them, which greatly surprised the pilots. According to N. Ignatyev, that was the first time in his life that he had received such a blessing before a flight.

The four I-185s took to the air and flew towards the front line. They headed for the Migalovo airfield near Kalinin, where the headquarters of the 3rd Air Army was located. The pilots introduced themselves to Army Commander Major General Gromov, who personally instructed them on how to conduct front-line tests of the I-185. For reasons of secrecy, the pilots were forbidden to fly across the front line, engage in air battles or take part in manoeuvring air combat. According to Ignatyev's recollections, they were told: "A fall of an I-185 on the territory occupied by the enemy will be regarded as high treason." The flights had to be performed at an altitude of 3,000–4,000 metres at a speed of 500–550km/h, depending on the weather conditions. For each flight, special clearance from Major General Gromov or Chief of Headquarters Colonel Dagayev was required.

The 728th Guards Fighter Air Regiment was stationed near the ancient Russian city of Staritsa, 60km from Kalinin up the Volga River. The situation in this sector of the front in late 1942 was somewhat tense but calm. The Rzhev–Sychyovka offensive operation, conducted in the summer, had amounted to nothing, in spite of the use of massive tank formations. The Rzhev operation at the Kalinin Front (between 24 November 1942 and 20 January 1943) also failed to bring any noticeable results. That was (according to a commonly mentioned version) a feint operation aimed to distract the enemy's attention from the main events at Stalingrad. The strategic operation conducted by Soviet intelligence proved successful, as the Germans kept a large group of troops in the Rzhev–Vyazma Salient until the summer of 1943. They were not only ground troops – in late 1942, it was there that the first batches of the *Luftwaffe*'s Fw 190 fighters on the Eastern Front began to arrive. Apparently, the tests of the I-185 on the Kalinin Front pursued the same goal of misleading the enemy.

The I-185s flew their first combat sortie on 9 December 1942, and their last combat sortie took place on 12 January 1943. They flew in two pairs, with the officer (Ignatyev or Kupin) usually as the leader and the sergeant (Borovykh or Tomilchenko) as the wingman. The fighters were often flown in conditions when aerial combat was going on above Soviet-held territory. In these instances, firing their cannons, the I-185s rushed through the formation of German aircraft, then made a turn and flew back to their home airfield. Two sorties were flown to provide cover for the Curtiss P-40 Kittyhawk reconnaissance aircraft operating near Rzhev. There was also a 'free hunt' sortie flown above Soviet territory. According to Ignatyev's recollections, pilot A. Borovykh shot down or damaged a German aircraft during the flight.

Kupin flew, for the most part, the M-71-powered I-185 prototype s/n 6204, while Ignatyev piloted the 'reference aircraft' and Borovykh and Tomilchenko were at the controls of the M-85A-powered I-185s. They had no occasion to encounter any Fw 190s in an aerial combat.

The group of I-185s often moved from one airfield to another, relocating to Staraya Toropa and returning to Staritsa again on numerous occasions. The aim was to create, among the German aviation command, an illusion of the presence of at least a regiment equipped with the I-185 fighters on the Kalinin Front, and to reduce the probability of strikes on fighter aircraft in case of possible enemy raids on the airfield.

In total, each pilot flew 10 or 11 combat sorties. For reasons of secrecy, these were in the majority of cases recorded in pilots' logbooks as training flights in the area around the airfield. Apart from Kupin, Ignatyev, Borovykh and Tomilchenko, the I-185s were test-flown in real training flights by Regiment Commander Vasilyaka and pilot Kustov.

In accordance with the command's instructions, reports on the operational tests had to be written only by officer pilots. Furthermore, such reports had to emphasise in every way that only training flights were performed in the I-185s. Commander of the 728th Guards Fighter Air Regiment Captain V. Vasilyaka wrote the following in his report:

> In the regiment, five pilots fly the I-185 aircraft. All five pilots take off and fly without any difficulties after flying Yak and I-16 fighters.
>
> Personally I have flown such aircraft as the I-16, Yak-1, Yak-7B, LaGG-3, La-5, Hurricane and I-185 powered by the M-71 and M-82 engines, and have come to the following conclusion:
>
> 1. Conversion from other fighter aircraft to the I-185 is simple, and does not cause any difficulties for pilots.
>
> 2. In flight, the aircraft is easily controllable, very stable, and behaves without any specific 'caprices'.
>
> 3. Performing take-off and landing is exceptionally easy.
>
> 4. The aircraft advantage consists of extremely high manoeuvrability in the vertical plane due to a good rate of climb. This enables the I-185 to conduct air combats with enemy fighters, that is not always possible in Yak-1, Yak-7B and La-5 aircraft.
>
> 5. In terms of horizontal speed, the I-185 has a considerable advantage over Soviet-built aircraft as well as enemy aircraft. The range of horizontal speeds near the ground is exceptionally wide, from 220km/h to 540km/h, which is an important factor for a modern fighter.
>
> In the horizontal plane, the aircraft picks up speed from the control speed to the maximum speed very quickly in comparison with LaGG-3, La-5 and Yakovlev aircraft; this means that it has good acceleration parameters. It performs aerobatic manoeuvres easily, quickly and energetically, like the I-16. The following are shortcomings as identified during service, which I recommend for the factory to rectify in course of new aircraft production:
>
> 1. The frontal portion of the canopy should be faceted.
>
> 2. Controls of the engine cooling shutters should be made simpler or easier.

3. Thimbles of the rudder control cables are not fit for performance of aerobatic manoeuvres such as rolls or half-rolls: the shoe heels catch the thimbles.

4. Aircraft handling at taxiing should be improved; making the U-turns should be made easier.

5. The throttle control lever should be relocated forward by at least 100mm; the existing arrangement of the lever does not allow throttling back entirely without making special moves.

6. A compressor should be installed in order to replenish air as required for landing gear and flaps retraction.

7. The manufacturer should be tasked with providing a system to start the engine with the help of compressed air.

8. A mechanism for the emergency opening of the canopy should be developed for the newly manufactured aircraft.

9. Cockpit ventilation should be improved (it is very hot in there).

In my opinion, the I-185 aircraft, powered by the M-71 or M-82 engine, and armed with three ShVAK cannons, meets all applicable requirements for conducting combat operations. It must be assumed that the I-185 is currently the best fighter aircraft in terms of ease of handling, speed, manoeuvrability (especially in the vertical plane), armament and survivability. Front-line pilots are looking forward to seeing this aircraft at the front.

Squadron Leader Senior Lieutenant Ignatyev also wrote his opinion of the I-185 aircraft:

I began to take part in combat operations at the front line of the Great Patriotic War in the I-16 and Yak-7 fighters. In over 320 combat sorties, I have destroyed up to 25 German aircraft, both in personal and group engagements.

Conversion to the I-185 aircraft presents no problems for a pilot of medium skills. The I-185 is in all cases simple and stable. Taking off is much easier than in the Yak-1; due to the high power of the engine, the aircraft quickly lifts off; gliding, landing and the landing run are easy to perform. Flying in the aerobatic area is simple; rolls, spins and half-rolls are performed energetically and do not require any effort. The I-185 has good horizontal and vertical speed performance. It is superior to all foreign and Soviet-built aircraft in terms of speed; for this reason, it is better to use it in vertical air combats. The horizontal manoeuvring performance is equal to that of the Yak-1. The I-185 was not used in combat operations in view of absence of the appropriate task. Training flights have shown that the I-185 aircraft is well fitted for conducting vertical air combats with enemy fighters. The aircraft armament consisting of three ShVAK cannons is quite sufficient; personally I recommend that the manufacturer should further use such armament on the I-185s. The M-71 and M-82 engines are quite suitable. They are powerful and robust; however, there are some issues to be resolved to improve their operation. Starting the engine in winter conditions is difficult. This is a general drawback of air-cooled engines; therefore, the ways of heating up the engine more quickly than it is done today should be considered. Arrangement of the engine filling device (filling gun) is inconvenient; I recommend placing the filling system near the instrument panel or behind it.

Shutter control is inconvenient and too stiff (it also needs to be modified in order to be similar to that of the I-16); with such arrangement, the system requires considerable effort and attention, both in the M-71-powered and in the M-82-powered aircraft.

The filler tank of the M-71-powered aircraft is inconvenient in terms of refilling; I recommend that the filling system be made like that of the Yak-1, from a common tank. This will facilitate engine starting. I recommend starting the engine using compressed air rather than the starter.

The following was the opiniion of Junior Lieutenant Kustov on the I-185:

In the combat operations at the front lines of the Great Patriotic War, I have always been flying an I-16 aircraft, in which I have flown over 100 combat sorties and shot down seven enemy aircraft personally and another seven in group engagements. Conversion from the I-16 to the I-185 was not difficult for me; for this reason, I believe that pilots who have good skills in flying the I-16 can freely convert to the I-185.

At take-off and landing, the aircraft behaviour is simple. After performing several flights in the I-185, I can conclude that, in terms of speed, it is superior to all types of aircraft currently in service with the Red Army Air Force. It has good vertical and horizontal manoeuvring performance. With such flight performance and powerful armament, with which the aircraft is equipped, it may well be reckoned among the best Soviet fighters.

Shortcomings of the aircraft are the following:

1. Spherical windscreen, which distorts the view considerably, should be replaced with a windscreen consisting of flat sheets.

2. Positioning of the throttle control lever is inconvenient; it should be relocated in the forward direction.

3. Controls of the engine shutters are inconveniently placed and too stiff.

4. Unavailability of the compressor.

I suggest that the manufacturer should supply such aircraft to the front-line units in the shortest possible time and in the maximum possible quantities.

Despite such flattering opinions of the I-185, the wishes of the front-line pilots remained unheeded. By mid-1942, the Soviet aviation industry had surpassed that of the Germans in terms of combat aircraft production rate; however, neither

Stavka nor NKAP were in a hurry to reconsider their policy regarding the qualitative composition of the Red Army Air Force. Any reduction in production rates, even a temporary one, was still deemed unacceptable. There were other factors at play too. Launching series production of the I-185, which was superior to other fighters in terms of flight performance, would bring up the issue of curtailing the production of such other fighters. This, for a number of reasons, was unpalatable both for certain circles among the leadership of the People's Commissariat and the Soviet Air Force, and of course for chief designers. Therefore, there was merely "a lot of leading-to-nothing fuss about the aircraft", as Polikarpov put it with a bitter smile.

The last attempt

In November 1942, before the beginning of the front-line tests of the four I-185s, NII VVS received the I-185 M-71, which was a reference aircraft for series production. State tests of the airplane were conducted until 26 December, and it was flown by test pilot P. Stefanovsky. While the engine was not running reliably (two power plants were replaced during the tests), notable results were obtained in terms of the flight speed, which was still regarded as the main criterion of a new aircraft's advantage. The maximum speed reached was 560km/h near ground level (600 km/h with augmented power) and 680km/h at an altitude of 6,000 metres. It was noted that in some flights Stefanovsky reached a speed of over 700km/h.

State tests of the reference aircraft were completed in January 1943. Given the truly aircraft's outstanding performance, several appeals were addressed to the higher authorities with a request to clear the I-185 for series production in the shortest possible time. In particular, pilots Stefanovsky, Loginov and Leading Engineer Lazarev directed the following report to Stalin:

> To: Central Committee of the All-Union Communist Party of Bolsheviks, Comrade J.V. Stalin.
> Dear Joseph Vissarionovich! We, test pilots of the Polikarpov I-185 fighter, are forced to appeal to you, Joseph Vissarionovich, with the following:
> 1. The I-185 fighter has passed the factory and state flight tests at the Red Army NII VVS. The factory tests were conducted by pilot Comrade Loginov; the tests in the Red Army NII VVS were conducted by pilot Comrade Stefanovsky. The following results were achieved in the course of the tests:
> a. Maximum speed near ground – 600km/h.
> b. Maximum speed at an altitude of 6,100m – 680km/h.
> c. Time to climb to 5,000m – 4.7 minutes.
> d. Average time to perform a turn at H=1,000m – 22–23 seconds.
> e. The fighter has high frontal firepower – it is equipped with three 20mm cannons and ammunition allowance of 600 rounds.
> f. The aircraft can be easily handled by a pilot of medium skills. This is confirmed by pilots who have flown it (12 persons; of them, four airmen of a guards regiment). The aircraft is the easiest-to-learn type for the majority of Soviet pilots.
> g. The fighter is simple in service. Its assemblies are easily accessible for maintenance in field conditions.
> 2. We know that Comrade Polikarpov has a project of the I-185 fighter version, implementation of which will allow achieving the following flight performance characteristics:
> a. Maximum speed near ground – 650km/h.
> b. Maximum speed at H=6,250m – 710km/h.
> c. Time to climb to 5,000m – 4.2 minutes.
> d. The frontal firepower may be increased up to four 20mm cannons.
> In terms of performance, the I-185 aircraft is currently reckoned among the best ones. For this reason, we are appealing to you with a request to authorise manufacture of an operational testing series, as well as testing the aircraft in combat conditions at the front.
>
> Test pilot of the Red Army NII VVS, Colonel Stefanovsky
> Leading Engineer of the Red Army NII VVS, Engineer Colonel Lazarev
> Test pilot of Factory No.51 of the NKAP Loginov.

On 4 February 1943, Polikarpov also personally addressed Stalin. He concluded his message with the following words: "The I-185 M-71 is awaiting your resolution in respect of clearing it for series production."

It is hard to tell whether the appeals to Stalin turned out to be of any help. However, in February and March 1943, under an assignment from the NKAP, preparation for production of the I-185 began at Aviation Factory No.81 in Moscow. The reference aircraft was handed over to the factory for repair and study (it had sustained minor damage during additional tests).

The work went on at a sluggish pace and was entirely discontinued in April. On 5 April, the I-185 M-71 prototype crashed due to engine failure, killing test pilot Stepanchonok. Under the resolution of the authorities, work on launching the series production of the type was discontinued. The reference I-185 M-71 was repaired to airworthy condition and returned to Factory No.51.

The last versions

While keeping working on improvements of the I-185 fighter, in spring 1943 Polikarpov completed design of a modified aircraft designated the I-187, which was intended to be powered by the M-71F uprated engine, with take-off power of 2,200hp. The aircraft had a lower gross weight and a teardrop-shaped cockpit canopy with flat frontal surfaces. A new original engine cowling with movable frontal shutters was developed, which combined optimal aerodynamics with uniform cooling of cylinder heads. According to calculations, the aircraft was expected to reach a maximum speed of 650km/h near ground level and 710km/h at an altitude of 6,250m.

The next project to appear was the I-188, to be powered by the M-90 engine with a take-off power of 2,080hp, which passed 50-hour tests in 1942. It was hoped that its successor, the M-95 engine with a take-off power of 3,300hp, would follow it in due course. With such an engine, the I-188's flight speed was planned to exceed 700km/h.

In late 1943, after returning from Novosibirsk to Moscow, Polikarpov was tasked with designing a fighter to be powered by a rocket engine developed by the Jet Scientific Research Institute (*Reaktivny Nauchno-Issledovatelskiy Institut*, RNII). The aircraft was dubbed *Malyutka* ('Little One'). An interesting fact is that the initial version of the *Malyutka* made use of many components of the I-185 fighter, which can be noted in the photographs of the model tested in TsAGI wind tunnels.

During the winter of 1943–44, the health of Nikolay Polikarpov began to deteriorate. In the spring, during the course of a thorough clinical examination, he was diagnosed with gastric carcinoma. In spite of receiving treatment and undergoing surgery, the designer's health kept worsening. On 30 July 1944, Polikarpov died.

After Polikarpov's death, V. Chelomey took over as head of his design bureau. With him, the team focused on creating cruise missiles with pulse jet engines. It is known that during the period of working on this topic in 1945, the design bureau developed an I-185 version which was fitted with the D-5 pulse jet engine in addition to the M-71 engine.

Flight performance and specifications of the I-185 aircraft								
Aircraft type	Project with the M-90	DIT-185 project	I-186 M-71 project	I-187 M-81	I-185 M-71 s/n 6202	I-185 M-71 s/n 6204	I-185 M-82A	I-185 M-71 reference aircraft for series production
Date of the project issue	6 January 1940	10 August 1940	5 May 1940	27 November 1940	–	–	26 May 1941	13 April 1942
Date of the first flight	–	–	–	11 January 1941	29 May 1941	8 April 1941	21 July 1941	10 June 1942
Engine power (rated/maximum) (hp)	M-90 1,500/ 1,750	1,500/ 1,750	1,700/ 2,000	1,280/1,500	1,625/ 2,000	1,625/ 2,000	1,390/ 1,600	1,625/ 2,000
Aircraft length (m)	7.25	7.55	7.68	7.765	7.74	7.68	8.1	8.05
Wing span (m)	9.8	9.8	9.8	9.8	9.8	9.8	9.8	9.8
Wing area (sq.m)	15.53	15.53	15.53	15.53	15.53	15.53	15.53	15.53
Empty weight (kg)	2,028.5	2,263.67	2,289	2,298.1	2,471	2,846	1,717	3,130
Gross weight (normal/with overloading) (kg)	2,708/ 2,908	2,900/ 3,254	2,984/ 3,489	3,120/3,325	3,119/ 3,534	3,500/ 4,015	3,328/ 3,418	3,735/ 3,825
Armament	2xBS* 2xShKAS 200kg of bombs	1xBS 1xShKAS 200kg of bombs	2xBS 2xShKAS 200kg of bombs	2xBS 2xShKAS 200kg of bombs	2xBS 2xShKAS 500kg of bombs	2xBS 2xShKAS 500kg of bombs	3xShVAK 20mm 500kg of bombs	3xShVAK 20mm 500kg of bombs
Maximum speed near ground (km/h)	576	576	571	506	505	556	549	600
Maximum speed (km/h) at altitude (km)	701/6	701/6	665/5	611/6.4	615/6.2	630/6.17	615/6.47	680/6.1

Flight performance and specifications of the I-185 aircraft								
Aircraft type	Project with the M-90	DIT-185 project	I-186 M-71 project	I-187 M-81	I-185 M-71 s/n 6202	I-185 M-71 s/n 6204	I-185 M-82A	I-185 M-71 reference aircraft for series production
Time to climb to 5,000m (mins)	4.5	5.0	4.3	6.4	5.7	5.2	6.0	4.7
Service ceiling (m)	10,250	10,250	10,750	9,900	10,000	–	10,450	1,000
Range (normal/maximum) (km)	680/1,100	680/1,100	780/1,100	962	900	895	1,015/1,380	835

* In 1940, the Berezin BS (Berezin, synchronised) large-calibre machine gun was designated the TKB-150.

Tests of the I-185 full-scale mock-up in TsAGI T-101 wind tunnel in the normal configuration (with full-scale wings). Fabric strips are attached on the wing, fuselage and empennage for visual demonstration of the air flow processes. The photo was taken on 5 September 1940.

Tests of the I-185 M-90 full-scale mock-up equipped with a cowling featuring a central cooling air intake in TsAGI T-104 wind tunnel in autumn 1940. The mock-up under study is fitted with the so-called 'short' wings, which are merely wing centre section fairings.

Designer Polikarpov (left) at the airfield during tests of the I-185.

204   The King of Fighters Volume 2

A sketch of the I-185 M-90 made by historian I. Sultanov in the late 1970s.

Installation of the PBP-1 collimator gunsight.

A spin recovery parachute installed on the I-185 M-71 s/n 6204. The fuselage tail fairing was replaced by a box-type cone, to which the parachute was secured.

The I-185 M-71 s/n 6204 before flight tests in March 1941.

The I-185 M-71 'reference aircraft' during tests at Novosibirsk in summer 1942.

The I-185 – the best fighter of designer Polikarpov 205

The I-185 M-71 'reference aircraft' before the tests in April 1942.

The I-185 M-71 with the engine cowling doors open and the propeller spinner removed.

Tests of the bombing armament (FAB-250 bomb) attachment under the I-185 M-71 s/n 6204 in September 1941 at the LII airfield in Ramenskoye.

A FAB-250 bomb being lifted using a BL-4 winch in order to attach the bomb to the underwing rack.

Two FAB-100 bombs mounted under the wing of the I-185 M-71. Note the fabric strips pasted over the empennage in order to detect spattering when VAP-6 chemical spray tanks were used. The photo was taken on 24 September 1941.

Rail launchers for four RS-82 rocket projectiles installed under the wing of a I-185.

206   The King of Fighters Volume 2

VAP-6 chemical spray tanks attached under the wing of a I-185.

The I-185 M-71 'reference aircraft' with the engine cowlings open.

The upper 20mm ShVAK cannon installed on the I-185 M-71 'reference aircraft'.

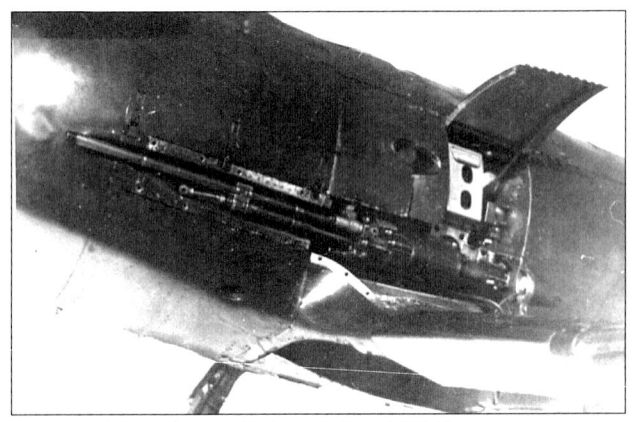

The side installation of the ShVAK cannon.

The upper portion of the power plant and armament of the I-185 M-82A.

The cockpit of the I-185 M-71 'reference aircraft'.

The I-185 – the best fighter of designer Polikarpov 207

The left side of the cockpit of the I-185 M-71 'reference aircraft'.

A view of the doors of the retractable landing gear.

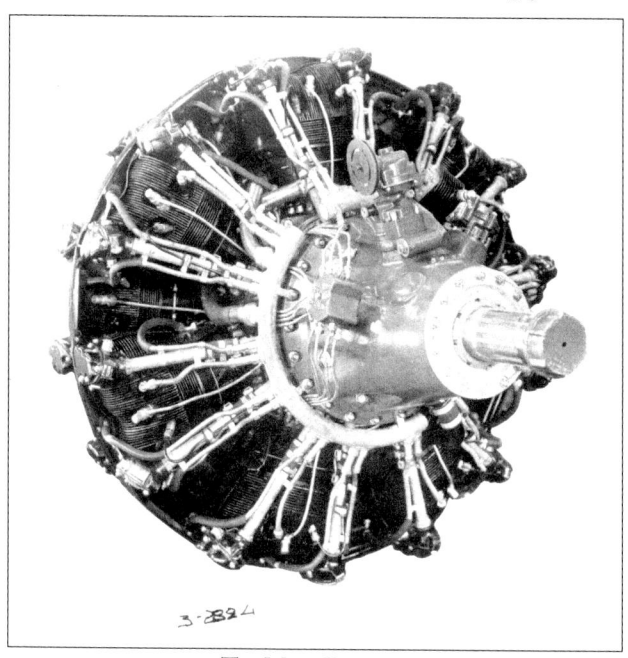

The M-82F engine.

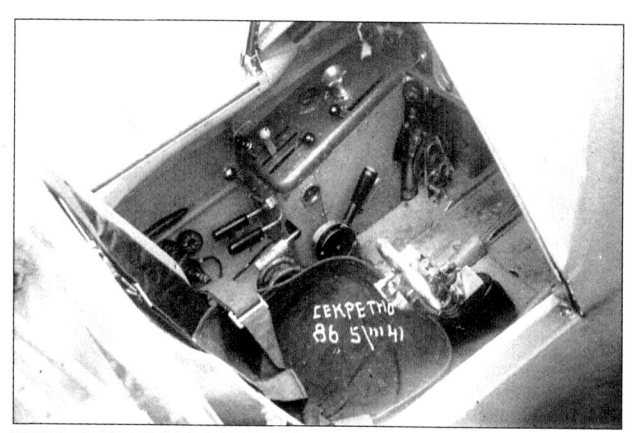

The cockpit of the I-185 M-71 s/n 6204.

The right side of the cockpit.

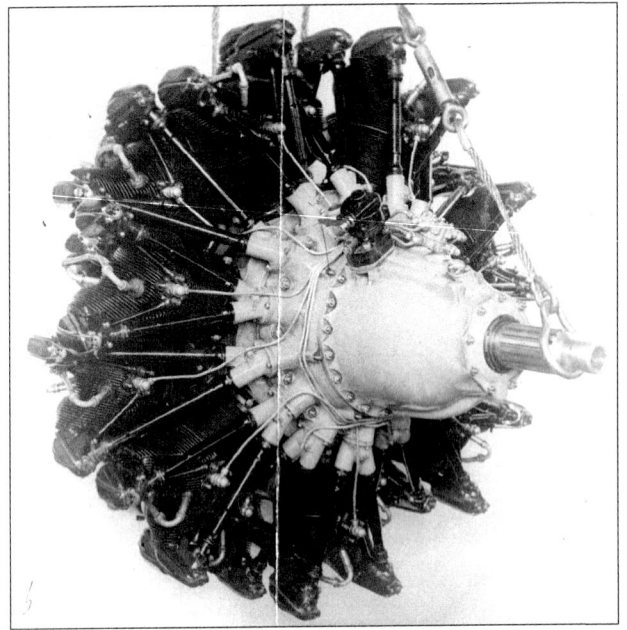

The M-90 engine.

The M-81 engine.

Designer Nikolay Polikarpov.

Pilot V. Stepanchonok.

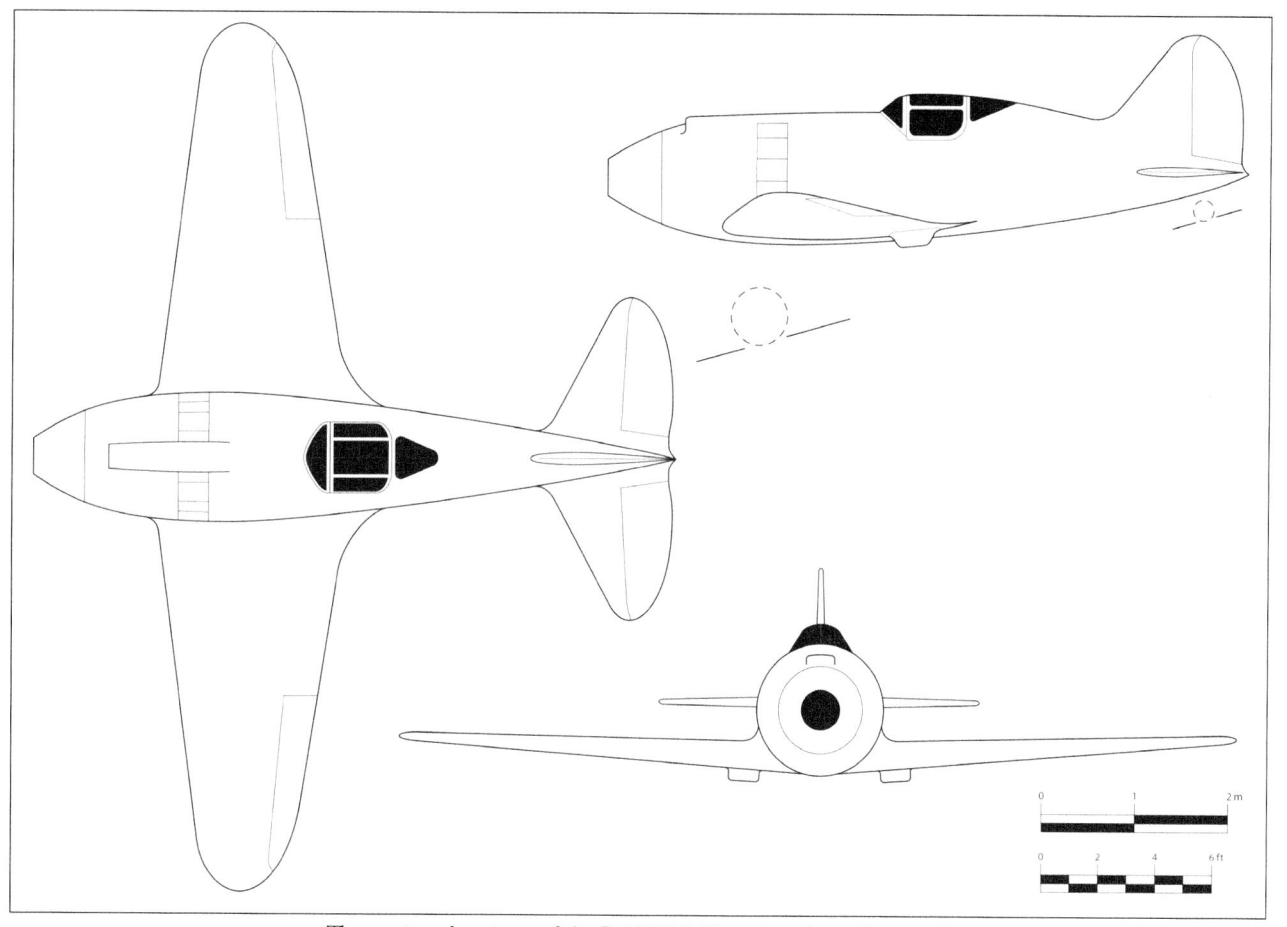

Three-view drawings of the I-185 M-90 project (initial version).

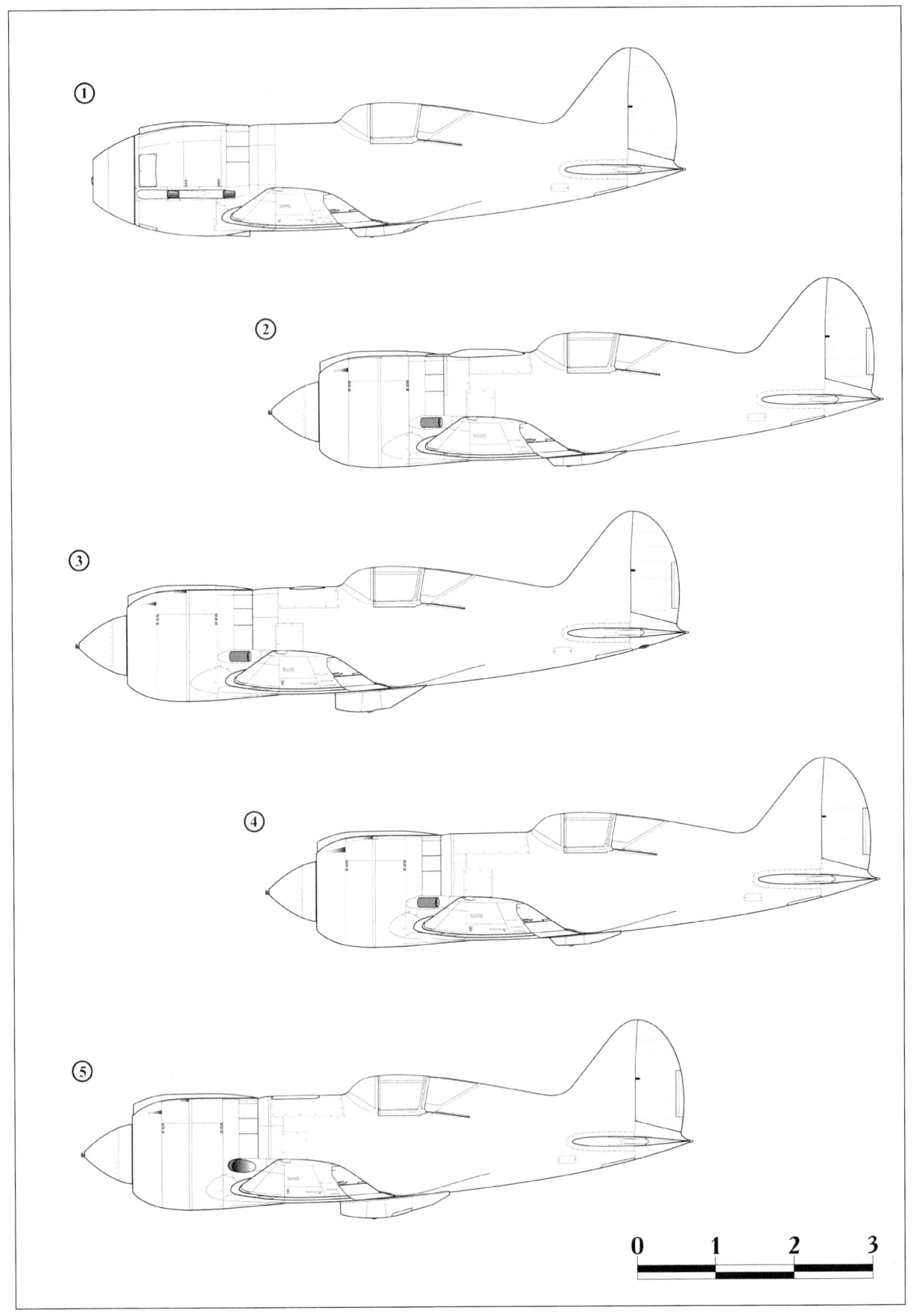

1. Side view drawing of the I-185 with M-90 engine, s/n 6201, during tests at TsAGI T-101 wind tunnel, September 1940.
2. Side view drawing of the I-185 with M-81 engine, s/n 6202, February 1941.
3. Side view drawing of the I-185 with M-71 engine, s/n 6202, October 1941.
4. Side view drawing of the I-185 with M-71 engine, s/n 6204, Moscow, March 1941.
5. Side view drawing of the I-185 with M-71 engine, s/n 6204, Novosibirsk, January 1942.

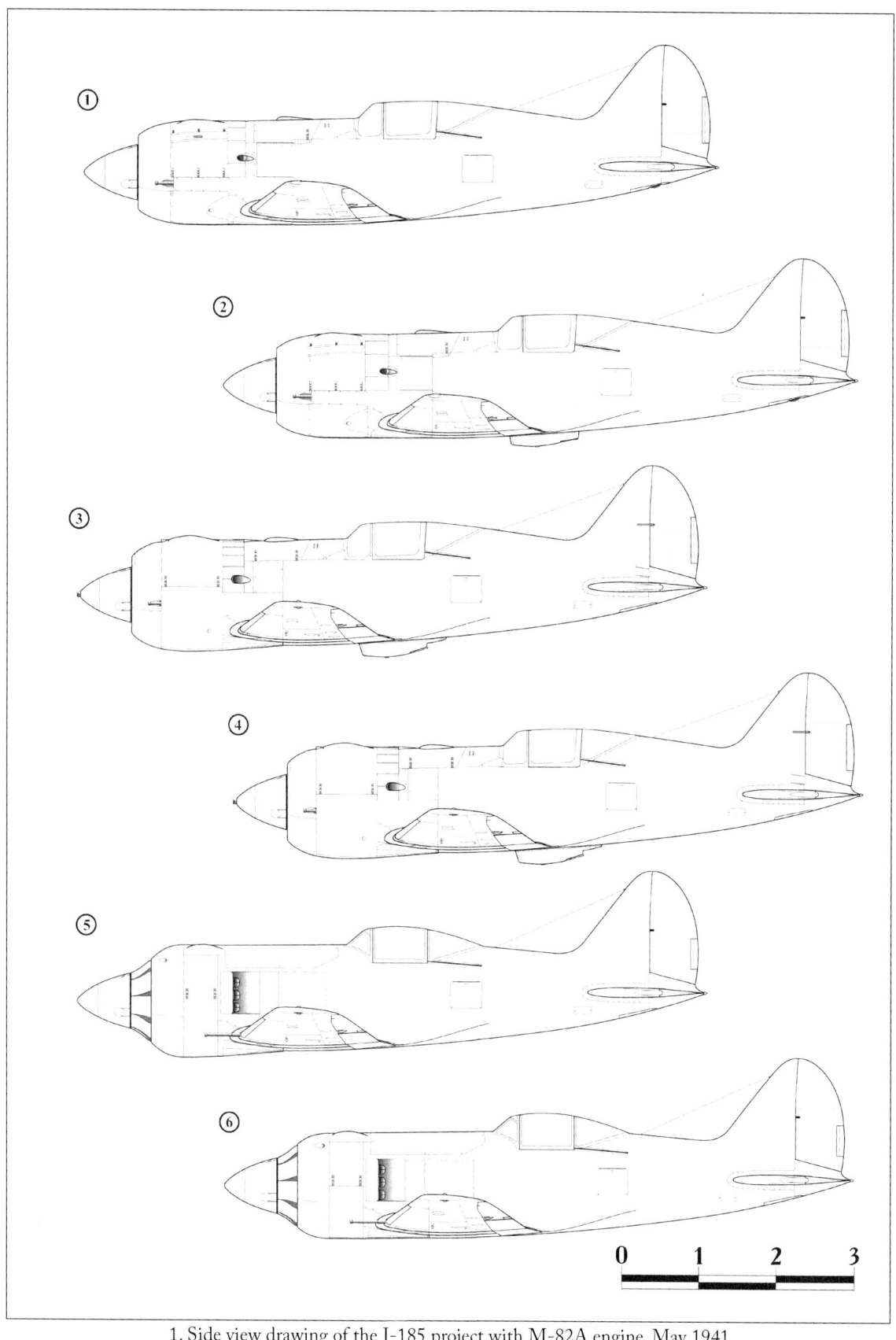

The I-185 – the best fighter of designer Polikarpov   211

1. Side view drawing of the I-185 project with M-82A engine, May 1941.
2. Side view drawing of the I-185 with M-82A engine, s/n 6203, Novosibirsk, April 1942.
3. Side view drawing of the I-185 with M-71 engine, the first reference aircraft
   built by the Factory No.51, Novosibirsk, June 1942.
4. Side view drawing of the I-185 with M-71 engine, the second reference
   aircraft built by Factory No.51, Novosibirsk, December 1942.
5. Side view drawing of the I-187 project with M-71 engine, February 1943.
6. Side view drawing of the I-188 project with M-90 engine, February 1943.

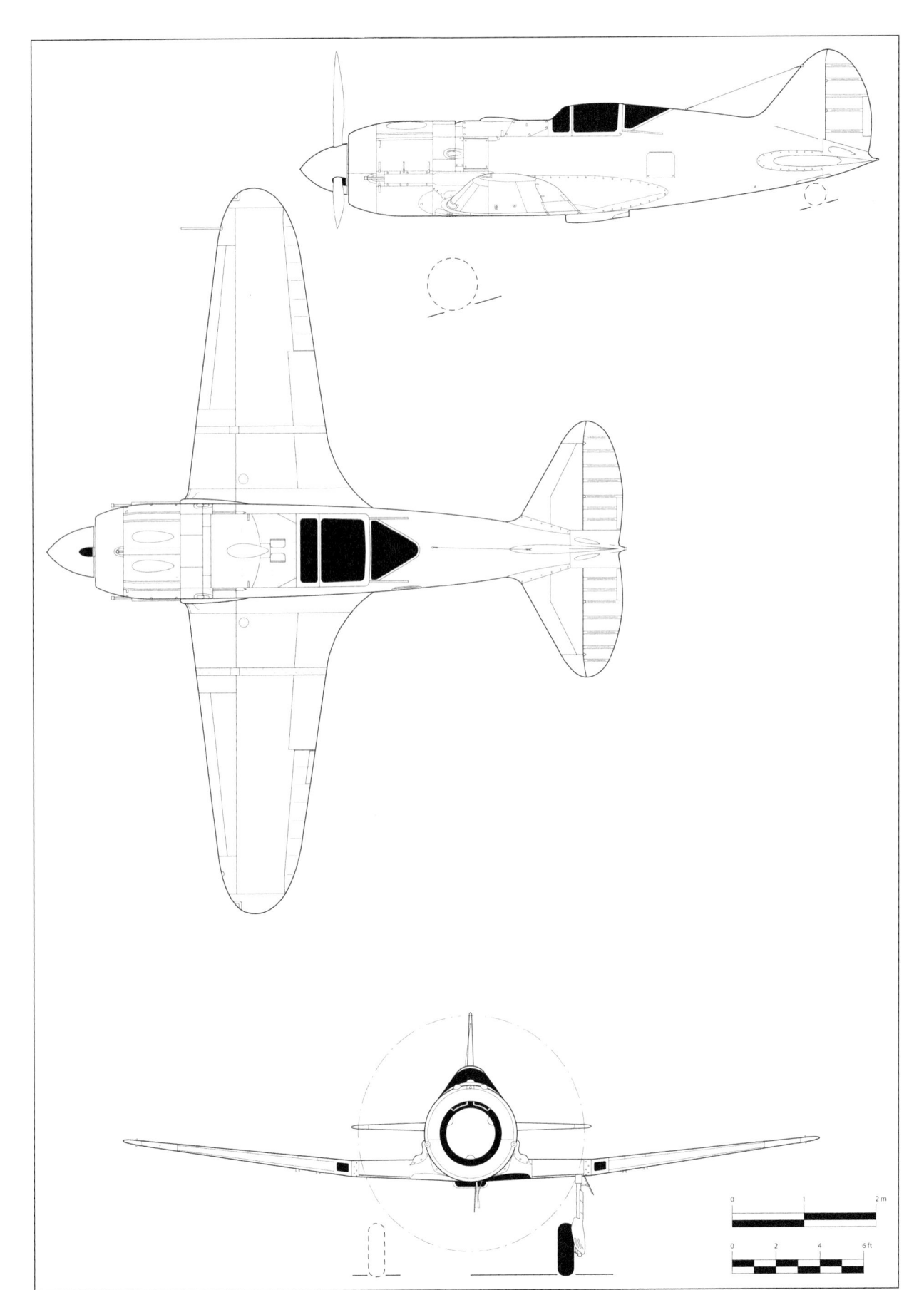

Three-view drawings of the I-185 with M-82A engine.

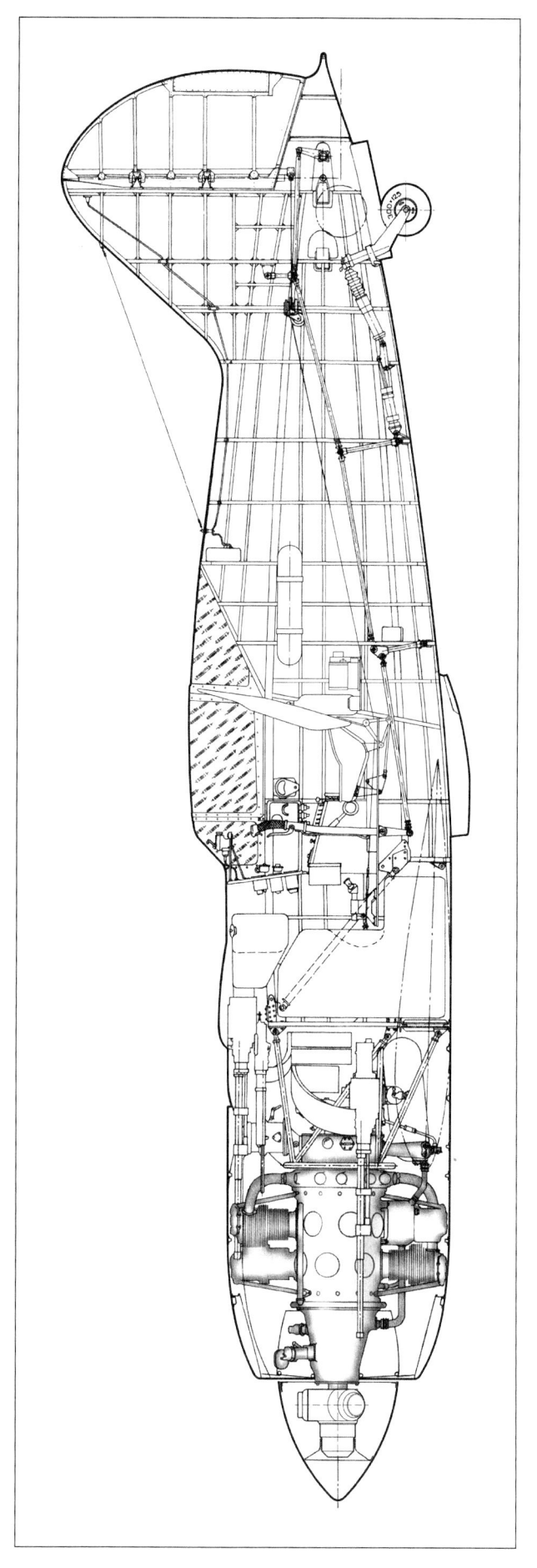

The I-185 – the best fighter of designer Polikarpov 213

Cutaway side view of the I-185 fighter.

5

The ITP fighter

Development of the fighter which was given the designation ITP (*Istrebitel Tyazholiy Pushechniy* – heavy cannon fighter) started after the first flights of the I-185 prototypes. The ITP was planned to be powered by the Mikulin AM-37P liquid-cooled engine (other options included Klimov's M-105P or M-107P) and equipped with powerful cannon armament. The explanatory note to the preliminary project specified that it was a single-seat fighter to be used for aerial combat with bombers and for attacks on ground targets. The aircraft armament consisted of a 37mm Shpitalniy cannon firing through the hollow shaft of the engine gearbox, and two synchronised ShVAK cannons. With the AM-37P engine, the estimated maximum speed was 670km/h at an altitude of 7,400m. With the M-105P engine, the maximum speed should reach 570km/h at an altitude of 5,000m. According to the project, the aircraft had a length of 8.95m, a wingspan 10.0m and a wing area of 16.45sq.m. The fuel reserve in the wing tanks was 760 litres. This ensured a flight range of 1,200–1,500km, which was sufficient to escort bombers.

The ITP was designed as an all-metal construction, with the airframe featuring a certain universality which provided for a possibility to install various liquid-cooled engines with minimum changes. Thanks to the thoroughly selected airframe proportions and precise aerodynamics, Nikolay Polikarpov hoped to have the best fighter in its class.

During the preliminary project review on 14 December 1940, the ITP was approved by the Expert Commission of the NKAP, which made the following conclusion: "It is of interest as our first front-line fighter with powerful cannon armament." The aircraft's development continued at a rather swift pace: the first meeting of the mock-up review commission was held on 8 January 1941. However, the conclusions of this commission concerned first of all the AM-37P engine, it being indicated that "there are no prospects for obtaining the AM-37P in the near future". Indeed, the works on this engine had been almost ceased due to the fact that it was not included in the plan of experimental activities. In response to Polikarpov's appeals to various authorities to speed up the process of creating the AM-37, designer Mikulin replied that the AM-41 requested by the People's Commissariat was under development, whereas the AM-37P engine was sidelined.

Under the circumstances, manufacture of the new Polikarpov fighter began with the M-107P engine, which developed 1,400hpd at take-off. In 1940, the M-107 was regarded as a promising and realistic engine, since it was the next – and more advanced – model after the M-105. Nearly all Soviet fighters designed or built with the M-105 were intended to be later fitted with the more powerful M-107. However, this engine never achieved acceptable performance. Later, in 1944–45, another engine with the M-107 designation appeared; however, it was in many respects a completely different engine.

Manufacture of the ITP, which received the in-house designation M or M-1, began at Aviation Factory No.51 in March 1941. The new and blatantly weak factory (in terms of equipment and specialists) could not cope with the manufacture of prototypes. Polikarpov tried – though without any noticeable success – to arrange manufacturing of the wing and empennage at Factory No.240. Therefore, until the evacuation, the ITPs were only being slowly built using Factory No.51's own resources. The M-107P engine was expected to arrive in autumn 1941, and was finally mounted on the aircraft only after the transfer of the factory team – together with the design bureau – to Novosibirsk.

The normal gross weight of the aircraft totalled 3,750kg, with a CG position of 22.3 percent MAC. Preparations of the ITP M-1 for the flight tests began on 14 February 1942. During subsequent days, the aircraft was taken to the airfield, where pilot Popelnushenko performed taxiing and take-off runs. Later, pilot Petr Loginov prepared to continue the testing. The aircraft first flew on 13 March 1942 from Novosibirsk airfield, with pilot A. Nikashin at the controls. During the landing approach, the oil line was damaged, causing a subsequent oil leak. Before 3 April, the pilots managed to perform five flights, but there were reports of unstable engine operation. The installed new M-107 also caused trouble with its uneven operation, and consequently, the flights were carried out with considerable interruptions.

By 22 July, only nine short check flights were made in the ITP. These showed that the considerable oil overheating and its constant release from the breather did not allow full power to be obtained and significantly reduced the aircraft's thrust performance. Due to constant engine overhauls and adjustments, armament was not installed at this stage. For the same reason, wing-mounted fuel tanks were not used, so the fuel system was not fully tested. Factory No.51 was tasked with bringing the aircraft to a stable airworthy condition and handing it over for testing to NII VVS. However, it turned out that this goal could not be achieved on schedule. On 26 August, pilot Zaitsev had to maee a forced landing at the airfield due to failure of the engine shaft bearings.

In late 1942, the ITP was transported to Moscow, where the new M-107PA engine, which had just been tested, was mounted. The installed armament consisted only of 20mm ShVAK cannons. Meanwhile, flights of the fighter prototype were still carried out in a sporadic manner. On 25 February 1943, an accident occurred involving an M-107A-powered Yak-9, after which series production of the engine was ceased and a decision was taken to continue its improvement. There followed a resolution by Deputy People's Commissar of NKAP for Experimental Aircraft Building A. Yakovlev to conduct static tests of the ITP. The aircraft successfully withstood all loadings up to 100 percent, but was no longer fit for flying. The life of this airplane, however, did not come to an end at that point – in 1944 the ITP (M) was used for the tests of pulse jet engines.

The second ITP (M-2) prototype was built in Novosibirsk and originally equipped with the AM-37 engine. It was only after delivery of the aircraft to Moscow in December 1942 that the AM-39 engine was mounted on it. This engine was waited for from April until 11 October 1943, so it was immediately installed on the aircraft upon receipt. On 23 October, the aircraft was handed over for testing.

The ITP (M-2) first flew on 23 November that year, while the second flight took place on 2 December. Unlike the previous version, the ITP (M-2) had only synchronised armament consisting of three fuselage-mounted ShVAK cannons. The aircraft was able to carry up to 400kg of bombs under the wings.

Despite the fact that the ITP fighter was originally designed for high flight speeds of approximately 700km/h, this value was never approached in practice due to a lack of suitable engines. Meanwhile, in 1943 and 1944, series production Lavochkin and Yakovlev fighters were already being fitted with powerful cannon armament. For this reason, further improvements of the ITP (M-2) were abandoned.

Main performance parameters of the ITP fighter		
ITP version	M-1	M-2
Wing span (m)	10.0	10.0
Length in the flight line (m)	8.95	9.0
Wing area (sq.m)	16.45	16.45
Empty weight (kg)	2,598	3,095
Gross weight (kg)	3,750 (3,366)	3,820
Wing loading (kg/sq.m)	227	232
Maximum speed near ground level (km/h)	541	540
Maximum speed near ground level with augmented power (km/h)	549	600
Maximum speed at an altitude of 5,000m (km/h)	645*	560**
Time to climb to 5,000m (mins)	5.4	6.0
Service ceiling (m)	–	11,500

* Speed at an altitude of 6200m
** Maximum speed at 2,500m with augmented power – 650km/h

A full-scale mock-up of the ITP.

216   The King of Fighters Volume 2

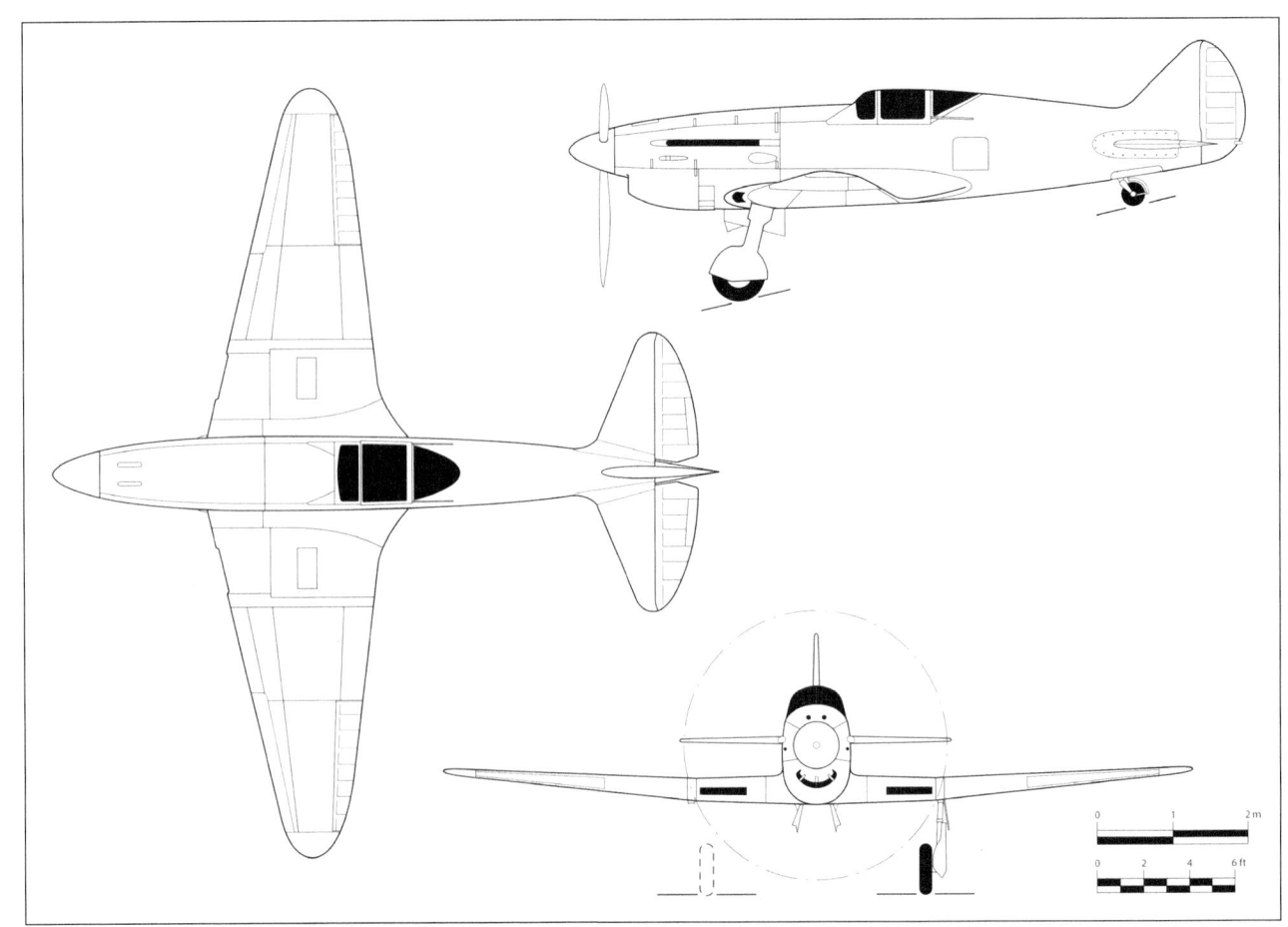

Three-view drawings of the ITP

The first ITP M-1 prototype in the course of testing.

The second ITP M-2 prototype.

The instrument panel of the first ITP prototype.

6

The last biplanes of Nikolay Polikarpov

Shortly before the Second World War, various design bureaus in the Soviet Union were developing approximately 20 types of single-engine fighters. Among these projects there were several biplanes, including the Borovkov-Florov I-207, Nikitin-Shevchenko IS fighter with a folding wing and Tairov OKO-4 multi-purpose aircraft. Nikolay Polikarpov also kept on developing manoeuvrable biplanes during that period.

6.1. The I-190

The I-190 fighter, which was determined under its technical task to be a manoeuvrable biplane with a maximum speed of 500–550km/h, was being developed concurrently with the I-180, starting from January 1938. Its development was brought about by the then existing notions of the nature of air combat, with monoplanes and biplanes interacting and complementing each other. The early period of the aerial war in Spain was seen as an illustrative and convincing example confirming the correctness of such judgments. Aerial combat had, by that time, changed very little from what it looked like in the First World War – it had the form of a disordered fight (to this day, such a combat is termed a 'dog fight') in which horizontal manoeuvrability was paramount. Soon, the nature of air battles began to change towards active use of vertical movement and high-speed attacks; however, the voices of those who had realised this fundamental truth were not heard at that time.

The development and manufacture of the I-180 monoplane was carried out at a quicker pace. In March 1938, under a governmental decree, the Chief Designer was ordered to complete the aircraft and to release it in its first flight before the end of the year. Development of the I-190 during that period was hardly progressing, which was no wonder given the fact that the team was busy preparing the I-153 drawings until May.

More active work on the new biplane began in the autumn, when the first two mock-up commissions were held. The next stage consisted of testing the aircraft models in TsAGI wind tunnels. The aircraft was designed as a further development of the I-153, with observance of the basic technology and using many subassemblies and production tooling of the earlier model. All this left some room for hope that the I-190 would enter series production promptly. The new features included the M-88 engine, fuselage contours, smooth plywood skin of the wings, cantilever horizontal tail and retractable tail skid.

At the next stage, the first prototype was to be built, but this seemed to cause difficulties. Aviation Factory No.156, which hosted Polikarpov and his team, was at that time overloaded with work. The production facilities were occupied with aircraft created by other designers. Being aware that a biplane fighter was a 'perishable' product, the designer decided not to begin building the I-190 at Factory No.156, and made an attempt to expedite the process. On 14 January 1939, he sent a request to the Head of the PGU NKOP, Paster, to authorise manufacturing of the I-190 at Aviation Factory No.1. People's Commissar of Aviation Industry M. Kaganovich came to know of the matter and personally gave permission to manufacture two I-190 prototypes at Factory No.1. After the third mock-up commission held on 19 February, building the aircraft was finally found to be expedient.

In fact, it was only in spring 1939 that work on the new fighter was launched – more than a year after the decision to create it had been made. The first I-190 was completed in October of that year, but its finalisation and refinements were carried out until mid-December. Almost immediately after the aircraft was rolled out of the assembly shop, manufacturing of the second prototype was started there. It was planned to equip the power plant of this prototype with two TK-1 type turbosuperchargers.

The first I-190 was powered by the M-88BRL non-geared engine and the AV-2 three-blade propeller, both of which were available in the form of single prototypes. As for the M-88 engine, it was mounted on the I-190 even earlier than on the I-180 (the first two I-180 prototypes flew with the M-87 engine).

Fitted with a ski landing gear, the I-190 was rolled out at Moscow Central Airfield on 23 November 1939. At the flight station of Factory No.1, the aircraft was painted, had all its frontal surfaces polished where possible and was subjected to thorough weighing. The take-off weight totalled 2,290kg – 184kg higher than the estimated weight. The engine runs began

The I-190 during tests in December 1939.

The I-190 in the assembly shop.

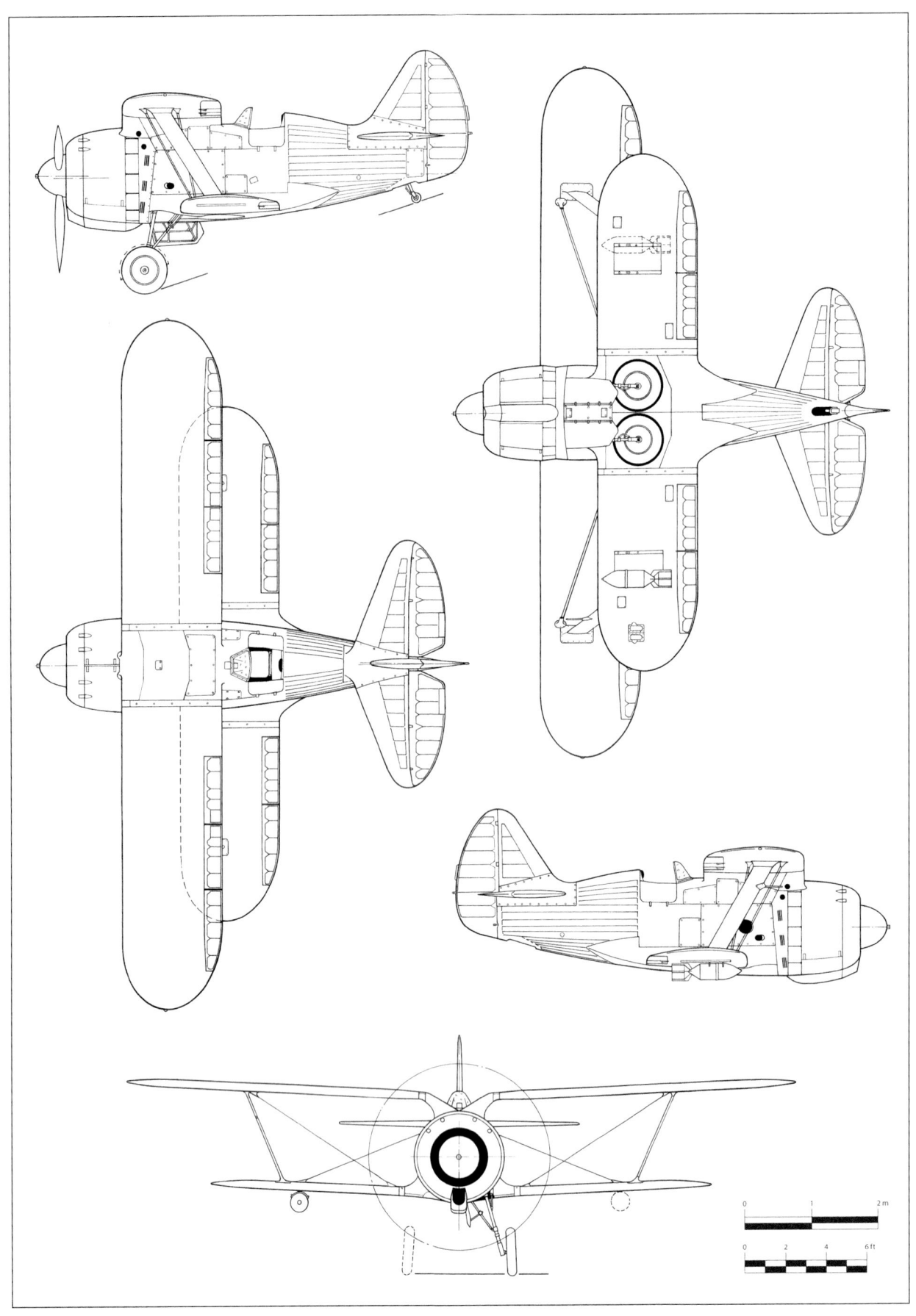

Five-view drawings of the the I-190 aircraft with the M-88BRL engine.

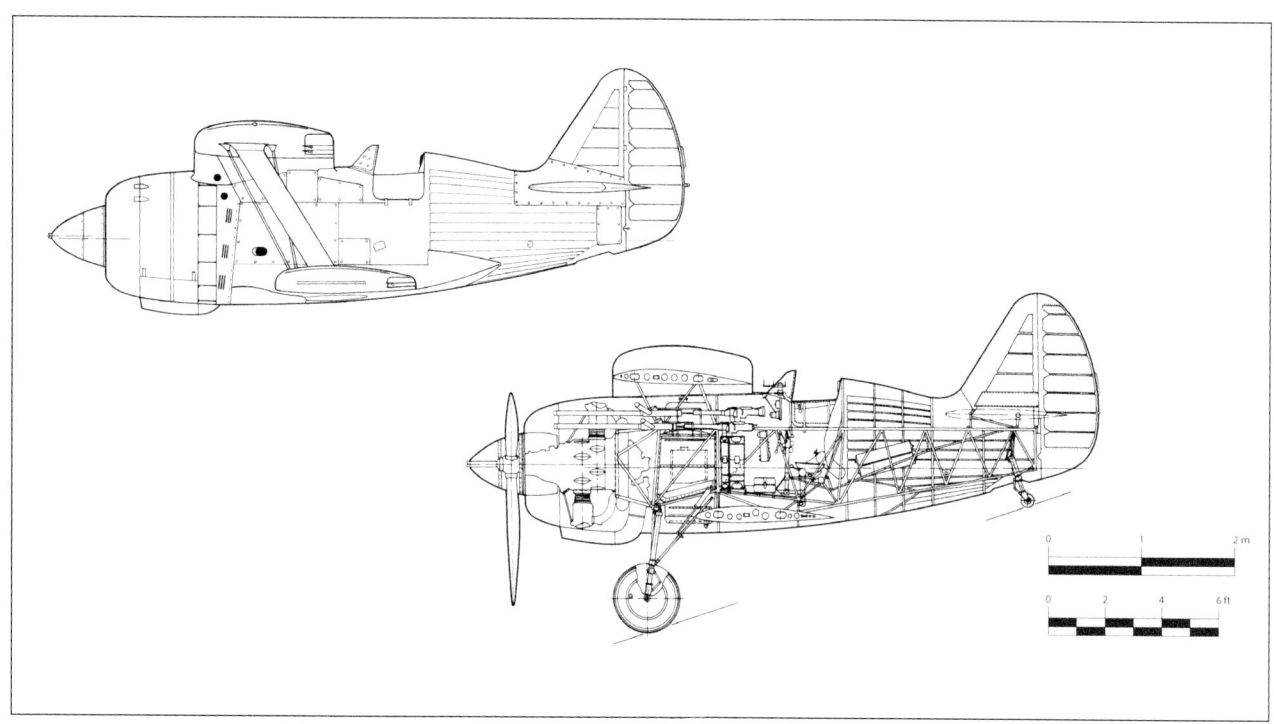

Side view and cutaway drawings of the I-190 with the M-88 geared engine.

in early December. On 15 December, the oldest test pilot at the Khodynka airfield, Alexander Zhukov, began to perform taxiing runs in the new aircraft, and even managed to make two minor liftoff manoeuvres on that day. With Zhukov at the controls, the aircraft first flew on 30 December 1939. All subsequent occasions that the aircraft took to the air were only brief ones, and were accompanied by numerous design improvements and refinements of the power plant. On 8 February 1940, pilot Ulyakhin joined the tests, with pilot Davydov starting test flying slightly later.

On 1 April, when Davydov was performing a flight, the right landing gear leg failed to extend completely and the aircraft sustained minor damage upon landing. The repairs were finished two weeks later, and the test flying resumed. Such flights, reckoned to be factory tests, continued until 6 June. There was one further incident, with the upper wing skin partially torn off in mid-flight. Throughout this period, three types of variable-pitch propellers were tested – a 2.75m-diameter AV-2L-1, 2.65m-diameter AV-2L-2 and 2.65m-diameter AV-2L-3. With the AV-2L-2 propeller, the maximum speed totalled 375km/h near ground level and 410km/h at an altitude of 5,000 metres. These performances were not acceptable, but there were hopes for obtaining the desired parameters with the new M-88R geared engine. The power plant, along with the new elongated and modified cowling, was, for the most part, borrowed from the I-180 fighter. In such a configuration, the aircraft performed several flights before the beginning of 1941. However, the expected maximum speed of 500km/h was not reached, and further improvement works were conducted only sporadically. Interest in the biplane-configuration fighter significantly decreased during that period.

A flight speed of 488km/h at an altitude of 5,000m was the maximum value reached in the I-190 before February 1941. On 13 February, the capricious M-88 engine failed during a scheduled flight from Moscow Central Airfield. Pilot Ulyakhin glided down to the runway, but the snow was deep during that winter, and the aircraft, which was fitted with wheeled landing gear, tipped up. Ulyakhin escaped unharmed, but the fighter sustained severe damage. The accident was made little of, and was soon forgotten. Yet the aircraft was never repaired and the second prototype was never completed. Thus ended the story of the I-190 biplane fighter.

To conclude, what follows is a brief description of the I-190, which was determined as a modification of the I-153 fighter. It was planned to be used as a ground-attack aircraft or, with external fuel tanks, in the role of an escort fighter.

The airframe had the same structure, with reinforced joints, as the I-153. The fuselage was a truss made of chromansil tubes. Forward of the cockpit, the fuselage was covered in duralumin sheets, while a fabric skin was used in the tail part.

The M-88 was a 14-cylinder double-row radial engine, measuring 1,296mm in diameter. The engine cowling had an adjustable rear slot (shutter), while the exhaust manifold consisted of two halves, with one exhaust pipe on each side of the fuselage. The oil cooler was installed on the right side of the fuselage aft of the engine cowling; the cooling air outlet had the same location.

The biplane cell featured I-shaped struts and was reinforced with four dual load-carrying bracing wires and two dual supporting bracing wires. Both the upper wing and lower wing were fitted with ailerons. Both wings had the Clark-YH profile, with a thickness-chord ratio of 10 percent. The two-spar wooden wings were covered in 1.5mm-thick plywood. The entire top surface of the wings was pasted over with fabric (marquisette) using cellulose dope, coated with several layers of aircraft dope and polished.

The empennage was of the cantilever type; however, provisions were made for installation of bracing wires between the vertical stabiliser and the horizontal stabiliser, with appropriate attachment fittings for this purpose.

The main landing gear, equipped with 700x150mm wheels, was almost identical to that of the I-153. The tail skid was retractable and had a 150x90mm solid rubber wheel. The firing armament consisted of four synchronised 7.62mm ShKAS machine guns. It was planned that two synchronised Berezin BS large-calibre machine guns would be installed later. The maximum bomb load was 200kg. To attach the bombs under the lower wing, integrated bomb racks were installed (in the same manner as in the I-153).

Technical specifications and flight performance parameters of the I-190	
Length in the flight line (m)	6.480 (6.60 after repair)
Upper wing span (m)	10.0
Lower wing span (m)	7.50
Height in the flight line (m)	3.554
Wing area (sq.m)	24.83
Empty weight (kg)	1,705
Gross weight (kg)	2,290
Wing loading (kg/sq.m)	92.2

6.2. The I-170

The project of a sesquiplane fighter under the designation 'M' was being developed at the Polikarpov Design Bureau in the second half of the summer of 1939. The beginning of work on this aircraft was associated with progress in the development

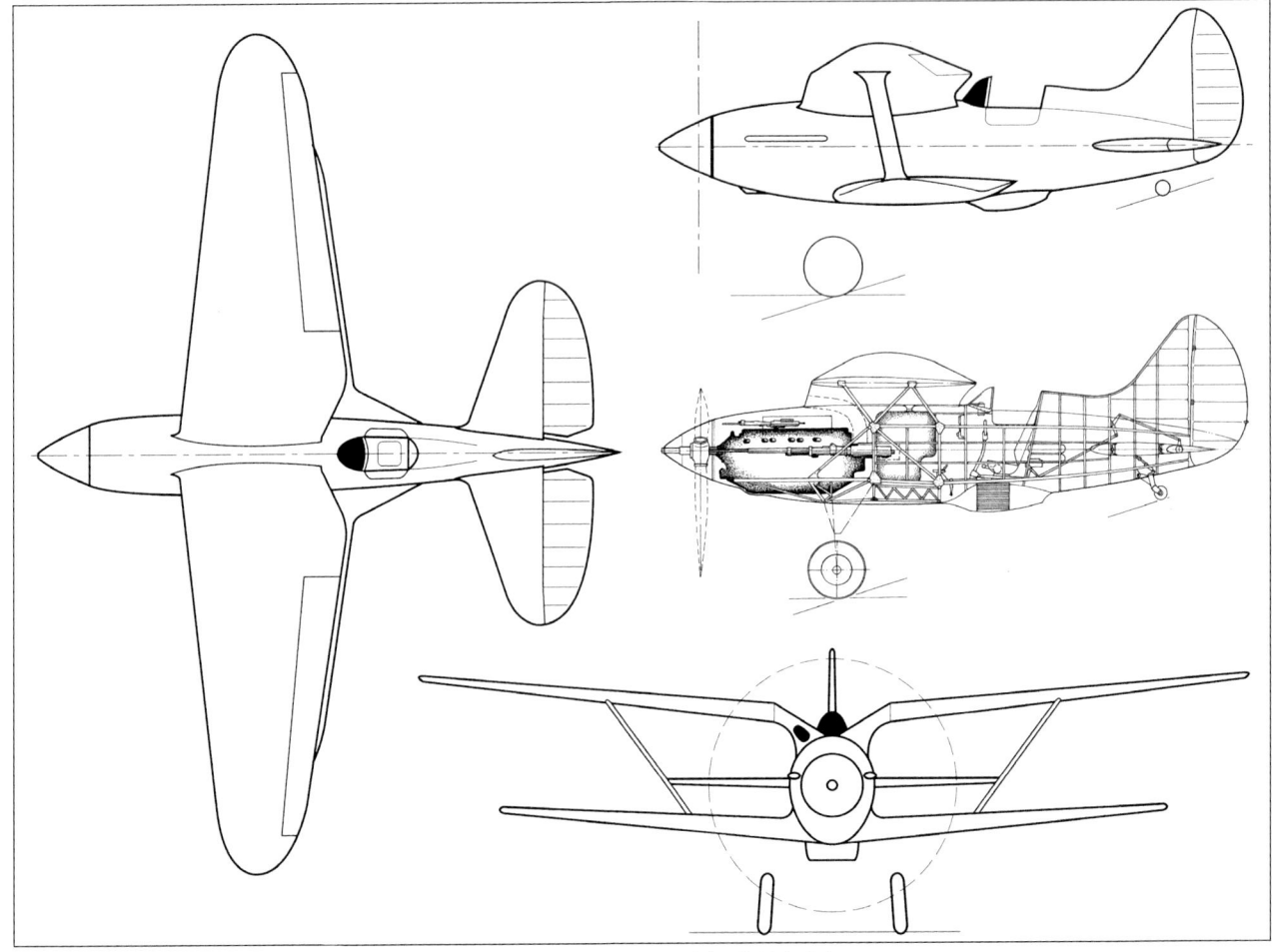

Three-view and cutaway drawings of the I-170 fighter project.

of inline liquid-cooled engines, on which the 'M' project was focused. Engine Factory No.26 in Yaroslavl (headed by Chief Designer V. Klimov) had been engaged for several years in development and improvement of such engines, based on the licensed (originally French-built) Hispano-Suiza engine. In 1936, the factory in Yaroslavl launched production of the 860hp M-100 engine, and less than a year later, the 960hp M-103 was presented for testing. In 1938, the factory was busy refining the 1,050hp M-105. Against this background of annual successes, the new, still more powerful M-106 engine was taken almost as an accomplished fact.

It was with the M-106 engine in mind that Polikarpov personally made the first preliminary calculations for the new fighter in August 1939. At the same time, the aircraft was given the designation I-170. With high manoeuvrability retained (the wing area was 25sq.m, which was nearly identical to that in the I-190 fighter), it was expected to reach a high maximum speed of over 500km/h.

In August 1939, concurrently with the beginning of the development works, consultations were held with representatives of the engine factory. In early autumn that year, Polikarpov decided to speed up work on the I-170. He intended to complete the development of the preliminary project no later than 15 October, and to build the aircraft mock-up a month later. On 29 September, engineer A. Karev was appointed Leading Designer for the I-170.

Polikarpov's subsequent departure on a business trip to Germany and the transfer, in his absence, of a considerable part of the staff to the newly formed A. Mikoyan design bureau, resulted in the discontinuation of many developments, including the I-170 fighter.

6.3. The I-195

The project involving this manoeuvrable biplane fighter was the last of Nikolay Polikarpov's known designs in this area. The beginning of development activities dates back to late winter 1940. Externally, the aircraft resembled a biplane version of the I-185 fighter, on which the designer had been working since January 1940. That was quite explicable, since, starting from 1932 and up to that period, new Polikarpov monoplane fighters had always had 'matching' biplane fighters, which were akin to the monoplanes in certain parameters.

In the explanatory note to the preliminary project of the I-195 manoeuvrable fighter, which was sent to the Chief Administration of the Air Force in spring 1940, Polikarpov wrote, "The role of a manoeuvrable fighter in modern warfare has not yet been thoroughly covered nor clarified … It can be expected that such [a] role will grow in importance with transition to multiple-aircraft engagements involving fighters and bombers, where speed will not play the decisive role to the same extent as manoeuvrability will." Apparently realising the controversy of such a statement, the designer further indicated that he intended to ensure "considerable and very up-to-date horizontal and vertical speeds" for the new aircraft.

It was planned that this biplane would use the power plant with a central cooling air intake, the fuselage tail portion – including the cockpit – and a number of other details from the I-185. Due to improved aerodynamics, a smooth skin, new NACA-230 wing profile, the absence of bracing wires and use of ejector exhaust pipes in combination with a powerful engine, it was envisaged the I-195 might have a design speed of 510km/h near ground level and 591km/h at an altitude of 7,000 meters, a landing speed of 103km/h and a service ceiling of 12,000m.

Armament was planned to consist of two 20mm ShVAK cannons and two large-calibre BS machine guns. In the ground-attack version, the I-195 was expected to carry up to 250kg of bombs. The aircraft had the following dimensions and weight parameters:

Length (m)	7.550
Upper wing span (m)	10.500
Lower wing span (m)	8.100
Height in the line of flight (m)	3.775
Wing area (sq.m)	28.9
Normal gross weight (kg)	2,916
Maximum gross weight (kg)	3,254

With such design characteristics, the I-195 project was reviewed in the summer of 1940, but no decision to build the aircraft was made. The era of manoeuvrable biplanes triumphing in aerial combat had come to an end, and they ultimately lost ground to high-speed monoplanes.

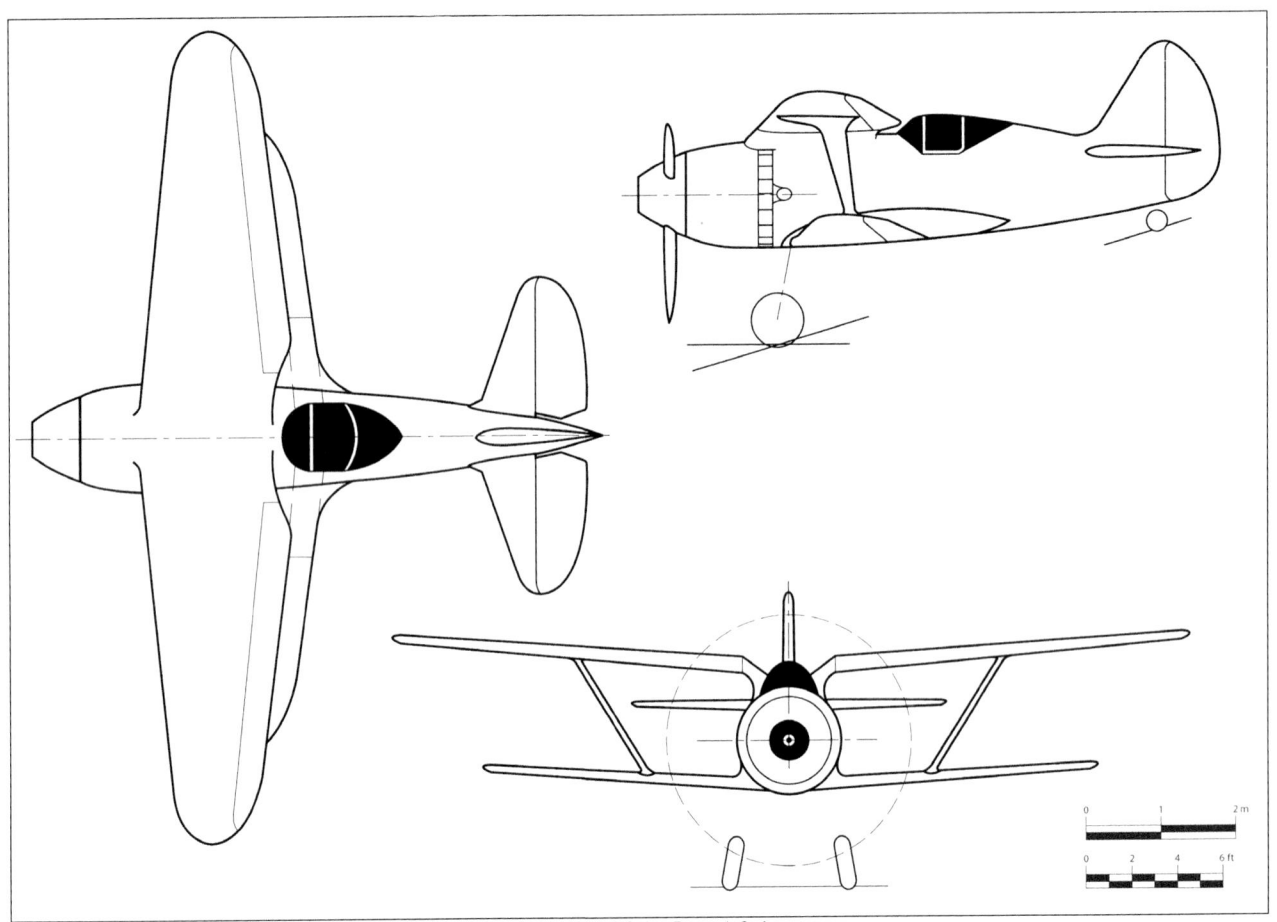

Three-view drawings of the I-195 fighter project.

7

The bomber designs of the 1930s

7.1. The VIT air destroyer of tanks

Among miscellaneous records of Russian aviation historian Vadim Shavrov, the following was found:

> In spring 1930, before TsKB was organised at Factory No.39, when our young group had just appeared at the factory and found the occupants of Hangar No.7 ('saboteurs', as they were referred to), I encountered Polikarpov almost every day. In one of our conversations about the TB-1 aircraft, which was just beginning to enter service with military units, Polikarpov said, 'As for this aircraft, it is no longer a modern one. Now we need to begin designing and building a bomber with the wing surface area twice as small as in this aircraft, with smooth skin, and with the flight speed twice as high.'

However, as is known, over the next several years Polikarpov did not address the subject of bombers, and was instead developing mostly fighter aircraft.

The first mention of the new Polikarpov two-engine aircraft capable of performing the role of a bomber dates back to the second half of 1936. It should be noted that it was initially referred to as the VT (*Vozdushniy Tank*, Air Tank). In the course of development, the designations MPI (*Mnogomestniy Pushechniy Istrebitel*, Multi-Seat Cannon Fighter) and SVB (*Samolyot Vozdushnogo Boya*, Airplane of Air Combat) were used. The aircraft was being built as the MPI-1 at Aviation Factory No.84 in the Moscow region, where Polikarpov's design bureau was accommodated from the second half of 1936. Later, during the course of building, the designation VIT-1 (*Vozdushniy Istrebitel Tankov 1*, Air Destroyer of Tanks, the First) began to be used. It was this designation that later became assigned to the completed aircraft.

The VIT-1 was a three-seat monoplane featuring good aerodynamic shapes, with smooth skin, a thin spindle-shaped fuselage, single-fin tail unit and retractable landing gear. The aircraft was powered by 860hp M-103 engines. The offensive armament of the VIT-1 was the most powerful of all Soviet-built combat aircraft. It included two 37mm Shpitalny K-37 cannons. The defensive armament, covering the rear hemisphere, initially had the TUR-10 turret with a ShKAS machine gun. Later, it was replaced with the SUDB-3 (*Srednyaya Oboronitelnaya Ustanovka Bombardirovshchika DB-3*, Medium Defensive Mount for the DB-3 Bomber), manufactured by Aircraft Armament Factory No.32.

In summer 1937, in parallel to the combat version, a civilian variant of the VIT was assessed, which was intended for participation in international air races across the Atlantic Ocean along the Paris–New York route. The racing, scheduled for 1938, never took place.

The manufacture of the VIT-1 was, for the most part, completed by mid-autumn 1937. With pilot V. Chkalov at the controls, the aircraft first flew on 31 October that year. On 16 November, during the third test flight, Polikarpov flew in the forward navigator's cabin. Later, NII VVS pilots G. Baydukov and M. Gromov took part in testing of the VIT-1. Tests of the K-37 cannons, which were mostly conducted at the Noginsk test range up to 1939, were deemed the project's most important aspect. It should be noted that the VIT-1 was initially regarded as a prototype intended to test the design and manufacture technology. Even before its first flight, development of the second, more advanced version was launched. Its main external difference from the first prototype consisted of the twin vertical tail. On 29 June 1937, Polikarpov signed the completed preliminary project of the VIT-2 aircraft, which was to become the embodiment of all the designer's ideas. The explanatory note to the preliminary project of VIT-2 listed its possible roles:

1. A high-speed medium bomber carrying 800kg of bombs inside the fuselage.
2. A dive bomber version with 900kg of bombs carried under the wings.
3. A ground-attack aircraft with armament consisting of six cannons, two machine guns and 300kg of bombs.
4. A long-range reconnaissance aircraft with powerful offensive and defensive armament (four ShVAK cannons).

5. A destroyer of major ground and air targets (two K-37 plus two ShVAK cannons).
6. An aircraft for escorting heavy bombers.

The VIT-2 was intended to be widely used in various overloading versions, including the role of a float-type torpedo bomber. The structural safety margin of 12 allowed performing all aerobatic manoeuvres and dropping bombs in a vertical dive. The option of defending the rear hemisphere with a 20mm ShVAK cannon was selected by Polikarpov after thorough research and consultations, and in accordance with common sense. He believed that, if the VIT-2 was attacked by cannon-armed fighters, fire would be applied at long distances, and a machine-gun turret would not be of use in such conditions. This circumstance became starkly evident during the Great Patriotic War, when Soviet bombers armed with ShKAS machine guns often proved unable to hit German fighters, which were firing at them from considerable distances. There was also a certain rationale to the limited firing angle of the VIT-2's aft mount: it was assumed that the speed advantage of the attacking fighters would be negligible if at all, so their attacks would occur in conditions of a chase, that is, at small heading angles. Hatch-mounted armament for firing in the lower hemisphere was, in Polikarpov's opinion, inefficient and even useless, because a single gunner could not fully control two cannons or machine guns simultaneously. On the other hand, making provisions for an additional gunner on an aircraft with such a dense arrangement of equipment was difficult.

Representatives of the Redmy Air Force did not agree with the designer's reasoning. Later, the design bureau had to develop a special under-fuselage remotely controlled mount accommodating twin ShKAS machine guns. In general, there were many disagreements regarding the VIT-2's armament, especially in connection with the mounting of the ShVAK cannons to provide defensive fire for the forward and aft hemispheres. As a result, a decision was made to build the first VIT-2 prototype with armament suggested by Polikarpov, and to fully replace the defensive armament with ShKAS machine guns in the second prototype.

Initially, the VIT-2 was intended to be fitted with M-105 engines, with which a maximum speed of 550km/h was reasonably obtainable. However, it took Engine Factory No.26 in Rybinsk a long time to perform refinement of the engines, so the series production M-103s were mounted for the test performance.

Manufacture of the VIT-2 began immediately after the commencement of tests of the VIT-1; however, full-scale activities were impeded due to the fact that Aviation Factory No.84 was busy mastering the production of the American Douglas DC-3 transport airplane, with all the major resources employed to perform work on the latter. Starting from 16 May 1938, Boris Kudrin began to fly the aircraft and conducted preliminary tests, mostly with a positive opinion. The pilot especially liked the aircraft's behaviour during landing: it was a classical three-point landing. Kudrin also praised the aircraft's controllability – the VIT steadily performed deep turns. The disadvantages of the aircraft included empennage vibrations with flaps extended, as well as miscellaneous minor design flaws.

From 11 July that year, the long-awaited M-105 engines were installed on the VIT-2. These were prototype engines, which had not yet passed the required tests in flight. However, speeding up the process of the VIT evaluation by military pilots was believed to be very important; for this reason, after several flights from the airfield in Khimki, the aircraft flew to the NII VVS airfield in Shchelkovo. During the period from 13 September to 5 October 1938, Major Stefanovsky completed almost the full scope of the tests. But only almost, because, after 35 flights, the M-105 prototype engines were toitally worn out, and a second pair of such engines did not exist. However, the main performance parameters of the aircraft were recorded; in particular, the maximum flight speed of 483km/h at an altitude of 4,300 meters. This value was deemed insufficient, since according to calculations, there had been hopes to reach a speed of 520–530km/h. Among the shortcomings, which had earlier been pointed out by Kudrin, were vibrations of the tail unit, heavy loads on the controls, insufficient efficiency of the rudders and a too-high landing speed of 130–140km/h. At the same time, the VIT-2 offered excellent visibility from all the cabins and great opportunities for further improvement. In terms of maximum speed, it was the fastest two-engine Soviet aircraft of 1938. In the final report on the state tests, it was suggested to rectify the defects which did not require major modification of the aircraft in the shortest possible time, and to then resume the aircraft's tests.

In late December 1938, after modifications were performed, the VIT-2 was prepared to resume flying; however, for some time it remained out of use. This was primarily connected with Valery Chkalov's death during the testing of the I-180 fighter prototype, and with Boris Kudrin's illness. Finally, on 9 February 1939, Stefanovsky test-flew the aircraft and then ferried it to Shchelkovo. Apart from Stefanovsky, the aircraft was flown by NII VVS test pilot Mikhail Nyukhtikov from 17 February. They performed flights until March, during which a maximum speed of 500km/h was reached. The pilots' opinions were exceptionally positive – at times even enthusiastic. The VIT-2 demonstrated excellent take-off and landing performance, could fly with only one operative engine and was, in many aspects, simply an appealing aircraft for the pilots to fly.

On the other hand, the aircraft had certain shortcomings, the most critical of which was the unacceptably aft centre-of-gravity position. In some loading variants, this reached 38.5 percent MAC. At the same time, the aircraft was found longitudinally stable at only 32 percent MAC. Subsequently, the question arose why the too-much aft CG position and the longitudinal instability of the aircraft had not attracted any attention earlier. There were several explanations for this. Firstly, general guidelines for designers (first and foremost, guidelines issued by TsAGI aerodynamics scientists) envisaged the aft CG position and even a certain instability, which was defined as a means to increase manoeuvrability. In addition, the first test flights were performed with an incomplete set of armament and equipment. Under such conditions, CG position figures were only slightly in excess of 30 percent MAC, and the aircraft had a quite acceptable flight performance. It was only during the building and testing of the VIT-2 that the Red Army Air Force requirements began to change in the direction of a more forward CG position and greater stability of the aircraft in all axes.

In April 1939, a special commission of the NKAP came to a conclusion that the VIT-2 aircraft had passed the first stage of state tests, and the project was recommended for series production provided that certain modifications were introduced. It was suggested that the wing span, wing area, fuselage length and vertical tail area should be increased, the CG position should be shifted forward by 7 percent MAC and new technologies should be used (welded joints should be avoided). A decision was made to build the aircraft under the designation VIT-2s (*Seriyniy*, series production) at Aviation Factory No.124 in Kazan. Polikarpov objected, since the factory in Kazan was at that time under a process of organisation and filling with production equipment. Furthermore, it was expected to focus the factory on manufacturing heavy bombers, in particular the TB-7. Aviation Factory No.84, which seemed preferable, was busy with mastering the licensed DC-3. Due to uncertainty about the manufacturing factory, the problem with the VIT-2s production programme was not resolved until summer 1939.

Changes to the aircraft's fate began after the annual May Day flypast above Red Square. The advantageous properties of the VIT, which overtook the SB bombers in flight, heightened interest in the aircraft. In midsummer, a government resolution on launching series production of the VIT-2s at Aviation Factory No.22 was issued. However, the resolution turned out to be the final point in the history of the air destroyer of tanks. In spite of the fact that interest in aircraft with heavy cannon armament remained, the aircraft that actually entered series production was the one requested by the commission of the NKAP as held in April. It was determined primarily as a dive-bomber. Before the end of summer 1939, the preliminary project of the aircraft under the working designation 'D' was completed and presented for review. Later, it was given the designation 'SPB'.

A brief technical description concludes the story of the VIT-2 aircraft.

The monocoque fuselage was made of metal and had elliptical cross-sections. In the fuselage-to-wing interface, the structure was made as a powerful steel truss taking up forces brought about by the firing of the K-37 cannons. The wing was of a two-spar design, with spar booms made of welded tubes. Welding was widely used in a number of structural joints. The wing centre section span totalled 3,250mm; its size was determined from the conditions of its transportation by rail. Each wing accommodated seven fuel tanks, four of which were integral with the wing centre section leading edges. All frontal portions of the fuselage, wing and empennage had flush riveting; in the rest of the skin, protruding head rivets were used. The internal space of the crew cabins was interconnected, thus providing for visual contact.

Dimensions and main technical specifications of the VIT-2	
Wing span (m)	16.5
Length in the flight line (m)	10.8
Wing area (sq.m)	40.76
Empty weight with the M-105 engines (kg)	4,083
Normal gross weight (kg)	6,300
Wing loading (kg/sq.m)	155
Service ceiling (m)	9,000
Flight range (km)	3,000
Maximum speed near ground level (km/h)	445
Maximum speed at 4,600m (km/h)	500
Time to climb to 4,000m (mins)	6.0
Normal bomb load (kg)	800
Maximum bomb load (kg)	1,400

7.2. The SPB high-speed dive-bomber

As we have just seen, during the course of the VIT-2s' preparation for series production, the aircraft was given the designation 'D' and underwent noticeable modifications. The engine compartment was rearranged, radiators of the engine cooling system were relocated to the sides of the engine nacelles, the fuselage became longer and the crew cabins received additional windows.

The VIT-1 model.

A general view of the VIT-2 fuselage centre section.

The VIT-2 right engine mount.

A RRAB bomblet dispenser suspended under the VIT-2 fuselage.

General views of the VIT-2 during tests in 1938.

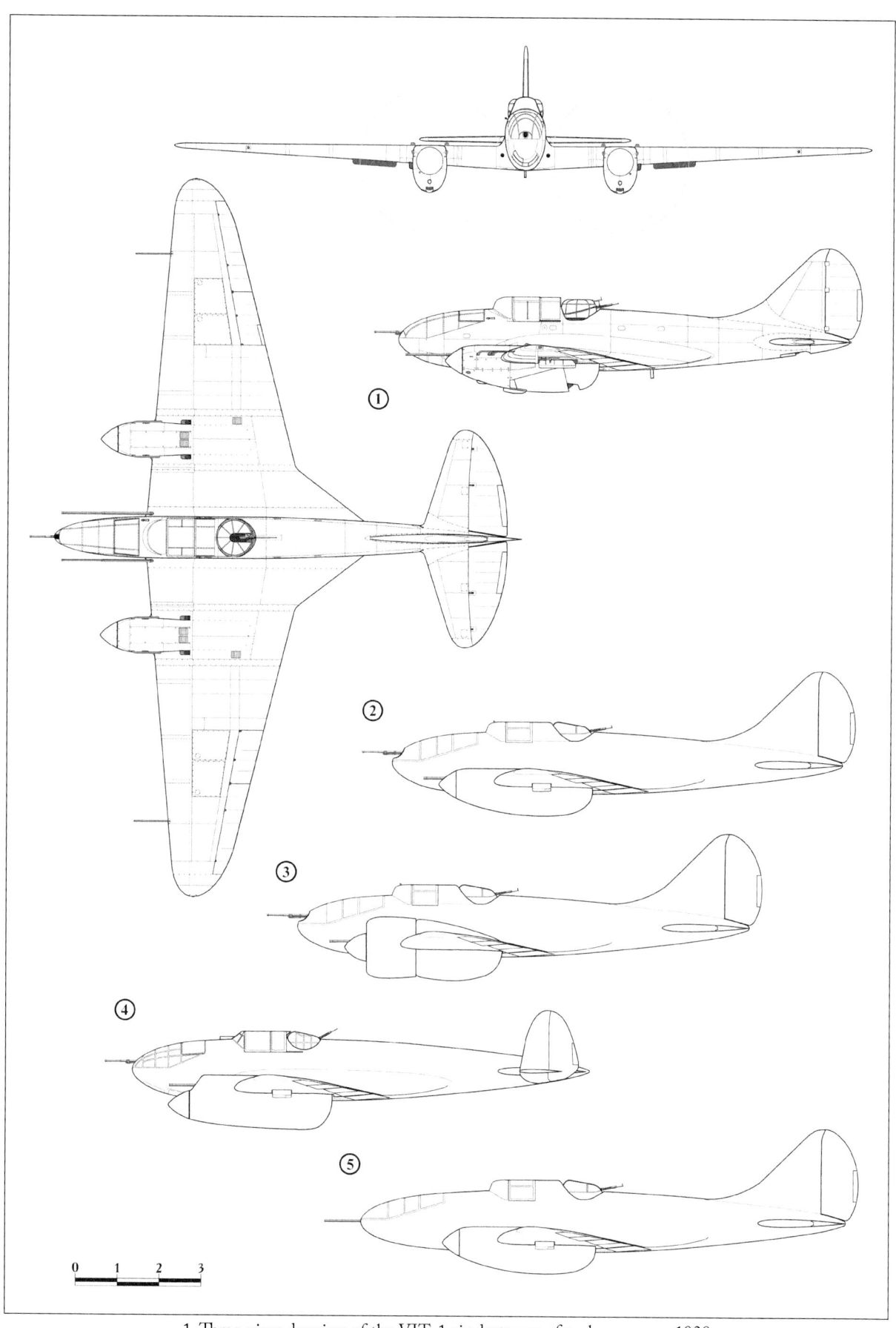

1. Three-view drawing of the VIT-1 air destroyer of tanks, summer 1939.
2. Side view drawing of the SVB project (airplane of air combat) with M-100 engines, September 1936.
3. Side view drawing of the SVB project with M-25 engines, September 1936.
4. Side view drawing of the SVB project with M-34FN engines, September 1936.
5. Side view drawing of the SVB project with M-100 engines and single Sh-37 cannon, September 1936.

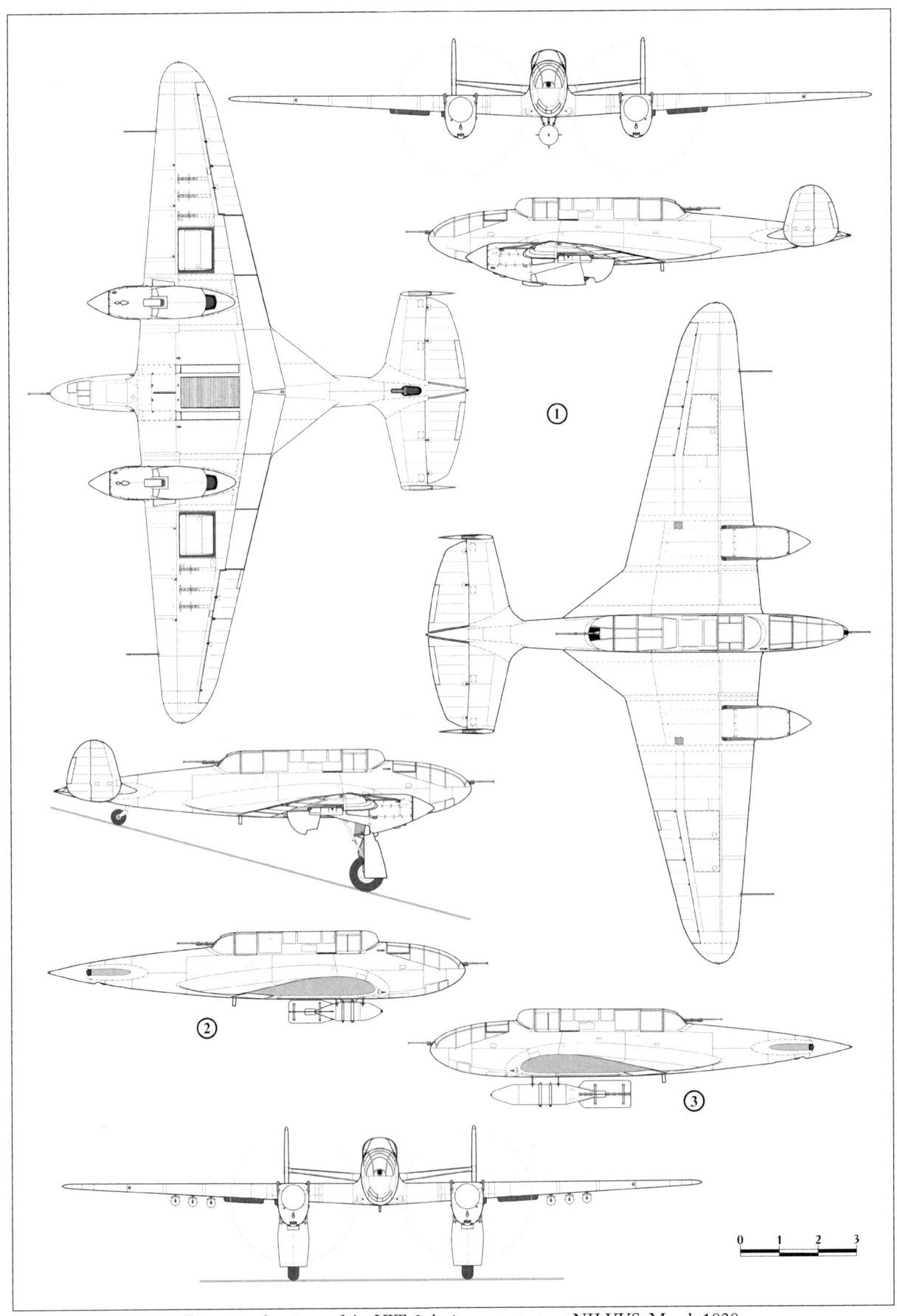

1. Five-view drawings of the VIT-2 during state tests at NII VVS, March 1939.
2. Side view drawing of the VIT-2 carrying FAB-1,000 bomb.
3. Side and front view drawings of the VIT-2 carrying FAB-500 bombs.

All the introduced changes were finally approved at a meeting on 28 July 1939, which was attended by the representatives of Aviation Factory No.1, Aviation Factory No.22, NII VVS and the First Chief Directorate of the NKAP. The aircraft had already been named the SPB (*Skorostnoy Pikiruyushchiy Bombardirovshchik*, High-speed Dive-Bomber), or sometimes the SBP. On 29 July, a government resolution was issued, under which the aircraft was to enter series production at Aviation Factory No.22. For this purpose, a separate production building was allocated in the territory of the factory. The building was intended to accommodate the OKO 'D' (*Obyedinennyy Konstruktorskiy Otdel*, Joint Design Department for the 'D' aircraft). Polikarpov's deputy, Nikolay Zhemchuzhin, was appointed head of the department. Under a separate order of the NKAP, employees from other enterprises (predominantly younger people) were delegated to join the newly formed team. By September and October 1939, the joint design bureau had become fully functional.

In addition to changes in external appearance and geometry, the aircraft's manufacturing technology was intended to be considerably revised. Welded steel tube structures, which had been used in its predecessor, were felt to be outdated and were replaced with open extruded sections and assemblies consisting of forgings, stampings and castings. The mould loft and templates method, which was beginning to enter into practice, was intended to be widely used in series production.

In October 1939, issues related to the layout of systems, equipment and armament were discussed on a full-scale wooden mock-up of the SPB. Representatives of the Soviet Air Force, in particular, demanded that the dorsal-mounted defensive large-calibre Berezin machine gun should be replaced with a standard turret accommodating a ShKAS machine gun. The designers, however, stood up for their original version.

It should be noted that even before starting the first prototypes' manufacturing, possible modification of the aircraft for use of various engine types had been studied. It was planned that the M-106, M-71, M-81 and M-120 engines would later on be used; nearly all calculations of the prospective power plants were done taking into account the use of turbosuperchargers, which should increase the aircraft's flying altitudes.

Among the proposed variants, the floated version of the SPB – intended for equipping naval aviation units – should be mentioned. According to the estimates, this version would reach a maximum speed of 435km/h at an altitude of 3,850m, which was considered to be a very good performance. Polikarpov, who insisted on a detailed study of this variant, believed that there was a possibility to create a universal aircraft to be used in both landplane and seaplane versions. An additional feature of the floated SPB was the installation of reverse-pitch propellers, which should have considerably shortened the length of the water-landing run. At the same time, it was suggested that the reverse-pitch propellers would be used as air brakes to reduce diving speed. Development of such propellers had already begun, so the possibility of their use was seen as quite realistic.

Initially, it was planned to build a prototype series of 10 SPBs with M-105 engines, with several aircraft to be used for operational tests. In practice, six aircraft were manufactured; five of them were actually flown.

The work on creating the SPB was going on at an accelerated pace. On 11 October 1939, the workshops began to manufacture parts and assembly tooling, while in late December, the first experimental SPB prototype No.1/0 was fully ready. On 30 December 1939, the aircraft was taken to the airfield to perform a test run of the engines. On 3 January 1940, the first taxiing runs took place at the airfield. However, the snow turned out to be too deep, so the wheels had to be replaced with skis from a Tupolev SB bomber. In the course of these activities, a considerable number of defects and shortcomings were revealed, as was usual, so it took another month to prepare the aircraft for the first flight.

The SPB first flew on 18 February 1940, with pilot Boris Kudrin at the controls. It was a short 10-minute circuit flight around the airfield. Kudrin later described the test flights as follows:

> We performed the first flight on an aircraft which had not been refined fully, as it was believed at that time that defects, which did not prevent an aircraft from flying for at least ten minutes, could well be rectified in the course of further testing … The next flight took place on 20 February. That was when a big trouble occurred. After take-off, at a height of 350–400 metres, the aircraft nosed down. I began to pull out but failed, in spite of the fact that I was pulling the control stick with all my might. At that point, a technician, who was seated in the observer's cabin, helped me. The matter was that snow was packing into recesses in our skis, and we had to take a technician along so that he would watch whether the wind was blowing the snow out from them or not.
>
> When the aircraft began to dive, the technician inserted an additional control stick [there was one in the navigator's cabin – *author's note*] and together we pulled out with much difficulty. Having no possibility to land either at our airfield or at Moscow Central Airfield, I decided to perform the landing at Shchelkovo airfield, which we did straight from the low-level flight.

Meanwhile, the next SPB prototypes were being completed. On 26 March, the second prototype (No.2/0) first took to the air; on 17 April, the SPB No.1/1 made its first flight. In general, the test flying was going fine, but the excessive haste took its toll. Numerous minor repairs and modifications were carried out at the airfield. Technical personnel were tinkering with the engine cooling system, replacing radiators and installing longer air intakes. On 7 April, the first serious incident occurred when both landing gear struts failed during the landing run in the aircraft No.2/0, but there were no injuries. As it turned out, this was due to a manufacturing defect.

At approximately the same time, the famous polar pilot Colonel Pavel Golovin joined the SPB tests at the factory airfield. In 1937, Golovin had been the first Soviet pilot to fly over the North Pole. During the Winter War with Finland, he took part in hostilities, flying a Tupolev SB bomber. Golovin took a keen interest in high-speed combat aircraft, and soon persuaded his superiors to transfer him to become a test pilot. On 1 April 1940, Golovin performed three familiarisation flights in one of the tested SPBs. On 26 April, aircraft No.2/1 first took to the air with Golovin at the controls. Another flight was planned to be conducted the following day to determine stability and controllability performance parameters. The aircraft took off from Moscow Central Airfield, being seen off by Polikarpov and Zhemchuzhin, who watched it leave for the test flying area of the NII GVF airfield (*Nauchno-Issledovatelskiy Institut Grazhdanskogo Vozdushnogo Flota*, Scientific Research Institute of the Civil Air Fleet) in northern Tushino.

It is not known what actually happened during the flight. Apparently, Golovin, who despite being energetic and courageous as a pilot was neither cautious nor experienced enough as a test pilot, began to enter a turn in the SPB at a high bank angle, and fell into a spin. Eyewitnesses watched the SPB fall out of the clouds, spiralling down in a flat spin. At a low altitude, the pilot attempted to bail out, but the distance to the ground was too small to parachute to safety. Together with Golovin, Leading Engineer K. Aleksandrov and Flight Mechanic N. Dobrov were also killed.

An accident commission found that the aircraft had fallen into a flat spin due to insufficient longitudinal stability. This drawback of the SPB was known; however, while the factory tests were underway, no one had placed any special emphasis on it.

In early May 1940, a decision was made to modify the first SPB prototype No.1/0 in order to reach a more forward CG position, and then to send it to TsAGI for full-scale testing in the T-101 wind tunnel. Flight tests continued with aircraft Nos.2/0, 1/1 and 3/1.

Misfortunes, however, kept occurring. On 6 May, the left engine of the SPB No.2/1 seized up in flight, and the aircraft made a forced landing at Shchelkovo airfield. On 16 May, after a new M-105 was mounted on the aircraft, it took to the air with Boris Kudrin at the controls. Later, he described the events that had taken place during the flight: "Once, the attachment eye of the left rudder trim tab broke off, and the aircraft rolled over. I reduced the speed, levelled off with difficulty, and then landed at the Central Airfield."

A few days later, a more serious accident occurred. On 27 May (a month after Golovin's fatal crash), test pilot Mikhail Lipkin took off in aircraft No.3/1. At an altitude of 2,000m, near Khimki, the right engine oil pressure dropped and the pilot had to shut down the engine. Lipkin aborted the mission and began to perform an approach descent to the airfield of Aviation Factory No.22 in Fili. There, as ill luck would have it, the entire northern portion of the airfield was crammed with SB bombers recently manufactured by the factory. Flying over these aircraft, the SPB clipped one of them, lost speed and struck the ground. As a result of the blow, the landing gear was destroyed and the aircraft found itself on its belly. Lipkin escaped unharmed.

It was expected that in further test flights, the maximum flight speed would be achieved, including that in dive conditions. Since the speed in a dive grows rapidly, a decision was made to conduct preliminary flutter tests within the speed range of 500–600km/h. Before that, the TsAGI group researching aircraft vibration drew up an expert report after studying the SPB documentation; the report indicated that the aircraft's critical speed was limited by the wing, and, provided that partial static balance of the ailerons was ensured, the critical speed would be defined as 658km/h. With unbalanced ailerons, the critical speed reduced to 500km/h. To increase the estimated critical speed, it was suggested that the mass balance of the ailerons should be increased by adding weight to their leading edges. In some of the SPB aircraft, the ailerons were actually modified. The aircraft which was intended to be used in the flutter tests, the No.1/1, did not undergo these modifications, and this fatal mistake led to another crash.

On 20 July, residents of Ramenskoe district near Moscow observed a two-engine aircraft at an altitude of about 2,000m which was flying with a slight descent at a very high speed (the descent was barely noticeable from the ground; for this reason, many eyewitnesses identified the flight as a horizontal one). Then, suddenly, the aircraft began to disintegrate in mid-air. The left wing, left engine and other parts came off, then the remaining debris crashed into the ground. Pilot Mikhail Lipkin and observer Grigory Bulychev were killed in the wrecked SPB No.1/1.

The investigation identified that the most probable cause of the crash was the wing flexure-aileron flutter. Head of the OKO 'D' Zhemchuzhin was found responsible for the tragedy and arrested. Later, through intercession of NII VVS leading specialists, he was released, with the blame then shifted to pilot Lipkin. He was alleged to have been increasing the speed in a dive too intensively and to have fallen victim to his own recklessness. Many years later, in the memoirs of test pilots P. Stefanovsky and M. Gallay, the circumstances of what had happened were interpreted in this very way. However, analysis of accident investigation reports allows the assumption that the aircraft was doomed from the start; furthermore, no one had seen any obvious dive.

There were also other mysterious points in this story. A thorough examination of the aircraft wreckage did not reveal any specific damage inherent to aileron flutter. There were no skin wrinkles, corrugations, buckling, burrs or stripped-off paint, nor any traces of collision between the ailerons and the wing in the aileron attachment area. Moreover, Polikarpov had opinions of his own in respect of the tragedy that had occurred. He believed that the crash might have been brought about by either separation of the wing leading edge, a rupture of the control rod under the action of the outboard aileron segment or the engine coming off the engine mount.

However, there remained very few people among the leaders of the Sovidt aviation industry and the Air Force who still took an interest in the causes of the death of the crew and the loss of the aircraft. On 29 July 1940, under an order of the People's Commissar of the NKAP, further testing and all production activities related to the SPB aircraft at Aviation Factory No.22 were discontinued. In view of this, on 7 August, a special commission calculated the costs of design and manufacture of the SPB type. In total, it was stated, some 33,330,000 roubles had been spent.

Data on the work performed and the results achieved were as follows:

Zero (prototype) series
1. Aircraft No.1/0 had been flown and was getting ready for wind tunnel tests.
2. Aircraft No.2/0 had been flown and was ready for further flying.
3. One airframe set in the form of subassemblies was handed over for static tests.

The 1st series
1. Aircraft No.1/1 had been flown and crashed under the control of pilot Lipkin.
2. Aircraft No.2/1 had been flown and crashed under the control of pilot Golovin.
3. Aircraft No.3/1 had been flown and damaged in an accident [and] crashed under the control of pilot Lipkin; the repair was 70 percent complete.
4. Aircraft No.4/1 was 100 percent complete and awaiting acceptance by the Technical Bureau.
5. Aircraft No.5/1 with TK-2 turbosuperchargers was at the final assembly stage; 90 percent complete.

The 2nd series
1. Aircraft No.1/2 – 75 percent complete.
2. Aircraft No.2/2 – 60 percent complete.
3. Aircraft No.3/2 – 75 percent complete.

The 3rd series – 40 percent of parts had been manufactured.
The 4th series – manufacture of parts had started.

In spite of apparent winding up of the works, Polikarpov believed that the SPB subject had not been exhausted. In his appeal to the government, he pointed out the need to check all calculations related to the aircraft, results of static tests, wind tunnel testing materials and other technical documentation. He hoped to resume, in the near future, the flight tests of aircraft No.4/1, to complete aircraft No.5/1 and 1/2, and to hand them over for testing. His confidence was boosted by a successful demonstration to Red Army Air Force representatives of a mock-up of the new SPB version with the AM-37 engines and a modified crew seating arrangement.

The SPB No.1/0 prototype during flight tests in winter 1940.

A view on the SPB wing centre section and the left engine.

The right side of the navigator's cabin. Note the additional control stick in the centre.

Views of the SPB cabin equipment.

The bomber designs of the 1930s 235

The SPB No.1/10 undergoing full-scale tests in the TsAGI wind tunnel.

The SPB after a crash landing on 27 May 1940.

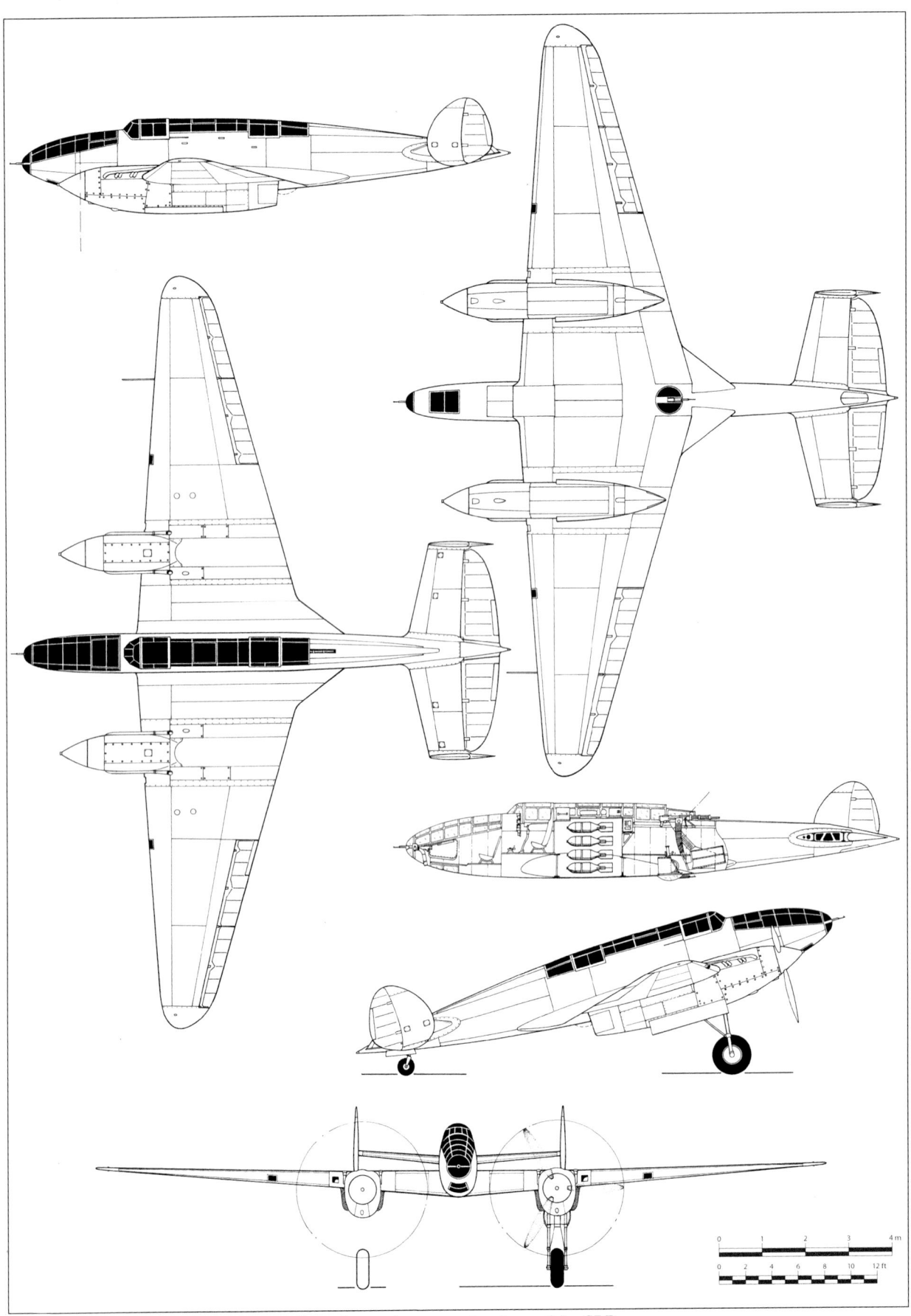

Five-view and cutaway drawings of the SPB.

The pilot was seated in the front in order to ensure better visibility in a dive. The navigator, together with the weapon mount, was seated behind the pilot. The number of clear panels over the entire nose section was increased. An air gunner to cover the lower rear hemisphere was added to the crew, thereby increasing it to four men.

However, no positive shifts occurred in the fate of the Polikarpov SPB. The new version was not developed any further. Taking any possible decision was postponed pending the results of the No.1/0 aircraft's wind tunnel tests. Despite being the very first prototype, this SPB underwent quite considerable modifications before the aerodynamic testing. The engine oil system was entirely rearranged, and air intakes for the U-shaped oil coolers were installed under the engine cowlings. Numerous minor changes including additional access hatches and reinforcements were implemented. But the most significant modification consisted in swept-back outer wing panels. For this purpose, additional load-carrying elements were inserted in the joint between the wing centre section and the outer wing panels; the empty space formed was covered with a large skin 'patch'. This was done in order to obtain a more forward CG position (26.93 percent MAC) and to improve longitudinal stability. In spite of the innovations, the wind tunnel tests showed that, in order to ensure sufficient longitudinal stability, the CG position of this aircraft in a flight should not exceed 21–22 percent MAC. At the same time, TsAGI experts concluded that the results of these tests should not be regarded as an obstacle for continuation of the flight tests. However, these conclusions appeared too late – in early 1941, when all works on the SPB were completely wound up.

Several causes of what happened may be mentioned; however, the appearance of the PB-100 dive-bomber (later known as the Pe-2) should be regarded as the most significant of them. In May 1940, it was suggested that the VI-100 high-altitude two-engine fighter should be converted into a dive-bomber. In late June, a government decree to launch production of the dive-bomber at Factory No.22 was issued. Test flights of the aircraft were being performed normally; for this reason, in early 1941, Aviation Factories No.22 and 39 in Moscow began to roll out the first production PB-100s. Under these conditions, there was no sense in continuing to hope for further development of the Polikarpov SPB.

A short technical description of the SPB aircraft:

The SPB was a twin-engine all-metal bomber intended for dive-bombing operations. The aircraft had a conventional arrangement, with a twin-fin vertical tail. The landing gear was retractable, with a pneumatic-mechanical retracting mechanism identical to that of the VIT-2.

The airplane was fitted with five racks for the bomb load attachment – two wing-mounted ones and three fuselage-mounted. To attach bombs inside the fuselage, the KD-2 bomb rack was installed. In a dive, bombs could be dropped only from the external racks. There were provisions for the aircraft to carry a single 1-ton bomb.

The SPB's firing armament consisted of the nose mount with a ShKAS machine gun in the navigator's cabin and the aft mount with a 12.7mm Berezin BT machine gun. To enable the gunner to fire the aft machine gun, the upper portion of the fuselage could be lowered. During the course of work on the aircraft, the firing weapons were complemented with the lower remotely controlled mount accommodating a ShKAS machine gun.

The SPB had self-sealing fuel tanks with an inert gas filling system. Among the aircraft's specific features should be noted installation of a control stick (like in fighters) at the pilot's station instead of a conventional control yoke.

The SPB was powered by the M-105 engines, with VISh-22E variable-pitch propellers.

Dimensions and main performance parameters of the SPB	
Wing span (m)	17.0
Length in the flight line (m)	11.4
Wing area (sq.m)	42.93
Normal gross weight (kg)	6,830
Wing loading (kg/sq.m)	159
Service ceiling (m)	9,550
Estimated flight range (km)	1,500
Maximum speed near ground level(km/h)	445
Maximum speed at 4,800m (km/h)	520 *

* A maximum flight speed of 517km/h was recorded during tests.

7.3. The *Ivánov* single-engine bomber

In the mid-1930s, an attempt was made in the Soviet Union to create a mass-production multi-purpose aircraft. These events went down in history as the Air Force contest codenamed *Ivánov*, the essence of which was to create an aircraft capable of performing the roles of a reconnaissance airplane and a light bomber. According to a widely spread opinion, the codename *Ivánov*, with the accent on the first syllable, was suggested personally by Stalin (this was one of his telegraph aliases). Allegedly, the Soviet leader suggested creating a special combat aircraft, which had to be reliable, unpretentious and omnipresent, like a simple Russian soldier Ivanov.

In early 1936, the Air Force administration proposed to several design bureaus the development, before the end of the year, a high-speed combat monoplane to be powered by the AM-34FRN engine. Generating take-off power of 1,200hp, this engine seemed, at that time, the most acceptable option for implementation of such a task, since it was a already existing product of the Soviet aviation industry. Within that year, design teams led by Grigorovich, Polikarpov, Neman, Kocherigin, Sukhoi and Ilyushin submitted their preliminary projects. It should be noted that the designations for these aircraft initially had absolutely nothing to do with the codename *Ivánov*. This name only began to be used in 1937, when the number of developers shrank to three (Sukhoi, Neman and Polikarpov). Furthermore, each of the designers was requested to create an aircraft using a specific manufacturing technology. Pavel Sukhoi was designing and building an all-metal aircraft at the facilities of the TsAGI Factory of Experimental Designs, and I. Neman was creating an all-wooden aircraft at Aviation Factory No.135 in Kharkov. Meanwhile, Polikarpov (he was at that time assigned to Factory No.21 in Gorky) was making use of both metal and wood in his new design.

The basic concept of the *Ivánov* project was understood to be its versatility, not only as far as combat application was concerned, but also in a much broader sense. Thus, it was intended that all three aircraft under construction should have a significant number of common unified assemblies, subassemblies and equipment. Among these interchangeable components were engines complete with cowlings and engine mounts, armament, equipment and even instrument panels. As for practical applications, the following designations were suggested and remained in use for some time:

Ivánov-1 (IV-1) – a ground attack aircraft;
Ivánov-2 (IV-2) – a bomber;
Ivánov-3 (IV-3) – a reconnaissance aircraft;
Ivánov-4 (IV-4) – an escort aircraft.

In accordance with the assignment given, Polikarpov, first and foremost, continued to improve the projects which were developed back in 1936 for the AM-34FRN engine. In 1936, his design bureau prepared two versions of the aircraft (low-wing and high-wing), the designation of which contained the common symbol 'R' (from *razvedchik* – reconnaissance aircraft). Afterwards, the low-wing version was studied in more detail; however, until autumn 1937, the designer kept turning to the high-wing configuration (in some cases, the term 'parasol' was used). The Chief Artillery Directorate of the Workers' and Peasants' Red Army took an interest in this version due to the good visibility ensured for the crew – all the more so because artillery spotters and reconnaissance aircraft of such configuration were already available or being built in the West. Polikarpov continued to improve the high-wing design version throughout 1937 under the designation AK-62 (from *artilleriyskiy korrektirovshchik* – artillery spotter), with the M-62 engine.

However, the Air Force administration finally decided to stay with the low-wing configuration, which was being discussed and studied by all three developers from early 1937. Working meetings, reviews and discussions on the configuration of aircraft structural elements were aimed at working out the most acceptable solutions. Consequently, the process of creating the *Ivánov* aircraft could hardly be named a 'competition'.

In spring 1937, when the full-scale wooden mock-ups were nearly completed in Moscow and Kharkov, an order to fit the *Ivánov* with the M-62 engine (which was, at that time, just planned for development) was received from the aviation industry authorities. In April that year, Polikarpov recalculated his design for the M-62; simultaneously, he made rough estimates in case of the use of the projected M-88 engine. He became absorbed in this project, especially in the issues of unification and lowering the production costs of a series aircraft. Impressed by positive reports on the use of the I-16 fighter in Spain (primarily with the issues of survivability and maintainability), Polikarpov suggested using, at the first stage of manufacture of the *Ivánov*, the same techniques that had been utilised in the production of the I-16. A wooden fuselage with moulded birch plywood skin and a wing of metal structure covered with fabric were intended to be used. Then, as production evolved, more advanced designs (for example, a wing with a smooth metal skin) were expected to be introduced on a step-by-step basis.

The work on building Polikarpov's *Ivánov* began at Aviation Factory No.84, with the active participation of designer Dmitry Tomashevich, who was Deputy Chief Designer for the aircraft type. The airplane in its final configuration was discussed using a full-scale wooden mock-up. After examining the mock-up and reviewing the presented calculations, representatives of the Air Force, as the key customer, expressed few objections or additional wishes. The designers were meeting the requirement to ensure a maximum speed of 350–400km/h, a service ceiling of 9–10km and a landing speed of 90–95km/h. The main controversy was the developers' refusal to ensure a range of 2,000km: this value was cut down by a quarter. As a result, the parties reached a mutual agreement, the aircraft design was finally approved and it was accepted for building at Aviation Factory No.21 in Gorky. In Polikarpov's opinion, the several hundred kilometres that separated Moscow and Gorky might slow down the manufacturing process noticeably. Furthermore, there were nearly no prototype aircraft production facilities at Factory No.21, whereas all the available workshops and areas were fully occupied with series production of other aircraft.

Within a short time, the Chief Designer's apprehensions were proved correct. Documentation sending, all kinds of approvals and trips that took up precious time brought about considerable delays in making the first prototype available. In late 1937, Polikarpov was appointed Chief Designer of Aviation Factory No.156. Formerly known as the TsAGI Factory of Experimental Designs, it was the creation and the true domain of Andrey Tupolev. After Tupolev was arrested, the Polikarpov Design Bureau and several other design teams were relocated to the factory facilities. The design bureau of Pavel Sukhoi, who was also developing and building his own version of the *Ivánov*, was accommodated at the same factory. Perhaps the 'home ground' was of some help to him – the aircraft, initially designated the ANT-51 and later renamed SZ (*Stalinskoye Zadaniye* – Stalin's Assignment), first flew on 25 August 1937, which was much earlier than Polikarpov's aircraft. After completing quite successful tests, the aircraft entered series production at several aviation factories under the Su-2 designation.

Due to the move of the design bureau, the manufacturing of the Polikarpov *Ivánov* also began to be carried out, for the most part, at the new location. On 29 February 1938, the completed fuselage was delivered from Gorky to Factory No.156 in Moscow. However, it took another month to resume the work – the assembly shop was busy and there was a lack of skilled workers. How could it have been otherwise, given that circumstances had brought together, under the same roof, people who were apparently more rivals than comrades-in-arms.

Nevertheless, the work was progressing. The Polikarpov *Ivánov* was completed by the scheduled date of 25 July 1938. On 2 August, test pilot Tuomas Susi performed trial taxiing in it, and on 3 August the aircraft first flew with him at the controls. In the second flight, the undercarriage was damaged during landing, and the aircraft was subsequently taken back to the factory for repairs.

The *Ivánov* of I. Neman was never completed as the chief designer was arrested. Some time later, it became pointless to resume work on this airplane as, when the M-62 engine was mounted on the already existing R-10 reconnaissance aircraft, the resulting aircraft was quite in line with the requirements set for the *Ivánov*. Modification of the R-10 for installation of the M-62 engine was carried out by designer Dubrovin. However, the aircraft, designated the KhAI-52, never entered series production.

The *Ivánov* multipurpose aircraft designed by Polikarpov during tests in summer 1938. Note the emblem of Aviation Factory No.156 painted on the vertical stabiliser.

The Polikarpov *Ivánov* was returned to the airfield a month after the August incident. The aircraft still had a considerable number of shortcomings; after nearly every flight, the factory technical crew had to carry out certain modifications. Furthermore, the assigned test pilots never stuck around long enough. On 2 September, the *Ivánov* was flown by Chkalov; on 9 September, military test pilot Shevchenko was at the controls; on 15 September, the flight was performed by TsAGI pilot Rybko; while on 4 November, test pilot Sakhranov flew the aircraft. The flights continued up to December 1938. Aside from the technical defects identified during the tests, the pilots' opinions of the aircraft were in general positive. Their comments included: "As far as piloting is concerned, the aircraft is simple and makes a good impression in flight" (Susi); "In flight, the aircraft behaves normally" (Chkalov); "The aircraft is easily controllable and stable enough; control stick forces are normal" (Rybko); "The landing is soft; the aircraft demonstrates no tendencies to stall" (Sakhranov).

On 15 December 1938, during the tests of the new Polikarpov I-180 fighter, pilot Chkalov was killed. No one dared to release another Polikarpov prototype aircraft to fly during the following days. On 25 December, a 'judgement of Solomon' was provided: the aircraft was sent back to the factory for the rectification of defects and the carrying out of routine repairs.

During the following two months, the aircraft stayed at Factory No.156. Throughout that period, it was equipped with skis instead of the wheeled landing gear, and fitted with the new M-63R engine. The M-63R was a prototype geared engine with an extension shaft; several such engines were manufactured, all of them not sufficiently refined. The Polikarpov *Ivánov* turned out to be one of the few Soviet aircraft to be equipped with the M-63R.

On 16 February 1940, when the transport team was ready to move the aircraft to the airfield, it turned out that there was nowhere to go. All test flights at Moscow Central Airfield were stopped, with the flight test station there being liquidated. Ramenskoye airfield, which became the base for TsAGI Department No.8, was in the middle of reorganisation process, so the airfield refused to accept the aircraft for testing. A week later, an agreement with TsAGI management was finally reached and the valuable cargo was taken to the airfield.

During the first flight, which took place on 21 March, the capricious M-63R engine failed. As another engine of this type was not available, a series production M-63 was mounted on the aircraft in late April.

Further events can be described as an 'attenuation of works'. By that time, the aircraft of Sukhoi had already entered series production, with all the aviation industry's efforts concentrated on its improvement. The Polikarpov *Ivánov* was laid up until better days, which, however, never came. Flight tests were not completed, and the story of the type came to an end.

Dimensions and main performance parameters of the Polikarpov *Ivánov*	
Wing span (m)	14.0
Length in the flight line (m)	9.4
Wing area (sq.m)	28.07
Empty weight (kg)	2,662
Gross weight (kg)	3,929
Maximum speed (km/h)	410

The accident in which the *Ivánov* aircraft's undercarriage was damaged on 3 August 1938.

The bomber designs of the 1930s 241

The instrument panel of the *Ivánov*.

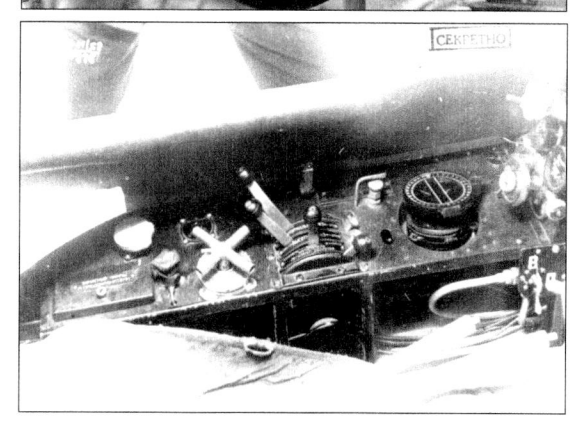

Components of the *Ivánov* aircraft.

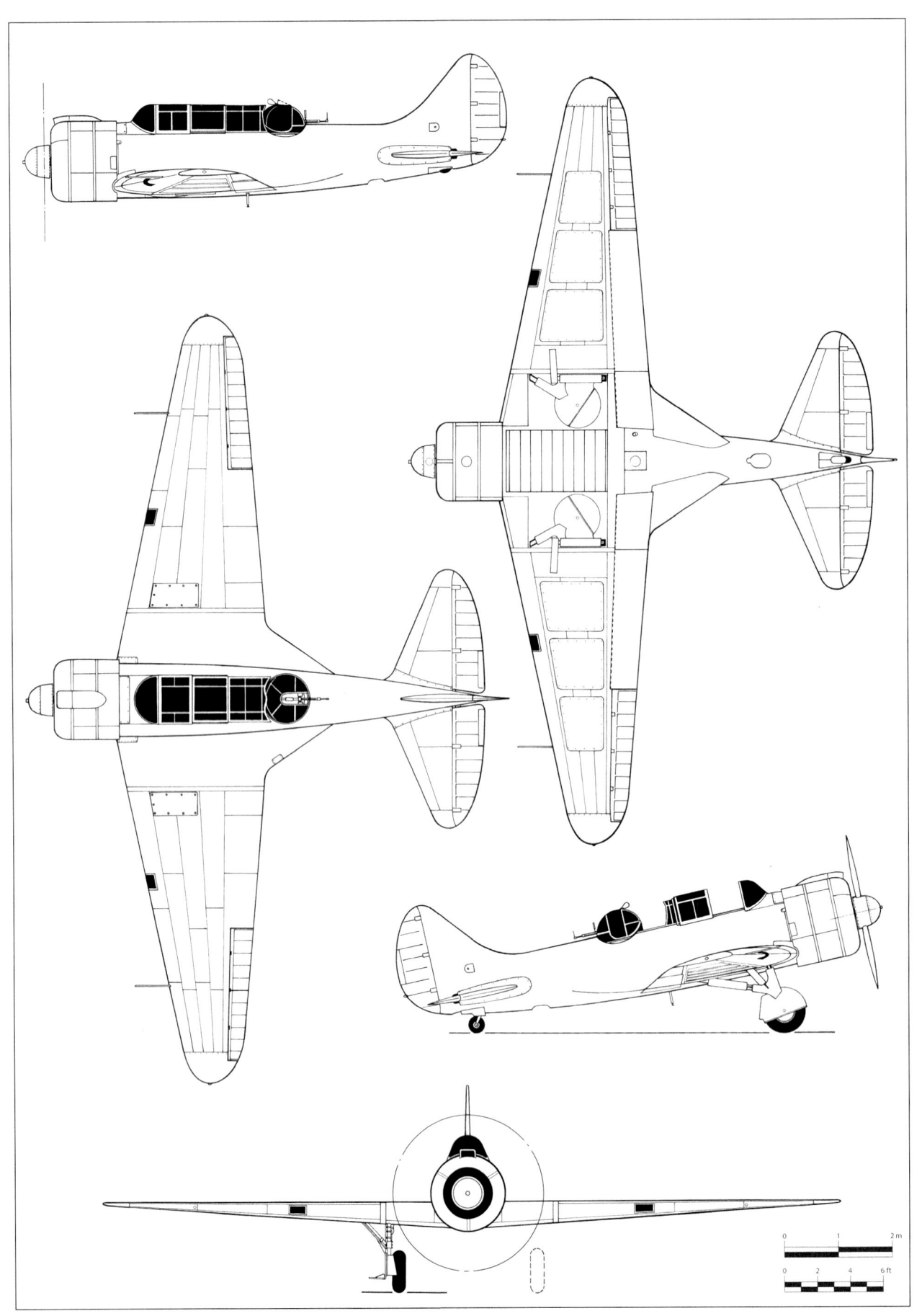

242 The King of Fighters Volume 2

Five-view drawings of the *Ivánov* aircraft.

8

Prototypes and projects of the 1940s

8.1. The ODB single-engine daytime bomber

The year 1940 saw a noticeable cooling in respect of Nikolay Polikarpov on the part of the state leaders and Soviet aviation industry bosses. This manifested itself in a considerable downsizing of his design bureau and its relocation to a new territory, which was barely suitable for full-fledged functioning. This was brought about, first and foremost, by a number of accidents and crashes involving Polikarpov prototypes. It was believed that, during the period from 1937 to 1939, the Polikarpov Design Bureau failed to bring at least one radically new aircraft to the series production stage. Polikarpov's reaction to this situation was, apparently, the only one possible for him – he continued to create new designs.

In response to the protracted story of creating the I-180, SPB and *Ivánov*, the designer offered more advanced projects – the I-185, TIS and ODB. Despite the fact that the TIS was planned as a heavy escort fighter – which was even reflected in its designation (*Tyazholyy Istrebitel Soprovozhdeniya* – Heavy Escort Fighter) – its role as a dive-bomber was considered to be of no less importance. At the same time, this aircraft served as a baseline for the development of the ODB (*Odnomotornyy Dnevnoy Bombardirovshchik* – Single-engine Daytime Bomber): in other words, a 'new edition of the *Ivánov* topic. Aerodynamic and technological solutions were borrowed from the TIS, together with several subassemblies including the nose part accommodating the pilot's and the navigator's cabin, and, naturally, the refined armament installations. The ODB was intended to be a dive-bomber as well.

The unusual feature of this project was the use of a single engine (the AM-37, AM-38 or M-120) positioned inside the fuselage, with the transmission of rotation to propellers located on the wing. A possibility to reverse the propellers in order to reduce the speed when diving and on landing was believed to be quite alluring. Furthermore, rotation of the propellers in the opposite directions helped to eliminate the old 'thorn in the side' of aviation – the reactive (gyroscopic) torque brought about by their rotation.

With regard to the power plant, it should be noted that Polikarpov had not previously been involved in the creation of such exotic designs. In his projects and developments, he was trying to achieve, above all, maximum simplicity and reliability. Therefore, selection of a complex system for engine torque transmission to propellers via extension shafts might seem unusual and even strange. The simplest explanation for this episode may be that Polikarpov was not alone in his choice. Shortly before the Second World War, many of the world's aircraft developers were following this route. New materials and more advanced calculation methods left quite enough room for hope for sufficient reliability of such systems. Polikarpov himself in particular expected to draw on the experience and developments of marine designers who made use of mechanical transmissions with various types of gearing in their ships.

In the design bureau, the ODB preliminary project was given the internal designation '3'. A NII VVS commission reviewed the preliminary project in 1941, and it aroused considerable interest, primarily due to the attractive combat layout (providing the convenience of offence and defence) and the possibility of reaching high flight performance parameters. Subject to replacement of ShKAS machine guns with large-calibre Berezin machine guns, the ODB project was recommended for further development, with a comment that the main task was to refine the power plant and the system of transmission to the propellers.

The development work on the ODB continued up to 1942. However, the difficult Soviet situation during the second year of the war prevented the full-fledged implementation of the project.

Dimensions and main design parameters of the ODB	
Wing span (m)	13.0
Aircraft weight (m)	10.85
Empty weight (kg)	3,335

Dimensions and main design parameters of the ODB	
Gross weight (with the AM-38) (kg)	5,238
Maximum speed at 9,000m (km/h)	645

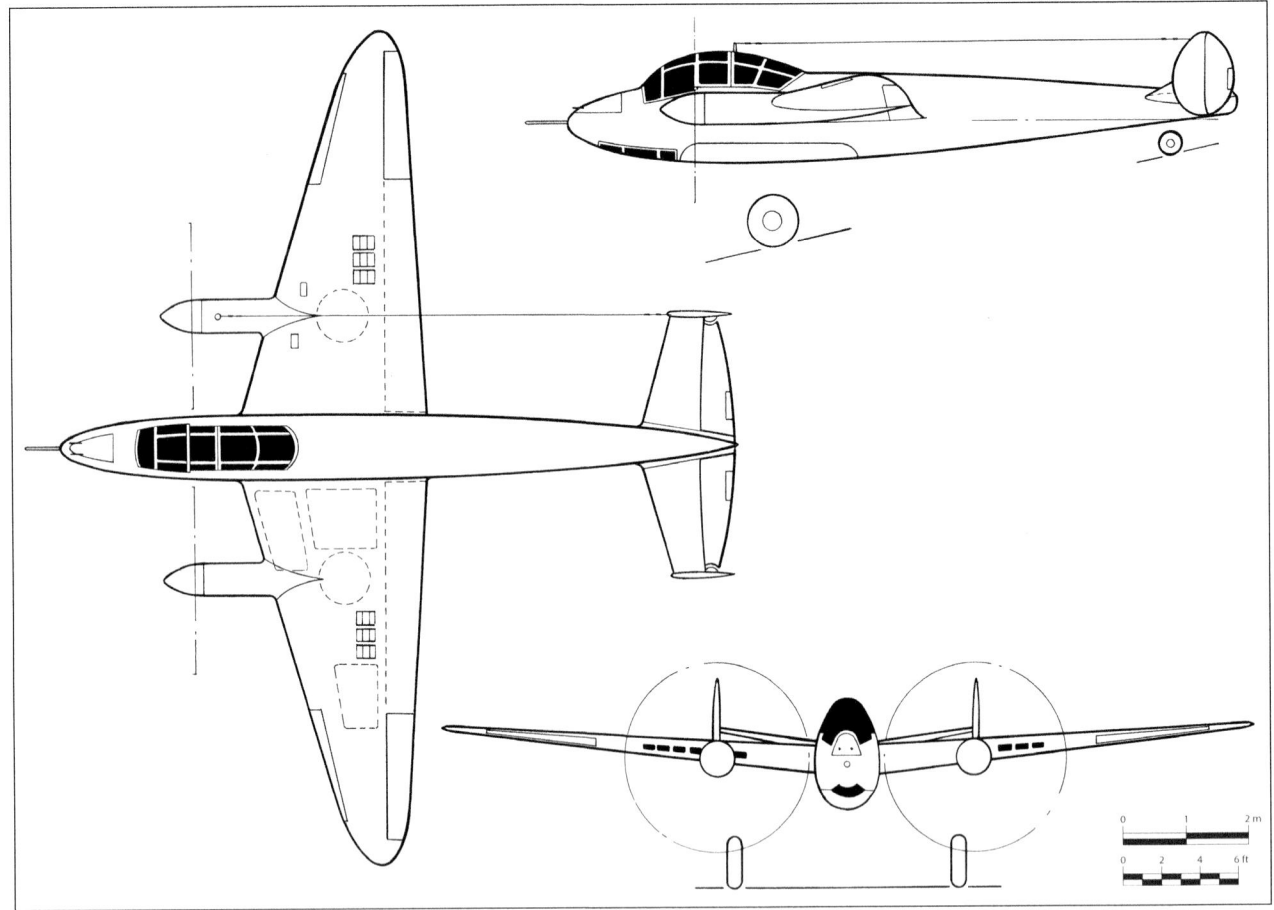

Three-view drawings of the ODB bomber project.

8.2. The NB night bomber

The hard wartime winter of 1941–42 brought about a need to revise views on the application of Soviet bomber aviation. In conditions of German air superiority and a lack of high-speed well-armed aircraft, bombing raids on the enemy were carried out, for the most part, at night-time. In such a situation, even the use of such outdated aircraft as the R-5 and R-Zet turned out to be quite efficient. War experience revealed the necessity to create a night bomber for series production, featuring high flight performance parameters. The requirements included a large internal volume in the fuselage in order to accommodate a bomb load of up to 4,000kg, good visibility for the crew, and stability and controllability performance parameters acceptable for pilots of medium skills. At the same time, these specialised wartime bombers had to be relatively cheap to produce and designed for only a short combat life. It was obviously not easy to solve such a difficult task; however, in late 1941, Nikolay Polikarpov decided to tackle it.

Development of the new aircraft began in Novosibirsk, where the Polikarpov Design Bureau and Experimental Factory No.51 were evacuated to in the autumn of 1941. In the design bureau, the aircraft was given the designation 'T', but in the accompanying documents it was referred to as the 'NB' (*Nochnoy Bombardirovshchik* – Night Bomber). The Chief Designer also called it *Nochnoy Bombovoz* (Night-time Bomb carrier).

The main design work, the scope and level of which corresponded to a preliminary project, were completed in January 1942. The aircraft was intended to be a two-engine high-wing monoplane, with a large cut-out in the fuselage to enable it to carry 2–5 tons of bombs, and was equipped with powerful defensive armament. The M-82, M-71 and M-90 engines were suggested for the power plant. Particular attention in the course of development was paid to improving the visibility for the pilot and navigator. The NB was also expected to be used in the role of a long-range daytime bomber; for this application, the number of air gunners was increased.

The NB design was created with a view to large-scale production in conditions of a shortage of stock and a lack of traditional aviation materials. Since the factories producing the bulk of Soviet aluminum had been in the currently occupied territories, the use of this metal had to be minimised. It was planned that the bomber would be made of steel (51 percent) and wood (38 percent), while some components in secondary structural assemblies were expected to be made of plastic.

Already by February 1942, Polikarpov had involved the evacuated TsAGI specialists in helping to determine the parameters of the propulsion system and selecting the most advantageous propellers. It was found that the best results in increasing the range and maximum flight speed could be obtained by using the TsAGI 3 SMV-14 four-blade propellers (in practice, these propellers were introduced just before the end of the war). The Chief Designer had to concern himself, *inter alia*, with revising the strength standards. According to the latest revision of these requirements, the standardised shock absorber load in the landing gear of aircraft intended for night flying had to be 1.5 times higher. In practice, meeting this requirement resulted in a considerable increase of the landing gear weight. In Polikarpov's opinion, there was no need for that, because aircraft usually performed landings without any bomb load and after having consumed a considerable portion of the fuel load.

Some problems also appeared in relation to special equipment to be used on the NB, such as bomb racks, gunsights, cameras, and communication and navigation devices. The task was not only to choose the best components and to 'guess' those most likely to succeed, but also to adapt this complex outfit to the aircraft.

Up until the summer of 1942, there was no particular interest on the part of the Soviet aviation industry management toward Polikarpov's initiative on the NB development. Operational requirements were not determined;, andthe preliminary project was not reviewed. These were hard times for the aviation industry, which for the most part continued to adapt itself to the conditions of evacuation, with the most vital task being to increase the output of the already existing aircraft to satisfy the front-line needs. It should be noted that, up until 1945, none of the concepts for new combat aircraft that were developed during the wartime actually entered production. The airplanes that were superseding the older ones were essentially versions of those that had been manufactured earlier. This happened not only because of a lack of manpower and funds, but also due to the existing 'alignment of forces' in the aviation industry.

In June 1942, the Soviet Air Force finally showed interest in Polikarpov's 'night-time bomb carrier'. This change of heart was connected with Stalin's decision to develop Soviet long-range aviation and to create, within a year, an air fleet consisting of around a thousand long-range bombers. However, as it turned out, the capabilities of the Soviet economy did not allow building such a number of aircraft, even over several years. It was in these conditions that Polikarpov's suggestion to build a cheap bomber using readily available materials was recalled. At the same time, the requirements of the aircraft also changed: now it had to be not just a night bomber, but also a long-range one. This demanded introducing noticeable changes into the design, studying the issues connected to the installation of additional fuel tanks and equipment, looking at the arrangement of the co-pilot's station and increasing the total number of crew members to five. As part of the improvement work to the NB, a series of consultations were held with a range of specialists, pilots, navigators, technicians and gunners. This was largely done in order to select the most effective equipment layout, to improve the crew operating conditions and to facilitate maintenance. As a result, installation of an autopilot was determined as mandatory, as well as the use of a heater for the crew's meals, and the aircraft structure was also reinforced to sustain an emergency landing.

During this period, along with the NB, intensive work on other types was going on at the Polikarpov Design Bureau and Factory No.51: four I-185s, two ITPs and a TIS aircraft were all being refined. These activities were expected to be completed by November 1942, after which all the resources were planned to be committed to the 'night-time bomb carrier'.

The mock-up review commission, which took place in Novosibirsk on 16 August 1942, can be considered as the point when full-fledged work on the NB began. The aircraft was presented to the review board with M-82A engines, which were intended to ensure a maximum speed of 472km/h near ground level (with the engines running at take-off power), and up to 525km/h at an altitude of 6,250m. The service ceiling was determined to be 8,000m, while the flying range would total 4,000km with a bomb load of 2,000kg. For a reduced range, the maximum bomb load could be increased to 4,000kg. In numerous versions of the considered layouts, the entire bomb load was placed inside the fuselage.

It was planned that the airframe structure and skin should be predominantly made of wood, while load-carrying components of the fuselage and the wing centre section, wing front spar and vertical and horizontal stabilizer spars were to be made of steel. Duralumin was to be used for the engine cowlings and nacelles, ailerons and control surfaces.

Defensive armament consisted of 12.7mm Berezin machine guns arranged in standard turrets and mounts. All crewmember stations, as well as the upper rotating turret, were protected with 13.5mm-thick armour.

The landing gear was retractable, with 1,200x450mm main wheels. The tailwheel leg was equipped with twin 450x150mm wheels.

After familiarising themselves with the presented design data and the full-scale wooden mock-up, members of the commission made a range of suggestions and requests for changes. Since there were a considerable number of Air Force flight personnel among the members of the commission, the recommendations that related to improvement of the crew stations were especially numerous.

After implementation of the proposed changes, the mock-up review commission examined the entire design again on 8 September, and this time approved it. This meant the end of the first stage of the route to creation of the bomber, and corresponded to an official inclusion of the work into the plan of the NKAP's activities. According to an estimate made in September 1942 by Polikarpov's deputy, Director of Aviation Factory No.51 N. Zhemchuzhin, the NB engineering drawings were 60 percent ready. Manufacturing of the mould lofts and templates was now started. During this period, the situation in Novosibirsk changed. Some of the personnel of the design bureau and experimental factory were returned to Moscow, where they were engaged in repairing combat aircraft. Meanwhile, some of the experienced workers and foremen were transferred to Aviation Factory No.153, which was building Yakovlev fighters on an increasing scale. Many series production workers, especially young ones, were also enlisted into the Red Army, while already in spring some machines and equipment from the factory in Novosibirsk had been transferred to Factory No.166 in Omsk in order to launch production of the Tu-2 bomber.

Having assessed the situation, Polikarpov appealed to the aviation industry management to transfer the final assembly and refinement of the NB to Moscow. It seemed possible to begin flight tests of the NB in spring 1943, provided that the facilities in both Moscow and Novosibirsk were used. In practice, however, the desired quick pace of building the aircraft was never reached. Engineering development activities and manufacturing of subassemblies were going on up until autumn 1943. At the same time, the thorough design of the NB airframe for the expected large-scale production also had an effect. The multi-stage breakdown of the aircraft was implemented with a high degree of accuracy: in the course of airplane assembly in Moscow, it was not required to perform adjustment of the subassemblies in order for them to fit each other.

During the winter of 1943–44, Factory No.51 and the Polikarpov Design Bureau were re-evacuated. Upon their arrival in Moscow, the team managed to conduct additional aerodynamic and structural tests of the bomber. The assembly of the prototype was completed in late 1943, and the NB first flew on 23 May 1944 from Moscow Central Airfield, with pilot Gavrilov at the controls. There then followed the usual process of aircraft modifications and refinements. The factory tests were resumed in August 1944, after the death of Polikarpov. The aircraft reached a maximum speed of 430km/h near ground level and 510km/h at an altitude of 5,000 metres. In terms of bomb load, the NB was noticeably superior to the Tu-2; however, it was inferior to the latter in terms of flight speed. It was expected that the aircraft would further be modified, in particular being fitted with turbosuperchargers, and that the tests would be continued in summer 1945.

The 'night bomb carrier' at Moscow Central Airfield during tests in 1944.

Unfortunately, the 'bomb carrier' never flew again. The NB remained laid up at the airfield all winter. Consequently, its plywood skin began to deteriorate because the airframe was only designed for a short service life. In March 1945, after the signing of the respective act, the NB was dismantled.

The aircraft had been through numerous versions and developments. In 1944, after the decision to use the NB as a daytime bomber, calculations were made for the installation of M-30F diesel engines and AM-39 high-altitude engines. The PTS-51 passenger/transport aircraft version powered by ASh-82 engines was also envisaged. First and foremost, the fuselage was modified, receiving a special hatch for the loading of oversize military equipment.

In late 1943 and early 1944, in accordance with plans for further development and improvement of long-range aviation, Polikarpov performed preliminary estimates of an NB-based four-engine strategic bomber, which was given the designation

Prototypes and projects of the 1940s 247

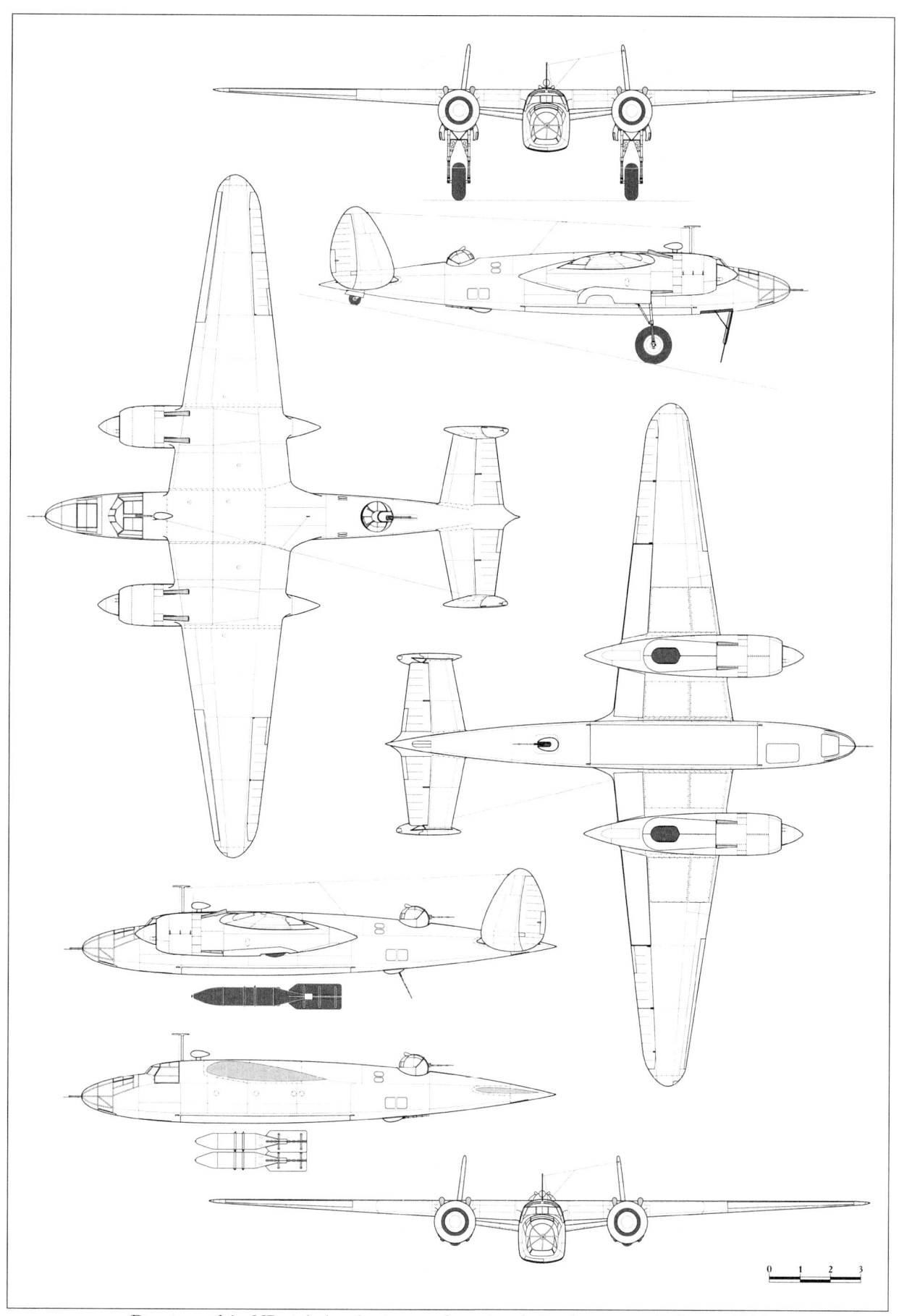

Drawings of the NB night bomber in a configuration during factory tests in August 1944.

BB (*Bolshoy Bombovoz* – Big Carrier of Bombs). The Klimov VK-107 engines were intended to be used as the power plant. The crew members for this version were accommodated in four separate pressurised cabins. Defensive armament consisted of 23mm, 25mm and 45mm cannons. The BB's take-off weight totalled 26 tons, and it had a wing area of 100sq.m and a maximum speed of 550km/h.

Dimensions and main performance parameters of the NB	
Wing span (m)	21.52
Length (m)	15.29
Wing area (sq.m)	58.1
Empty weight (kg)	6,767
Gross weight (kg)	12,640
Maximum speed near ground level (km/h)	436
Maximum speed at altitude (km/h)	515
Service ceiling (m)	6,150
Load ratio	46.4 percent

8.3. The BDP combat troop-carrier glider

The starting point in the history of Soviet multi-seat unpowered military aircraft can be considered to be 23 January 1940, on which day the Directorate for Production of Troop-Carrying Gliders was established within the NKAP. In autumn the same year, at a special meeting attended by Stalin, a decision was made to arrange a competition in order to identify the most successful models of a glider with a view to the subsequent launch of their series production. As a result, gliders were proposed by designers O. Antonov, V. Gribovsky, P. Tsybin and N. Kurbala. The most likely of them – the Antonov A-7 and Gribovsky G-11 – entered production and were successfully used in the Great Patriotic War.

Nikolay Polikarpov had not previously taken part in the designing of unpowered aircraft, so when his proposal was submitted in early June 1941, it apparently came as a surprise to many. For many years after these events, aviation industry specialists have wondered why the eminent designer had felt the need to enter someone else's domain, to engage in designing a structure that had little prestige from the start, and to delve into topics which were essentially on the sidelines of mainstream aviation development. It should be noted that production of gliders was planned to be carried out not at aviation factories, but at secondary facilities such as woodworking and furniture plants. The cause of Polikarpov's unexpected interest probably lay in him having his own view of this problem, in which he conceived something new and original.

Unlike other designers, he proposed a glider not just for carrying cargoes or troops in the rear, but as a means of actively attacking the enemy. It can be supposed that such a direction of the designer's thoughts was influenced by what had happened in late May 1941, when the Germans launched an attack to capture the island of Crete from the defendeding British troops. The attack on the island was carried out from the air and involved the use of assault gliders. While the airborne assault had succeeded in its mission, the German casualties were very heavy. Analysing this operation from the point of view of aviation participation, Polikarpov came to the conclusion that the attacking side could avoid such high losses by using special well-armed and armour-protected landing devices. In line with this idea, he designed a special-purpose glider where the paratroopers inside it could fire their hand-carried weapons at the enemy on the ground during the course of gliding. Adequate protection in the air was ensured by removable armour plates, which after landing in open terrain could be used as shields.

Development of the glider, which was given the designation BDP (*Boyevoy Desantnyy Planer* – Combat Troop-carrier Glider), was performed by Polikarpov and his design bureau team in June 1941. The preliminary project of the glider (within the design bureau, it was given the designation 'S') was completed a few days before the fateful day of 22 June, the start of Operation *Barbarossa*. It was a cantilever high-wing glider with a wing span of 20 metres and a smooth spindle-shaped fuselage without the protruding cockpit canopy. The glider was of an all-wood construction, which was the cheapest and the easiest to manufacture. The size of the glider, which was capable to carry 16 men with weapons, was selected so that it could be towed by Tupolev SB or Ilyushin DB-3 bombers. It was also planned that the paratroopers would be able to use their firearms in mid-air to defend attacks by enemy fighters.

Once the BDP project was approved by aviation industry authorities, the glider's manufacture was started at Experimental Aviation Factory No.51. By late summer 1941, the glider was already completed and prepared for flight tests. Flights of the first BDP prototype began in September at the LII airfield near Moscow. An SB bomber powered by M-103 engines was used as the towing aircraft. The glider was flown by experienced pilot V. Fedorov, who performed 14 flights. On 14 October, the tests were halted due to the serious combat situation on the approaches to Moscow and the beginning of the subsequent evacuation.

According to the test results, the BDP was stable in flight along all axes, allowed hands-off flying and offered sufficient efficiency of the controls both in flight and upon landing: "In terms of piloting technique, it is very simple and pleasant, and does not require high piloting skills. It can easily be flown by a pilot who has completed a course of training in instruction gliders."

At the same time, insufficient structural strength of joints in the wings and fuselage was highlighted. For this reason, during the tests the BDP's gross weight was limited to 2,200kg, and the flying speed to 220km/h (the glider had been designed for 3,200kg and 320km/h, respectively). The pilot noted that the curved front windows created considerable distortion, and recommended installing a conventional canopy with a faceted windscreen. Meanwhile, the extension of flaps was accompanied by empennage buffeting.

It was recommended that the BDP should be cleared for series production after implementation of changes and structural reinforcements. No difficulties with this were expected; it was believed that the glider could be manufactured at the facilities of small woodworking factories. However, TsAGI specialists noted that its cost as a series production glider was somewhat high.

In October 1941, a decision was made to evacuate the first BDP prototype from Moscow. The glider was thus taken in tow by an SB bomber, but the flight was not successfully completed. Fighters of the Moscow Air Defence Forces intercepted the unusual 'air train' and forced it to perform a landing near Kashira. At the site of the forced landing, the glider was ransacked by local residents and only then returned to Moscow for repair. The subsequent fate of the first prototype is not traceable.

The second prototype of the glider, which was given the designation BDP-2, was completed in Novosibirsk, home to the evacuated Aviation Factory No.51 and Polikarpov Design Bureau. The glider was handed over to the LII branch for flight testing on 6 February 1942, and was flown by I. Shelest. The BDP-2 structure was reinforced, based on the results of the first prototype's testing, and its gross weight became slightly higher. Its appearance also changed, with the cockpit canopy provided with a faceted windscreen, some structural components becoming simpler and the trailing edges of the rudders and elevator being made of steel wire, in the same manner as had been done in the early days of aviation.

The BDP-2 was tested with skis, with the tests lasting until 14 March. During that period, actions were taken to reduce empennage buffeting. To a certain extent, this problem was resolved by cutting openings in the flaps in order to reduce air flow disturbance. The test report again pointed out the simplicity of handling the BDP-2, its high payload, sufficient manoeuvrability and stability within a wide range of centre-of-gravity positions (27–41 percent MAC). The glider was thus recommended for series production.

Nearly concurrently with the commencement of flight testing, a search for facilities to launch series production of the BDP began. Having inspected several small facilities near Novosibirsk, representatives of the Polikarpov Design Bureau selected the workshops of the Siberian Military District. Until recently, the workshops had served as auxiliary production facilities for Aviation Factory No.153, manufacturing skis for aircraft. That was where production of the BDP was planned to be launched, with the first series amounting to 1,000 gliders. The cost per glider in the series was estimated at 41,125 roubles.

While approvals were going on, a new location for the BDP production was found – Factory No.490 in Stalingrad. Throughout the summer of 1942, the engineering drawings, mould lofts, templates and fixtures began to arrive to Stalingrad from Novosibirsk. However, in view of the situation at the front, with the Red Army retiring and the German forces approaching Stalingrad, arrangements for the gliders' production there had to be discontinued. At that point, the expedience of building the BDP gliders also became dubious. The war was clearly taking a protracted and exhausting form, in which a need for special missions, for which the glider had been designed, seemed unlikely. Furthermore, the Antonov A-7 and Gribovsky G-11 gliders had already been introduced into series production.

In the meantime, the history of the BDP continued. In July 1942, the second BDP-2 prototype was handed over to the Moscow–Irkutsk air route administration for trial operation as a transport aircraft. Several flights were performed along the Novosibirsk–Omsk–Sverdlovsk route and back, with the BDP-2 towed by a Tupolev SB bomber. Together with the BDP, several A-7 gliders were also flying this route. Civil aviation representatives were enthusiastic about the tests conducted; the gliders allowed carrying bulky cargoes, and the Tupolev SB (PS-40) airplanes to which they were attached were mostly used for mail delivery. It was planned to build several transport gliders for civil air routes based on the positive results of the flights performed.

In 1943, production of 10 BDP gliders was launched at Factory No.51. It is known that two gliders were delivered before the end of the year. Readiness of the third and fourth gliders was estimated at 98 percent, of the fifth at 80 percent, of the sixth at 28 percent and of the seventh at 10 percent. The further fate of these gliders is not known to the author.

The other projects of Polikarpov in the area of unpowered aircraft were the DP-30 large troop-carrying glider (capable of carrying 30 persons) and the BP bombing glider. The BP was suggested by the designer back in 1941. Such gliders were planned to be delivered to the target by bomber aircraft, being intended for application at night-time or in areas of Soviet air supremacy. The BP bomb bay accommodated up to 2,000kg of bombs, and the crew included a pilot, a bombardier/gunner and an air gunner. Defensive armament consisted of a TAT turret with a large-calibre BT machine gun and a ShKAS machine gun.

Description of the BDP glider
The glider fuselage, which was of all-wood construction, provided for the accommodation of 17 persons, including the pilot. The pilot's cockpit was equipped with a jettisonable canopy, with its frame made of wood. In the lower part of the cockpit, additional windows were arranged in order to improve visibility.

The paratroopers' seats were arranged along the fuselage sides and constituted an integral part of the structure. In the middle there was an aisle that was 600mm wide. For entrance and disembarkation, two doors were made – 900mm and 950mm wide – one of them in the forward part of the fuselage on the right, and the other in the rear part on the left. On the first BDP prototype, there were two narrow doors on the right side and two on the left side. Later, the left rear door was made wider. In the lower portion of the fuselage, behind the paratroopers' compartment, an additional hatch for bailing out was provided. Near the wing leading and trailing edges, special hatches were cut out for firing infantry machine guns in the upper hemisphere. To protect the tail, a fragment of the fuselage in the upper portion was capable of lifting and becoming the gunner's fairing.

The BDP had a single-spar all-wood wing with a NACA 230 profile. The wing leading edge and local reinforcements were covered in plywood, whereas the rest of the wing areas were covered in fabric. To reduce the landing speed, Schrank-type flaps were positioned in the area between the ailerons and the fuselage.

The empennage was of cantilever type, all-wood, covered in plywood and fabric. The landing gear was arranged as two skis made of glued ashwood and secured on rubber-block shock absorbers. The interface between the skis and the fuselage was covered by a fairing made of aviation cloth. For take-off, the BDP was equipped with a jettisonable dolly that had four 400x150mm wheels.

The glider was not equipped with any armament but had provisions for mounting seven DP machine guns, including two machine guns for firing in the upper hemisphere, one machine gun in the lower hatch and two machine guns on each of the fuselage sides. For passive protection, u12 removable 5.5mm-thick 480x550mm armour shields were installed inside the glider. The pilot was provided with a foldable armored backrest. The total weight of the BDP's armour was 127kg.

Specifications of the BDP	
Length (m)	13.60
Wing span (m)	20.0
Wing area (sq.m)	44.72
Airframe weight (kg)	1,470
Gross weight (kg)	3,408

Satisfied with the results achieved during the trial operation of the BDP, Polikarpov decided to upgrade his glider so that it would no longer be dependent on a towing aircraft. Thus appeared the MP (*Motoplaner*) powered glider fitted with two M-11F engines. The MP had a fuel reserve for seven hours of flying, could be used as a small transport aircraft and was able to carry 12 paratroopers with weapons or a corresponding amount of cargo. With a higher load, take-off and delivery to the target were carried out with the help of a towing aircraft. The MP had an advantageous difference from other gliders – usually transport gliders did not return to their base and were destroyed after cargo delivery, but a powered glider without load was able to return home on its own.

State tests of the MP were conducted at Moscow Central Airfield, although the glider also flew to Medvezhyi Ozyora Airfield – which belonged to the Red Army Airborne Forces – and to the airfield of the LII NKAP in Ramenskoye. The flights were performed by test pilot Captain S. Anokhin of the Separate Testing Air Squadron of the Red Army Airborne Forces.

Between 12 July and 10 September 1943, 70 flights were made, with a total flying time of 40 hours and 10 minutes. With the glider towed by an SB bomber, an altitude of 4,500m was reached, while the actual airspeed was 270km/h. In the opinion of the pilots who took part in the flight tests (V. Yuganov, V. Rastorguyev, G. Shiyanov, A. Grinchik, P. Fedrovi, P. Stefanovsky, V. Shevchenko, A. Dolgov, Gavrilov, Borodin, Romanov and P. Savtsov), the MP had good stability, was easy to pilot and could be flown by pilots with only low skills. With a gross weight of 3,300m and with one engine operative, the powered glider was able to continue horizontal flying, and was easily kept from turning by applying the rudder.

During the period from 10–13 September, the MP was further tested for suitability of use by airborne forces. Based on the estimated overload gross weight of 4,000kg, several variants of loading were checked:

Prototypes and projects of the 1940s   251

Wooden frame of the BDP glider fuselage during the course of manufacturing.

The first BDP prototype during tests near Moscow on 16 September 1941.

The cockpit of the BDP glider.

Two Degtyaryov machine guns mounted in the upper liftable fuselage section of the glider, offering the possibility to fire in the upper hemisphere.

The BDP-2 glider during tests in Novosibirsk in the winter of 1941–42.

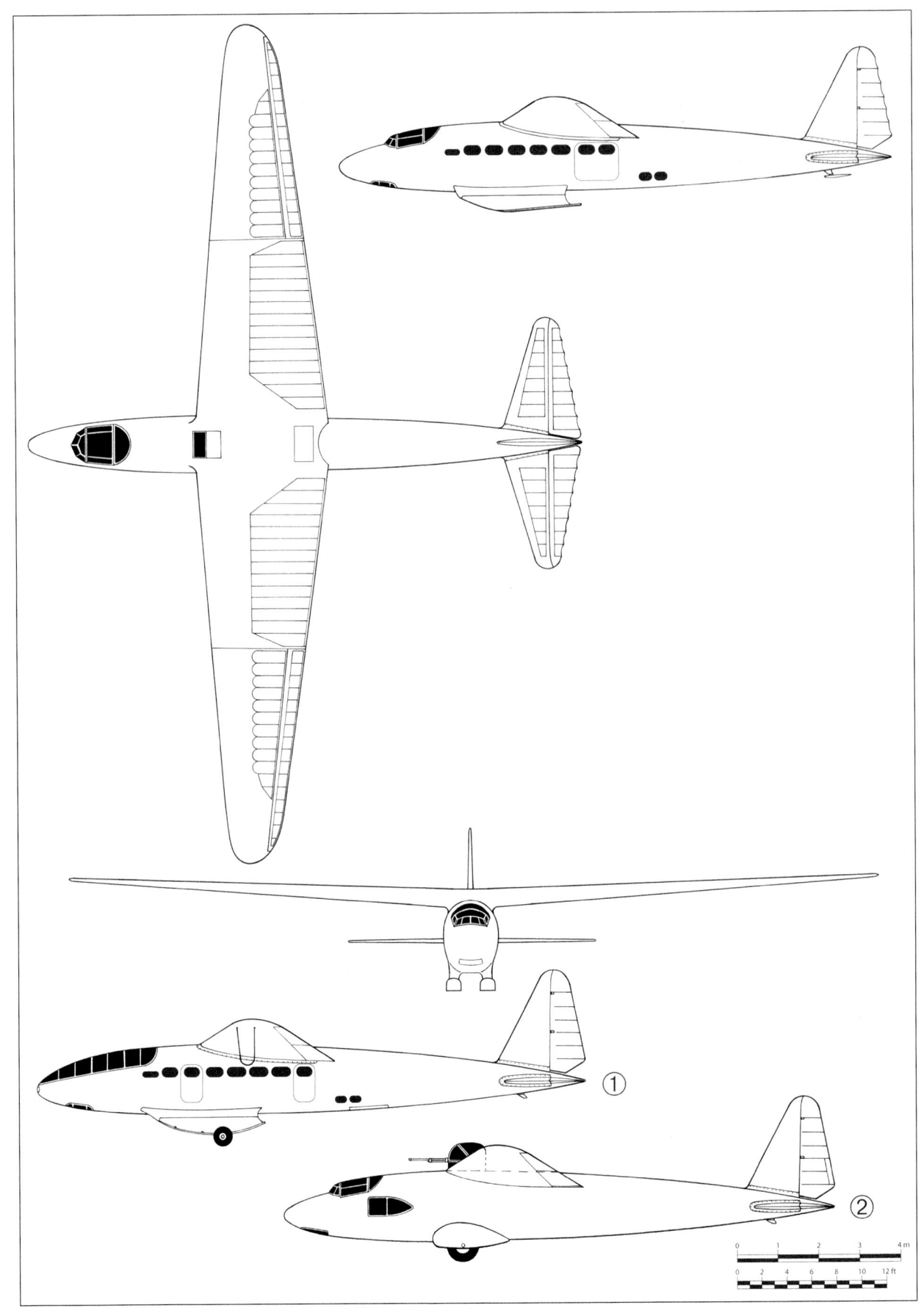

1. Four-view drawings of the BDP glider.
2. Side view drawing of the BP bombing glider project.
8.4. The MP powered glider

The MP powered glider during tests in summer 1943.

1. A squad of riflemen (11 persons).
2. An anti-tank crew of six persons, a 45mm anti-tank cannon in a dismantled condition and two boxes of shells (40 pieces). Assembly and deployment of the cannon took between eight and 10 minutes.
3. A DShK anti-aircraft machine-gun with a crew of five persons and ammunition.
4. An anti-tank rifle squad of 10 persons and three anti-tank rifles.
5. Two or three motorcycles (three Veloset motorcycles or two Indiana motorcycles).

It was pointed out that the MP had passed all the tests successfully, and was recommended to be introduced into service of the air units of the Red Army Airborne Forces and transport aviation. The glider was intended to enter series production.

Despite the positive opinions of the test pilots, production of the MP was never launched. This was largely connected with the fact that the Red Army liberated many areas where partisans were operating, and the need to use troop assault gliders was no longer regarded as urgent. Furthermore, the Shcherbakov Shche-2 and Yakovlev Yak-6 light transport aircraft, each of which were powered by two M-11 engines, were already in series production.

Main performance parameters of the MP glider	
Maximum speed near ground level (km/h)	185
Maximum speed at an altitude of 1,000m (km/h)	179
Time to climb to 1,000m (mins)	12.5
Service ceiling (m)	2,700

Absolute range (km)	930
Gross weight (kg)	3,500–4,000
Take-off run with a weight of 3,500kg (m)	400–480

Comparison of the MP, TS (Shche-2) and Yak-6 s/n 013 built by Factory No.47			
	MP	TS-1	Yak-6
Full length (m)	13.60	13.515	10.350
Height in parked condition (m)	3.20	4.80	4.110
Wing span (m)	20.0	20.54	14.0
Wing area (sq.m)	44.70	64.0	29.6
Engines	M-11F	M-11D	M-11D
Empty weight (kg)	2,420	2,235	1,400
Normal gross weight (kg)	3,500	3,400	2,300
Full payload (kg)	1,280	1,165	872
Load ratio (percent)	44.5	38	43
Wing loading (kg/sq.m)	78.5	53	77.5
Maximum speed near ground level (km/h)	185	157	177
Time to climb to 1,000m (mins)	12.5	13	5.5
Take-off run (m)	400	350	285

8.5. The TIS heavy escort fighter

In 1940 and 1941, nearly all active design bureaus of the Soviet aviation industry were involved in the development of two-engine combat aircraft capable of performing the roles of long-range and heavy fighters. All these hypothetical aircraft in the form of preliminary projects, with appropriate supporting documents, were submitted for review to the Expert Commission of the NKAP chaired by Boris Yuryev. There were quite a number of well worked-out projects: proposals were submitted by Kocherigin, Mikoyan, Grushin, Polikarpov, Tairov, Sukhoi and Bisnovat. As a result, Yuryev decided to stem this tide of creative proposals, and inscribed on one of the projects: "Since seven rather similar designs have been submitted, the work should be entrusted to no more than three Chief Designers, namely, Polikarpov, Mikoyan and Grushin."

The preliminary project by Nikolay Polikarpov, designated as a Heavy Escort Fighter (*Tyazholyy Istrebitel Soprovozhdeniya*, TIS) powered by two AM-35 or AM-37 engines, was submitted for review on 18 September 1940. The developer announced high flight performance parameters: the maximum speed was expected to reach 625km/h at an altitude of 8,000m with the AM-35A engines, and 652km/h at an altitude of 7,400m with the AM-37 engines. The flight range was intended to be between 1,200 and 1,920km.

Offensive armament was planned to consist of two ShVAK cannons, two large-calibre Berezin machine guns and four ShKAS machine guns. Two ShKAS machine guns, each on a separate mount, were used for defence of the rear hemisphere. The TIS had several roles, being intended to escort bombers, fight enemy aircraft, support ground forces and carry out dive bombing. In general, the preliminary project suited the Red Army Air Force; therefore, after a review of the proposals for the TIS aircraft, the NKAP Commission found further development expedient.

The TIS was designed as an all-metal aircraft, with load-carrying assemblies made of 30KhGSA steel. All the other structural components and the skin were made of duralumin. The thin, elongated fuselage accommodated two crew members in the nose and could carry 400kg of bombs in the internal bomb bay. To improve the visibility for the pilot, additional transparent sections were arranged in the nose of the fuselage. The crew entered the aircraft via a deployable ladder hatch. In an emergency, this rather large hatch could be jettisoned, enabling the pilot and the rear gunner to bail out almost unhindered. To ensure protection for the crew, installation of armour plates in various configuration options was envisaged.

The TIS had a two-spar wing, which, according to the production breakdown conditions, consisted of five parts: the wing centre section, two engine sections and two outer wing panels. Automatic slats were provided in the outer wing leading edges, while the trailing edges accommodated three sections of flaps.

The TIS's design and production technology were based on the previous aircraft created by the design bureau, the SPB. However, mention of the SPB led to a more critical assessment of the new project. It was felt that the TIS, in which the relative ratios between the wing area and the empennage area (with the total wing area reduced by 8sq.m) were retained, might also prove to be unstable both longitudinally and laterally. Afterwards, such suspicions brought about a constant concern on the part of the design team, led by Sigayev, about creating, first and foremost, a stable aircraft. In order to meet

The scene of the crash involving pilot Gavrilov on 29 June 1944 at Moscow Central Airfield.

this requirement, the TIS had an elongated fuselage and a powerful twin vertical tail. The efforts to ensure the desired centre-of-gravity position (22.8 percent MAC) during development of the aircraft's structural layout often resulted in compromising its aerodynamics. Thus, the original intention to install oil coolers in the root portion of the wing had to be abandoned; to shift the CG position forward, the radiators were arranged under the engine cowlings.

During 1940 and 1941, several peculiar episodes occurred. In the summer of 1940, a new standard for main landing gear wheels was established for the newly designed aircraft. For airplanes having a gross weight of up to 7,000kg, 900x300mm wheels had to be used; aircraft with a gross weight of over 7,000kg had to be equipped with 1,100x400mm wheels. At that time, the TIS's normal gross weight was determined to be approximately 7,000kg. For this reason, Mikhail Yangel, who had been appointed Leading Engineer for the aircraft, tried to insist on the smaller wheels. However, that was not to be. Deputy People's Commissar of Aviation Industry Sergey Yakovlev immediately thwarted these attempts, and stated with authority: "Comrade Yangel, we must strictly adhere to the standard." Finally, the issue was settled; 1,000x350mm wheels were found, which suited everyone. The interesting thing about this episode is that the Yakovlev BB-22 aircraft was originally equipped with rather small (600x250mm) main landing gear wheels. After entering production, the BB-22 was redesignated the Yak-4 and became noticeably heavier. As a result, the designers had to think again and to mount a special landing gear leg with twin 750x175mm wheels.

On 22 October 1940, a full-scale TIS mock-up was reviewed. After a detailed discussion, the manufacture of three new two-engine fighters was included into the NKAP experimental aircraft building plan for 1941. In spring and summer 1941, building of the aircraft was carried out at the new Aviation Factory No.51. Since the factory itself was only in the formation stage, individual TIS assemblies and subassemblies were manufactured at other production facilities. In particular, outer wing panels were made at Aviation Factory No.84.

256 The King of Fighters Volume 2

A wooden mockup of the TIS aircraft.

The TIS 'A' at the airfield in Novosibirsk in the spring of 1942. The flaps are extended and the gunner's canopy is opened.

The TIS 'A' during tests in 1942.

A view of the instrument panel in the cockpit of the TIS 'A'.

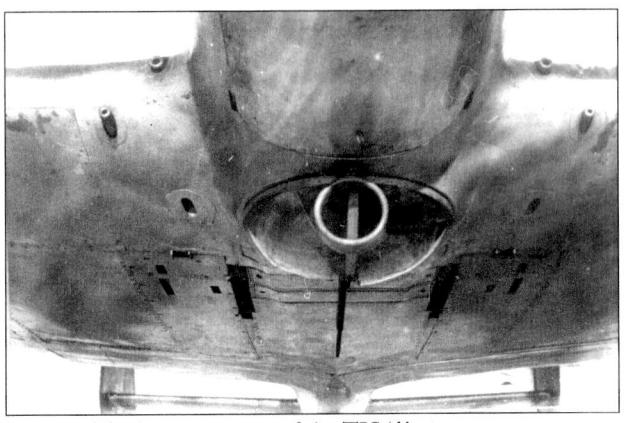

The lower portion of the TIS 'A' wing centre section. Note the ShVAK cannons, BK machine gun, lower defensive turret with the ShKAS machine gun and the bomb attachment racks.

The TIS 'A' in 1942.

The entrance hatch for the TIS crew.

The first prototype, powered by AM-37 engines and designated the TIS 'A', was for the most part completed before summer 1941. It was towards autumn of that year that the aircraft was taken to the airfield of the LII NKAP in the settlement of Stakhanovo near Moscow. The first flight took place on 2 September, the TIS taking to the air with G. Shiyanov at the controls. In total, seven flights were performed before 11 October. After nearly each of them, certain modifications and rectification of defects were carried out. Flight performance parameters were not measured. On 29 September, the aircraft flew to Moscow, where, according to the factory report, it had enlarged vertical stabilisers installed. However, it turned out not to be possible to resume testing in the near future. In accordance with the decision to evacuate in the face of the advancing German armies, the TIS flew to Arzamas on 13 October, and then to Kazan, where it was dismantled and sent by rail to the new location of Factory No.51 in Novosibirsk. The in-process stock for the other two TIS prototypes (with the readiness of subassemblies and parts for the second and third prototypes estimated at between 50 and 60 percent) was also sent to Novosibirsk.

Test flights of the aircraft, which after a number of improvements and the mounting of the enlarged vertical tail was given the designation TIS '2A', were resumed on 16 February 1942. The power plant consisted of two AM-37 engines with 3.2m-diameter VISh-61FS propellers. The aircraft was flown by test pilot N. Gavrilov. No specific conclusions were expressed after this first stage of the tests, but it was believed that the aircraft had not been refined enough to continue testing.

In April, the TIS was again taken to the airfield, where flights continued until 8 May. A specific mention was made of the aircraft's armament, which included a wing centre section-mounted battery of two ShVAK cannons (with total ammunition of 700 shells) and two 12.7mm Berezin machine guns (800 rounds), a nose-mounted battery of four ShKAS machine guns (40,000 rounds), a TSS-1 mobile mount with a ShKAS machine gun to defend the upper part of the rear hemisphere (750 rounds) and a mobile mount with a ShKAS machine gun to defend the lower hemisphere (500 rounds). Two racks providing for carrying 500kg of bombs on each were arranged under the fuselage.

In the course of the resumed flights with a normal gross weight of 7,849kg, the aircraft developed a maximum speed of 455km/h near ground level and 555km/h at an altitude of 5,800 metres. It took the aircraft four minutes to climb to an altitude of 3,000 metres; at higher altitudes, it turned out not to be possible to determine the rate-of-climb due to poor engine performance. To achieve higher flight performance figures, certain modifications had to be implemented, including installation of special-purpose high-altitude magnetos on the engines (the BSM-12Sh magnetos were suggested), changing the design of intake pipes and enhancing the rigidity of slats, flaps and landing gear doors, etc. Assessing the aircraft's behaviour in flight, Gavrilov concluded that the TIS was not stable enough and had no elevator setting margin at landing.

It was suggested that longitudinal stability should be improved by installing counterweights or springs in the control system. To enhance directional stability, the vertical stabilisers had to be further enlarged, while aileron load could be decreased by reducing the wing dihedral.

The aircraft was again returned to the factory for modifications. This time, the changes proved to be more noticeable. The dihedral of the outer wing panels was reduced from 7° to 4° by means of replacing upper attachment fittings; the area of the vertical fins was further enlarged; the area of the rudder and the elevator was enlarged respectively; and the stabiliser setting was changed. Among other things, the landing gear doors control mechanism was modified, the trailing edge of the gunner's canopy was enlarged and the shape of the oil cooler tunnels was changed. An attempt was made to upgrade the power plant: new AM-37 engines with a gear reduction rate of 0.59 were mounted, and the 3.4m-diameter AV-5-172 propellers were covered with new spinners. With a normal gross weight of 8,086kg, the CG position with the landing gear extended was 21.4 percent MAC; with the landing gear retracted, it was 27 percent MAC. The wing loading totalled 238kg/sq.m.

Nevertheless, the next stage of the tests showed that the problems still persisted. In the course of taxi runs on 6 October 1942, one of the engines failed and had to be overhauled. On 15 October, the first flight at the LII took place. On 30 October, a more serious incident occurred, which consisted of a left engine seizure. In March 1943, the testing of the TIS had to be interrupted since no new AM-37s were available.

The tests, though full of problems, yielded some positive results. The pilots pointed out the good behaviour of the TIS during take-off and landing runs, found that the aircraft was stable in flight about all axes and noted that the aircraft could be flown by pilots of medium skills.

The further fate of the aircraft remained undecided for a reason which was a common one for Soviet aviation – unavailability of a suitable engine. Polikarpov counted on the AM-39 engines, but there was serious doubt about the future availability of such engines. In 1943, the TIS was transferred to Moscow, where the series production low-altitude AM-38F engines were mounted and several additional improvements was implemented. In particular, water cooling radiators were installed in the outer wing panels.

In spring 1944, the aircraft was again handed over for flight tests, under the designation TIS 'MA'. On 29 June, the TIS 'MA' made a crash landing at Moscow Central Airfield. Following an investigation, the accident board concluded that pilot N. Gavrilov had performed the landing calculations incorrectly (as a result, the landing occurred beyond the landing strip) and had failed to extend the flaps. Consequently, the aircraft had run off the airfield. During the landing run, the brakes had turned out to be inefficient, the aircraft had ended up in a ditch (the ditch of the aircraft shooting range on the outskirts of the airfield) and the left main landing gear leg had collapsed. In the conclusion of the accident report, it was stated that "the flying time of the prototype, built in 1941 and subjected to subsequent modifications in 1942 and 1943, totalled 36 hours". Despite the fact that the TIS had achieved the status of a quite refined aircraft, there were no further developments and the project was abandoned.

Dimensions and main performance parameters of the TIS	
Wing span (m)	15.5
Length in the flight line (m)	11.70
Wing area (sq.m)	34.85
Empty weight with the AM-37 engines (kg)	5,970 (6,261*)
Normal gross weight (kg)	7,849 (8,086*)
Wing loading (kg/sq.m)	225 (238*)
Service ceiling (m)	10,000 (calculated)
Flight range (km)	1,070 (calculated)
Maximum speed near ground level (km/h)	455
Maximum speed at 5,800m (km/h)	555
Time to climb to 3,000m (mins)	4.0
Normal bomb load (kg)	1,000

* for the TIS 'MA' aircraft

8.6. The last projects

After returning from Novosibirsk to Moscow, the Polikarpov Design Bureau resumed the refinements and flight tests of the I-185, ITP, TIS and NB aircraft. Concurrently, during that period, Polikarpov joined the work on solving the problem of creating the 'VP' (*Vysotniy Perekhvatchik*) High-altitude Interceptor powered by the M-71TK engine. Within the design bureau, the project was given the designation 'K'. Work on this aircraft, which was a logical development of the I-185 family, began in September 1943. The following month, due to the fact that there was no hope of obtaining the M-71 engine, the development continued with a proposal to use the AM-39 fitted with turbosuperchargers. The change in the power plant entailed a considerable revision of the design; as a result, the preliminary project of the VP (K) was ready only in summer 1944, and the due date for handover of the aircraft for tests was shifted to December 1944.

The VP was a classic low-wing airplane of mixed construction utilising the wooden fuselage tail part, which was a conventional solution for Polikarpov's team. The aircraft was designed to have a ventilated-type pressurised cabin, which provided the most comfortable conditions for the pilot at high altitudes. The wings were all-metal, with a span of 11.0m and an area of 16.2 square metres, and made use of all the design solutions fully tested in the earlier types of the I-185 and ITP. In the process of determining performance parameters, a decision was made to replace the initially proposed NACA-230 airfoil with an innovative laminated airfoil, which was more suitable for high-altitude flying. The estimated gross weight of the fighter was 3,320kg. Its armament consisted of two 23mm cannons.

Calculations showed that, with the AM-39A engine, the VP would be able to develop a maximum speed of 500km/h at low altitudes and 715km/h at an altitude of 13,750m. With the AM-39B engine, the estimated speed near ground level was 586km/h, while it should rise to 680km/h at an altitude of 13,000m. The service ceiling was to reach 14,500–14,750m. It should take the aircraft 24.48 minutes to climb to 14,000m with the AM-39A engine, and 18 minutes with the AM-39B engine.

The VP performance parameters as submitted for review were found to be realistic. It was planned that four prototypes would be built. From late 1943 t0 early 1944, test benches for testing the propulsion system and the pressurised cabin began to be manufactured at the experimental aircraft production facilities of Factory No.51. In August 1944, the readiness of engineering drawings of the interceptor was estimated at 95 percent, and manufacturing of the first prototype began. In September, however, all work on the VP interceptor was discontinued.

At the same time as creating the piston engine powered fighter, high-altitude problems were expected to be solved by making use of rocket engines. The relatively successful flying of the Bolkhovitinov BI prototypes left room for hopes to successfully develop this subject. In late 1943, after returning from Novosibirsk to Moscow, Polikarpov was tasked with designing a fighter to be powered by a rocket engine developed by the Jet Scientific Research Institute (*Reaktivnyy Nauchno-Issledovatelskiy Institut*, RNII). The aircraft, which was dubbed *Malyutka* ('Little One'), initially made use of many design elements of the I-185 fighter. In the process of the project's improvements, the aircraft changed noticeably – it was a

7.0m long low-wing monoplane, with a straight wing having a span of 7.5m, and with a nosewheel landing gear. The aircraft had a ventilated pressurised cabin. The armament consisted of two 23mm cannons.

The *Malyutka*'s power plant, which had a maximum thrust of 1,400kg and a rated thrust of 1,100kg, consisted of two combustion chambers. The two chambers operated together at take-off, climb and acceleration to maximum speed; to maintain the flight speed, just one chamber was used. Kerosene served as fuel, with nitric acid used as the oxidising agent. Fuel components were placed in four fuselage tanks and fed to the engine by a turbo-pump assembly in accordance with a specific sequence. To ensure the required stability, the forward kerosene tank and the aft oxidiser tank were depleted first; then followed the aft kerosene tank and the forward oxidiser tank. The change in the centre-of-gravity position as fuel components were consumed was compensated by a release of water from a special tank. After completion of an interception mission and the depletion of fuel, the aircraft was expected to glide down onto the airfield with the engine turned off.

The *Malyutka* aircraft was intended to reach a maximum speed of 890km/h near ground level and 845km/h at an altitude of 15,000m. It was projected to take the aircraft a minute to climb to 5,000m and two-and-a-half minutes to climb to the design altitude. The maximum estimated service ceiling was determined to be 16,000m. After reaching an altitude of 15,000m, the interceptor was able to continue flying at the maximum thrust for one minute and at the minimum thrust for nine minutes.

The development of the interceptor preliminary project continued in 1945. Shortly afterwards, however, the project was abandoned by order of the NKAP.

Another new project during this period was the development of a jet-powered missile aircraft similar to the German V-1. This activity continued after the death of Nikolay Polikarpov, when V. Chelomey was appointed Chief Designer of Factory No.51. His deputy was D. Tomashevich, who continued the work on aviation projects.

In September 1944, a specialised design bureau was organised using the resources of Polikarpov's team, tasked with the development of pulse-jet engines and unmanned missile aircraft. For this purpose, all the captured samples of the type which were brought from Germany began to be collected at Factory No.51. The preliminary project of this aircraft was given the designation '10X'. In late 1944, factory tests were started of the D-3 pulse-jet power plant, which was designed by Chelomey. In January 1945, an order was issued by the State Defence Committee to build a prototype series of 100 10X aircraft and to present the first prototypes for testing. This work continued for several years and resulted in the creation of the 14X, 16X and other missile aircraft. Later, Chelomey's team was transferred to another factory, where the missiles continued to be improved.

By a government decree of 19 February 1953, the design bureau and experimental aircraft production facilities of Factory No.51 were handed over to A. Mikoyan's OKB-155 Design Bureau. For a certain period of time, the facilities were referred to as a branch. In October 1953, Factory No.51 was allocated as an experimental aircraft production facility for the restored P. Sukhoi Design Bureau. The main assembly shop of the factory, which once was the hangar of the TsAGI Department of Operation, Flight Tests and Refinements, is still to this day a part of an active aviation production enterprise.

The wind-tunnel test model of the *Malyutka* aircraft with the wing and empennage from the I-185.

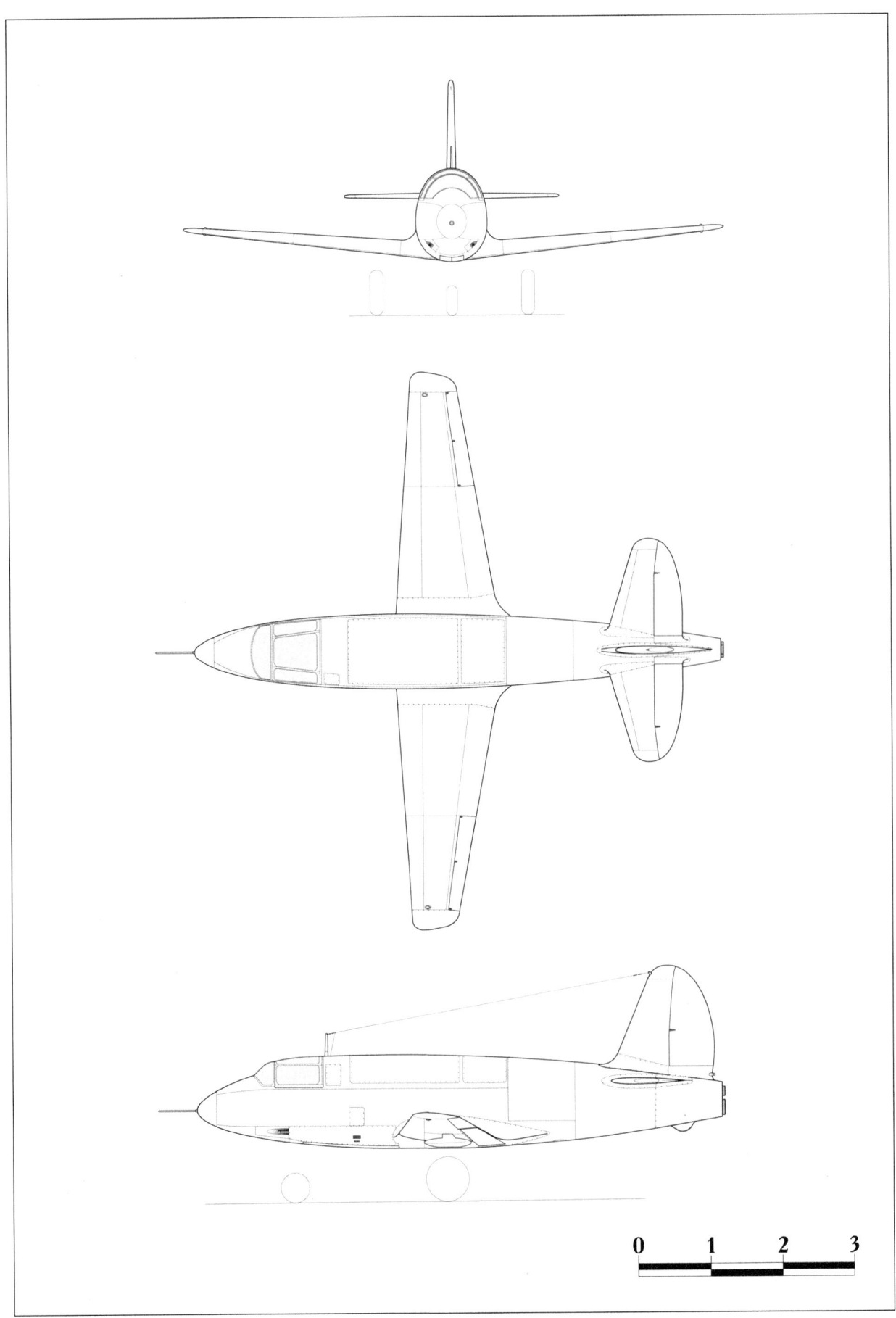

Three-view drawings of the *Malyutka* rocket aircraft project from 1944.